OUR LOST EXPLORERS:

THE NARRATIVE OF THE JEANNETTE ARCTIC EXPEDTION

OFFICERS OF THE
Jeanette Arctic Expedition.
COPYRIGHT SECURED 1882. AMERICAN PUBLISHING COMPANY.
MOSS-TYPE.

OUR LOST EXPLORERS:

THE NARRATIVE

OF THE

JEANNETTE ARCTIC EXPEDITION

AS RELATED BY THE SURVIVORS, AND IN THE RECORDS AND
LAST JOURNALS OF LIEUTENANT DE LONG.

REVISED BY

RAYMOND LEE NEWCOMB,
NATURALIST OF THE EXPEDITION.

WITH GRAPHIC DESCRIPTIONS OF
ARCTIC SIBERIA, THE LENA AND ITS DELTA, THE NATIVE AND EXILED
INHABITANTS OF THE COUNTRY, ETC.; AND MR. NEWCOMB'S NAR-
RATIVE OF A WINTER OVERLAND JOURNEY FROM
THE ARCTIC OCEAN TO ST. PETERSBURG.

ALSO

AN ACCOUNT OF THE JEANNETTE SEARCH EXPEDITIONS, THEIR
DISCOVERIES, THE BURNING OF THE RODGERS, &c., &c.

WITH AN INTRODUCTION BY

Rev. W. L. GAGE, D.D.

MAPS, PORTRAITS, AND NUMEROUS ENGRAVINGS.

PUBLISHED BY SUBSCRIPTION ONLY.

HARTFORD, CONN.:
AMERICAN PUBLISHING COMPANY.
1888.

Copyright, 1882,
AMERICAN PUBLISHING COMPANY,
HARTFORD, CT.

OUR LOST EXPLORERS:
THE NARRATIVE OF THE JEANNETTE ARCTIC EXPEDITION

By George W. De Long

As Published in 1882

Trade Paperback ISBN: 1-58218-282-5
Hardcover ISBN: 1-58218-283-3
eBook ISBN: 1-58218-281-7

All rights reserved, which includes the right to reproduce this book or portions thereof in any form whatsoever except as provided by the U. S. Copyright Law. For information address Digital Scanning, Inc.

Digital Scanning and Publishing is a leader in the electronic republication of historical books and documents. We publish many of our titles as eBooks, as well as traditional hardcover and trade paper editions. DSI is committed to bringing many traditional and little known books back to life, retaining the look and feel of the original work.

©2001 DSI Digital Reproduction
First DSI Printing: April 2001

Published by DIGITAL SCANNING, INC.
Scituate, MA 02066
www.digitalscanning.com

INTRODUCTION.

The Arctic Ocean has been for years the nursery of heroic deeds. And had the results of enterprise been even less than they have been in that region of frost and ice, and months-long night, what has been shown there of that which is noblest and most admirable in man would have been worth all that it has cost. The story of war and of battle brings to light much bravery, much endurance,—often much magnanimity; yet the record is stained with so much of bloodshed, and of cruelty, that not infrequently it seems more like a transcript of the baser human passions than of heroic courage and noble achievement. And Arctic discovery, too, is full of pain, for its course is tracked with hardships, and its field is sown with graves. Yet there is so much of brightness, of hope, of mutual helpfulness, and of novel experience in the record, that we turn to the stories of polar adventure with the same zest with which boys breathe in the probabilities and glorious recklessness of such adventurers as Tom Sawyer.

The book now before the reader falls not a whit behind its predecessors. Indeed, as an unbroken current of hardship, disappointments, perils, and final disaster, uncheered with scarce a gleam of that success which was fondly hoped at the outset, the work is without a rival. From the time when this little company of about one-third of a hundred souls, became entangled in the ice masses off Herald Island and Northeastern Siberia, and then embedded in the floes, on and on, through the long winters of 1879, 1880, and 1881, and through the brief summers of 1880 and 1881, down to the discovery of some of the survivors, and in their immense and unparalleled feats of courage, strength, and endurance in crossing the ice-fields after the Jeannette went down, till they reached the Siberian villages and towns, there is one continuous strain of heroism, one incessant and good-humored story of that which is best and most hopeful in the human soul. And so the book becomes in its revelations of character, a work of singular and thrilling interest. Those sturdy men of many nationalities and many languages, embracing not only the best known European people, but the Chinese and the North American Indians, all working in harmony, and for the common good; those rude and primitive Tunguses of Northern Asia, hospitable and kindly; the Cossacks, and even the exiles who had been driven to Siberia for their offences, warming into charity and hospitality towards the sufferers from a distant land; the zeal of the surviving men of the Jeannette to learn, to the last particular, the fate of DeLong and of Chipp; the earnestness and eagerness of the officers to attain to all possible scientific results; the loyalty of all to their superiors in office, and the fidelity to the great fact of law,—all this invests the book with a delightful and incessant charm.

And as the interest of the world grows breathless to catch the last words of this intrepid band, and the remotest whispers of their fate, the sense of their endurance, their courage, and their high and manly hope, becomes more inspiring. No audience is larger than that which now awaits each voice that can tell us of the fortunes of the Jeannette and her crew. The discovery of the dreadful fate which met the DeLong party comes to us as the crowning agony of a long series of distresses. But while such disasters win universal sympathy, the story of such a retreat as that of the boat-loads of men whose untiring efforts during the summer of 1881, after they left the Jeannette, this volume records, will be read with the interest which is only given to deeds of sustained courage and manly striving. And we have no fear that the modest tale will fail of finding its thousands of readers.

CONTENTS.

CHAPTER I.

THE JEANNETTE AND HER CREW—VOYAGE TO THE ARCTIC OCEAN.

PAGE.

The Pandora bought, renamed, and fitted out—Officers and Crew—Departure from San Francisco—Anequin and Alexai—Arrival at Northeastern Siberia—Good-bye to Civilization—Last tidings of the Jeannette. 17

CHAPTER II.

A SEARCH FOR MISSING WHALERS AND THE JEANNETTE.

The Mt. Woolaston and Vigilant—Reminiscence of Captain Nye—Sailing of the Corwin—Indian Village at St. Michaels—Bear-hunters of Alaska—The starved Islanders—Deserted Villages—Capture of whisky-trading schooners—Cruise in Arctic waters—Interesting incidents—The northern pack and its fatal drift. 28

CHAPTER III.

SEARCHES FOR THE JEANNETTE—SECOND CRUISE OF THE CORWIN.

Search Expeditions of 1881—The Jeannette Relief-Board—The Corwin starts north—Landing of search party on Siberian coast—Fate of the lost whalers discovered—Exploration of Herald Island—Professor Muir's narrative—Landing on Wrangel Island—Wreck of the Webster—The Golden Fleece and Ray's Expedition—Excursion to the Reindeer Chukches—The Diomedes—An Esquimaux Long Branch—No traces of the missing explorers. 39

CHAPTER IV.

SEARCHES FOR THE JEANNETTE—CRUISE OF THE RODGERS.

The Mary and Helen renamed the Rodgers—Officers and crew—Departure from San Francisco—The 180th Meridian—Description of the Bay of Avatcha, Petropavolvsk, and Commander's Island—Slaughter of sea-bears at Copper Island—Voyage to Cape Serdze—Visit to a Ckukcke village—Wrangel Island explored—An exciting bear-hunt—Waring's adventures—Putnam's winter camp—The Rodgers goes into winter quarters in St. Lawrence Bay. 54

(v)

CHAPTER V.

SEARCHES FOR THE JEANNETTE—CRUISE OF THE ALLIANCE.

PAGE.

The Steamship Alliance and her officers—The start from Norfolk Navy-Yard—Voyage to Iceland and Norway—Exciting news—Voyage to Bear Island and Spitzbergen—The midnight sun as seen near Horn Sound—White whales—Walrus hunters at Bell Sound—Beyond the 80th Parallel—In a fog—A fairy-like scene—View from the crow's nest—Exciting times at Dane's Island—Return to Hammerfest, and home—A phenomenal cruise—Results of the Voyage. 71

CHAPTER VI.

PLANS FOR AN INTERNATIONAL SEARCH.

No news from the Jeannette—Lost in the Arctic—Lehigh Hunt's Expedition—Action of London Geographical Society—Reminiscence of the Franklin Search—Plans of operation—Opinions of Arctic travelers. 79

CHAPTER VII.

FIRST TIDINGS FROM THE EXPLORERS.

Startling news from Irkutsk—Arrival of some of the Jeannette's crew on the Siberian coast—Official telegrams—Prompt action of Russian officers—Second Cutter missing—A season of suspense—"By Baikal's Lake." 83

CHAPTER VIII.

THE SIBERIAN TUNDRA.

A land of desolation—The Tundra in summer—An animated scene—Arctic moss—Graphic description of the Tundra in winter—Dreariness, cold, and solitude—Frozen in mammoth and rhinoceros—Curious legends of the natives—Fossil ivory—The "isle of bones." 91

CHAPTER IX.

THE LENA RIVER AND ITS DELTA.

A mighty river—Its head-waters and tributaries—Ledyard's travels, and voyage down the stream—Hospitable Russians—Valley of the Lower Lena, and its inhabitants—Description of the Delta—Immense sea-coast—Seven great arms of the Lena—A wonderful sight—The Vega and Lena—A disappointing pilot—Johannesen's voyage up the river—Amusing incidents—Curious customs and ceremonies—Ludicrous thanksgiving service—Extinguishing a 'clerk.' 98

CONTENTS.   vii

CHAPTER X.

ENGINEER MELVILLE'S NARRATIVE.

PAGE.

Melville in command of whale-boat—His story of the voyage and sinking of the Jeannette, the retreat south, the separation of the boats, and the landing of his party—The discovery by natives, who conduct them to a village where startling news from Nindermann arrives—Searches for De Long—The survivors at Yakutsk. 111

CHAPTER XI.

LIEUTENANT DE LONG'S RECORDS.

Copies of four records found in huts along the North channel of the Lena, which were left there by De Long as he retreated southward. 125

CHAPTER XII.

EXPERIENCES OF NINDERMANN, NOROS, AND LEACH.

Verbatim copy of Nindermann's letter written at Bulun—Noros's story of his parting with De Long when he and Nindermann were sent on for relief—The narrative of Mr. Leach. 130

CHAPTER XIII.

YAKUTSK.

The 'City of the Yakuts'—The Cossack conquerors of Siberia—The Province of Yakutsk—Natives, Russian peasants, and exiles—Yakuts and Tonguses—Ostyak tents—Winter dwellings—Customs of the country—Priests—The 'Pole of Cold'—Interesting notes of travelers—A story of Russian jealousy—Ledyard's eulogy of women—Life at Yakutsk. 140

CHAPTER XIV.

IRKUTSK.

The capital of Eastern Siberia—A cheerful resting-place—Description of the city and its suburbs—Lake Baikal—Valley of the Angara—Account of the great fire of 1879—The fire brigade—Ludicrous scenes and incidents—Religious processions—Mr. Jackson's journey to Irkutsk—Meeting with the Jeannette crew. 154

CHAPTER XV.

LIEUTENANT DANENHOWER'S NARRATIVE.

The story of the expedition—Sailing of the Jeannette—Daring the ice-pack—Frozen in—Drifting—Life on ship—A break-up—Anequin's discovery—Tremendous pressures—Severe gales—A bad leak—Starting the pumps—Hunting excursions—Chipp's experiments—Exciting bear chases—De Long's adventure. 169

CONTENTS.

CHAPTER XVI.

LIEUTENANT DANENHOWER'S NARRATIVE—(CONTINUED.)

The Jeannette in winter quarters—Constant danger—Bear-hunting on the floes—Melville's Canal—Scurvy—Discovery of Jeannette Island—An excursion to Henrietta Island—A curious mistake—Mount Sylvie—Breaking up of the ice—An even keel—A fascinating danger—The hunters' recall—A fatal nip—Abandoning the ship—Encamped on the ice—Sinking of the Jeannette. 191

CHAPTER XVII.

LIEUTENANT DANENHOWER'S NARRATIVE—(CONTINUED.)

Preparations for a long journey—Sleds, boats, and outfit—Order of march—The start southward—A discouraging outlook—Startling discovery—Ferrying the fissures—The hospital tent—Heroism of men—Land ahead—A dash for the shore—Annexation of Bennett Island—Land-slides—Dunbar's exploring trip. 207

CHAPTER XVIII.

LIEUTENANT DANENHOWER'S NARRATIVE—(CONTINUED.)

Launching the boats—Start for Bennett Island—Deserting dogs—Working south between ice-fields—Fatal delay at Ten Day Camp—Among the New Siberian Islands—Hunting on Thaddeoffsky—A terrible situation—Halt on Kotelnoi—Hunting parties—Stalbovoi—Hunting on Semenoffski—Last interview with Chipp—A start for Siberia—Fearful gale, which separates the boats—Launching a drag—An eventful night—Another day and night. 222

CHAPTER XIX.

LIEUTENANT DANENHOWER'S NARRATIVE—(CONTINUED.)

Off the coast—Attempts to reach shore—Enter and proceed up a river—A night of agony in a hunting-camp—A delightful Sunday—Reconnoitering—First meeting with natives—Piloted south by Cut-eared Wassili—At Spiridon's village—The voyage continued. 238

CHAPTER XX.

LIEUTENANT DANENHOWER'S NARRATIVE—(CONCLUDED.)

Arrival at Geemovialocke—The chief's house—Visited by a Russian exile—Attempt to proceed—Return to the village—Decayed geese—Sojourn at the Tunguse village—A native feast day—Arrival of another exile—Entertained at Kusmah's house—The exile starts for Bulun—Danenhower's search for De Long—Startling news—Melville starts to search for De Long—Arrival of Cossack commander—Journey to Bulun and Yakutsk. 250

CHAPTER XXI.

LIEUTENANT DE LONG'S LOG-BOOK.

A copy of the Jeannette's log kept by the commander from May 17th to June 12th, 1881, when the ship sunk.   262

CHAPTER XXII.

A ROLL OF HONOR.

Report of the Ispravnik of Verkhoyansk—Nicholai censured—Generous natives, exiles, and officials—Danenhower's letter.   270

CHAPTER XXIII.

MR. NEWCOMB'S NARRATIVE.

Incidents of the voyage north—Ougalgan Island—Kolyutschin Bay—Skating off Herald Island—Adventure with bears—Singular phenomenon—Sea-gulls—Grand auroral display—Christmas and New Year's entertainments—Indian superstitions—At the pumps—Dangerous excursion—Entomological specimens.   277

CHAPTER XXIV.

MR. NEWCOMB'S NARRATIVE—(CONTINUED.)

Conflict of the floes—Jeannette Minstrel Troupe—Christmas entertainment—Fac-simile of programme—Mr. Collins's poem—A dream of home—Discovery of new lands—Animal life—A tremendous nip—The Jeannette doomed and deserted—A night on the ice—The ship sinks—A dreadful blank.   292

CHAPTER XXV.

MR. NEWCOMB'S NARRATIVE— (CONTINUED.)

Appearance of camp—The retreat begun—Landing on American soil—Tramps on Bennett Island—Among the birds—Interesting volley—Building a cairn—Sailing southward—Adventures among the New Siberian Islands—Start for Siberia—Gales and tempests—On the big land once more—A luxurious hut.   308

CHAPTER XXVI.

MR. NEWCOMB'S NARRATIVE—(CONTINUED.)

A start up the Lena—Meet natives—A dinner with Theodore, Tomat, and Carinie—Pictures of 'saints'—Horse-hair nets—Old Bushielle—A voyage south—Arrival and long residence at a Tunguse village—Friendly exiles—Dwellings, dress, and customs—Routine of life—Religious feasts—Kusmah, the exile—A present from the Pope of Bulun—De Long in distress—Melville's departure—Journey to Bulun by dog-teams.   320

CHAPTER XXVII.

MR. NEWCOMB'S NARRATIVE—(CONTINUED.)

Good-bye to Bulun—Reindeer teams—Nights in a povarnia—Lassoing reindeer—Experiences on the road—Meeting with exiles—Arrival at Verkhoyansk—Russian officials—The outposts of civilization—The famous vodka—A village of exiles—Customs of the country—Journey resumed—Cross the Arctic Circle—Retrospective—Exiled Poles—Russian traders—Descending the mountains—Novel sight—Fine scenery—Accidents—Visit to Reindeer Tunguses—A night attack—Curious scenes and incidents along the road by night and day—Odd customs. 332

CHAPTER XXVIII.

MR. NEWCOMB'S NARRATIVE—(CONTINUED.)

Approach to Yakutsk—The Mecca of my hopes—Hospitable reception—Sight-seeing—An old fortress—Life at Yakutsk—Evening recreations—New Year's day—The Russian Christmas—Churches and priests—Curious fire-engines—A peculiar people—The start homeward—'Jining the army'—Reception at Irkutsk—Dr. Ledyard—Life in the metropolis—Arrival of Jackson—Noros returns east—A sample of the 'boys.' 343

CHAPTER XXIX.

MR. NEWCOMB'S NARRATIVE—(CONTINUED.)

Leave Irkutsk—Meet Harber and Scheutze—Seamen turn back—Journey through Siberia—Sights at Tomsk—The Siberian women—Omsk—Life on the Kirghesian steppes—Easter Sunday at Throisky—Village entertainments—Russian superstitions—A wedding—Fanciful dresses—A capsize—The Ural River—Osk—The Ural Mountains—Fine views—Kirghese hunters—Cossack villages—Orenburg and the 'iron horse'—An interesting city—Ride along the Volga—Agricultural scenes—Moscow—St. Petersburg—Interview with the emperor and empress—Cronstadt—Hull—Liverpool—'Home again.' 353

CHAPTER XXX.

DE LONG'S FATE DISCOVERED—THE GRAVES ON THE LENA.

The search renewed—Melville at Cath Carta—Visit to Cape Bykoff—Fearful storms—An account of the search for and finding of De Long and his men—The rifle in the snow—'All dead'—Removal of the lost explorers—Description of their mausoleum—Inscription on the cross—The tragedy on the Delta—Strange incidents—The nightly alarm fire—De Long's last effort. 366

CONTENTS. xi

CHAPTER XXXI.

LIEUTENANT DE LONG'S DIARY.

PAGE.

A melancholy relic—Copy of De Long's diary extending from October 15th to the end—A terrible story of hardships, sufferings, and death, and of heroic bravery and Christian resignation. 379

CHAPTER XXXII.

NEW SEARCHERS IN THE FIELD.

The search for Chipp—Travelers from the East and the West—Berry, Hunt, and Gilder—Harber and Scheutze's expedition—Preparations at Vitimsk—Hunt and Bartlett join Harber—Meeting of steamers—Homeward journey of the returning explorers. 394

CHAPTER XXXIII.

BURNING OF THE RODGERS—AN ICE-FLOE TRAGEDY.

The Rodgers at St. Lawrence Bay—'Fire'!—Burning of the Ship—Escape to the shore—A grand sight—At home with the Chukches—Grace's narrative—Putnam missing—Alarming discovery—Drifting on the ice—Putnam's sad fate. 401

CHAPTER XXXIV.

LIFE AMONG THE CHUKCHES.

Hunting for a living—Fisherwomen, medicine-men, dwellings, customs and superstitions—Visit to Reindeer Chukches—Death of a girl—Life at Camp Hunt—Three strangers—Zane's adventure—Retreat south—Arrival of the North Star and Corwin—Rescue of the castaways—Loss of the North Star. 414

CHAPTER XXXV.

MR. GILDER'S TRAVELS IN SIBERIA.

The start from Camp Hunt—Traveling companions—Waiting for Wanker—Chukche amusements—Dancing girls—Love-sick Constantine—Journey to Cape North—A genuine 'poorga'—A night in the snow—The Chukche caravan—A brilliant sight—Ornamental bells—Lost in a snow-storm—Carried over a precipice—Badly frozen—Loss of dogs—On the borders of civilization—A night in a deserted hut—An abandoned village—Picture of life in a cottage—Down the Kolyma—Arrival at Wanker's house—Surprising changes—An old hypocrite—The powerful stranger—Escape from Wanker—Friendly villagers—Arrival at Nishni Kolymsk—Journey to Middle Kolymsk—Description of the town and its people—Curious sights—Antiquated implements—Inside the houses—Interesting exiles—An unpardonable offence—A convenient religion—Pictures of saints—Household devotions—'Dear little Nanyah' and her guardian—A beautiful sight—'Vodka,' and the custom of the country—Journey to Verkhoyansk. 428

CHAPTER XXXVI.

THE STORY OF THE FORLORN HOPE.

Additional particulars respecting the parting of Nindermann and Noros from De Long, and of their journey to Bulun. 449

CHAPTER XXXVII.

ENGINEER MELVILLE'S NARRATIVE—(CONTINUED).

The voyage from Semenoffsky and separation of the boats—The November search for De Long—Opinion as to Chipp's fate—Finding of the first cutter. 462

APPENDIX.

An account of the arrival and reception of Melville and his companions. 470

LIST OF ENGRAVINGS.

	PAGE.
PHOTOGRAPHIC PORTRAITS OF THE OFFICERS OF THE ARCTIC STEAMER JEANNETTE,	*Frontispiece.*
GROUP OF EXPLORERS IN ARCTIC COSTUME,	17
ALEXAI AND HIS WIFE— THEIR LAST INTERVIEW,	24
ESQUIMAUX FAMILY NEAR CAPE PRINCE OF WALES,	36
TATTOOED WOMAN OF ST. LAWRENCE ISLAND,	38
THE CORWIN SEARCH PARTY— SLEDGING ON THE SIBERIAN COAST,	44
A BIRD NURSERY,	47
PETROPAVLOSK— REPULSE OF THE ALLIES,	57
COMMANDER'S ISLANDS— SLAUGHTER OF SEA-BEARS,	58
CHUKCHES VISITING THE RODGERS IN SKIN BOATS,	60
INTERVIEWING A DENIZEN OF WRANGEL LAND,	62
PREPARING FOR WINTER,	70
HUT OF WRECKED NORWEGIANS AT BEAR ISLAND,	73
GLACIERS AT BELL SOUND, SPITZBERGEN,	74
SAMOYEDES OF ARCHANGEL,	78
THE " RESCUE,"	82
LIMIT OF TREES IN SIBERIA,	92
MAMMCTH SKELETON IN THE MUSEUM AT ST. PETERSBURG,	95
NATIVE OF THE TUNDRA, WITH SIBERIAN RHINOCEROS-HORN,	96
SIBERIAN RIVER BOAT,	99
YAKUSTK, EASTERN SIBERIA, IN THE SEVENTEENTH CENTURY,	101
THE VEGA AND LENA SALUTING CAPE CHELYUSKIN,	104
LANDING A SEA-SICK OFFICIAL,	109
WINTER YOURT,	110
THE JEANNETTE FASTENED TO A FLOE,	113
GRAVES IN THE PRIMEVAL FORESTS OF SIBERIA,	124
LIEUTENANT DE LONG AND HIS MEN WADING ASHORE,	126
THE PARTING ON THE LENA,	133
SIBERIAN VILLAGE CHURCH,	141
SIBERIAN PEASANT, WITH SAMOVAR,	142
OSTYAK TENTS MADE OF BIRCH-BARK,	143
NATIVE GIRLS OF YAKUTSK IN WINTER COSTUME,	146
YAKUTSK IN OUR DAYS	147
A WINTER JOURNEY— AMONG THE DRIFTS,	153

LAKE BAIKAL, EASTERN SIBERIA, IN WINTER,	155
VIEW IN IRKUTSK,	157
A CITY ON FIRE,	161
EXILED CRIMINAL IN CHAINS,	166
LIEUTENANT DANENHOWER TELLING HIS STORY,	168
NORDENSKIÖLD'S WINTER QUARTERS, KOLYUTSCHIN BAY,	172
WHALERS STOPPED BY THE ICE,	174
SKATING ON THE YOUNG ICE,	176
THE ICE IN MOTION,	178
ARCTIC AURORAS,	185
DE LONG'S ADVENTURE— A MUTUAL SURPRISE,	187
IN THE CROW'S-NEST,	190
BEAR-HUNTING ON THE FLOE,	193
JEANNETTE ISLAND,	194
ARCTIC GLACIER,	197
THE JEANNETTE CREW ABANDONING THEIR SHIP,	203
THE SINKING OF THE JEANNETTE,	206
FIRST CAMP AFTER STARTING SOUTH,	213
VIEW OF BENNETT ISLAND,	220
EXPLORATION OF BENNETT ISLAND,	221
WORKING SOUTH THROUGH THE ICE,	223
THADDEOFFSKY ISLAND,	226
STOLBOVOI ISLAND,	230
THE SEPARATION OF THE BOATS,	234
CHILD IN ARCTIC RIG,	237
FISHERMAN'S HUTS,	249
WINTER RESIDENCE OF THE RUSSIAN EXILE,	253
ARCTIC YOUNGSTER,	261
OUTLINES OF JEANNETTE ISLAND,	263
EFFECTS OF A NIP,	269
ON THE RETREAT,	273
GLAUCOUS-WINGED GULLS,	278
WALRUS,	281
EFFECT OF ICE PRESSURES,	283
"MORE FRESH MEAT,"	289
AN ARCTIC SKETCH,	291
CONFLICT OF THE FLOES,	292
THE JEANNETTE IN HER LAST DOCK,	301
A VISION OF HOME,	303
OLD-WORLD POLAR DRESS— FROM A PAINTING IN THE STOCKHOLM MUSEUM,	307
A SUCCESSFUL HUNTER,	309
ANNEXATION OF BENNETT ISLAND,	310
CAIRN ON BENNETT ISLAND,	313
SEAL AND SEAL-HOLE,	314
LAND-SLIDE AT BENNETT ISLAND,	315

LIST OF ENGRAVINGS.   XV

ARCTIC DUCKS,	317
LOG CABIN ON THE LENA,	319
SIGHTING THE FIRST NATIVES,	321
OUR DEPARTURE FROM GEEMOVIALOCKE,	330
YAKUT HUNTER,	331
GOOD-BYE TO BULUN,	333
NOVEL DESCENT OF THE MOUNTAINS,	338
REINDEER TUNGUSES AND SUMMER TENT,	340
RUSSIAN KIBITKA,	342
RUSSIAN PRIEST,	346
SURVIVORS OF THE EXPEDITION AT YAKUTSK— FROM A PHOTOGRAPH,	347
SUMMER YOURT,	352
JUMPING CRADLE-HOLES,	354
A SIBERIAN SPINNER,	356
A RUSSIAN WEDDING PARTY,	358
A SIBERIAN TARANTASS,	359
THE GREAT BELL OF MOSCOW,	363
BOUNDARY STONE BETWEEN EUROPE AND ASIA,	365
THE RIFLE IN THE SNOW,	369
MELVILLE DISCOVERING DE LONG AND HIS COMPANIONS,	370
THE TOMB ON THE LENA,	371
NEW-WORLD POLAR DRESS,	378
A TIME OF TROUBLE,	382
"SUCH A DREARY, WRETCHED NIGHT,"	385
BURIAL OF ERICKSON IN THE LENA,	387
BURNING OF THE RODGERS,	400
RODGERS SEAMEN ATTEMPTING TO RESCUE PUTNAM,	410
CHUKCHE COUNTRY HARES,	415
CHUKCHE WOMAN ANGLING,	416
THE STAROST OF THE REINDEER CHUKCHES,	418
A CHUKCHE DWELLING,	420
INTERIOR OF TENT,	421
MAN AND WOMAN OF TIAPKA,	425
SEALS SPORTING,	427
CAPE NORTH,	440
BEAKER SPONGES FROM SEA-BOTTOM AT MOUTH OF THE KOLYMA,	445

MAPS, PLANS, ETC.

MAP OF EASTERN SIBERIA, SHOWING EXPLORERS' ROUTES,	16
MAP OF THE LENA DELTA,	16
PLANS OF THE BOATS,	228
WASSILI'S CHART,	246
FAC-SIMILE OF ENTERTAINMENT PROGRAMME,	294, 295
PLAN OF DE LONG'S LAST CAMPING PLACE,	374

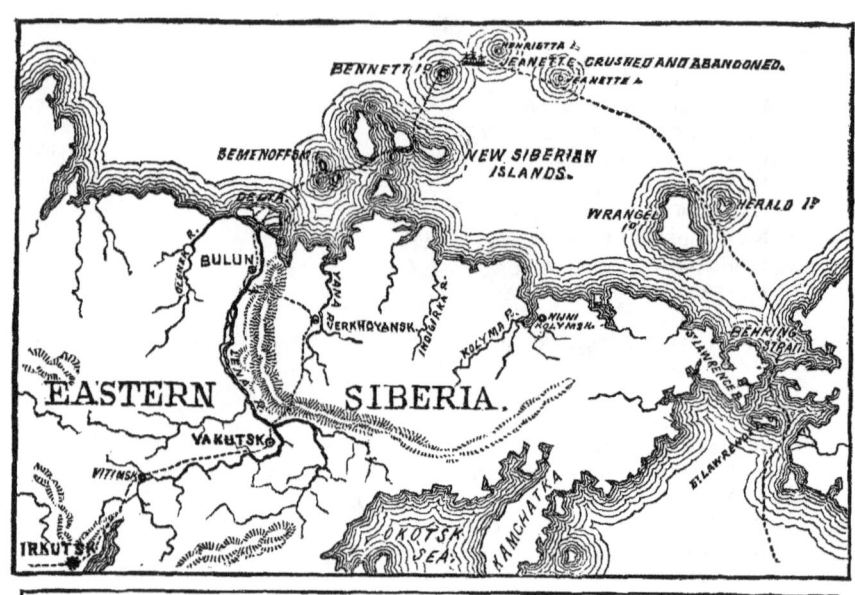

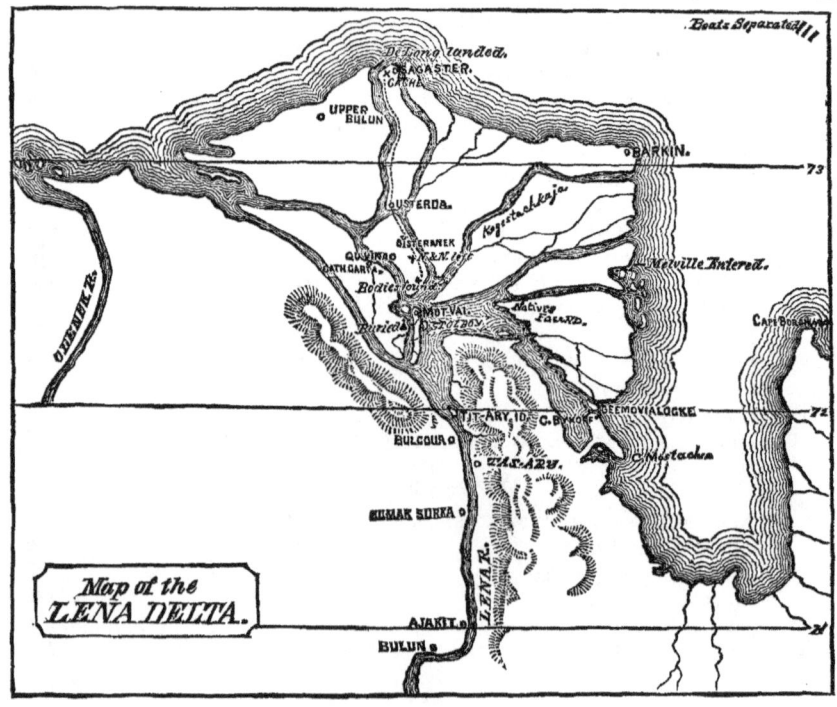

TONG SING. LEACH. NEWCOMB. DANENHOWER. WILSON. COLE.
FROM A PHOTOGRAPH TAKEN ON THEIR ARRIVAL AT YAKUTSK.

CHAPTER I.

THE JEANNETTE AND HER CREW—THE VOYAGE TO THE ARCTIC OCEAN.

THE American Arctic Expedition, commanded by Lieutenant George W. DeLong of the United States Navy, which left San Francisco, July 8th, 1879, was projected by James Gordon Bennett, proprietor of the New York *Herald*. After the return of the last of the two successful expeditions which he had sent to Africa under Henry M. Stanley, Mr. Bennett longed for new worlds to conquer, and decided to send out, at his own expense, an expedition to attempt to reach the North Pole by way of Bering's Straits. Lieutenant DeLong became interested in the undertaking, and the Pandora, owned by Captain Allan Young, was selected and bought as a suitable vessel to convey the explorers.

The Pandora was built in England in 1862. She was a bark-rigged steam yacht of 420 tons burden, with an engine of 200 horse-power, and a wide spread of canvas. She was strongly constructed, and had seen considerable service in the northern seas. In 1873 she conveyed her owner to the Arctic regions for the purpose of searching for records of Sir John Franklin's expedition; and in 1876 Captain Young cruised in her about the northern part of Baffin's Bay,—having been deputed by the English Admiralty to search for Captain Nare's expedition.

By special act of Congress the vessel was allowed to sail under American colors, to assume a new name—the Jeannette—and to be navigated by officers of the United States Navy, with all the rights and privileges of a government vessel. The Secretary of the Navy was authorized to accept and take charge of the ship for the use of the proposed expedition, and to use any material on hand in fitting her for the voyage; but upon condition that the Department should not be subjected to any expense on account thereof.

The Jeannette was taken from Havre, in France, through the Straits of Magellan to San Francisco, by Lieutenant DeLong, with Lieutenant Danenhower as navigating officer, and there delivered to the naval authorities at Mare Island After a thorough examination it was deemed advisable, on account of the hazardous nature of the contemplated voyage, that her capacity to resist the pressure of the ice should be increased. "This conclusion," says the Secretary of the Navy, "was precautionary, merely, inasmuch as she had been well constructed, and was believed to possess ordinary strength."

A large amount of work was subsequently done upon the ship at the expense of Mr. Bennett. She was furnished with new boilers; iron box beams were put in abaft and forward of the boilers to strengthen her sides; trusses were strengthened; additional wooden hooks were introduced and fastened through and through; her extreme fore end, to the extent of about ten feet from the spar deck down, was filled in with solid timber and caulked; additional strakes and planks six inches thick were introduced to strengthen her bilge; and her deck frame was renewed wherever required. The cabin and forecastle were padded with layers of felt to keep out the cold, and the poop deck was covered with several thicknesses of stout painted canvas. Boats, tents, extra sails, two extra propellers, extra pumps, a distilling apparatus, a hoisting engine rigged on the spar deck to be employed in warping, all kinds of machinery that might possibly be of use, and everything that could be devised to give safety to the explorers and efficiency to the expedition, were provided. The vessel was fully provisioned and equipped for a three years' voyage.

The following letter was written by Lieutenant DeLong just before the expedition started:—

ARCTIC STEAMER JEANNETTE,
SAN FRANCISCO, CAL., JULY 8th, 1879.

Hon. R. W. THOMPSON, Secretary of the Navy:—

SIR,—I have the honor to inform you that the Jeannette, being in all respects ready for sea, will sail at three o'clock this afternoon on her cruise to the Arctic regions.

I have also the honor to acknowledge the receipt of your orders of the 18th of June in relation to the movements of the Arctic expedition under my command; and while I appreciate the grave responsibility intrusted to my care, I beg leave to assure you that I will endeavor to perform this important duty in a manner calculated to reflect credit upon the ship, the navy, and the country at large.

I beg leave to return thanks for the confidence expressed in my ability to satisfactorily conduct such a hazardous expedition, and I desire to place upon record my conviction that nothing has been left unprovided which the enterprise and liberality of Mr. James Gordon Bennett and the experiences of our Arctic predecessors could suggest.

Your obedient servant,

GEORGE W. DELONG,

Lieutenant United States Navy, commanding Arctic steamer Jeannette.

The officers and crew of the Jeannette were as follows:—

Lieutenant George W. DeLong, U. S. N., Commander.
Lieutenant Charles W. Chipp, U. S. N., Executive Officer.
Lieutenant John W. Danenhower, U. S. N., Navigator.
George W. Melville, Chief Engineer. J. M. Ambler, Surgeon. Jerome J. Collins, Meteorologist. Raymond L. Newcomb, Naturalist. William M. Dunbar, Ice Pilot. James H. Bartlett, First-class Fireman. John Cole, Boatswain. Walter Lee, Machinist. Alfred Sweetman, Carpenter. George Lauderback, Walter Sharvell, Firemen.

George W. Boyd, Adolf Dressler, Hans H. Erickson, Carl A. Gortz, Nelse Iverson, Peter E. Johnson, George H. Kuehne, Henry H. Kaack, Herbert W. Leach, Frank Mansen, Wm. F. C. Nindermann, Louis J. Noros, Edward Star, Henry D. Warren, Henry Wilson, Seamen.

Ah Sam, and Charles Tong Sing (Chinese), Cook and Cabin Stewards.

Lieutenants DeLong and Chipp were officers of the U. S. steamer Juniata on her northern cruise in search of the crew of the lost Polaris. Mr. Melville was engineer of the steamer Tigress when she went north on the same errand. All of the crew were volunteers, selected with great care from many applicants. Ninderman was a member of the Polaris ice-drift party.

A complimentary reception was given by the California Academy of Sciences to the officers of the Jeannette, a few days before their departure. The meeting was largely attended, and many eminent scientists of the Pacific coast were present. In response to an invitation to address the audience, Lieutenant DeLong spoke as follows:—

"When the officers of the expedition which I have the honor to command were invited to be present this evening to listen to the discussion of the Arctic problem, I replied for them and myself that nothing would give us greater pleasure than to be present. At the same time, however, I asked that we might be excused from any active participation in the discussion until after our return from within the Arctic circle. This humble peculiarity of ours, it would seem, is not to be tolerated; and however unfit I am to reply with any degree of propriety to the very kind remarks that have been made to us this evening, it seems that it is one of the duties that is forced upon the commander of the expedition, as well as a great many other duties. As far as this part of the expedition is concerned, there is really very little to say. By the act of Congress it has been placed under the charge of naval officers, and it has, since the passage of the act of Congress, received the fostering care and encouragement of the Navy Department. It is peculiar as being the first expedition fitted out to penetrate the highest regions of the north by way of Bering's Straits. Ships have heretofore passed through Bering's Straits, rounding Point Barrow, and going to the northward to rescue and relieve Sir John Franklin; but this is the first purely polar expedition that has ever been despatched by way of Bering's Straits.

"I dare say that after we have left San Francisco, in our passage to the northern seas, we shall experience very much the same difficulties and hardships and trials that have been experienced by everybody who has gone before us. It is one of the most difficult things—in fact, it is an impossible thing—for one starting out on an expedition of this kind to say in advance what he is going to do. The ground which we are going to traverse is an entirely new one. After reaching the seventy-first parallel of latitude we go out into a great blank space, which we are going to endeavor to delineate and to determine whether it is water or land or ice. You will excuse me, therefore, from attempting to explain what we are going to do. If you will be kind enough to keep us in memory while we are gone we will attempt to tell you what we have done on our return, which, I dare say, will be more interesting than attempting to tell you what we hope to do. I can only return to you my sincere thanks for the kind reception you have given us and for the interest you manifest in our peculiar undertaking."

On the 30th of June the San Francisco Chamber of Commerce, specially convened for the purpose of expressing the deep interest felt in the expedition by that body, adopted the following resolutions:—

"Whereas the San Francisco Chamber of Commerce is desirous of expressing its deep interest and good-will toward all measures calculated to forward and extend any scientific explorations likely to benefit the commerce, navigation, or agricultural interests of our country; therefore, on behalf of the mercantile industry of the Pacific slope of the United States of America, be it

"*Resolved:* That we earnestly offer our cheering words of hearty approval to encourage the well-planned American Arctic expedition about to prosecute from our Pacific coast a continuance of that noble work of polar exploration so gallantly inaugurated and fearlessly advanced by the nations bordering on the Atlantic. On behalf of our city, as a future seat of national wealth and extended commerce, we desire to foster scientific enlightenment; and this Chamber views with marked interest an enterprise of national importance, sailing from its Golden Gate, fully equipped with a picked band of brave and resolute men possessed of Arctic experience, whom we feel are capable of winning a successful and glorious record for the nation whose banner floats over them, and whose blessing goes with them. While recognizing with admiration the fact that this expedition is wholly paid for and supported by private munificence, we rejoice that this enterprise is officially endorsed by the United States government, who accord it the national rights necessary to proper discipline, and the suitable dignity intrusted by a great and growing nation whose knowledge it will increase, and to whose honor it will redound. As a national work it will extend the geographical survey and topographical knowledge of our northern boundary; in the interests of commerce, navigation, and national agriculture it may determine laws of meteorology, hydrography, astronomy, and gravitation, reveal ocean currents, develop new fisheries, discover lands and people hitherto unknown; and by extending the world's knowledge of such fundamental principles of earth-life as magnetism and electricity, and various collateral branches of atmospheric science, solve great problems important to our common humanity.

"*Resolved:* That as the well-merited offering of an appreciative nation, our people would rnost heartily approve of and endorse the use of a national vessel to convoy the Jeannette to her most northern port of departure, whence, leaving the shores of solemn pine, she will traverse the northern seas alone, followed by the earnest hopes of friends to progress and the world of science.

"*Resolved:* That we tender to her brave and accomplished commander, Lieutenant George W. DeLong, United States Navy, to his efficient staff of able specialists in various departments of science, and to his hardy and gallant crew, one and all, our hearty good wishes for their safe return, and for the entire success of the American Arctic Expedition from the Pacific."

The departure of the Jeannette from San Francisco, on the 8th of July, 1879, was a notable event in the history of that city. As the vessel moved slowly toward the Golden Gate, the friendly waving of hats and handkerchiefs from the wharves, the shipping, and Telegraph Hill, told the explorers that the good people of the city, as well as the men of the sea, were giving them a hearty send-off. A salute of ten guns fired from Fort Point greeted them at the Narrows, and several steamboats crowded with spectators, and the white-sailed craft of the San Francisco Yacht Club convoyed the Jeannette till she was out on the bosom of the broad Pacific, and fairly started on her voyage to the unknown north. Mrs. DeLong, the devoted wife of the commander, remained on her husband's ship till the last moment, and received his parting farewell as he assisted her from the Jeannctte's boat to the deck of the last returning craft.

The Jeannette proceeded direct to Ounalaska, one of the Aleutian Islands, and anchored in the harbor of Illiouliouk, August 2d. This place is the headquarters of the Alaska Commercial Company, and its agent and other officials showed the explorers much kindness and attention. Additional stores and supplies of coal and fur from the storehouses of the company were taken on board.

On the 6th of August the Jeannette resumed her course, and on the 12th of August anchored opposite the little settlement and blockhouse known by Americans as St. Mlichael's, Alaska, and by Russians as Michaelovski. The explorers were welcomed by Mr. Newmann, agent of the Alaska Commercial Company, and by Mr. Nelson, an employee of the Smithsonian Institute and observer of the U. S. Signal Service, who were philosophical enough to live contentedly in that isolated place. A drove of about forty trained dogs, three dog-sleds, and fur clothing were here taken on board ship, and two native Alaskans, named Anequin and Alexai, were hired to accompany the expedition as dog drivers and hunters. Alexai was a married man, and both could speak a little English.

"Mrs. Alexai," wrote Mr. Collins, "a chubby-faced, shy, but good-humored looking young female, came on board to see her husband off on his long cruise. She behaved with great propriety under the circumstances. Alexai behaved also with stolidity tempered by affection for his spouse.

THE LAST INTERVIEW.

They sat together, hand in hand, on some bags of potatoes near the cabin-door, and probably exchanged vows of eternal fidelity. I was greatly touched, and got up on the bridge with my sketch-block, on which I outlined their figures. I had to take them as they sat with backs toward me, for Mrs. Alexai was too modest to face the pencil. Before leaving the ship Captain DeLong gave the bereaved one a cup and saucer with gilt letters on it. She seemed overpowered with emotion at the possession of such unique treasures, and at once hid them in the ample folds, or rather stowage-places, of her fur dress."

On the 18th of August the schooner Fanny A. Hyde, conveying coal and extra stores for the expedition, arrived from San Francisco, and on the evening of the 21st both vessels resumed the voyage northward. As they started out, the guns at the old Russian fort and at the Agency of the Western Fur and Trading Company belched forth a parting salute.

On the 25th the Jeannette arrived at St. Lawrence Bay, East Siberia, some thirty miles south of East Cape, where DeLong learned from the natives that a steamer, supposed to be the Vega, had gone south. The schooner arrived the next day, and her stores were transferred to the Jeannette. In a letter dated August 26th, Engineer Melville wrote home as follows:—

"We did not send our convoy back from St. Michael's as we expected, because we were too deeply laden already to take on our stores. It was very fortunate for us we had her to carry our extra coal and stores over here, for on the way we were caught in a terrible gale of wind, and, owing to the condition of the ship, and deeply laden as we were, the sea had a clean sweep over us. It stove in our forward parts, carried away the bridge, caved the bulkheads, and in fact just drowned us out. Had we the other stuff on board we must have foundered, or else got it overboard in time. We leave here for East Cape to-day, having taken on board all our stores, and we are in even much worse sea-condition than we were before; but we think that maybe, when we get into the ice where the wind can't raise a sea, we will be all right."

From St. Lawrence Bay the Jeannette continued her journey alone. Just before starting, Mr. Collins, as special correspondent of the New York *Herald,* wrote to that journal as follows:—

"All before us now is uncertainty, because our movements will be governed by circumstances over which we can have no control. If, as I telegraphed, the search for Nordenskiold is now needless, we will try and reach Wrangel Land, and find a winter harbor on that new land, on which, we believe, the white man has not yet put his foot. At the worst, we may winter in Siberia, and 'go for' the Wrangel Land mystery next spring. I am in great hopes we will reach there this season.

"We are amply supplied with fur clothing and provisions, so that we can feed and keep warm in any event for some time. Our dogs will enable us to make explorations to considerable distances from the ship and determine the character of the country. Feeling that we have the sympathy of all we left at home, we go north, trusting in God's protection and our good fortune. Farewell."

After rounding East Cape, Lieutenant DeLong touched at Cape Serdze, on the northeast coast of Siberia, and left his last letter home. It was dated August 29th, and reached Mrs. DeLong over a year afterward. In this letter he expressed his intention of proceeding to the southern end of Wrangel Land, touching on the way, if practicable, at Kolyutschin Bay, where the natives informed him Nordenskiold had wintered. "If," he wrote (referring to the probability that a ship would be sent to obtain intelligence of him the following year), "the ship comes up merely for tidings of us, let her look for them on the east side of Kellet Land and on Herald Island."

On the 2d of September, 1879, when about fifty miles or so south of Herald Island, Captain Barnes, of the American whale-bark Sea Breeze, saw the Jeannette under full sail and steam, and attempted to communicate with her, but both vessels were in heavy ice, and a dense fog was setting in, which prevailed up to the following day. These vessels, having approached to within less than four miles of each other, held their courses without communication. On the following day, September 3d, 1879, Captain Kelley, of the bark Dawn, Captain Bauldry, of the Helen Mar, and several others of the whaling fleet, then somewhat northward of the Sea Breeze, saw smoke issuing from a steamer's smoke-stack, in range of Herald Island. The Jeannette, having pressed forward, was hull down north of these whalers; hence they only saw her black smoke. She was standing north. The weather was quite clear at this time. These were the last tidings of the Jeannette, or any of her crew, received for over two years.

Lieutenant DeLong's plans were to reach Wrangel Land the first season, spend the winter in exploration there, and then to push on northwardly as far as possible. "I shall go," he said, before starting, "to the extreme limit of possible navigation that I am able to attain. If the current takes me to the west, you will hear of me through St. Petersburg; but if it takes me eastward and northward, there is no saying what points I may reach; but I hope to come out through Smith's or Jones's Sound."

From Ounalaska Lieutenant DeLong sent to his friend, Lieutenant Jacques, a long letter, teeming with the interest and enthusiasm his great work had inspired. "We are started," he wrote, "and we shall try to do our best. We have a good, solid ship, and everything that money and experience could provide. We go to Ounalaska, thence to St. Paul's Island, thence to St. Michael's, and thence to as high a latitude as God will let us reach in two years—keeping the third year in reserve to get back. Keep us in mind, old fellow, and pray for my success, for my heart is set on this thing. Ninderman is with me, and keeps the bridge watch. Have a good time, and be careful of your health, and I pray God to bless you."

CHAPTER II.

A SEARCH FOR MISSING WHALERS AND THE JEANNETTE.

(Cruise of the Corwin, 1880.)

IN the autumn of 1879, two whaling ships, the Mt. Wollaston, commanded by Captain Nye, and the Vigilant—which, with a score of others, left San Francisco in the spring—failed to return, and were reported as having been seen entangled in the ice by Captain Bauldry, whose bark, the Helen Mar, was the last to get away. Another vessel, the Mercury, was also caught in the ice, and her crew were rescued by the Helen Mar.

Tempted by favorable weather and the hope of success in catching whales, these vessels had prolonged their stay in the Arctic Sea till after the middle of October, and Captain Bauldry escaped with difficulty, forcing a passage through the new ice which formed rapidly around him. A sudden change of wind drove the missing whalers northwesterly into open water, while a heavy body of ice south of them prevented all escape. Their crews numbered about twenty men each, and the desperate condition in which they were placed may be inferred from the fact that during the eight previous years no less than thirty-three vessels, out of the small fleet there engaged in whaling, had been caught in the pack and drifted to the northeast, carrying with them sixty men who had remained by their ships in the vain hope of saving them, and of whom nothing has since been heard. During the same period, over thirty other whalers of the same fleet had also been crushed or otherwise wrecked.

The following reminiscence of Captain Nye is furnished by Mr. William Bradford, the eminent marine artist:—

"A short time before Lieutenant DeLong's departure I suggested to him that we call together all the whaling captains then in port—most of whom I knew well personally—and avail ourselves of whatever information their experience might afford and suggestions they might have to make. He accepted the idea and arranged the meeting, and they all attended. One by one they gave their opinions, mainly upon the point of their greatest interest, the probable direction of the winds and currents at the time when Lieutenant DeLong expected to reach Wrangel Land. But there was one among them who kept ominously silent, not venturing an opinion or offering a suggestion. I finally said: 'Captain Nye has not given us his opinion, and we would like to hear from him.' He said: 'Gentlemen, there isn't much to be said about this matter. You, Lieutenant DeLong, have a very strong vessel, have you not? Magnificently equipped for the service, with unexceptionable crew and aids? And you will take plenty of provisions, and all the coal you can carry?' To each of these questions, as it was asked, Lieutenant DeLong replied affirmatively. 'Then,' said Captain Nye, 'put her into the ice and let her drift, and you may get through or you may go to the devil, and the chances are about equal.' Poor Captain Nye! He ventured in there after Lieutenant DeLong —into those same Arctic regions, in the prosecution of his enterprise as a whaler—and was never heard of again. He was from New Bedford, Mass., was one of the oldest, bravest, and best men in the service, and there was no man sailing to the frigid seas who knew more of their perils than he who made that ominous forecast of the probable fate of the Jeannette, if not of her commander."

Much anxiety for the missing barks was felt in San Francisco, and merchants and citizens of that city petitioned the Secretary of the Navy to send out a government vessel to search for the whalers, and also for the Jeannette, as in the opinion of returned whalemen Captain DeLong had not succeeded in reaching Wrangel Land when winter set in.

Subsequently, Captain C. L. Hooper, of the revenue cutter

Corwin, was ordered on a trip northward to search for tidings of the missing vessels. He was also instructed to cruise in the waters of Alaska for the enforcement of the revenue laws, to visit St. Lawrence Island, where many natives had died of starvation, and to endeavor to suppress the traffic in whiskey, which was the principal cause of so much misery.

Captain Hooper sailed from San Francisco, on his mission of good-will, May 22d, 1880. After touching at Ounalaska, June 9th, the Corwin met heavy ice pitching and grinding along the edge of the pack, and found refuge in a good harbor on the north coast of Nunivak Island, off a native settlement.

"The inhabitants," says Captain Hooper, "all ran away to the hills as we approached, but on the next day we succeeded in capturing them—one man, three women, and three children. They were very much alarmed, and evidently thought they were to be killed. A present of some tobacco soon quieted their fears, and the man was persuaded to come on board, and seemed very much interested in all he saw. A looking-glass astonished him more than all the rest. At first he was alarmed at it, and then, after overcoming his fears, was greatly amused. He did not know the taste of brandy or whiskey, and when offered some made a wry face and spat it out in evident disgust. Having lived away from civilization, his tastes had not been educated to such a degree. He put his hands upon the stove, and seemed astonished that it burned him, and even tried it a second time to make sure. The houses of the settlement, ten in number, were built of mud and all connected by a subterranean passage. They were arranged in a circle, with a common entrance to the passage in the center."

Following the track of the Jeannette, Captain Hooper next visited St. Michaels, June 22d, where he met Messrs. Newman and Nelson, two Americans residing there. "These gentlemen," wrote Hooper, "live quite comfortably. They have about a dozen log-houses, which they use for dwellings and storehouses, enclosed in a stockade. Some of the more civilized natives are employed as domestics. An Indian village about half a mile from the trading-post consists of about thirty houses and a dance-house. These houses contain two rooms. The first, or outer one, is built half under ground and has a frame roof covered with earth. The inner room is entirely under ground, and is reached through a small opening in the back of the front room. These natives are a lazy, worthless people. The only sign of civilization noticeable among them is their fondness for whiskey and tobacco."

Two weeks later Captain Hooper again visited St. Michaels, and found the place much changed in appearance. The snow and ice were all gone, the hillsides were covered with wild flowers, and the air was thick with mosquitoes. The traders of the two companies located here had also arrived from the different trading-posts of the interior, some of which are 2,000 miles from the coast. These traders come to St. Michaels every spring as soon as the ice leaves the rivers; they bring in the furs purchased during the winter, get a new supply of trade goods, and return apparently satisfied with their lot.

"I was," says Captain Hooper, "particularly impressed with the fine physique of the Indians whom they brought down with them. They are very much superior to the coast Indians, resembling more in appearance the Indians seen on the plains, having piercing black eyes, long, muscular limbs, and erect figures, showing courage, strength, and endurance.

"These Indians live by hunting bears, moose, wolves, and reindeer, and trap mink and foxes. In the summer they hunt with guns; in the winter, when game cannot run fast on account of the snow, the bow and arrow are used. Black bears are killed with a knife or spear. It is considered disgraceful to shoot them. When an Indian meets a black bear, he approaches within a few feet; the bear stops, faces him, and rises on his haunches, prepared to give him a hug. The

Indian then draws his knife with great deliberation, and addressing the bear says: 'I know you are not afraid; but neither am I. I am as brave as you are.' Then advancing cautiously, he improves the first opportunity when Bruin is off his guard to give him a thrust with the knife in a vital spot, and the savage has one more deed of valor to boast of to his friends when they gather in their dance-house to 'ung-to-ah,'—a ceremony which consists of dancing around the fire and relating, in a kind of song or chant, to the music of a drum, their deeds of daring in the past, and indulging in promises of still more glorious ones in the future.

"The result of the conflict, however, is not always entirely in the Indian's favor; the bear sometimes gets the best of it, and handles the savage very roughly. We saw several natives who bore the marks of very severe scalp wounds received in encounters with bears."

After his first visit to St. Michaels, Captain Hooper steamed westward to St. Lawrence Island, to investigate the reported wholesale starvation of the natives during the two or three preceding winters.

"We stopped," he says, "off the first village, about midnight of June 25th, and found the village entirely deserted, with sleds, boat-frames, paddles, spears, bows and arrows, etc., strewn in every direction. We found no dead bodies, probably missed them in the faint twilight, as we subsequently learned at the west end of the island that they had all died. From the number of houses, boats, etc., we estimated the number of those who had died to be about fifty.

"On the 26th we followed along the north side of the island, examining the villages as we came to them. At Cape Siepermo we found the village deserted, not a sign of life remaining. I counted fifty-four dead bodies, and as these were nearly all full-grown males, there can be no doubt that many more died. The women and children doubtless died first, and were buried. Most of those seen were just outside the village, with their sleds beside them, evidently having been dragged out by the survivors, as they died, until they, becoming too weak for further exertion, went into their houses and, covering themselves with skins, lay down and died. In many of the houses we saw from one to four dead bodies.

"About fifteen miles west of Cape Siepermo we found another village, also entirely deserted. Here we saw twelve dead bodies, all full-grown males. As at the other villages, the women and children had probably been buried, as we saw none. The number of dead at this place was estimated at thirty. At a large settlement on the northwest end of the island, which we next visited, we found about three hundred natives alive. Two hundred had died, and the entire population had barely escaped starvation by eating their dogs and the walrus-hides covering their boats and houses. At a settlement on the northwest end the natives said a large number had died, but how many they could not tell. They said the weather was cold and stormy for a long time, with great quantities of ice and snow, so that they could not hunt walrus and seal; and as they make no provision for the future, but depend upon what they can get from day to day, of course failure means starvation.

"These people live directly in the track of vessels bound into the Arctic Ocean for the purpose of whaling or trading. They make houses, boats, clothing, etc., of the skins of walrus and seals, and sell the bones and ivory to traders for rum and breech-loading arms. As long as the rum lasts they do nothing but drink and fight. They had a few furs, some of which we tried to buy to make Arctic clothing; but, notwithstanding their terrible experience in the past, they refused to sell for anything but whiskey, rifles, or cartridges."

It is gratifying to know that Captain Hooper succeeded in capturing two whiskey-trading schooners, and that they were dealt with according to law.

The season for northern search having now arrived, Captain Hooper passed through Bering's Straits into the Arctic Sea, and made five distinct attempts to reach high latitude, but without extraordinary success. On the 20th of August he was within three miles of Herald Island, and on the 11th of September he was within twenty-five miles of Wrangel Land; but even these positions were only attained after steaming long distances through labyrinthian lanes, and coming in contact with large bodies of floating ice.

The Corwin sailed hither and thither, across the open portions of the Arctic basin, and much interesting information relating to the native tribes, natural history, and geology of the region was gathered; but no trace of the Jeannette or missing whalers was found, and at the close of the Arctic summer the Corwin returned to San Francisco.

The following extracts are from Captain Hooper's account of his voyage:—

"In that part of the Arctic visited by the Corwin the ice is quite different from the ice in the vicinity of Greenland. No immense icebergs raise their frozen peaks hundreds of feet in the air. The highest ice seen by us during the season would not exceed fifty feet in height. The average height of the main pack is from ten to fifteen feet, with hummocks that rise twenty or thirty feet. The specific gravity of sea ice is 91; hence only about a tenth is visible above the surface of the water. A field of twenty feet in height may have a depth of nearly two hundred feet. This enormous thickness is caused by one layer of ice being forced upon another by the action of wind and current. The greatest thickness it attains by freezing is about eighteen feet. At that depth ice ceases to be a conductor of temperature.

"Along the edge of the pack, during the summer, is generally found a belt of drift ice varying in width according to the direction of the wind. When the wind blows off the pack, drift ice is frequently found fifteen or twenty miles from the main body. At times the pack itself opens in leads, by which it may be penetrated for several miles. In venturing within the limits of the pack, however, a sharp watch must be kept on the movements of the ice, and a retreat made at the first indication of its closing.

"A vessel beset in the pack is as helpless as if she were far inland, while there is imminent danger of being crushed at any moment. When the wind blows on the pack, the drift ice becomes as close as the pack itself. In addition to the constant twisting, turning, breaking, and piling up of the ice, the whole body has a northern set, moving very slowly, but none the less surely.

"Having visited every part of the Arctic that it was possible for a vessel to reach, penetrating the icy regions in all directions fifty to one hundred miles further than any vessel succeeded in doing last year, without being able to find the slightest trace or gain the least tidings of the missing whalers, we were forced to the conclusion that they had been crushed and carried north in the pack, and that their crews had perished. Had any of them survived the winter it seems almost certain that they would have been found either by the Corwin or by some of the whalers, all of whom were on the lookout for them during the summer. It was thought possible that the crews might have escaped over the ice and reached Herald Island, but a sight of the perpendicular sides of that most inhospitable-looking place soon banished even this small hope.

"I have no fears for the safety of the officers and crew of the Jeannette. The fact that they have not been heard from seems to indicate that the vessel is safe, and that they consider themselves able to remain another year at least."

Many of the desolate places which the Corwin sighted or touched at had been visited and named by English navigators in search of Franklin. A correspondent of the New York *Herald* speaks of some of them as follows:—

"Notable among those on the Asiatic coast is Emma Harbor, Plover Bay, Siberia, where Captain Moore wintered in the Plover in 1848–49. It is surrounded on nearly all sides by lofty, barren mountains, whose summits, reaching into the clouds, give them an air of desolate grandeur. Their geological formation is quite remarkable, seemingly nothing more than colossal piles of broken bowlders and fragments of rock.

"On the American side, the western extremity of the New World, Cape Prince of Wales, terminates as a bold, ragged promontory, whose celebrated peak, being joined to the mainland by a low ridge of hills, gives it at a distance the appearance of standing alone in the ocean.

ESKIMO FAMILY NEAR CAPE PRINCE OF WALES.

"Near the head of Kotzebue Sound we found on Chamisso Island, about two hundred feet above the sea level, an astronomical station, composed of a mound of earth and stones, on the top of which was a wooden shaft about twelve feet high, and bearing carved inscriptions of several English ships—Blossom, Herald, Plover. To these was added the 'Corwin—1880.' Near by was another shaft with the names of some Russian vessels.

"About forty miles south of Bering's Straits is a remarkable rocky island, named King's Island by Captain Cook. Its cliffs, almost perpendicular on all sides, rise to the height of 750 feet. It is surrounded by bold water, enabling ships to approach to within a very short distance of the shore. This Arctic Gibraltar—minus the fortifications—has a ragged outline, and its surface is composed principally of stone covered with mosses and lichens, but neither tree nor shrub nor grass is to be found. Noticeable on the most elevated points are a number of stone columns resembling the remains of a Druidical place of worship, or the ruins of some old feudal castle.

"But the most noteworthy feature of the island is the village, composed chiefly of houses excavated in the rocks on a slope of somewhat less than forty-five degrees, and from one to two hundred feet above the sea. At a distance it looks not unlike the resort of some of the sea-fowl who choose these isolated spots to hatch and rear their young. The wonder naturally arises, what are the attractions and capabilities of such a place, that the simple-minded Esquimaux should select it as an abode? All of which can be answered in one word—walrus. Near the village is a cave, used by the natives as a store-house or crypt for food, the entrance to which is not unlike an immense gable window.

"More space might be devoted to a detailed description of what may not inappropriately be called an Esquimaux eyrie, rivaling in interest the lacustrine villages of Switzerland, so remote and unique is its position; but we will only conclude by saying that the traveler and the archæologist may go far in their journeyings and researches before finding a place that shall equal in grotesqueness this far away Walhalla of the walrus family."

The fact that nothing was heard of the Jeannette during the season of 1880 did not cause general serious apprehensions for her safety, and some Arctic navigators considered it a good omen—a promise that the expedition would be a successful one, and that the purposes for which it was sent out would be accomplished. On this subject Lieutenant Weyprecht, of the Austro-Hungarian Arctic expedition of 1872, wrote as follows:—

"I cannot see any reason for being more anxious about

the Jeannette now than on the day when she entered the ice. A ship, whose object is discoveries in uninhabited regions, cannot be expected to remain in communication with home. I know the Jeannette to be well adapted for Arctic service, and she is provisioned for three years,—so Mr. DeLong has no reason to linger about the outer ice for the benefit of those who are expecting news. The absence of news, and the failure of the Corwin to obtain information, must be contemplated as a symptom of success, the Jeannette having probably wintered in regions inaccessible to trading ships. With all the resources at his disposition, Mr. DeLong cannot be expected to return so early without having completely fulfilled his task, if not compelled by very pressing motives, such as scurvy among his crew, or the loss of the ship."

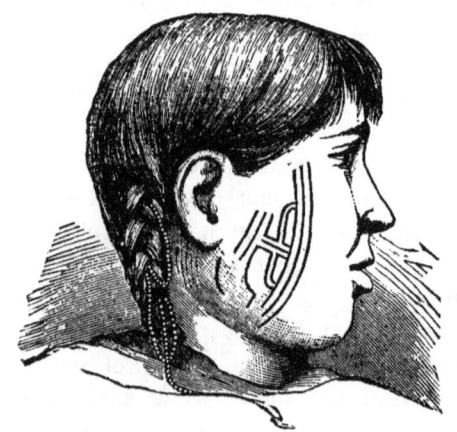

TATTOOED WOMAN OF ST. LAWRENCE ISLAND.

CHAPTER III.

SEARCHES FOR THE JEANNETTE—1881.

(SECOND CRUISE OF THE CORWIN.)

AS the spring of 1881 drew on without bringing any news of the Jeannette, it was deemed wise to carry out some concerted plan of action for the discovery of the whereabouts of the ship and her crew. Petitions for government aid and action were presented to Congress, and Hon. Charles P. Daly, President of the American Geographical Society, in an eloquent letter to the President of the United States, urged the sending out of a search expedition.

Subsequently, early in March, Congress authorized the Secretary of the Navy to expend $175,000 for a suitable ship and its equipments, to be manned wholly by volunteers from the navy, and to be sent north to search for the Jeannette. A little later, Secretary Hunt convened at the Navy Department a board of officers, to whom the duty was intrusted of suggesting and advising as to the best plan for conducting the government searches for the Jeannette.

The Jeannette Relief Expedition Board was composed of Rear-Admiral John Rodgers, Captain James A. Greer, Lieutenant-Commander Henry C. White, Lieutenant William P. Randall, Lieutenant R. M. Berry (recorder), Paymaster Albert S. Kenny, and Surgeon Jerome S. Kidder. They were officers of great experience, and most of them had been identified with earlier Arctic expeditions and explorations in that region. After thoroughly investigating the whole subject, they made a full report, in which they stated their views as to the direction of the search, and the best means for carrying it out.

During the summer of 1881, three well-appointed expeditions—in the Corwin, the Rodgers, and the Alliance—sailed northward from the United States expressly to search for the Jeannette. Two other expeditions, also, which went out primarily for scientific purposes, were instructed to keep a sharp lookout for the Jeannette, and to consider it an important part of their duty. The first of these was under the command of Lieutenant Greely, with a station at Lady Franklin Bay, in Smith Sound; and the second was located at Point Barrow, the northern extremity of Alaska, under command of Lieutenant Ray.

Nor were the Search Expeditions of 1881 confined to the United States. England was represented by Mr. Leigh Smith, a private gentleman, who, in his little yacht, the Eira, gallantly took upon himself the task of searching in the region of Franz Josef Land; an exploring expedition under Dutch auspices, in the ship Wilhelm Barentz, volunteered to make the search for the Jeannette a part of its programme; Russian men-of-war were directed to do what they could for the discovery and relief of the lost, explorers; the nomad inhabitants of Northern Siberia were requested to be on the lookout for any survivors of the expedition who might reach their coast; and M. Soulkowsky, a Russian, traveled overland from Irkutsk to Bering's Strait, through Siberia, on the same errand.

The first Jeannette Search Expedition to leave the United States in the year 1881, steamed out of San Francisco harbor in the revenue steamer Corwin, on the 4th day of May. The occasion was one of much friendly interest, and thousands of people assembled to witness the departure of the explorers. The officers of the Corwin on this voyage were as follows:—

Captain Charles L. Hooper, Commander.
First Lieutenant, W. J. Herring. Second Lieutenant, E. Burke.
Third Lieutenants, O. B. Myrick, George H. Doty, Wm. E. Reynolds.
Chief Engineer, J. T. Wayson. Assistant Engineers, C. A. Laws, E. Owen.
Surgeon, Irving C. Rosse. Scientist, Professor John Muir.

Ten days after leaving San Francisco the Corwin was within sight of the Aleutian Islands, and a little later was anchored in the bay at the southern end of Ounalaska, to the leeward of a high mountain. The natives came out from the shore to welcome back the little cutter which had visited them the preceding year.

The next halt was made at Seal Islands, May 23d; ice was sighted on the 24th; and the Corwin arrived at St. Lawrence Island on the 28th. The natives appeared to be well supplied with food, but lamented the non-arrival of trading vessels with whiskey, as in former years. The voyage was resumed the same night.

Having been informed that a story was in circulation among the natives along the coast to the effect that a party of seal-hunters, while on the ice near Cape North, in November, 1880, had discovered and boarded two wrecked vessels (supposed from the description given of them to be the missing whalers, Mount Wollaston and Vigilant), Captain Hooper resolved to fit out a land party to follow the coast north and west, to investigate this report, and search for the Jeannette. He stopped at St. Lawrence Bay to procure dogs for the party, but the natives would neither sell nor lend any. When told of the object of the excursion, they shook their heads, and said: "No use; all dead"; and would have nothing to do with it. At a village a little beyond Cape Serdze, Captain Hooper was more successful.

"Following the coast," he says, "to the westward, we came to a settlement of Chukches, behind an island called by the natives Tupkan, which is about one mile long, one-fourth of a mile wide, and 150 feet high. It lies a mile off shore. Along the coast we found a rim of ice from five to thirty feet high, and extending from two to ten miles off shore. At our landing-place it was quite narrow, but so rough and hummocky that it seemed to us impassable, and we were about to give up the attempt and return to the ships when we saw some natives going in the direction of the vessel, about a mile further north. Taking our boat we rowed to a point opposite them, and getting out on the ice we waited for them to approach, which they did with some caution, as if they were not quite sure what our intentions were. However, a few words from our interpreter, Joe, and a present of some tobacco, soon quieted their fears and established friendly relations between us. At first they denied all knowledge of the report in regard to the wrecks, but subsequently, having acknowledged that they had heard of it, they told so many wonderful tales that we were inclined to doubt them all.

"After some persuasion and promises of liberal rewards, two of them consented to accompany us if we would shoot walrus for their families to subsist upon during their absence. This we readily promised, provided we could find the walrus; but as none were in sight, and we could not spare the time to hunt for them, we compromised by giving them a few pounds of tobacco. One of them proved to be such a great talker that Joe, who was a man of very few words, said, after listening to him awhile, 'I think its more better we don't take this fellow; too much talk,' and in deference to Joe's wishes the loquacious Tupkan was left behind. The other, a large, quiet, good-natured fellow, accompanied us, and was found useful, although given to romancing. He seemed to think we were in search of information which it was his special province to supply, and some of the flights of imagination he indulged in were truly surprising, considering that he had never received any of the advantages of a civilized education."

The Corwin now steamed northward through a lane of open water, between the pack and the shore ice, until June 1st, when, in latitude 68° 10' north, longitude 176° 48' west, the end of the lead was reached. They had run up this lead for over one hundred miles, and it had been foggy or snowing most all of the time since they entered it, so that often they could not see more than the length of the vessel.

The Corwin now stood to the eastward under sail. No land could be seen, a dense snow-storm prevailed, and a hard gale from the north brought down large quantities of ice. During the night the rudder was broken off by coming in contact with heavy ice.

The next day the explorers steamed southeast along the edge of the shore ice, keeping a sharp lookout for land. The lead was closing rapidly behind them, and there was danger of being frozen in. Toward night it stopped snowing, and an island was in full view. The ship was stopped, and the land party, consisting of Lieutenants Herring and Reynolds, one seaman, and two natives, were put ashore. They took with them twenty-five dogs, four sleds, a skin boat, provisions for two months, etc. They were directed to go as far westward as Cape Yakan, if possible, and to rejoin the Corwin at Cape Serdze.

After seeing the party fairly started, the Corwin was headed south for Plover Bay, Siberia. The approach to this place, and the appearance of the coast, is thus described:—
"In the afternoon of the 12th the sea became smooth and glassy as a mountain lake, and the clouds lifted, gradually unveiling the Siberian coast up to the tops of the mountains. First the black bluffs standing close to the water came in sight, then the white slopes, and then one summit after another until a continuous range, forty or fifty miles long, could be seen from one point of view, forming a very beautiful landscape. Smooth, dull, dark water in the foreground; next a broad belt of ice, mostly white like snow, with numerous masses of blue and black shade among its jagged, uplifted blocks. Then a strip of comparatively low shore, black and gray; and then back of that the pure, white mountains, with only here and there dark spots, where the rock faces are too steep for snow to lie upon."

After visiting St. Michael's, Norton Sound, Captain Hooper returned to Cape Serdze, and took the land excursionists on board. "They had been absent twenty-eight days, and had been along the Asiatic coast to a place called Cape Wankerem, where they found the parties who had boarded the wreck, and obtained from them a number of articles taken from it, which have since been identified as belonging to the missing whaling-bark Vigilant, and others to Captain Nye, of the Mount Wollaston, which would seem to indicate that both crews had been on board the Vigilant. It is not unlikely that, both vessels being caught, it was decided by their captains, who were both skillful sailors and men of great courage and energy, to unite their forces on the best vessel, and that a subsequent break-up of the ice released it, and enabled them to reach some point near where the wreck was discovered before again becoming embayed.

SLEDGING ON THE SIBERIAN COAST.

"The statement made by the natives was, that they were out sealing on the ice, when, seeing a dark object, they approached it, and it was found to be the hull of a vessel, with masts, bulwarks, and boats gone, and the hold partly filled with water. In the cabin were four corpses, three on the floor and one in a berth. After taking what they could carry home, night coming on, they left the wreck, with the intention of returning in the morning; but during the night the wind, which had been from the northward, changed to southwest, and the wreck was not seen again, having drifted away or sunk.

"The sledge party had also met traveling parties of Chukches from the vicinity of Cape Yakan, on their way to East Cape, and from them learned that no white men had been seen on the coast. These people are constantly traveling back and forth, and it would be almost impossible for any one landing on the coast to escape their notice."

From Cape Serdze Captain Hooper went to Cape Lisburne, a bold, rocky promontory on the northwestern coast of Alaska, to get a supply of coal from a mine in that vicinity. He then headed northwesterly, and succeeded in getting within half a mile of Herald Island. The ship was anchored to the shore ice July 30th, and a party immediately landed. Professor John Muir, the scientist of the expedition, describes the exploration of the island as follows:—

"After so many futile efforts had been made to reach this little ice-bound island, everybody seemed wildly eager to run ashore and climb to the summit of its sheer granite cliffs. At first a party of eight jumped from the bowsprit chains and ran across the narrow belt of margin ice, and madly began to climb up an excessively steep gully, which came to an end in an inaccessible slope a few hundred feet above the water. Those ahead loosened and sent down a train of granite bowlders, which shot over the heads of those below in a far more dangerous manner than any of the party seemed to appreciate. Fortunately nobody was hurt, and all made out to get down in safety.

"While this remarkable piece of mountaineering and Arctic exploration was in progress, a light skin-covered boat was dragged over the ice and launched on a strip of water that stretched in front of an accessible ravine, the bed of an ancient glacier, which I felt assured would conduct by an easy grade to the summit of the island. The slope of this ravine, for the first one hundred feet or so, was very steep; but, inasmuch as it was full of firm, icy snow, it was easily ascended by cutting steps in the face of it with an axe that I had brought from the ship for the purpose. Beyond this there was not the slightest difficulty in our way, the glacier having graded a fine, broad road.

"Kellet, who discovered this island in 1849, and landed on it under unfavorable circumstances, describes it as an inaccessible rock. The sides are, indeed, in general, extremely sheer and precipitous all around, though skilled mountaineers would find many gullies and slopes by which they might reach the summit. I first pushed on to the head of the glacier valley, and thence along the backbone of the island to the highest point, which I found to be about one thousand two hundred feet above the level of the sea. This point is about a mile and a half from the northwest end, and four and a half from the northeast end, thus making the island about six miles in length. It has been cut nearly in two by the glacial action it has undergone, the width at this lowest portion being about half a mile, and the average width about two miles. The entire island is a mass of granite, with the exception of a patch of metamorphic slate near the center, and no doubt owes its existence with so considerable a height to the superior resistance this granite offered to the degrading action of the northern ice sheet, traces of which are here plainly shown. . . . This little island, standing, as it does, alone out in the Polar sea, is a fine glacial monument.

"The midnight hour I spent alone on the highest summit, one of the most impressive hours of my life. The deepest silence seemed to press down on all the vast, immeasurable, virgin landscape. The sun near the horizon reddened the edges of belted cloud-bars near the base of the sky, and the jagged ice-bowlders crowded together over the frozen ocean stretching indefinitely northward, while more than a hundred miles of that mysterious Wrangel Land was seen blue in the northwest—a wavering line of hill and dale over the white and blue ice-prairie and pale gray mountains beyond, well calculated to fix the eye of a mountaineer; but it was to the far north that I ever found myself turning, where the ice met the sky.

"I would fain have watched here all the strange night, but was compelled to remember the charge given me by the captain, to make haste and return to the ship as soon as I should find it possible, as there was ten miles of shifting, drifting ice between us and the open sea. I therefore began the return journey about one o'clock this morning, after taking the compass bearings of the principal points within sight on Wrangel Land and making a hasty collection of the flowering plants on my way. . . .

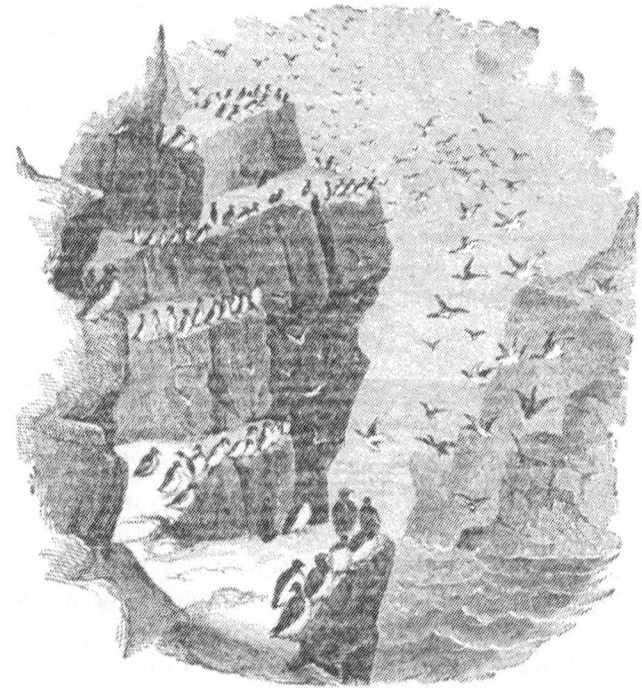

A BIRD NURSERY.

"Innumerable gulls and murres breed on the steep cliffs, the latter most abundant. They kept up a constant din of domestic notes. Some of them are sitting on their eggs, others have young; and it seems astonishing that either eggs or the young can find a resting-place on cliffs so severely precipitous. The nurseries formed a lively picture, the parents coming and going with food or to seek it, thousands in rows, standing on narrow ledges like bottles on a grocer's shelves, the feeding of the little ones, the multitude of wings, etc."

Another member of the exploring party described his experiences as follows: "Selecting what was conceived to be the most favorable spot for ascending the cliff, several persons made the attempt, occasionally detaching huge bowlders, which came bounding down like a bombardment, and recalling some old army esperiences. The attempt had to be abandoned after getting up a few hundred feet. In company with several others, the writer tried what seemed to be a more practicable way—a gully filled with snow—up which we had gone scarcely a hundred feet when, looking back with affright and forward with despair, we literally backed down with failing hearts and trembling limbs. In the meantime the skin boat had been brought over the ice; and, one of the men pointing out another place where he thought we might ascend, it was the work of but a few minutes to cross a small bit of open water which led to the foot of a steep snow-bank, somewhat discolored from the gravel brought down by melting snow from above. We climbed several hundred feet up the snow and ice, having to cut steps before reaching the top. It was like scrambling over the dome of the Washington capitol with a great yawning cliff below. A ravine was next reached, through which tumbled, with loud noise and wild confusion, over broken rocks and amid some scant lichens and mosses, a mountain stream of pure water, which had hollowed out a shaft or tunnel, forming a glacier mill or moulin. It was over the roof of this tunnel that we had passed.

"All sense of fatigue vanished on reaching this summit. The grand view there revealed like an apocalypse made one halt with feelings of mingled delight and astonishment. In front the midnight sun shone with gleaming splendor, coloring all the waste of ice, sea, and granite. To the left Wrangel Land appeared in well-defined outline, and to the northward an open sea led we knew not whither. From the middle of the island two or three points of the land bore southwest by west deceptively. In shape the island is something like a boot, with a depression at the instep. In the extreme west were seen a number of jagged peaks and splintered pinnacles of granite, some of them resembling giant remains of ancient sculpture, all worse for exposure to the weather."

The island was searched carefully for traces of the missing ships, but none were found, or anything to indicate that the island had ever before been visited. The only signs of life seen, excepting the birds, were a small fox and a polar bear. On a high promontory, at the northeast point, a cairn was erected, in which was placed a bottle containing written information and a copy of the New York *Herald*.

After leaving Herald Island, July 31st, the Corwin cruised for several days off the coast of Wrangel Land, following along the edge of the ice-pack, running into leads, and trying to reach the land, but never being able to approach nearer than twenty miles. As it was impossible to effect a landing until there was a decided change in the condition of the ice, Hooper withdrew southerly, moving through floating ice, and reached the mouth of Wankerem River, on the Siberian coast. While skirting along the coast they fell in with a number of wandering Yoraks, who had herds of reindeer.

The 10th of August found the explorers again on the edge of the ice-pack, off the south end of Wrangel Land. On the evening of the 11th they entered a lead, and had approached to within eight miles of land, when a dense fog stopped further progress. The next morning, after squeezing through heavy ice for two hours, they reached a small space of open water, and anchored about three hundred feet from the beach. The cutter was lowered, and Captain Hooper, Lieutenant Reynolds, Engineer Owen, and others started for the shore.

The party landed, and looked anxiously around for traces of the missing seamen, but they looked in vain; their own voices alone broke the solitude. On a high cliff Lieutenant Reynolds set up a pole of drift wood, to which was attached an American flag, and a bottle containing a record of the visit. The country was taken possession of in the name of the United States of America, and rechristened New Columbia. As the flag fluttered in the breeze a salute was fired from the ship, and cheers were given by the crew and the land party.

"The great distance to which slight sounds are sometimes transmitted in the Arctic regions is remarkable. Amid the grim silence of Wrangel Land, at a time when the air was acoustically opaque for that latitude, the voice of the boatswain giving orders two miles away was distinctly heard by the land party, while laughter and words spoken above the ordinary tone were heard with such amazing distinctness as to suggest telephonic communication."

The river where the Corwin anchored was named Clark River, in honor of Mr. E. W. Clark, the Chief of the Revenue Marine. It was about one hundred yards wide, and deep and rapid, and from the top of the cliffs near by it could be seen extending back into the mountains a distance of forty miles. The mountains, devoid of snow, and seen under very favorable circumstances through a rift in the clouds, appeared brown and naked.

"Our stay on shore," says Captain Hooper, "was necessarily short, on account of the strong northerly current which was sweeping the ice-pack along with irresistible force. At half-past nine A.M., being unable to hold our position any longer, we commenced to work out toward the lead, which we reached at eleven A.M. We examined the shore line with our glasses while approaching and leaving the land, north and south, and saw nothing but perpendicular cliffs of slate, from one to three hundred feet high, the sloping banks of the river being the only place for miles where a party traveling over the ice would be able to affect a landing."

Captain Hooper now sailed to the eastward, and on the 16th reached Point Barrow, where he found a portion of the crew of the whaling-ship Daniel Webster, which had been crushed by the closing of a lead, to the north end of which it had sailed. The captain of the Webster only realized his danger when it was too late. In half an hour after the lead began to close behind him, his ship was crushed, and thrown over on the ice, a wreck. The crew escaped to the shore, and some of them had gone overland to Icy Cape. Nine of the crew were taken aboard the Corwin.

Leaving Point Barrow, August 18th, the Corwin ran southerly to Plover Bay, Siberia, a distance of 600 miles, and arrived there the 24th. The Golden Fleece was anchored in the harbor, having on board Lieutenant Ray and his party, bound for Point Barrow to establish a signal station, and from them Captain Hooper first learned of the assassination of President Garfield. The natives were very friendly, and reported that the Rodgers had been there eight days previous, and that a Russian man-of-war had gone up the coast.

An excursion up the bay is thus described by the *Herald* correspondent: "Having turned over to Lieutenant Ray two of our dog-sledges and a quantity of furs, we towed his vessel to sea, and returning took the steam-launch, with two natives, and started up the bay to visit some Reindeer Chukches, about twenty miles off. Soon the busy little launch was spinning through the water, and the rhythmic grind of her machinery greatly astonished the natives. I asked one of them, by way of banter, 'Why don't you people build a boat like this?' To which he replied, pressing his hand on his forehead, 'Ah, too much think—too much think."

"Arrived at the deer-man's, we found his house, or rather his ovoidal tent, between two high mountains, and at the foot of a valley, which extended back in the clear air many miles of picturesque distance amid other mountains, remarkable if not unique on account of their desolate grandeur. On making known the object of our visit, the old man despatched two of his sons, lithe, nimble fellows, who started off in a trot, each with a long spear, over the mountains in the direction of the deer pasture. As they were gone some five or six hours, I amused myself in the meantime by climbing over 2,000 feet up the steep side of the nearest mountain. It may be the amusement of a small mind, but it was great fun to detach several large bowlders of a ton or more and see them go tearing and thundering down the rocky incline. Among other things there was noticeable on the side of this mountain a tunnel under the snow of several hundred feet in length. It had been caused by a brisk stream, and reminded one of a sewer some eight or ten feet in height.

"After exploring this somewhat curious sight, my attention was next directed to the herd of deer coming slowly down the valley. Pretty, quiet, meek-looking animals they were as they stood chewing their cuds, and allowing themselves to be photographed without the least fear. So tame and gentle were they that I patted and stroked a number of them. The herd, numbering something less than two hundred, were of different colors, several being perfectly white, and others fawn-colored, while several were spotted like circus-horses, and most of them were shedding the hairy muffle from their horns, which, in several instances, was hanging in shreds, and obstructing their eyesight.

"Selecting two young males from the herd, they were killed and skinned, and one of the young men, stripping himself to the waist, and being assisted by two others, took the carcasses to the boat for us; and after paying him in tobacco, flour, and several small articles, we hastened down the bay as fast as the little launch could run."

August 27th found the Corwin returning northward. A short stop was made at the Diomedes on the 28th. Over the tops of these islands hung dense, misty clouds, unmoved by a sharp northeast gale, which seemed only to have the effect of producing the phenomena known as cloud banners. Among other things seen at the Diomedes was a collection of ivory carvings—toys, spinning-tops, chairs, etc. As the boat approached shore a number of girls stopped playing, and sat their dolls up in a row, so that they might get a good look at the strangers.

At noon, on the 30th of August, the blue peaks of Wrangel Land were again in view; but progress toward them was stopped by ice when twenty miles distant from land. During the night the Corwin stood along the ice-pack, and the next morning found her hove to off Herald Island. A fierce gale was blowing, during which the iron ice-breaker was lost; and as the oak sheathing was entirely gone around the bows (leaving nothing to break ice with but three-and-one-half-inch Oregon fir plank), it was not deemed prudent to venture into the ice again. The gale lasted several days, and, after it had subsided, the Corwin cruised leisurely eastward, into the vicinity of Kotzebue Sound.

Near the entrance of Hotham Inlet is an Esquimaux Long Branch, where the natives resort in summer for trade and pleasure, and about six hundred were there assembled when the Corwin arrived.

"Here the Captain and the *Herald* correspondent, entering into competition with the natives in several kinds of athletics, and coming out ahead, were invited to shoot with a bow and arrow at a mark which had been missed several times. It was not an archery club, composed of young ladies and spooney men, against which we had to contend, but the real live, primitive man, who procured his dinner by means of the spear and feathered shaft. So the captain, resolving himself into a toxopholite, and pulling himself together for a mighty effort, discharged his arrow, and, through pure accident, succeeded in driving it into the target the first shot—of course refusing to shoot a second time—to the great surprise of the unsuspecting bystanders."

On the 14th of September the voyagers left the Arctic sea and started for home. At St. Michaels they were obliged to take on board the already over-crowded ship a party of shipwrecked men, who, after twenty-one days of privation, had reached St. Michaels from Golovin Bay. On the 21st of October they arrived at San Francisco.

CHAPTER IV.

SEARCHES FOR THE JEANNETTE—1881.

(SUMMER CRUISE OF THE RODGERS.)

ON the 16th day of June, 1881, two United States steamships, commanded and manned by officers and seamen of the United States navy—all of whom had volunteered for the perilous service—started north to join in the search for DeLong. One of them—the Alliance—went from Norfolk navy yard, on the Atlantic, and the other one—the Rodgers—steamed out through the Golden Gate of the Pacific coast.

Only three months before her departure, the Rodgers was known in San Francisco as the Mary and Helen, a staunch and ice-tried steam-whaler of 420 tons. She was built in Bath, Maine, in 1879, was bark rigged, and carried a great spread of canvas. Her length was one hundred and fifty-five feet, breadth of beam thirty feet, depth sixteen feet. She was bought by the Secretary of the Navy for $100,000, and re-named the Rodgers, in compliment to the distinguished naval officer who was the president of the Jeannette Relief Board.

The Rodgers was overhauled and strengthened at the navy yard, Mare Island, and ample provisions and supplies for her own crew during a long voyage, and for the relief of any shipwrecked seamen who might be fallen in with, were taken on board. The command of the expedition was given to Lieut. Robert M. Berry, a native of Kentucky, an officer in whom the Navy Department had the greatest confidence. All of the officers, as well as the crew, were volunteers; and, as on previous occasions, when bold and hazardous services have been required of our naval officers, it was difficult for the Department to make a selection out of the many gallant men who volunteered for this adventurous expedition.

The officers and crew of the Rodgers were as follows:

Lieutenant Robert M. Berry, Commander.
Master Howard S. Waring, Master Charles F. Putnam.
Ensigns, Henry J. Hunt, George M. Stoney.
Surgeons, Meredith D. Jones, Joaquin D. Castillo.
Engineer, Abraham V. Zane. Pay Clerk, W. H. Gilder.
H. P. DeTracey, Joseph F. Quirk, W. F. Morgan, Frederick Bruch, Joseph Hodgson, W. Rohde, Frank Burk, Hans Schumann, Fred Smith, Patrick Cahill, George Gardner, S. W. Morrison, Richard Bush, Julius Huebner, Jacob Johansen, Thomas Loudon, Frank McShane, Frank F. Melm, Olaf Petersen, Otto Polte, Owen McCarthy, W. H. Derring, Edward O'Leary.
Dominic Booker, steward. Robert Morelli, Wm. Grace, cooks.

Mr. Gilder, the pay clerk, who was also the special correspondent of the New York *Herald,* accompanied Lieutenant Schwatka on his overland journey in King William's Land in 1879, and was the historian of that expedition. Frank F. Melm was also a member of Schwatka's party. The crew were fine-looking, hardy men, and most of them crossed the continent by railroad to join the expedition.

A short time before starting on his voyage Lieutenant Berry received a letter from the Hon. W. H. Hunt, Secretary of the Navy, from which the following is an extract:—

"In the pursuit of your adventurous and arduous voyage you carry with you the sympathy and entire confidence of the department. Nothing that can be done to contribute to your well-being and success shall be omitted. As soon as you are fully ready you will sail.

"The eyes of your fellow countrymen, of the scientific men of all the world, and especially of those interested in Arctic explorations, will follow you anxiously on your way through the unknown seas to which you go. May Heaven guard and bless you and your officers and men, and crown your heroism with success and glory."

The Rodgers was escorted out to sea by a fleet of pleasure yachts, steamboats, and tugs. Thousands of eager spectators witnessed her departure, waving handkerchiefs and giving cheers, while the whistles of the steamers in the harbor and factories along the shore sounded out their noisy farewell.

On the 27th of June the Rodgers was on the Pacific Ocean, one thousand miles from San Francisco. "On the 29th," wrote a correspondent, "we sighted Ounalaska's high mountains, and on the next day passed within fifty miles of Umnak, and saw the peak of its snow-crested volcano, 5,000 feet high, burst through a cloud and tinged with the glory of the setting sun. It was a gorgeous spectacle. Near it we saw the smoke arising from one of the burning volcanoes of the Four Mountains. The following day we passed into Bering's Sea.

"On the 14th of July we crossed the 180th meridian, and were in east longitude. Here is where the mariner takes up one day when sailing toward the west, or drops one if going east. As we were to recross the same meridian in a few days, Lieutenant Berry concluded that we might as well retain our old reckoning. The only difference it made was that we found the religious people of Petropavlovsk holding service on Saturday instead of Sunday, and we were constantly in doubt as to whether to-day was really to-day or tomorrow."

The Rodgers arrived at Petropavlovsk July 19th, and found anchored there the Alaska Commercial Company's steamer Alexander, Captain Sandman, and the Russian corvette, the Strelock, commanded by Captain DeLivron. DeLivron informed Lieutenant Berry that he had been directed to assist the searchers for the Jeannette in every way in his power; and during the stay of the Rodgers the Russians extended to her officers the most cordial hospitality. At this place a native was hired as dog-driver, and forty-seven dogs were taken on board, whose howls for many hours afterward were something to be remembered by all who heard them.

Petropavlovsk (Ports of Peter and Paul) is the capital of

the Kamchatdales, and the only town on the eastern coast of the Kamchatka peninsula. It is situated on the right shore of the splendid Bay of Avatcha, which may claim, with that of San Francisco, to be one of the finest harbors in the world. This little town of 500 inhabitants points with pride to its two monuments of Bering and La Perouse; and its old fortifications, now covered with grass and flowers, serve to recall the defeat of the English and French allies, who attacked the village during the Crimean war.

REPULSE OF THE ALLIES.

It was from Avatcha Bay that Captain Vitus Bering, the first Russian navigator of the strait which bears his name, sailed, in June, 1741, on his last voyage. After discovering the American coast, and the magnificent peak which he named Mount St. Elias, scurvy broke out among his crew, and his ship drifted about at random until November, when it was wrecked on the uninhabited island which still bears his name. Bering and many of his men died on this island, in December, and the survivors, thanks to the invincible energy and sanguine disposition of Steller, the physician of the expedition, escaped to Kamchatka, the next summer, in a little ship which they built from the wreck of the St. Paul.

Bering Island lies to the northeast of Avatcha Bay, and, together with Copper Island and some small islands and rocks lying round about, forms a peculiar group of islands, separated from the Aleutian Islands proper, named, after the rank of the great seafarer who perished there, Commander's Islands. Though belonging to Russia, the American Alaska

SLAUGHTER OF SEA-BEARS.

Company has acquired the right of hunting there, and maintains on the main islands two commercial stations, which supply the inhabitants, several hundred in number, with provisions and supplies; the company buying of them in exchange, furs—principally the skin of an eared-seal (the sea-cat or sea-bear), of which from 20,000 to 50,000 are killed annually in this region. Some Russian officials are also settled on the island, to guard the rights of Russia, and preserve order.

Leaving Petropavlovsk, July 24th, the vessels in the harbor dipping their flags as a parting salute, the Rodgers headed for St. Michael's, Alaska, and came to anchor toward night, August 3d, under the shelter of Stuart Island, in Norton Sound, to wait for daylight, as the wind was blowing a gale, and the sea was running high.

"The next morning," wrote the *Herald* correspondent, "we got under way and steamed slowly on our course, in a dismal rain and fog. The lead was kept going constantly, the quartermaster calling in a dreary, monotonous voice the depth of water found at each cast of the lead. Again we were compelled to drop anchor on account of shallow water and the concealment of the few known landmarks under the mist. About eleven o'clock the fog lifted a little, and we could see the small settlement of St. Michael's about seven miles distant, and shortly afterward dropped anchor beyond the point of land that forms a shelter for the harbor, a few antiquated iron guns bellowing forth a salute. The fort of St. Michael's, as it is called, is an enclosure of dwellings and warehouses, the interstices filled with a high wooden fence, that was originally erected as a protection against the assaults of hostile Indians. The fence of the present day is, however, maintained rather as a shelter against the wind than to guard against savages."

From St. Michael's Lieutenant Berry crossed over to Plover Bay, Siberia, and then proceeded north to St. Lawrence Bay, where he found the Strelock anchored in the harbor. After taking on board two Chukches, as hunters and dog-drivers, the Rodgers again started north August 19th, accompanied by the Russian corvette. The next day was stormy, and the wind blowing so hard that it was difficult to make any headway against it. The Strelock was seen working in shore, but was soon lost sight of, and was seen no more by the crew of the Rodgers.

The following morning was clear and pleasant, and Cape Serdze Kamen soon appeared in view. "When we came near the land," says the correspondent, "a skin boat filled with Chukches came alongside for the purpose of trading.

They took us to a place which proved to be Kolyutschin Island and bay, where there is a large Chukches settlement. The village consisted of seven large circular dome-like tents, of about twenty feet in diameter, made of seal-skins sewed together, and supported by an intricate arrangement

CHUKCHES BOATS.

of poles of drift-wood. On the side opposite the entrance were arranged three or four sleeping apartments, shut off from the main tent and each other by curtains of reindeer skins. These were the separate tenements of as many families, the savage semblance of flats in an apartment-house. The skin drapery of several of these rooms was raised, and upon the beds, which were also of reindeer skins and covered the entire floor of each, sat women engaged in household duties or attending to the wants of a colony of dirty, half nude children.

"We sailed the same evening for Herald Island, and at seven P. M., August 23d, obtained our first view of Cape Hawaii, Wrangel Island, about twelve miles distant to the northwest, with the ice extending about ten miles off the shore. The next morning both Wrangel Island and Herald Island were in plain sight, and we arrived off the latter at noon the same day. A boat was sent on shore to search for tidings of the Jeannette and missing whalers. An examination of the western extremity of the island was made, and the remainder scanned from the summit of the highest land with glasses without discovering any traces.

"The island was found to be a narrow ridge, between five and six miles long, and not over a quarter of a mile wide at the base. The crest of the western half of the island was so narrow that one could straddle it, while the eastern portion was lower and more rounded at the top. The island is not more than about six hundred feet high at the highest point, but from it, the atmosphere being perfectly clear, we could see a long distance. Wrangel Island was in plain view, but no land could be seen to the northward of it as far as the eye could reach.

"After the return of the boat we steamed along the southern shore of the island without discovering any cairn, and then headed for Cape Hawaii. We sighted the cape at ten A. M., August 25th, and shortly after made the ice along the starboard beam, densely packed; skirted it, and at four P. M. discovered from the masthead a lead, and followed it in. At ten P. M., having passed through about ten miles of ice, we dropped anchor about half a mile from shore in six fathoms of water. Two boats were lowered at once, and several of the officers landed on a low, gravelly beach, and gave three hearty cheers, which were responded to by those on board. Two sky-rockets were sent aloft, and when the party returned, one of the officers cut a Christmas cake in honor of the event."

Early the next morning, 26th, a boat was sent in to examine a lagoon which had been seen by the landing party, and at its mouth was found an excellent small harbor. The vessel was moored in this harbor, and preparations made for the exploration of the island.

Three search parties were organized. Lieutenant Berry, Surgeon Jones, and four men were to proceed overland to the northern coast; Master Waring was to go north in a whale-boat and skirt the eastern coast; and Ensign Hunt, with a whale-boat, was to explore the southern coast. The boat parties were provided with fifteen days' provisions, and instructed to encircle the island if possible. The three parties got off August 27th, between three and four P.M., and three cheers were given by those remaining on board as each one left the ship's side and started upon its separate route.

INTERVIEWING A DENIZEN OF WRANGEL ISLAND.

The vessel was left in charge of Master Putnam, who was also intrusted with the magnetic observations, assisted by Ensign Stoney, to whom was assigned the task of surveying the harbor and adjacent coast lines.

"The next day, Sunday, the 28th of August," says the correspondent, "was one of the most delightful days ever experienced in this land of storms.

"About six o'clock, September 3d, we were about to sit

down to dinner, when two white objects were seen on the mainland near the shore, which the glass showed to be a she bear and her cub. In a short time the dingy was lowered, and two of the officers jumped in, armed with rifles, and were rowed ashore against a strong gale. When the boat struck the beach all jumped ashore and started in pursuit, headed by Mr. Tracey, the carpenter, who, though drenched to the skin in effecting a landing, abated not his energy in the chase. After going several miles with little prospect of coming up with the game, all returned to the ship except the carpenter, who, pointing ahead and shouting, 'Excelsior,' kept up the pursuit. Success attended his efforts, and he returned at ten o'clock at night, after traveling about ten miles and killing both bears."

At eleven o'clock the same night a voice from the sand spit hailed the ship, and was recognized through the howling of the gale as that of Captain Berry, who had just returned from his inland journey. He was accompanied by one of the men, and said the others of his party were suffering from lame feet, and had lagged behind. A boat crew, in charge of Mr. Hodgson, pulled to the beach and started to find the wayfarers. A severe snow storm and hard gale tended to make the search a difficult one; but they returned at three o'clock in the morning with two of the men (Dominic and Petersen), who were found sleeping about five miles from the ship.

As nothing had yet been seen of Dr. Jones, Ensign Stoney, with a boat's crew, landed at the head of the bay, some four miles from the ship, and searched the shores for several miles in each direction. They got back to the ship in the afternoon. Meantime Dr. Jones, accompanied by Melms, had reached the harbor and been taken on board ship. He had passed the night without much discomfort, under a shelter which Melms had constructed.

Lieutenant Berry had reached a point about twenty miles inland, where, from a mountain 2,500 feet high, he was enabled to see open water entirely around the island, except between west and south-southwest, where his view was obstructed by a high range of mountains, which, however, appeared to terminate the land in that direction. The interior was found to be entirely devoid of animal life and of other plants than those growing near the coast. Two ridges of mountains followed the trend of the northern and southern shores, between which a rolling country existed, traversed by small streams, evidently fed by the melting snow from the mountains.

Master Waring was accompanied on his expedition by Dr. Castillo and a crew of five seamen. He started off toward the east with a breeze which sent him swiftly along under reefed mainsail; but the wind soon died out, and he encamped on shore for the night. After rounding Cape Hawaii, the following morning, 28th, he pulled up to a small island near the mouth of a creek, where were the skeletons of a whale and walrus. "His attention was attracted by some pieces of wood sticking up in the sand, evidently by intention, and he then noticed footprints leading to the cliff near by. Following them, he came upon a flag-staff, from which drooped what appeared to be a United States flag, and attached to the staff was a bottle containing documents which had been left by the officers of the Corwin."

After leaving copies of the originals, which were brought away, Waring continued on, and in the afternoon "rounded a point marked by a perpendicular column of rock about one hundred feet high. Here heavy pack ice was encountered, extending as far to the eastward as he could see. Near the shore it was somewhat broken, and permitted his advance through a narrow channel where only short paddles could be used. At a quarter to six o'clock the ice drew so close that he was compelled to haul up on the beach and encamp for the night. The next day, 29th, the ice still held him, and, accompanied by Dr. Castillo, he scrambled to the top of a hill north of his camp, from which his eyes were rewarded by observing the trend of the coast toward the west. This he found to be the extreme northeast cape, and no land could be seen to the northward. Toward the west the land was low near the water, and ran out in long, low points, forming deep bays, which held the ice packed in dense masses against the shore.

"The following morning the weather was clear, and Herald Island appeared in plain view from the beach. By nine o'clock the ice opened sufficiently to allow the boat to move slowly by the aid of paddles, and, after six hours' hard work, they had rounded the cape, and made about five miles to the westward.

"At five o'clock another effort was made to proceed, but after laboring an hour and a half, and narrowly escaping being crushed by two large masses, by backing out from between them just as they came together with a force that no boat could have withstood, a narrow lead let them in to the beach. Within five minutes after they landed not a vestige could be seen of the opening by which they had so narrowly escaped. Nothing but a grinding and crunching sea of ice met the view."

The next day, 30th, opened with a strong northerly wind and flurries of snow. The ice remained densely packed against the shore opposite the camp, and a reconnoissance along the beach showed that it was in the same condition both to the northward and westward.

September 1st was a gloomy day for the party; no movement of the ice occurred to indicate the liberation of the boat, and its abandonment and a march overland to the ship seemed the only alternative.

Early the next morning a party went westward about fifteen miles to a point from which they could see the land trending to the south and west. Preparations were made for abandoning the boat, which was hauled high up on the beach and turned bottom side up. The boat mast was erected on a neighboring hill, and a record deposited indicating the route taken by the retreating crew.

"A dismal snow storm was prevailing when, at five o'clock

on the morning of the 3d inst., they started upon their journey. It was intensely cold, and the wind blowing in squalls. Their course was directed toward the eastern coast, where they could find shelter behind the hills, and driftwood from which to make a fire and cook some food on reaching camp at night. The traveling, with heavy loads on their backs, was intensely disagreeable, while, to add to their discomfort, the snow changed to rain, which drenched their clothes and increased the weight of their burdens. The route lay over a series of hills, which were very fatiguing to men unaccustomed to land journeys. At night they rested only a few hours, when it was too dark to see to travel.

"As soon as it was sufficiently light to see, they started again, with sore and stiffened limbs, and feet torn by the sharp stones that covered the ground. At seven A. M. they reached the beach, where a rousing fire was started and a hot breakfast prepared, which put new life into the weary travelers, and then, through the snow and rain, they plodded until reaching the head of the bay, where they were overjoyed to find a boat, which had gone there to bring in the skins of Mr. Tracey's bears. An hour later they were welcomed on board ship.

"Almost at the same time that Waring started toward the east with a fair wind, Ensign H. J. Hunt pulled away upon his course to the westward. He was accompanied by Engineer Zane, and his crew consisted of five men. It was hard pulling against the wind, and at nine o'clock, when he encamped for the night, he was not more than about nine miles from the harbor. The oars were brought into requisition the following day, but the progress was not very rapid.

"During the day they saw what looked like a cairn upon the beach, and Hunt landed to examine it. His praiseworthy curiosity came near bringing him into trouble, however, for he found himself within about six feet of a huge polar bear taking a siesta, before he was aware of it. As the ponderous brute raised his head and turned toward the intruder, they gazed at each other in a dazed sort of way for a few minutes, when Hunt cut short the interview by facing about and starting for the boat at a marvelous speed, shouting loudly for his rifle. In the meantime the bear arose in a dignified and leisurely manner, and slowly walked toward the sea, when Hunt sent a bullet through him that caused him to turn again for the beach; another shot brought him to the ground, and a third so disabled him that Johansen ran up and gave him the *coup de grace* with the muzzle of his rifle at the animal's ear.

"The third day out they rounded the southwest point of the island, and their course lay somewhat east of north. The wind was strong and carried away their main boom. Plenty of ice was encountered the next day, and, though working hard, they only succeeded in making about four miles upon their course by paddling and hauling. Next day they could only proceed by towing along shore and cutting a way through the ice, and were finally compelled to tie up in lee of a large piece of ice and bail out. They had finally, however, accomplished about four miles after a hard day's work. Day after day this labor was repeated until they reached the northern point of the island, where they encountered a succession of sand spits running toward the north and east beyond the mainland, and with miles of open water between, which proved to be only shallow lagoons, where they constantly grounded, and extricated themselves with difficulty. In some instances the spits extended between twenty and twenty-five miles from the land.

"September 5th, they reached the most northerly point of Wrangel Island, and could distinctly see the northeast cape bearing to the southward and eastward of their position; but the same heavy pack that brought Waring's party to grief, baffled their most strenuous efforts to encompass the island. Often, while working through the ice, they found themselves compelled to follow leads that carried them far out from the land, and closed behind them. Sometimes midnight found them still at their oars, or wading through lagoons, sounding in that way for a channel to reach the land, or cross the water in the direction of their course.

The run home, when reluctantly enforced, was made in five days. The 10th of September, the day assigned for reporting back, had passed, and the day of grace was drawing to a close, when a little whale-boat was seen beating in from the south and west, and we were soon cheering the returned explorers as they drew along side. The result of their labor was perfectly satisfactory, as they had reached positions within easy view of each other's furthest points, and, though no traces that we could identify as of the Jeannette or the lost whalers were found, an accurate survey had been made of this land, and its character ascertained. The necessary scientific data had been collected, and a harbor found which may sometime be of inestimable value to ice-imprisoned whalemen.

Along the sand spit, near the Rodger's harbor, as well as on the entire coast of Wrangel Island, is strewn driftwood, among which may often be found utensils of wood, made by the natives of the Siberian or American coast, and some are of very ancient date, as are attested by their venerable appearance. A number of specimens were gathered by members of the expedition as relics. Among them can be recognized portions of vessels and articles of civilized manufacture, but whether keeping the sad tale of wrecks and human suffering, or merely washed from the deck of some passing whaler, it would be difficult to tell.

The explorers left Rogers Harbor, September 13th, and the same evening visited the bay, where the whale-boat had been left, but were unable to get near the land owing to ground ice and shoal water.

An attempt was made to examine Herald Island, but no landing could be effected. The ship was then headed due north, and, on the morning of the 16th, ran into loose ice, and soon came up to a dense pack. A lead to the northwest was entered, but it ended in an impenetrable pack, with smooth, new, unbroken field ice beyond, as far as the eye could reach. A retreat into open water was effected, and the pack ice was skirted to the eastward.

On the 17th another lead was entered, and the ship forced its way through floating ice for fifteen miles, when, at five P. M., a dense pack was again encountered. As darkness came on the ship was secured to a floe. During the night the temperature fell to eight degrees below freezing, and new ice, from one to three inches thick, was formed, cementing the floes together.

At three A. M., 18th, the ship was cast loose, and, after steaming for more than an hour through the ice which had closed around it, a lead was reached which brought the explorers to open water. Another lead was entered and followed to its end on the 19th.

Having now reached latitude 73 deg. 44 min. north, longitude 171 deg. 48 min. west, without discovering any traces of land; and, finding that the main pack from that point trended well to the southeast, Lieutenant Berry returned to Wrangel Land, and, on the 22d, succeeded in picking up the abandoned whale-boat. He then headed to the north and west, and reached a position, the latitude of which is 73 deg. 28 min. north, and the longitude 179 deg. 52 min. east.

It was now late in the season, and, as a longer stay would have endangered the ship, Lieutenant Berry turned south to search for winter quarters. The Siberian coast was sighted just east of Cape Jakan; but a strong northwest wind was blowing at the time and a heavy sea running, so that it was not possible to send a boat on shore. Berry then coasted to the eastward, examining the shore from the ship. Toward evening the wind freshened, and falling snow shut out the land altogether.

After standing off from the coast and laying to for forty-eight hours without any improvement in the weather, Lieutenant Berry gave up the attempt to examine the shore at that place, and headed for Tiapka Island, situated about twenty miles west of Cape Serdze, where he succeeded in putting up a house; and at this place he left Master Putnam in command of a party, consisting of Surgeon Jones, Pay-Clerk Gilder, Petersen, Melms, and Constantine Taternoff. The party was fully supplied with Arctic clothing and provisions for one year, besides a large quantity of pemmican. They had also a boat and a supply of dogs and sledges, with which they were expected to make journeys westward along the shore of the Arctic Ocean. Lieutenant Berry and the balance of the officers and crew left Putnam's winter camp October 8th, and steamed southeasterly to St. Lawrence Bay, experiencing stormy and thick weather throughout the voyage, and a violent gale from the westward on the 13th and 14th. In a letter to the Secretary of the Navy, written at St. Lawrence Bay, October 16th, 1881, Lieutenant Berry said:—

"I shall now proceed to put the ship into winter quarters here, and render all as comfortable as possible. Our provisions have all proved to be of excellent quality, and we are in every respect well provided for the winter. All well on board."

CHAPTER V.

SEARCHES FOR THE JEANNETTE—1881.

(CRUISE OF THE ALLIANCE.)

THE sending out by the Secretary of the Navy of a United States ship to cruise in the waters of Spitzbergen in search of the missing expedition, was one of the results of the labors of the Jeannette Relief Board. It was supposed that if DeLong had landed on Wrangel Land and sledged his way to the Pole, he would return by the way of Smith's Sound or Spitzbergen, where he would be likely to meet whalers and walrus-hunters much sooner than he would if he returned to Wrangel Land, as the first-named places are several hundred miles the nearest to the Pole. An expedition in that direction, to ask the co-operation of the whalers and walrus-hunters, and to bring home the Jeannette's men if they were found, was accordingly decided on.

The steamship Alliance, having been designated for the service, was hastily equipped at the Norfolk navy yard, and started on her long voyage June 16th, 1881—the same day on which the Rodgers left San Francisco. Drawing away from abreast the famous frigate Kearsarge, which fought the rebel cruiser Alabama outside Cherbourg, she passed gracefully down the stream, while the sailors of the receiving-ship Franklin and other war-vessels manned the rigging and cheered her adventurous crew. The officers of the Alliance were as follows:—

Captain George H. Wadleigh, Commander; Lieutenant C. H. West, Executive Officer; Lieutenant C. P. Perkins, Navigator; Lieutenant Elliott, Master Schwenk, Chief-Engineer Burnap, Surgeon Eckstein.

The crew numbered nearly two hundred men. Mr. Harry

Macdonna accompanied the expedition, and from his very interesting letters to the New York *Herald* the following account of the voyage is principally compiled.

The Alliance touched at St. Johns, N. F., and her officers there gave a farewell breakfast to Lieutenant Greeley's party, who were awaiting transportation to their station at Lady Franklin Bay, to which place they were subsequently taken by the steamer Proteus.

Starting onward, June 29th, the Alliance proceeded to Reykjavik, Iceland, and was the first American man-of-war to enter that harbor. The Icelanders were much interested in their visitors, and particularly so in the colored men among the crew, several of whom went galloping through the town on ponies, to the great delight of the youth of the ancient capital. "One of the negro sailors who went ashore became a victim to the seductions of Danish whiskey. For two days he was missing, and the master-at-arms went ashore and advertised a reward of ten dollars for the lost man. The town turned out to find him, and he was found. Subsequent to this, every time a negro seaman appeared on shore he was hunted as a lost man or as an escaped curiosity from a museum."

From Iceland, the Alliance went to Hammerfest, Norway, the most northern city of Europe. "Here," wrote Mr. Macdonna, "we heard of the shooting of President Garfield. The first news we had of the event was from a captain who came up from Tromsöe, and told some one on board that the president was recovering slowly.

" 'You mean the president's wife, don't you?' said the party informed. 'She was quite ill when we left the States.'

" 'No; I mean the president himself,' said the skipper, with decision. 'He has been shot, and it is feared he may die.'

" 'When was he shot? Who shot him? What for? How did it happen? Where was he shot?' and a volley of other questions were launched at the almost bewildered captain, who could give no further information than that President

Garfield had been shot by some one—where he did not know, and for what he could not tell. He had just one cheerful fact, that the President was recovering."

HUT OF WRECKED NORWEGIANS, BEAR ISLAND.

On the 29th of July the travelers left Hammerfest and started north. On the second day out they sighted Bear Island, and endeavored to work around to the westward of it, but were stopped by ice. Turning back, they cruised westward, but what seemed an impenetrable barrier of ice opposed their passage to the north. They then returned to Bear Island, and finally made their way slowly north to Spitzbergen and along its western coast. When near Horn Sound they had their first view of the midnight sun. It was on a clear, bright night, with not a fleck of cloud as big as a mustard-seed in the amber sky. In the clear water astern, several white whales sported about.

"The sun looked like a great disk of molten gold, which seemed, through the smoked snow-glasses, to throb and pulsate, sending waves of light from its center to its rim.

These soft rolling ripples of light seemed to depart from the periphery with irregularity, although they started from the center as if a pebble had been dropped there. Sometimes they would depart from the rim with the same regularity as they started; and then again they seemed to hurry off on one side and delay on the other, giving the sun, for an instant, an oblong appearance. This midnight sun was not alone sensible to the eye; one could feel its rays, which burned the skin with the copper warmth of Indian summer days."

At Bell Sound, where they arrived August 3d, three walrus-hunting schooners were anchored in the gale that was

GLACIERS AT BELL SOUND.

blowing on a lee-shore, just in front of a magnificent glacier; and, viewed across the bay, they seemed mere specks against the marble-white face of the towering ice. A whaleboat was sent to one of them to deliver circulars respecting the Jeannette; and then the Alliance steamed onward to Green Bay, Ice Fiord, where a Norwegian steamer and several sailing vessels were anchored. Another vessel, which had been wrecked only two days previously, lay stranded on the shore near by. The sunshine was warm and bright, the bay was clear of ice, and the mountains around were decked in green.

Continuing on to a position northwestward of Spitzbergen, the ship again approached the ice-pack, and steamed slowly forward in a dense fog. As it grew colder the fog condensed on the ship's rigging, froze, and hung in fringes of icicles from every rope. About ten P. M. the fog suddenly disappeared, and the soft sunlight illuminated the glistening fringes of icicles, and seemed to change them into raining diamonds. The scene was dazzling and fairy-like.

The ship was now at the foot of the ice-pack, and the navigator announced a latitude of 80 deg. 0 min. 55 sec. north, longitude 11 deg. 22 min. east. "The effect of this news on a company of men who were informed before they left the States that they could not get to Iceland, and when they got to Iceland were told they would never reach Spitzbergen, and who in Norway were pleasantly smiled at and told they would be back there again in a fortnight, was quite exhilarating."

"We were," says Mr. Macdonna, "in fact, 590 geographical miles from the North Pole; but who that has seen this desert of ice, piled up in hummocks and forced into mountainous ridges by a force that the mind cannot comprehend, will venture an opinion as to the years of dreary endeavor yet to be endured before man shall reach that supreme spot?

"Of all the desolate sights the human eye has rested on, this desert of ice, stretched out like a gaunt, bleached beggar, hand to heaven, is the most subduing. Even the sea loses its music as it beats against the barrier. It moans monotonously and melancholy all the dreary years, and frets against a hydra-like impediment that, in centuries flown, was overcome and overcome only to present itself again, season after season, rejuvenated and incorrigible. The dominion of the ice is not disputed here."

From his elevated position in the crow's nest Captain

Wadleigh could see no opening to the north or northeast, and, after moving up and down the edge of the pack for a few hours, he turned back and anchored near Dane's Island, off the northwest coast of Spitzbergen, August 6th. "During the second day of the stop at Dane's Island loud noises were constantly heard, which reverberated through the valleys inland and over the great interior sea of ice, until lost in the distance. The first noise was like the rattle of artillery, and then it boomed along to thunder loudness, and so decreased again. Investigation proved that the noise proceeded from the great glaciers abutting into South Gat, and those around in Smeerenburg Bay, twenty miles away. The third day of the stop here, in addition to other excitements, afforded one from danger of being run into by icebergs, that came rushing down with the swift current through the Gat.

"The Alliance remained in South Gat until the 12th, when, having completed the collecting of 'specimens' and done much dredging for deep-sea organisms, Commander Wadleigh weighed anchor and sailed north again. For six weary days we groped about in the fog, which came down upon us as soon as we were off shore, occasionally meeting great isolated ice-floes, which caused considerable anxiety. On the seventh day out—the 19th of August—we encountered the first heavy snow-storm, accompanied with a brisk breeze and considerable floating ice.

"The 21st came clear and bright, with a cloudless sky and warm sunlight, and from the crow's nest the ice-pack could be seen far away on the northern horizon. Commander Wadleigh resolved to make for the ice again; and during the afternoon we fell in with the advance floes just south of the eightieth parallel. Several promising openings appeared, however, and, as it was suggested by the ice pilot that there was open water beyond this belt to the north, the captain resolved to make an attempt to reach it. He only succeeded in making twelve miles through the ice, however, when the way was blocked again by the solid pack, in which not an opening could be seen. Far as the eye could reach to the northward, one flat, monotonous expanse of ice was all that could be seen, with here and there a seal or a walrus basking in the sun."

From this position, in latitude 80 deg. 10 min. north, Captain Wadleigh turned back and went to Hammerfest for a supply of coal. On the 16th of September he again started north, and proceeded to Spitzbergen, cruising under sail, and getting as far north as 79 deg. 36 min. The weather for several days was a succession of gales, snow, sleet, and dense fogs. On the 25th he headed for Reykjavik, and arrived there October 10th. Five days later he started homeward by way of Halifax, and reached New York in November.

Mr. Macdonna considers the cruise of the Alliance the most phenomenal one ever made in the Arctic seas. He declares that the ship was utterly unfit for the dangerous work mapped out for her, and that no sufficient preparation for the voyage had been made—notwithstanding which, she reached the highest point ever attained by a man-of-war. This success he regards as an evidence of good luck rather than anything else, and he thinks that experience in Arctic explorations is no guarantee against failure. "If," he wrote, "Commander Wadleigh had had a ship that could have withstood the ice, there is no doubt, under the favorable circumstances, that we could have carried the American flag beyond the eight first parallel of latitude. Tempting as was the chance, Commander Wadleigh did not take the risk; for had any accident overtaken the ship, its results would have been without parallel in the history of Arctic navigation. Never before has any ship with two hundred souls on board ventured so far north as the Alliance; and, with such a number to feed, in case the ship was lost and the crew compelled to winter, famine would have had a race with scurvy for the men and officers."

In summarizing the results of the voyage Captain Wadleigh says: "At sea, near the land or ice, a careful watch has been kept for anything that would throw any light on the object of the cruise, and fishing vessels have been communicated with and furnished with a description of the Jeannette. The ship's position in a sealed bottle has been thrown overboard every day, the temperature and specific gravity of the water noted every two hours, and all observations made as carefully as possible with the means at our disposal. Great interest in the search has been shown by the officers and generally by the crew; and I think it my duty to ask the attention of the department to the unusual expense to which they have been subjected. The ship has been particularly fortunate in having the services of Lieutenant C. H. West, executive officer, Lieutenant C. P. Perkins, navigator, and Chief-Engineer Burnap. I take pleasure in commending them to the department for the very efficient manner in which their duties have been performed."

SAMOYEDES OF ARCHANGEL.

CHAPTER VI.

PLANS FOR AN INTERNATIONAL SEARCH IN 1882.

THE several United States expeditions which went north to search for the Jeannette in the year 1881 had returned home or gone into winter quarters, and not the slightest clue to the whereabouts of the missing ship or to the fate of the adventurous men who sailed in her so gaily out through the Golden Gate nearly two and one-half years previously had been discovered. As cold weather came on the thoughts of all friends of humanity turned painfully northward, in sympathy with DeLong and his men, who, if still alive, seemed doomed to pass a third weary and sunless winter amid the cold, darkness, and desolation of the remorseless frost-land which held them in its icy grasp.

Meantime new plans for solving the mystery which surrounded the lost explorers were being projected and discussed both at home and abroad, and it was felt that, owing to the failure thus far of all attempts to gain any information respecting them, nothing less than international search could cover the field.

The fact that Leigh Hunt had not returned home and might himself need relief, and gratitude for the part taken by the United States in the search for Franklin, served to intensify the feeling of the English people. The Colonial Department addressed a letter to the governors of the Hudson Bay Company, urging upon them the importance of a thorough search by the trappers and employees of the company along the northern coast of North America; and the Geographical Society of Great Britain was actively engaged in devising plans for relief expeditions. At a meeting of the society, held in the London University, December 12th, 1881, Mr. C. R. Markham, C. B., spoke as follows:—

"The deepest sympathy has been felt here for the missing expedition. We cannot forget the noble way in which Mr. Grinnell and the United States government and people came forward, not merely with sympathetic words, but active deeds, during the search for Sir John Franklin and his ill-fated but heroic followers. I was myself on board one of the English searching ships that were moored to the ice-floe barring the way westward on September 10th, 1850, and well remember our feelings of grateful admiration when the two gallant little American schooners, the Advance and Rescue, put out their ice anchors alongside us and remained there during a gale of wind, and then beat up through the fast-closing ice to the western end of Griffith Island, in company with our squadron.* DeHaven, Dr. Kane, and the others nobly represented the feeling of their country—that feeling of generous sympathy which is filling our hearts now, and making us as anxious for news of the Jeannette as Americans were then about the fate of Franklin.

"The American people may be assured that not only do English geographers feel the deepest sympathy for the gallant explorers on board the Jeannette, but that we shall gladly and actively do what lies in our power to make the search complete, and give any aid that may, after due con-

---

*The Englishman's memory is good, as the following extracts from Dr. Kane's history of the First United States Expedition, commanded by Lieutenant Edwin DeHaven, will show. These extracts are copied from "The Frozen Zone and its Explorers," published at Hartford:

"September 10.—Here we are again all together, even Ommanney with the rest. The Resolute, Intrepid, Assistance, Pioneer, Lady Franklin, Sophia, Advance, and Rescue; Austin, Ommanney, Penny, and De-Haven, all anchored to the 'fast' off Griffith's Island, the way to the west completely shut out.

"September 13, 10 A. M.—We are literally running for our lives, surrounded by the imminent hazards of sudden consolidation in an open sea. All minor perils, nips, bumps, and sunken bergs, are discarded. We are staggering along under all sail, forcing our way while we can.

"4 P. M.—We continued beating toward Griffith's Island, till, by doubling a tongue of ice, we were able to force our way. The English seemed to watch our movements, and almost to follow in our wake—a compliment, certainly, to DeHaven's ice-mastership."

sideration, appear likely to be useful. The debt of gratitude which we owe to the nation which sent the Rescue and Advance to search for Franklin can never be forgotten."

The probability that DeLong would retreat to the coast of Northern Siberia, in case of disaster to his ship, had been repeatedly affirmed by Mr. George Kennan, author of "Tent Life in Siberia," who has traveled over four thousand miles in sledges in Northeastern Siberia. As early as November, 1880, Mr. Kennan suggested that the Secretary of the Navy should request the governor of Eastern Siberia to take measures to have natives of the North Siberian coast look out for the Jeannette and her crew; and, in subsequent letters, he earnestly urged the importance of making preparations on the coast for the prompt discovery and relief of the Jeannette's survivors, in case they landed there.

Lieutenant Howgaard, a Danish naval officer who had made the northeast passage with Nordenskiöld, also believed that the Jeannette should be looked for in that direction, and was actively engaged in collecting funds to enable him to go over the track which he had sailed in the Vega, for the purpose of searching the northern coast of Siberia. He laid his plans before the Royal Geographical Society, at their meeting above referred to, December 12th, and soon afterward started for the United States on the same errand.

"For a second time," wrote a correspondent of the New York *Herald,* "in the history of polar research, an expedition is probably lost in the Arctic. There is to be another great Franklin search, with this difference,—that was an English and American search of a limited segment of the polar circle; this will be a universal search of the whole border of the 'unknown region,' participated in by nearly all the civilized nations of the earth. The whole Siberian coast will probably be searched by Captain Berry, Nordenskiöld, Lieutenant Howgaard, and the Russians. The Russian international polar station, at the mouth of the Lena or at the New Siberian Islands, will be very important; for I believe De Long built cairns and left notice of his progress there, if he was not prevented from landing by heavy weather or ice. Spitzbergen and Nova Zembla will be international stations, and England will search Franz Josef Land on all its coasts and sounds with a large government expedition, for the Jeannette and for Leigh Smith. Five hundred whalers, walrus-hunters, and sealers will search for the Jeannette at the edge of the pack in all the seas that they frequent, from the Kara Sea to Spitzbergen and East Greenland, up Lancaster Sound, and in Bering Sea. Lieutenant Ray, at Point Barrow, will probably be able to search half way to the mouth of the Mackenzie River, and Lieutenant Greely, at Lady Franklin Bay, will probably go northwest to Cape Joseph Henry."

Only three days after the above extract was published, tidings of the missing explorers startled the civilized world and rendered further search for the Jeannette unnecessary.

CHAPTER VII.

FIRST TIDINGS FROM THE EXPLORERS.

ALMOST two and one-half years had elapsed since the sailing of the Jeannette, when, near the close of the year 1881, dispatches from an inland Siberian city, coming nearly ten thousand miles by telegraph and cable, via St. Petersburg, London, and Paris, were received by the New York *Herald,* as follows:—

LONDON, December 20th, 1881.

The *Central News'* London correspondent has called at the *Herald* office, and has given us a copy of a telegram from the *Central News'* St. Petersburg correspondent, which reads as follows:—

"Gouverneur Sibérie Orientale annonce bâteau polaire Américain Jeannette trouvé. Equipage secouru."

[The Governor of Eastern Siberia announces that the American polar vessel Jeannette has been found, and that its crew has been saved.]

PARIS, December 20th, 1881.

Our St. Petersburg correspondent telegraphs this morning, that General Ignatieff has just received the following telegram, which I transcribe literally:—

"IRKUTSK, Dec. 19th, 6.55 P. M.

"The Governor of Yakutsk writes, that on the 14th of September three natives of Hagan Oulouss de Zigane, at Cape Barhay, 140 versts north of Cape Bykoff, discovered a large boat with eleven survivors from the shipwrecked steamer Jeannette. They had suffered greatly. The Adjunct of Chief of the District was immediately charged to proceed with a doctor and medicines to succor the survivors at Yakutsk, and to search for the rest of the shipwrecked crew. Five hundred rubles have been assigned to meet the most urgent expenses. The engineer, Melville, has sent three identical telegrams,—one addressed to the London office of the *Herald,* one to the Secretary of the Navy, Washington, and the third to the Minister of the United States at St. Petersburg. The poor fellows have lost everything. Engineer Melville says that the Jeannette was caught and crushed by the ice on the 23d of June, in latitude 77 degrees north, and 157 degrees east longitude. The survivors of the Jeannette left in three boats. Fifty miles from the mouth of the Lena they lost sight of each other during a violent gale and dense fog. Boat No. 3, under command of Engineer Melville, reached the eastern mouth of the Lena on the 12th of September, and was stopped by icebergs near to the hamlet of Idolaciro-Idolatre. On the 29th of October there also arrived at Bolenenga boat No. 1, with the sailors, Nindermann and Noras. They brought the information that Lieutenant DeLong, Dr. Ambler, and a dozen other survivors, had landed at the northern mouth of the Lena, where they are at present in a most distressing state, many having their limbs frozen. An expedition was immediately sent from Bolonenga to make diligent search for the unfortunates, who are in danger of death. No news has as yet been received of boat No. 2. In the communication addressed to Mr. Bennett, Melville adds a request that money should be sent immediately, per telegraph, to Irkutsk and Yakutsk. Will you urgently request that 6,000 rubles be transmitted immediately to the Governor of Yakutsk for researches for the dead and assistance and care, as well as for the return and conveyance of the shipwrecked men to the house of the governor. There is a surgeon who will bestow upon them all possible care.

(Signed) PRESIDENT PEDASCHENKI."

LONDON, December 22d, 1881.

The following telegram was received at the London office at twenty minutes past two this morning:—

LIST OF THE THREE BOATS' CREWS. 85

"IRKUTSK, December 21st, 2:05 P. M.

"Jeannette was crushed by the ice in latitude 77 deg. 15 min. north, longitude 157 deg. east. Boats and sleds made a good retreat to fifty miles northwest of the Lena River, where the three boats were separated in a gale. The whaleboat, in charge of Chief-Engineer Melville, entered the east mouth of the Lena River on September 17th. It was stopped by ice in the river. We found a native village, and as soon as the river closed I put myself in communication with the Commandant at Bolonenga. On October 29th I heard that the first cutter, containing Lieutenant DeLong, Dr. Ambler, and twelve others, had landed at the north mouth of the Lena. The Commandant at Bolonenga sent instant relief to the whaleboat party, who are all well. Nindermann and Noros arrived at Bolonenga on October 29th for relief for the first cutter, all of whom are in a sad condition and in danger of starvation, and all badly frozen. The Commandant at Bolonenga has sent native scouts to look for them, and will urge vigorous and constant search until they are found. The second cutter has not yet been heard from. Telegraph money for instant use to Irkutsk and Yakutsk. The list of people in the boats is as follows:—

FIRST CUTTER (SAFE).

Lieutenant George W. DeLong, Dr. James M. Ambler, Jerome J. Collins, William Nindermann, Louis Noros, Hans Erickson, Henry Kaack, Adolf Dressler, Carl Gortz, Walter Lee, Nelse Iverson, George Boyd, Alexai, Ah Sam.

SECOND CUTTER (MISSING).

Lieutenant Charles W. Chipp, Captain William Dunbar, Alfred Sweetman, Henry Warren, Peter Johnson, Edward Star, Sharvell, Albert Kuehne.

WHALE BOAT (SAFE).

Engineer Geo. W. Melville, Lieutenant J. W. Danenhower, Jack Cole, James Bartlett, Raymond Newcomb, Herbert Leach, George Landerback, Henry Wilson, Mansen, Anequin, Tong Sing. (Signed), MELVILLE."

A cable message from Engineer Melville, identical with the one copied above, was also received by the Secretary of the Navy, and he replied to it by cable as follows:—

"NAVY DEPARTMENT,
WASHINGTON, D. C., December 22d, 1881.
To Engineer MELVILLE, U. S. N., IRKUTSK:—

Omit no effort, spare no expense, in securing safety of men in second cutter. Let the sick and the frozen of those already rescued have every attention, and as soon as practicable have them transported to milder climate. Department will supply necessary funds.

HUNT, Secretary."

A dispatch from Mr. Hoffman, *chargé d'affaires* of the United States at St. Petersburg, conveying the news and the assurance that the most energetic measures would be taken by the Russian authorities for the discovery and relief of the missing men, was received by the Secretary of State at Washington, December 20th. On the next day the *Herald* correspondent at St. Petersburg telegraphed as follows:—

"General Anutschin, the Governor-General of Eastern Siberia, who happens to be at present in St. Petersburg, having received information of the arrival of the shipwrecked crew of the Jeannette in the region under his command, immediately proceeded to Gatschina and saw the Emperor, who personally ordered that all supplies that were necessary for food, clothing, money, and transportation should be placed at their disposal." General Anutschin also gave orders by telegraph that the inhabitants of the shores of the provinces of Yakutsk and Yeniseisk should be at once informed of the loss of the Jeannette, and requested to make active research for the discovery of the missing shipwrecked men.

Messages from General Pedaschenki, subsequently received by Governor Anustchin, gave assurance that the search would be continued during the winter by the Cossack commandants of Bulun and Yakutsk, under direction of Gen. Tschernieff, the Governor of Yakutsk, and that nothing that could be done for the relief of the distressed seamen would be omitted.

Immediately upon receipt of the first news about the Jeannette, Mr. James Gordon Bennett, who was residing in Paris at that time, transferred the sum of 6000 roubles by telegraph, through the Messrs. Rothschilds, to General Ignatieff at St. Petersburg, with a request that he would draw on Mr. Bennett for any further sums required for the succor and comfort of Lieutenant DeLong and his party. About the same time Mr. Bennett received from General Ignatieff the following telegram:—

"Have hastened to communicate to your correspondent the news received from Yakutsk, and have given orders to the governor to take the 'most energetic measures for the rescue of the shipwrecked crew, together with authority to undertake all necessary expenses, for which I have promised to reimburse him.

IGNATIEFF."

The following are copies of dispatches from the State Department, transmitted by cable, to Mr. Hoffman, at St. Petersburg:—

"DEPARTMENT OF STATE,
WASHINGTON, December 20th, 1881.

HOFFMAN, Chargé, St. Petersburg:—

Tender hearty thanks of President to all authorities or persons who have in any way been instrumental in assisting unfortunate survivors from Jeannette, or furnishing information to this government.

FRELINGHUYSEN."

"DEPARTMENT OF STATE,
WASHINGTON, D. C., December 23d, 1881.

HOFFMAN, St. Petersburg:—

Convey the thanks of the President to the imperial government for its liberal and generous action in advancing the necessary funds to render assistance to the members of the Jeannette expedition, and inform Mr. DeGiers that you are authorized to draw on me to reimburse that government if it will kindly inform you of the amount.

FRELINGHUYSEN, Secretary of State."

The opening months of the new year were a season of painful suspense as to the fate of the gallant commander of the Jeannette, his brave first officer, and other missing men of the expedition. Briefly stated, about all that was known of them in the United States was as follows:—

Three boats, carrying the Jeannette's crew, left Semenoffski Island, September 12th, for the mouth of the Lena, and were separated during a hard gale when about fifty miles from land. The whale-boat party, commanded by Engineer Melville, landed near the east mouth of the Lena, September 16th, and on the 26th reached a native settlement called Bykoff, where they had to wait till the river was frozen over solid before proceeding south.

On the 29th of October a native arrived from Bulun (a settlement further south) with a letter written by Noros and Nindermann, two of the men who accompanied Lieutenant DeLong in the first cutter. This letter stated that DeLong had landed on the Siberian coast and needed prompt assistance. Melville went to Bulun, where he saw the two men, and learned that when they left their comrades, October 9th, they were out of food and in a deplorable condition, and one of them had died. Mr. Collins had volunteered to stay behind with the sick man, but they had all kept together.

Mr. Melville immediately procured the services of some natives with dog-sledges, and went north to search for his distressed comrades. He visited the place where the first cutter landed, and found some records which DeLong had left behind as he retreated slowly south. The last of these records was dated October 1st. He traced the party to the edge of a desolate and uninhabited region, which the natives refused to enter, and was then obliged to return to Bulun. Thence he proceeded to Yakutsk, 1,200 miles distant, and after organizing several search-parties and arranging a plan of operation he started to return north with two of his own men, Russian, a Cossack, and some natives.

Meantime Lieutenant Danenhower, the second officer of the Jeannette Expedition (who had been relieved of his command by DeLong on account of the bad condition of his eyes), had arrived at Yakutsk with his eyes badly affected, and acting under orders from the Secretary of the Navy, and against his own wishes, had started homeward with nine of his companions.

It was apparent that DeLong and the balance of his boat's party when last heard of, way back in October, were even then in imminent danger of speedy death from cold and starvation, and that one of their number had died from exposure. Nothing had been heard of Lieutenant Chipp, and it was supposed that his boat with all on board had gone down in the gale which separated him from his commander, or that a worse fate had befallen him if he reached the land. It was just the time of year when the Arctic storms begin to sweep down on the Siberian coast, and all living things move toward the interior to escape their fury. It is no trifle to be thrown on this coast without food and shelter or means of transportation, even in summer. It is vastly worse in winter, when the sea and river channels are closing with ice, and when heavy storms and falling snow obscure the landscape.

Months elapsed before a tolerably full, connected and intelligible account of the voyage of the Jeannette, and of the adventures and sufferings of the survivors of the expedition, was received at home. Meantime the Lena became a familiar word where it had never been spoken before, and its fatal delta the subject of deep interest and scrutiny. During this period of weary waiting the following verses were contributed to the Philadelphia *Times:*—

> By Baikal's lake, on wild Siberia's plain,
> Where howling blasts from Arctic's frozen main
>   Sweep over the arid wastes;
> Where zero marks the mild degrees of cold,
> And man to live must be of native mold,
>   A shipwrecked boat's crew rests.

By Lena's tide, whose waters never sleep,
And hyperborean blasts perpetual revel keep,
    And cold and death combine;
Where nature spreads her icy mantle o'er
The desert steppes and wilds forever more,
    DeLong and Melville pine.

Two nations vie in competition brave
The lost to trace, the rescued few to save,
    Frost-bitten, maimed and blind;
Whilst far away, where western breezes blow,
Where Minnesota's fertile prairies glow,
    A woman waits resigned.

A world looks on with sad and anxious gaze,
And Science gropes anew in troubled maze,
    And men begin to doubt;
Since Norsemen sailed, full twice five hundred years
Have rolled away, and strewn the floes with tears,
    To trace the pole about.

And still they die, and still the years roll on;
Bold Franklin erst, and now perchance DeLong—
    Two of a burdened roll.
'Fair Science' mourns, but must not, cannot stay
In such a strait, nor falter in the way,
    Till found the Northern pole.

Before continuing the narrative, it will be well to say something of the great Siberian river, which DeLong chose as his objective point on leaving the New Siberian Islands; and of the Siberian tundra, on whose northern edge he was thrown by the fortunes of exploration at an inclement season of the year.

CHAPTER VIII.

THE SIBERIAN TUNDRA.

THE shores of the Arctic Ocean lying between Nova Zembla and Bering's Strait are perhaps the most desolate on the whole Arctic circle. The great Siberian rivers—the Obi, the Yenisei, the Lena, the Indigirka, and the Kolyma—rise in the Altai Mountains, and flow, in their upper courses, through forests of tall trees. But before they reach the Arctic Ocean they traverse, for hundreds of miles, a dreary and barely habitable region of frozen deserts and swamps—great desolate steppes, known to the Russians as *tundras*.

In summer these tundras are almost impassable wastes of brown Arctic moss saturated with water; and in winter trackless deserts of snow drifted and packed by northern gales into long, hard, fluted waves. The ground is frozen to a great depth, but in summer thaws out for a distance of from two to three feet.

Nothing can be more melancholy than the aspect of the tundra, where, says Wrangel, endless snows and ice-covered rocks bound the horizon, nature lies shrouded in all but perpetual winter, and life is an unending struggle with privation and with the terrors of cold and hunger; where the people, and even the snow, emit a constant smoke, and this evaporation is immediately changed into millions of icy needles, which make a noise in the air like the crackling of thick silk; where the reindeer crowd together for the sake of the warmth derivable from such contiguity; and only the raven, the dark bird of winter, cleaves the sombre sky with slow-laboring wing, and marks the track of his solitary flight by a long line of thin vapor.

"The tundra," says another writer, "is the very grave of nature, the sepulchre of the primeval world, which occasionally reveals to the astonished gaze the forms of colossal animals long since extinct. Often trunks of trees split asunder with a loud noise; masses of rock are loosened from their sites; the ground in the valley is rent with yawning fissures. Dense grows the atmosphere; the stars wane and flicker; all nature sleeps a sleep that resembles death, and which is only interrupted in the summer by a short interval of spasmodic activity.

LIMIT OF TREES IN SIBERIA.

"In winter, when animal life has mostly retreated south or sought a refuge in burrows or in caves, an awful silence, interrupted only by the hooting of a snow-owl or the yelping of a fox, reigns over the vast expanse; but in spring, when the brown earth reappears from under the melted snow and the swamps begin to thaw, enormous flocks of wild birds appear upon the scene and enliven it for a few months. Eagles and hawks follow the traces of the natatorial and strand birds; troops of ptarmigans roam among the stunted bushes; and when the sun shines, the finch or the snow-bunting warbles his merry note. About this time, also, the reindeer leaves the forests to feed on the herbs and lichens of the tundra, and many smaller animals migrate thither.

"Thus during several months the tundra presents an animated scene, in which man also plays his part; for birds, beasts, and fishes must all pay tribute to his various wants. But as soon as the first frosts of September announce the approach of winter, all animals, with but few exceptions, haste to leave a region where the sources of life must soon fail. The geese, ducks, and swan return in dense flocks to the south; the strand bird seeks in some lower latitude a softer soil; the water-fowl forsakes the bays and channels which will soon be blocked by ice; the reindeer once more returns to the forest; and in a short time nothing is left that can induce man to remain. Soon a thick mantle of snow covers the hardened earth, the frozen lake, the icebound river, and conceals them all under its monotonous pall, except where the furious northeast wind sweeps it away and lays bare the naked rock."

The following graphic description of the region of the Lower Lena is from the pen of Mr. George Kennan, author of "Tent Life in Siberia":—

"Underlying the great moss tundras which border the Lena River north of Yakutsk, there is everywhere a thick stratum of eternal frost, beginning in winter at the surface of the earth, and in summer at a point twenty or thirty inches below the surface, and extending to a depth of many hundred feet. What scanty vegetation, therefore, the tundra affords, roots itself and finds its nourishment in a thin layer of unfrozen ground—a mere veneering of arable soil—resting upon a substratum five or six hundred feet in depth of permanent and impenetrable ice. This foundation of ice is impervious, of course, to water, and as the snow melts in summer the water completely saturates the soil to as great a depth as it can penetrate, and, with the aid of the continuous daylight of June and July, stimulates a dense luxuriant growth of gray Arctic moss. This moss in course of time covers the entire plain with a soft, yielding cushion, in which a pedestrian will sink to the knee without finding any solid footing. Moss has grown out of decaying moss year after year and century after century, until the whole tundra for thousands of square miles is a vast, spongy bog. Of other vegetation there is little or none. A clump of dwarf berry bushes, an occasional tuft of coarse swamp-grass, or a patch of storm-and-cold-defying kedrovnik, diversifies, perhaps, here and there the vast brownish-gray expanse; but, generally speaking, the eye may sweep the whole circle of the horizon and see nothing but the sky and moss.

"An observer who could look out upon this region in winter from the car of a balloon would suppose himself to be looking out upon a great frozen ocean. Far or near he would see nothing to suggest the idea of land, except, perhaps, the white silhouette of a barren mountain-range in the distance, or a dark sinuous line of dwarfed bushes and trailing pine stretching across the snowy waste from horizon to horizon, and marking the course of a frozen Arctic river.

"At all seasons and under all circumstances this immense border-land of moss tundras is a land of desolation. In summer its covering of water-soaked moss struggles into life only to be lashed at intervals with pitiless whips of icy rain until it is again buried in snow; and in winter fierce gales, known to the Russians as *'poorgas,'* sweep across it from the Arctic Ocean and score its snowy surface into long, hard, polished grooves called *'sastrugi.'* Throughout the entire winter it presents a picture of inexpressible dreariness and desolation. Even at noon, when the sea-like expanse of storm-drifted snow is flushed faintly by the red gloomy light of the low-hanging sun, it depresses the spirits and chills the imagination with its suggestions of infinite dreariness and solitude; but at night, when it ceases to be bounded even by the horizon, because the horizon can no longer be distinguished when the pale green streamers of the aurora begin to sweep back and forth over a dark segment of a circle in the north, lighting up the whole white world with transitory flashes of ghostly radiance and adding

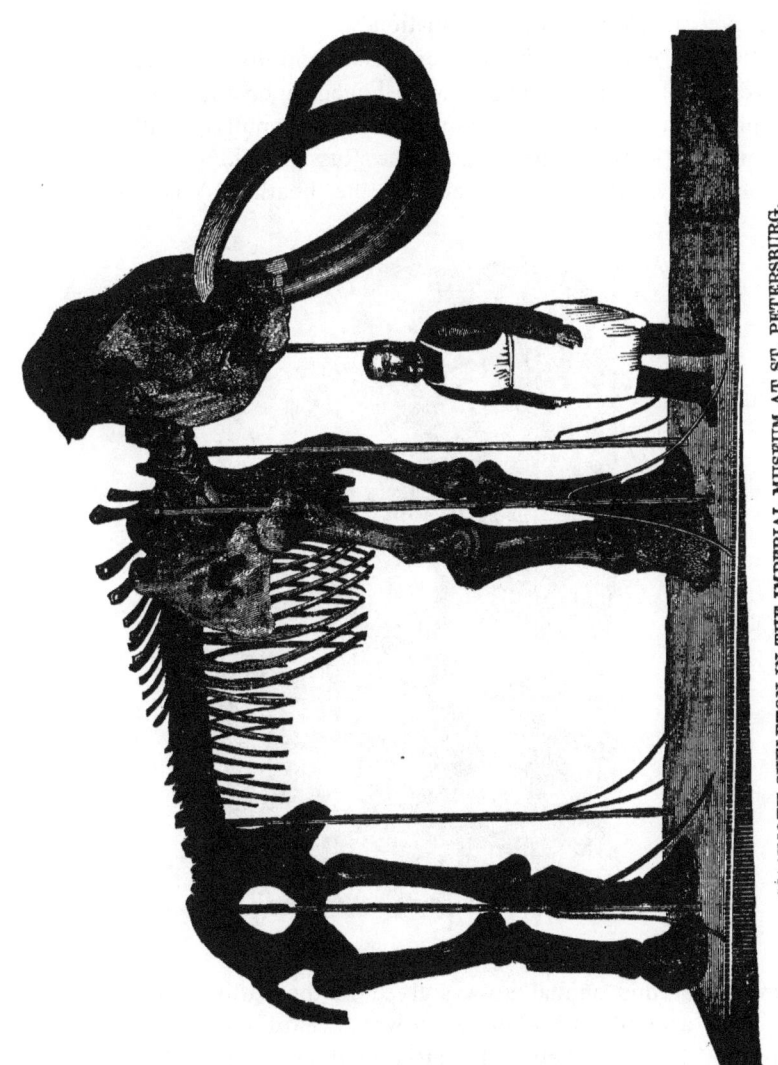

MAMMOTH SKELETON IN THE IMPERIAL MUSEUM AT ST. PETERSBURG.

mystery to darkness and solitude,—then the Siberian tundra not only becomes inexpressibly lonely and desolate, but takes on a strange, half terrible unearthliness which awes and yet fascinates the imagination."

In the region of the Lower Lena, and to the westward, have been found specimens of a huge rhinoceros, and of an elephant larger than that now existing—popularly called the mammoth. It is so named from the Russian *mamont,* or Tartar *mamma* (the earth), because the heathen Yakutes be-

SIBERIAN RHINOCEROS HORN.

lieved that this animal always lived in the earth, and worked its way around like a mole, however hard the ground was frozen. They also believed that it died on coming in contact with the outer air. As for the rhinoceros, the natives supposed that its horn was the talon of a species of gigantic bird, regarding which many wonderful stories were told in the tents of the Yakuts, the Ostyaks, and the Tunguses. Their legends tell of fearful combats between their ancestors and this enormous winged animal.

In the year 1799, a Tunguse found on Tamut Peninsula, which juts out into the sea from the delta of the Lena, a frozen-in mammoth, and he waited patiently five years for the ground to thaw so that the precious tusks could be uncovered. The skeleton of this mammoth is now in the Imperial Museum at St. Petersburg. Its tusks are remarkable for exhibiting a double curve,—first inward, then outward, and then inward again. They are each nine and one-half feet in length (measured along the curve), and the two weigh 360 pounds.

The tundra is in summer completely free of snow, but at a short distance from the surface the ground is always frozen. At some places the earthy strata alternates with strata of pure, clear ice, and it is in these frozen strata that the carcases of mammoths and rhinoceroses are found, "where," says Nordenskiold, "they have been protected from putrefaction for hundreds of thousands of years."

The nearer we come to the Polar Sea the more plenty are the fossil remains of the mammoth, but nowhere are they found in such quantities as on the New Siberian Islands. Every year, in early summer, fishermen's boats direct their course from the Siberian rivers to the "isle of bones"; and during winter, caravans drawn by dogs take the same route, and return with loads of fossil ivory, which finds its way into China and Europe.

CHAPTER IX.

THE LENA RIVER AND ITS DELTA.

THE head waters of the Upper Lena have their sources spread out for 200 miles along the counter slopes of the hills that form the western bank of Lake Baikal, and the main stream rises within seven miles of that lake, and not far from Irkutsk, the capital of Eastern Siberia. At Kachugskoe, about sixty miles from Lake Baikal, the Lena is as wide as the Thames at London, and in spring time its deep and clear waters have a very rapid current. The next station after Kachugskoe is Vercholensk, a town of 1,000 inhabitants.

After flowing 500 miles further through a hilly country, with high banks always on one and sometimes on both sides, on which are thirty-five post-stations and more villages, the river passes Kirensk, the chief town of the section. Here cultivation of the ground practically ceases, except for vegetables. At this point, too, the river receives on its right the Kirenga, which has run nearly as long a course as the Lena. The stream thus enlarged now flows on for 300 miles to Vitimck, where it is joined by its second great tributary, the Vitim, from the mountains cast of Lake Baikal. Another stretch of 460 miles, through a country still hilly, but with villages less frequent, brings the traveler to Olekminsk, a town of 500 inhabitants, where the Lena receives from the south the Olekma, which rises near the Amoor River. It then continues on for 400 miles through a sparsely-populated district till it reaches Yakutsk, where it is four miles wide in summer, and two and one-half in winter. At this place it is usually frozen over about the first of October, and not free from ice till near June. The course of the river thus far has been northeasterly.

Nearly one hundred years ago, John Ledyard, the great American traveler of that period, after walking from London to St. Petersburg, through Norway, Sweden, Denmark, and Finland, made his way to Irkutsk, where he became acquainted with a Swedish officer. On the 26th of August, 1787, the two travelers embarked on the Upper Lena in a

SIBERIAN RIVER BOAT.

small boat, at a point 150 miles distant from Irkutsk, with the intention of floating down with its current 1,400 miles to Yakutsk—just as Ledyard, in his college days, had floated down the Connecticut River in a small canoe, from Hanover, N. H., to Hartford.

When they started, says Sparks, there had been a hard frost, and the forest trees had begun to drop their foliage and put on their garb of winter. The stream was at first no more than twenty yards broad, with here and there gentle rapids, and high, rugged mountains on each side. They were carried along from 80 to 100 miles a day, the river gradually increasing in size, and the mountain scenery putting on an infinite variety of forms, alternating sublime and picturesque, bold and fantastic, with craggy rocks and jutting headlands, bearing on their brows the verdure of pines, firs, larches, and other evergreens and Alpine shrubs.

All the way to Yakutsk the river was studded with islands which added to the romantic appearance of the scenery. The weather was growing cold, and heavy fogs hung about the river till a late hour in the morning. They daily passed small towns and villages, and went ashore for provisions as occasion required. The following are extracts from Ledyard's journal:—

"August 30th. We stopped at a village this morning to procure a few stores. They killed for us a sheep, gave us three quarts of milk, two loaves of bread, cakes with carrots and radishes baked in them, onions, one dozen of fresh and two dozen of salted fish, straw and bark to mend the covering of our boat, and all for the value of about fourteen pence sterling. The poor creatures brought us the straw, to show us how their grain was blasted by the cruel frost, although it had been reaped before the 21st of August.

"September 4th. Arrived at the town of Keringar at daylight, and staid with the commandant till noon, and was treated very hospitably. Some merchants sent us stores. It is the custom here, if they hear of the arrival of a foreigner, to load him with their little services. It is almost impossible to pass a town of any kind without being arrested by them. They have the earnestness of hospitality; they crowd their tables with everything they have to eat and drink, and, not content with that, they fill your wallets. I wish I could think them as honest as they are hospitable. The reason why the commandant did not show his wife was because he was jealous of her. I have observed this to be a prevailing passion here."

On the 18th of September, Ledyard arrived at Yakutsk, after a voyage of twenty-two days, during which he had passed from a summer climate to one of vigorous cold. When he left Irkutsk it was just in the midst of harvest time, and the reapers were in the fields; but when he entered Yakutsk the snow was six inches deep, and the boys were whipping their tops on the ice. He debarked from his batteau two miles above the town, and there mounted a sledge, drawn by an ox, which had a Yakute on his back, and was guided by a cord passing through the cartilage of his nose.

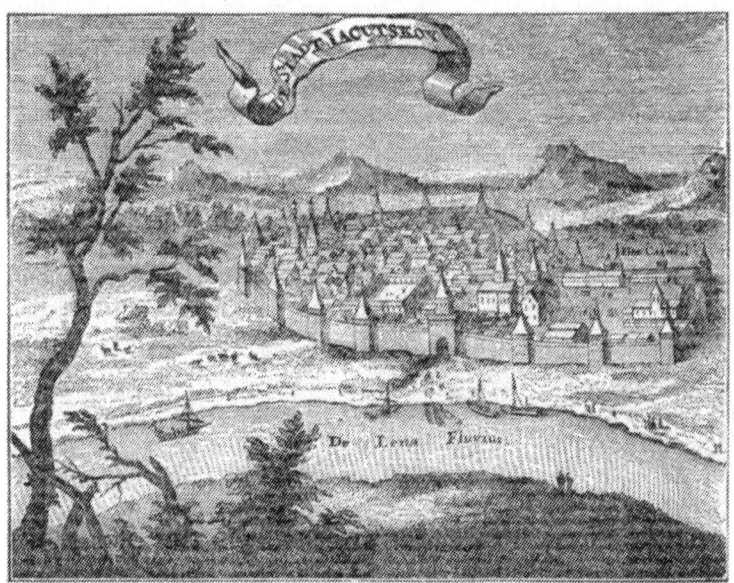

YAKUTSK IN THE SEVENTEENTH CENTURY.

At Yakutsk the Lena makes a bend and runs due north, receiving on its right, 100 miles below Yakutsk, one of its largest tributaries, the Aldan, which rises in the Stanovoi range, bordering on the Sea of Okhotsk. Yakutsk is only 270 feet above the sea, and the current, henceforth, is sluggish. About fifty miles further the Lena receives its largest tributary from the left, the Vitui, and then proceeds majestically through a flat country, with an enormous body of water, to the Arctic Ocean, into which it enters among a delta of barren islands formed of the debris brought down by the river. In times of flood, uprooted trees and driftwood are swept down in vast quantities, portions of which are left upon the labyrinth of islands which form the delta, and the remainder are carried into the Polar Sea, to be drifted away with the current which flows from east to west along the Siberian coast.

The delta of the Lena has a frontage on the sea, from the eastern channel around to the western channel, of nearly 200 miles, and, according to Latkin, it is crossed by seven great arms. The westernmost arm is called Anatartisch, and it debouches into the sea at a cape fifty-eight feet high, named Ice Cape. Next comes the river arm Bjelkoj; then Tumat, at whose mouth a landmark erected by Laptev in 1739 is still in existence. Then come the other three main arms, Kychistach, Trofimov, and Kischlach, and finally the very broad eastmost arm, Bychov, which is fouled by shoals. The river divides into these several arms at a point distant about 100 miles from the sea.

The total length of the Lena is about 2,500 miles, with a fall of 3,000 feet. Its waters are drained from an area of 800,000 square miles, and the river, with its numerous affluents, occupies an area of over 40,000 square miles.

North of Yakutsk, in the valley of the Lower Lena, there are no towns, but only a few miserable settlements or villages, hundreds of miles apart, and scattering huts, in which a comparatively few natives—Yakuts, Tunguses, and Yukaghirs—hibernate through the long winter, and wait for the return of summer, when they can renew their hard-earned supplies of provisions by hunting and fishing. There are also a few unhappy exiles, banished mostly for their crimes, and some Russians. Bulun, Schigansk, and Kumak Surka are the best known of the settlements. Tas Ary is on the delta, and is the most northern fixed dwelling-place on this part of the coast; it is inhabited entirely by Tunguses. Bulun is about 100 miles further south, and boasts of a priest and two Crown officials.

Between Bulun and Yakutsk are stations at intervals, constructed of logs. Lieutenant Danenhower describes one of

THE VEGA AND LENA SALUTING CAPE CHELYUSKIN.

these stations, only seventeen miles from Yakutsk, as a small building of only one room, with a cow-shed attached. When the travelers arrived there were about twenty people in the room, and also the carcass of a horse which had been killed for food, and brought into the room to thaw out.

The shores of the Siberian tundra witnessed a wonderful sight in 1878, when, for the first time in the history of the world, two steam vessels ploughed their way from Europe around Cape Chelyuskin. A brief account of the navigation of the Lena by one of these vessels will be of interest, when taken in connection with events which transpired along the river three years afterward.

When Nordenskiöld made his famous Northeast Passage, his ship, the Vega, was accompanied as far as the mouth of the Lena by a small steamer of the same name, owned by Mr. A. Sibiriakoff, and commanded by Captain Johannesen. Leaving Tromsöe, Norway, July 21st, 1878, they arrived at the mouth of the Yenisei, August 6th, and on the 18th were anchored in a splendid harbor situated between Taimyr Island and the main-land. The ground was free of snow, and covered with a gray-green vegetation consisting of grasses, mosses, and lichens.

On the 19th the vessels continued their course along the coast of the Chelyuskin Peninsula, through a dense fog, which occasionally lightened up so that the contour of the land could be distinguished. They steamed past an extensive field of unbroken ice occupying a bay on the western side of the peninsula, and at length an ice-free promontory glinted out through the fog in the northeast. In a short time the Vega and Lena were anchored in a little bay, open to the north and ice-free, that cuts the promontory in two. Flags were hoisted and a salute fired. The first object of the voyage had been attained; the northernmost point of the old world, variously called Cape Chelyuskin, Cape Severo, and Northeast Cape, had been rounded by vessels for the first time.

The air had cleared, and the cape lay before them lighted

up by the sun and free from snow. A large Polar bear was seen parading the beach, with eyes and nose turned toward the bay to inspect the new arrival; frightened by their salute, it took to flight and escaped the balls of the Swedes.

At noon on the 20th the vessels sailed on, meeting with much drift-ice, and the floes soon increased in size till progress through them was almost impossible. Open water was again reached on the 23d, and with a fresh breeze the vessels moved rapidly along without the aid of steam, over a perfectly smooth sea. High, picturesque mountains were seen inland. On arriving at the mouth of the Lena, a favorable wind and an open sea induced Nordenskiöld to continue on without stopping, and the Vega and the Lena accordingly parted on the night of August 27th—the former to continue its eastward course; the latter to ascend the Lena.

Before the Lena left Tromsöe, the agent of the owner entered into a formal contract with a Yakut pilot, who agreed to meet the vessel at the north point of the delta and take it up the river to Yakutsk. He was to travel to the Arctic Ocean in May, and to erect on some eminence near the shore of Tumat Island a signal-tower of drift-wood or earth, like a Cossack mound, not lower than seven feet. On this foundation he was to erect a pyramidal frame of three or more thick logs, on the top of which was to be fixed a flag-staff with a pulley-block for a flag, which was to be hoisted at least 42 feet from the ground. He was to guard the landmark thus erected until the river froze in the autumn, and when the nights became dark he was to light fires on the land and hang lanterns to the flag-staff.

It was also provided in the contract, that during his whole term of service the pilot, and his interpreter, "must be always sober (never intoxicated), behave faithfully and courteously, and punctually comply with the captain's orders." He was to receive as pay for all these services and self-denials the sum of 900 roubles, one-third of which was to be paid in advance.

The contract had been entered into with the friendly co-operation of the Governor and Bishop of Yakutsk, who were much interested in the proposed voyage. But notwithstanding all this, the affair was attended with no better success than that the pilot celebrated the receipt of the large sum of money by getting thoroughly intoxicated; and while in that state he broke one of the bones of the fore-arm, and was unable to start for the appointed rendezvous.

After the Lena had parted with the Vega she steamed toward land, and came the same day to the northernmost cape of the Lena delta, where the pilot's landmark was to have been erected; but there was no pilot there, and no flag-staff was visible. Johannesen then sailed westward along the shore, but as his search in this direction was not attended with success, he turned back to the first-mentioned place and landed there. On the shore stood a very old hut, already completely filled with earth. It probably dated from some of the expeditions which visited the region in the beginning of the century. Wild reindeer were seen in large numbers.

Left thus to his own resources, Captain Johannesen steamed again to the westward, as near to the land as possible, but as the water became shallower and shallower he determined to search for the broad easternmost arm of the river (named Bychov), and on the 1st of September he anchored in a bay on the main-land in the neighborhood of its mouth.

On the 3d of September, Johannesen continued his course up the river, but the Lena soon got aground, and it was several hours before the water rose enough so it could be got off. While the vessel was aground, nine Tunguses came on board. They paddled small boats, which were made of a single log of soft wood, hollowed out, and could just carry a man each. Johannesen endeavored in vain to induce some of the Tunguses to pilot the steamer. He did not succeed in explaining his wish to them, notwithstanding all the attempts of the Russian interpreter—a proof of the slight contact these Tunguses had had with the rulers of Siberia, and also of the difficulty and unwillingness with which the savage learns the language of the civilized nations.

The sailing through the delta was rendered difficult by the maps, which were made 140 years ago, being now useless: for the delta has undergone great alterations since then. Where at that time there were sand-banks, there are now large islands, overgrown with wood and grass. At other places, again, whole islands have been washed away by the river. It was not until the 7th September that the delta was finally passed and the Lena steamed in the river proper, where the fair-way became considerably better. Johannesen says, in his account of the voyage, that it is improbable that any of the western arms of the Lena are of importance; partly because the mass of water which flows in an easterly direction is very considerable in comparison with the whole quantity of water in the river; partly because the western and northern arms, which Johannesen visited, contained only salt water, while the water in the eastern arm was completely free from any salt taste.

On the 8th, early in the morning, the first fixed dwelling-place on the Lena, Tas-Ary, was reached. Here the voyagers landed to get information about the fair-way, but could not enter into communication with the natives because they were Tunguses. In the afternoon of the same day they came to another river village, Bulun. Impatient to proceed, and supposing that it also was inhabited wholly by "Asiatics" (a common name used in Siberia for all the native races), Johannesen intended to pass it without stopping. But when the inhabitants saw the steamer, they welcomed it with a salute from all the guns that could be got hold of in haste. The Lena then anchored. Two Crown officials and a priest came on board, and the latter performed a thanksgiving service.

"Even at that remote spot," says Nordenskiöld, "on the border of the tundra, the Asiatic comprehended very well the importance of vessels from the great oceans being able to reach the large rivers of Siberia. I, too, had a proof of this in the year 1875. While still rowing up the river in my own Nordland boat, with two scientific men and three hunters, before we got up with the steamer Alexander we landed among others, at a place where a number of Dolgans were collected. When they understood clearly that we had come to them, not as brandy sellers or fish-buyers from the south, but from the north, from the ocean, they went into complete

A SEA-SICK OFFICIAL.

ecstacies. We were exposed to unpleasant embraces from our skin-clad admirers, and finally one of us had the misfortune to get a bath in the river, in the course of an attempt which the Dolgans in their excitement made to carry him almost with violence to the boat, which was lying in the shallow water some distance from the shore. At Dudino, also, the priests living there held a thanksgiving service for our happy arrival thither. Two of them said mass, while the clerk, clad in a sheepskin caftan reaching to his feet, zealously and devoutly swung an immense censer. The odor from it was at first not particularly pleasant, but it soon became so strong and disagreeable that I, who had my place in front of the audience, was like to choke, though the ceremony was performed in the open air. Soon the clerk was completely concealed in a dense cloud of smoke, and it was now observed that his skin cloak had been set fire to at the same time as the incense. The service, however, was not interrupted by this incident, but the fire was merely extinguished by a bucket of water being thrown, to the amusement of all, over the clerk."

At nine in the morning the Lena continued her voyage up the river, with the priest and the Crown officials on board, but they had soon to be landed, because in their joy they had become dead drunk. On the 13th, Schigansk was reached, and samples of the coal found there were taken on board. On the 21st the Lena reached Yakutsk. The first vessel which, coming from the ocean, reached the heart of Siberia, was received with great good-will and hospitality, both by the authorities and the common people. Johannessen continued his voyage up the river until, on the 8th of October, he came to the village Njaskaja. Here he turned back to Yakutsk, and laid up the steamer in winter-quarters a little to the south of that town.

WINTER YOURT.

CHAPTER X.

ENGINEER MELVILLE'S NARRATIVE.

WHEN the Jeannette's crew was retreating over the ice towards the New Siberian Islands, after the loss of their ship, Lieutenant Danenhower suffered severely from trouble with his eyes, and in consequence thereof was relieved from duty. Engineer Melville succeeded him as commander of the whale-boat party, and received orders from Lieutenant DeLong as follows:—

"U. S. ARCTIC EXPEDITION, CAPE EMMA,
BENNETT ISLAND, LAT. 76.38, LON. 148.20 E.,
August 5th, 1881.

To P. A. ENGINEER GEORGE W. MELVILLE, U. S. N.:—

SIR—We shall leave this island to-morrow, steering a course (over ice or through water as the case may be) south magnetic. In the event of our embarking in our boats at any time after the start, you are hereby ordered to take command of the whale-boat until such time as I relieve you from that duty or assign you to some other. Every person under my command at the time who may be embarked in that boat at any time is under your charge and subject to your orders, and you are to exercise all care and diligence for their preservation and the safety of the boat. You will under all circumstances keep close to the boat in which I shall embark; but if unfortunately we become separated you will make the best of your way south until you make the coast of Siberia, and follow it along to the westward as far as the Lena River. This river is the destination of our party, and without delay you will, in case of separation, ascend the Lena to a Russian settlement from which you can communicate or be forwarded with your party to some place of security and easy access. If the boat in which I embark is separated from the other boats, you will at once place yourself under the orders of Lieutenant C. W. Chipp, and so long as you remain in his company obey such orders as he may give you.

Very respectfully,
GEORGE W. DELONG,
Lieutenant U. S. Navy, Commanding Arctic Expedition.

Mr. Melville's personal narrative, made up from his letters and reports to the Secretary of the Navy, describes the voyage and wreck of the Jeannette, and subsequent events, as follows:—

We arrived in the harbor of Lütke, Bay of St. Lawrence, on the 25th of August, and on the 27th completed our supply of stores from the schooner, and sailed for the Arctic Ocean, to visit Kolyutschin Bay to search for Nordenskiöld, and then to continue our voyage of discovery. We arrived at Kolyutschin Bay on August 31st, and having found satisfactory proof of the safety of Nordenskiöld we continued our voyage to the northward.

On September 3d we came up with the ice, and on the 4th sighted Herald Island. We continued to work through the ice until the 6th of September, when we became finally fixed in the ice. On September 13th an attempt was made to land on Herald Island, but it was unsuccessful, and the traveling party returned to the ship on the 14th. We continued to drift with the ice toward the northwest, and on October 21st sighted Wrangel Land, bearing south. We continued fast in close-packed ice until November 25th, when, after several days' severe crushing of the ice and nipping of the ship, she was forced into open water, and drifted northwest without control until the evening of the same day, when we brought up against a solid floe piece and made fast, where we again froze in, and remained until the vessel was eventually destroyed.

On January 19th, after several days' anxiety from the crushing strain of the ice on the ship and the noise made by the rising and bursting of the floe, we finally discovered that the ship, after receiving several severe shocks, was leaking badly. Steam was got on the engine boilers, and both steam and hand pumps were worked day and night until the ship

FASTENED TO A FLOE.

was partially repaired. Stores were hoisted out of the hold, and all preparations made to make good our retreat to Wrangel Land if forced to abandon the ship. We continued to drift northwest, and steam was necessary to pump the ship until May 18, 1880.

In the meantime a water-tight bulk-head had been built into the forward part of the ship, and the spaces between the ship's frames filled in with meal, tallow, ashes, and oakum to keep out the water. After May 18th, 1880, the water was pumped out night and day by hand pump or windmill pump until the ship was destroyed.

Long and dreary months of close confinement to the ship, and anxiety for her safety continued until May 17th, 1881, when we were enlivened by our first sight of land since March, 1880, when we lost sight of Wrangel Land; and as no land was laid down in any chart in our possession, we concluded it to be a new island. The island was named Jeannette Island, though not landed upon. Its position was latitude 76 deg. 47 min. north, longitude 158 deg. 56 min. east.

The ship drifted rapidly northwest, and on the 24th of May a new land was discovered, and as we were drifting toward it no effort was made at the time to land upon it. The ice in the vicinity of the ship was much broken up and thrown into chaotic masses in all directions and in all forms imaginable. Great anxiety was now felt for the safety of the ship, as the whole ice-field, pack and floe, seemed in rapid motion. We gradually approached the island until the 1st of June, when a party, consisting of C. E. Melville and five men, with a boat mounted on a McClintock sled drawn by fifteen dogs, and equipped with guns, ammunition, tent, and provisions for seven days, left the ship to make a landing, which was accomplished on the evening of June 3d. We hoisted the national standard, and took possession of the island in the name of the United States of America, naming it Henrietta Island. It is situated in latitude 77 deg. 8 min. north, and longitude 157 deg. 43 min. east. It is high, mountainous, and of volcanic origin, and is covered by a perpetual dome of ice and snow. The traveling party returned to the ship on June 6th.

The ship and ice continued to drift to the west and northwest, the whole ice-field being broken up in all directions. On the night of June 10th several severe shocks were felt, and the ship was found to have raised several inches in her bed There was evidence of an approaching break-up of our friendly floe-piece. At ten minutes past twelve A. M., June 11th, the ice suddenly opened alongside the ship, completely freeing her, and she floated on an even keel for the first time in many months.

The ice continued in motion, but no serious injury occurred to the ship until the morning of the 12th, when the ice commenced to pack together, bringing a tremendous strain on the ship, heeling her over to starboard, and forcing the deck-seams open. This continued during the day at intervals until evening, when it was evident the ship could not much longer hold together. The boats were lowered on the ice, and provisions, arms, tents, alcohol, sledges, and all necessary equipment for a retreat securely placed on the floe. By six P. M. the ship had entirely filled with water, and lay over at an angle of about twenty-two degrees, being kept from sinking by the opposing edges of the floe. On the morning of the 13th of June, about 4 o'clock, the ice opened and the ship went down, with colors flying at the masthead.

We remained six days on the ice organizing our system and line of march south, during which time we had resumed a rapid drift to the northwest. On June 24th, having marched south one week and obtained observation for position, we found we had drifted to latitude 77 deg. 42 min. north—a loss of twenty-four miles northwest.

We continued our march south and west, and finally landed on Bennett Island, July 29th. Hoisted the national flag and took possession of the island. It is located in north latitude 76 deg. 38 min., east longitude 150 deg. 30 min. We traversed the eastern end of the island. Left it August 6th, and sighted the north side of Thaddeus (Faddeyev) Island, one of the New Siberia group, and remained there ten days ice-bound. Landed on the south side of Thaddeus Island August 31st. Left south end of Kotelnoi Island September 6th. Camped in sight of Stolbovoi Island September 7th. Landed on Semenoffski Island September 10th.

We left Semenoffski Island, September 12th, in three boats for Barkin, at the Lena's mouth. Separated by a gale of wind the same night. Made the shoals off Barkin on the morning of September 14th. Made eastern entrance of Lena River September 16th, and camped in a vacant hut. Made two days' journey, and on the 19th fell in with three natives, who would not pilot us to a village.

On the 20th I tried to proceed up the river, but found the

shoals too difficult, and was compelled to return to the house where we slept on the 19th. On returning to the house we found Bushielle Koolgiak, who voluntarily offered to pilot me to Bulun, but after three days' hard work stopped at the house of Spiridon. Next day set out, and brought up at the house of Nicoli Chagre. The ice was forming in the river, and the natives informed me that we could not proceed south until the sledding season commenced, which would be in about fifteen days.

On the next day I made an effort to get up the river with three native pilots, but after grounding very often the pilots insisted on returning, and the condition of the party did not warrant me in advancing, for most of us were very much exhausted, were suffering from frozen feet and legs, and lack of food, the majority being unable to walk. The natives gave us quarters, and a limited quantity of fish and decayed geese.

On October 8th a Russian exile, named Koosmah Eremaoff, discovered us accidentally. He gave us salt and all the food his scanty supply allowed, and agreed to go to Bulun to inform the commandant of that place of our presence and distressed condition, and obtain food and transportation.

Koosmah started for Bulun October 16th, and took Chagre with him, and was to have returned in five days; but he did not return until the evening of October 29th, when he brought a small supply of food and a letter from Baishoff, Commandant of Bulun, who was to be at Bykoff on November 1st, with reindeer and sleds to carry the whole party to Bulun. Koosmah also brought a letter from two of the first cutter's crew, whom he met at Kumak Surka in charge of three natives, who were transporting them to Bulun. This letter was the first intelligence I had of the first cutter; the following is a copy:—

"NOVEMBER 6TH.

Arctic steamer Jeannette lost on the 11th of June; landed on Siberia the 25th of September, or thereabouts;

want assistance to go for the captain and doctor and nine other men.   [Signed]
WM. C. F. NINDERMANN,
LOUIS P. NOROS,
Seamen U. S. N.

Reply in haste; want food and clothing."

I immediately started with dog-sleds for Bulun, October 30th, hoping to intercept the commandant on the way; but he had reindeer, and traveled by a different route. Master John W. Danenhower, having recovered the use of his eyes, had been placed in charge of my party, with orders to follow me to Bulun as soon as transportation could be obtained.

I arrived at Bulun at five P. M., November 2d, and found the two men in a very exhausted condition. From them I learned the following particulars of what transpired subsequent to October 1st, the date of the latest of Lieutenant DeLong's records.

The party (DeLong's) crossed the Lena to the west bank on October 1st, at a summer hunting-lodge called Usterda. The toes of seaman H. H. Erickson having been amputated, he was placed upon an improvised sled, which was hauled by his comrades, several of whom were hardly able to walk, owing to frozen feet and legs. They proceeded south slowly for two days, and crossed a small branch of the Lena, which they had to wade. On October 6th they stopped at a small hut, where Erickson died the next day, and was buried in the Lena.

By this time they were in a deplorable condition, having eaten their last dog-meat, and being on an allowance of three ounces of alcohol per man per day. They proceeded south until October 9th, when Lieutenant DeLong decided to send two men ahead to seek relief.

The feet of Nindermann and Noros were better than those of the others, and they were supplied with blankets and a Remington rifle (forty rounds of ammunition), and six ounces of alcohol, which was a per capita division of the whole stock of the latter. They were ordered to proceed south on the west bank of the Lena, and to send relief if found, being told that the others would follow their footsteps. When the two men started, the party was at a halt on the north bank of a large western branch of the Lena. The two men ascended that branch about five miles to make a crossing, and then traveled southeast to a hut situated on the Lena bank. After fourteen days of intense suffering and slow progress they reached Bulcour, and were found by three natives, who supplied them with food and transported them to Bulun by deer-sleds, arriving at that place October 27th.

The commandant of Bulun took good care of Nindermann and Noros, but was unable to understand them. He gave them material, and they wrote a long dispatch addressed to the American Minister at St. Petersburg, which the commandant took with him to Bykoff. Mr. Danenhower immediately sent it to me by special courier, together with an order from the commandant to a subordinate at Bulun to furnish me with an outfit, and appointing Kumak Surka as a rendezvous, at which place I met him and the remainder of my party on November 5th. After a consultation, I ordered Mr. Danenhower to proceed south with all the party except James H. Bartlett, first-class fireman, who was to remain at Bulun to communicate with me.

I started north on that evening, November 5th, to the relief of Lieutenant DeLong, having with me two natives and two dog-trains, with provisions for ten days. Stopped at Kumak Surka, November 5th. Traveled fifty versts November 6th, and reached Bulcour.* Found two deserted houses and traces of the two men, Nindermann and Noros. Weather-bound November 7th; traveled sixty-five versts on November 8th; examined small hut where the two men had slept, and where a number of sleds were stowed. Slept in snow-bank that night. November 9th, travelled eighty-five

---

* A verst is two-thirds of a mile.

versts, visiting the huts at the two crosses, the shoal at Astolira, and reaching Mot Vai after midnight.

The next morning I found in the hut a waist-belt that had been made on board the Jeannette, and there were good indications that one or two of Lieutenant DeLong's party had slept in the hut. On November 10th, our provisions running short, I decided to go to Upper Bulun, a distance of 120 versts to the northwest, in order to renew them. Reached Upper Bulun about midnight on the 11th, having stopped at the deserted hunting-station of Cath Conta on the 11th, and also having visited eight huts on the route. Considerable stale fish and deer-meat were found at Cath Conta, but no signs of it or the huts having been visited by DeLong's party.

On my arrival at Upper Bulun the natives brought in Lieutenant DeLong's record, dated October 1st, and I learned that others had been found. I sent to a neighboring village for them, and the next morning records dated September 22d and 26th, with a Winchester rifle, were brought to me. On November 12th, we were weather-bound. The only provisions to be obtained were deer-meat and fish, there being a scarcity of the latter, the natives having to send 250 versts for their own supply.

On November 13th I obtained four days' supply of fish, and with fresh dog-teams and natives started for Ballock, a hut in which record No. 3 and the Winchester rifle were found. Slept there that night; found both huts filled with snow. On November 14th I followed the east bank of the Lena to the coast; followed the coast about three miles to the east, and found the cache that had been made by Lieutenant DeLong on September 19th, 1881. I made a thorough search and gathered up everything. The sleighs being too heavily laden to carry it, I searched for the boat both east and west of the cache for a distance of five miles each way, and to a distance of one mile and a half off shore, and saw no signs of it. The ice was very much broken, and was shoved up in masses to within twenty-five feet of the cache.

I returned about midnight to Ballock, and to Upper Bulun the next day, November 15th, during a heavy storm. Was obliged to wait there two days to rest and feed the dogs. During this time I overhauled everything obtained in the cache, and the following is a correct list, viz.:—

One box containing refuse medical stores; one box of small articles (mess-gear); one box for navigation books and sextant; one box chronometer; two tin cases containing four log-books; two cook-stoves; two pieces of rope; seven old sleeping-bags, condemned; one lot of old clothing (worn out); one Winchester rifle; one repeating rifle (both broken); one boat-breaker; one boat-bucket; one box specimens from Bennett Island.

Some of these articles were left at Upper Bulun, and the others were taken to Yakutsk. There was no list of articles found in the cache, but record No. 1 was found in the navigation-box,

On November 17th I left Upper Bulun with fish for ten days' food, and with three dog-teams driven by three natives. I visited the place at which DeLong's party crossed the Lena, and traced the party to Sisteraneck, from which place I wished to search for the hut in which Erickson died; but there was a storm raging, and the natives insisted on returning to either Bulun or Upper Bulun, because there was a lack of food and the dogs refused to work. We had only raw frozen fish to eat, so I determined to return to Bulun, and arrived there November 27th, in a nearly exhausted condition—feet, hands, legs and face badly frost-bitten—having been ten days in a continuous storm, remaining two nights and one day in one hole in a snow-bank without shelter of any kind.

From my knowledge of the country, and from the evidence of Noros and Nindermann, I am convinced that Lieutenant DeLong and party are somewhere to the westward of the Lena, and between Sisteraneck and Bulcour, which are separated by an extent of about one hundred and fifty versts of a barren and desolate region, devoid of sustenance. To search that region a large force will be required, with proper authority from the Russian officials. I therefore came to this place to communicate with the United States, and immediately, with the aid of the authorities, to organize searching parties.

In the meantime the commandant of Bulun is searching with all the force his small town affords. The governor of this province has sent a general order throughout the entire region, from the Lena to Kolyma, to search for and render assistance to both parties that are missing. I am now completing my arrangements, and will start north in a few days. The Governor-General, G. Tschernieff, is rendering every assistance in his power.

The general health of the whole party is excellent, but Mr. Danenhower's eyes are badly affected. John Cole, seaman, suffers from aberration of the mind, and Herbert Leach, seaman, from frozen toe. To-morrow, Mr. Danenhower, with nine men, will proceed to Irkutsk and thence to the Atlantic seaboard.

I will keep James H. Bartlett, first-class fireman, and W. F. C. Nindermann, seaman, with me. Mr. Danenhower will carry to the United States the records and the articles found in the cache.

In conclusion, I call the attention of the department to the upright and manly conduct of Master J. W. Danenhower, who cheerfully rendered the most valuable assistance under the most trying circumstances, and whose professional knowledge I availed myself of on all occasions. We were in perfect accord at all times, although an unfortunate circumstance deprived him of his legitimate command.

The conduct of first-class fireman James H. Bartlett is worthy of special notice. His superior intelligence, cheerful disposition and energy are highly commendable. Also seaman Herbert Leach, who was at the helm for eleven hours in the gale, during which time his feet and legs were badly frozen; after which he worked manfully at the oars without a murmur, enduring the most intense pain.

Yours respectfully, GEORGE W. MELVILLE,
Passed Assistant Engineer, United States Navy.

Before leaving Bulun for Yakutsk in December, 1881, Mr. Melville gave Gregory M. Baishoff, the Russian commandant at Bulun, verbal directions to commence at once a search for the missing seamen; and to stimulate the natives, a reward was offered for the recovery of the people, books and papers. While on his way to Yakutsk he also wrote to the commandant a letter of instructions, which was translated by an exile and conveyed to Bulun. The following is a copy thereof:—

It is my desire and the wish of the government of the United States of America, and of the projectors of the American expedition, that a diligent and constant search be made for my missing comrades of both boats. Lieutenant DeLong and his party, consisting of twelve persons, will be found near the west bank of the Lena River.

They are south of the small hunting-station which is west of the house known among the Yakuts as Qu Vina. They could not possibly have marched as far south as Bulcom. Therefore, be they dead or alive, they are between Qu Vina and Bulcour. I have already traveled over this ground, but I followed the river bank. Therefore, it is necessary that a more careful search be made on the high ground back from the river for a short distance, as well as along the river bank.

I examined many huts and small houses, but could not possibly examine all of them. Therefore it is necessary that all—every house, large or small—be examined for books and papers or the persons of the party. Men without food and with but little clothing would naturally seek shelter in huts along the line of march, and if exhausted, might be in one of the huts.

They would leave their books and papers in a hut if unable to carry them further. If they carried their books and papers south of that section of the country between Mot Vai and Bulcour, they will be found piled up in a heap, and some prominent object erected near them to attract the attention of searching parties. A mast of wood or pile of wood would be erected near them, if not on top of them. In case books and papers are found, they are to be sent to the American minister resident at St. Petersburg. If they are found in time, and can be forwarded to me before I leave Russia, forward them to me.

The persons of the dead I wish to have carried to a central position most convenient of access to Bulun, all placed inside of a small house, arranged side by side for future recognition, the hut then securely closed and banked up with snow or earth, and to remain so until a proper person arrives from America to make final disposition of the bodies. In banking up the hut, have it done in such a manner that animals cannot get in to destroy the bodies.

Search for the small boat containing eight persons should be made from the west mouth of the Lena to and beyond the east mouth of the Yana River. After the separation of the three boats no information has been received concerning the small boat, but as all three boats were destined to Barkin and then to go to the mouth of the Lena River, it is natural to suppose that Lieutenant Chipp directed his boat to Barkin if he managed to weather the gale. But if from any cause he could not find a Lena mouth, he would continue along the coast from Barkin west for a north mouth of the Lena, or south for an eastern entrance or mouth of the Lena River. If still unsuccessful in getting into the Lena River he might, from stress of weather or other cause, be forced along the coast toward the Yana River.

Diligent and constant search is to commence at once, and to continue till the people, books and papers are found, care being taken that a vigilant and careful examination of that section of the country where Lieutenant DeLong and his party are known to be is made in early spring-time, when the snow begins to leave the ground, and before the spring floods commence to overflow the river banks. One or more American officers will, in all probability, be in Bulun in time to assist in the search; but the search mentioned in these instructions is to be carried on independently of any other party, and to be entirely under the control of the competent authority of Russia.

GRAVES IN THE PRIMEVAL FOREST OF SIBERIA.

CHAPTER XL

LIEUTENANT DeLONG'S RECORDS.

THE records written by Lieutenant DeLong, which Mr. Melville secured during his November search, extend over a period of twelve days, and the last one was written eight days before Nindermann and Noros were sent ahead for assistance. The terrible story of hardships and privation told by these records, the statements of Nindermann and Noros as to the condition of the party eight days after the last record was written, and his own fearful experiences while searching for his comrades, must have extinguished in Melville's mind all hope that they would ever be rescued alive-unless they had found food and shelter in some native settlement.

COPY OF RECORD NO. 1.

[This record was found in the cache at the landing-place of the first cutter, by Mr. Melville, on the 14th day of November, 1881.]

ARCTIC EXPLORING STEAMER JEANNETTE,
LENA DELTA, Monday, Sept. 19th, 1881.

The following-named fourteen persons belonging to the Jeannette, which was sunk by the ice on June 12th, 1881, in latitude north 77 deg. 15 min., longitude 155 deg., landed here on the evening of the 17th inst., and will proceed on foot this afternoon to try to reach a settlement on the Lena River.

GEORGE W. DELONG,
Lieutenant Commanding.

1. Lieutenant DeLong.
2. Surgeon Ambler.
3. Mr. Collins.
4. W.F.C. Nindermann.
5. A. Gortz.
6. Ah Sam.
7. Alexy.
8. H. H. Erickson.
9. H. H. Kaack.
10. G. H. Boyd.
11. W. Lee.
12. N. Iverson.
13. L. P. Noros.
14. A. Dressler.

Whoever finds this paper is requested to forward it to the Secretary of the Navy, with a note of the time and place at which found.

[Copies of the above in six languages followed.]

A record was left about one-half mile north of the southern end of Semenoffski Island, buried under a stake. The thirty-three persons composing the officers and crew of the Jeannette left that island in three boats on the morning of the 12th inst. (one week ago). That same night we were separated in a gale of wind, and have seen nothing of them since. Orders had been given, in the event of such an accident, for each boat to make the best of its way to a settlement on the Lena River, before waiting for anybody. My boat made the land in the morning of the 16th inst., and I suppose we are at the Lena Delta. I have had no chance to get sight for position since I left Semenoffski Island. After trying for two days to get in shore without grounding, or to reach one of the river mouths, I abandoned my boat and waded one-and-a-half miles, carrying our provisions and outfit with us. We must now try, with God's help, to walk to a settlement, which I believe to be ninety-five miles distant. We are all well; have four days' provisions, arms and ammunition, and are carrying with us only ship's books and papers, and blankets, tents, and some medicines; therefore our chance of getting through seems good.

GEORGE W. DELONG,
Lieutenant United States Navy, Commanding.

COPY OF RECORD NO. 2.

[This record was found in a hut by a Yakut hunter, and given to Mr. Melville at Upper Bulun, on the 12th day of November, 1881.]

ARCTIC EXPLORING STEAMER JEANNETTE,
AT A HUT ON THE LENA DELTA,
BELIEVED TO BE NEAR TCHOLHOGOJE,
Thursday, 22d of September, 1881.

DE LONG AND HIS MEN DING ASHORE.

The following-named persons, fourteen of the officers and crew of the Jeannette, reached this place yesterday afternoon, on foot, from the Arctic Ocean.

GEORGE W. DE LONG,
Commander of Expedition, Lieutenant U. S. Navy.

Whoever finds this paper is requested to forward it to the Secretary of the Navy, with a note of the time and place at which it was found.

[Copies of the above in six languages followed.]

Lieutenant DELONG.	A. GORTZ,	L. P. NOROS.
P. A. Surgeon J. A. AMBLER.	G. H. BOYD.	W. LEE.
Mr. J. J. COLLINS.	N. IVERSON.	AH SAM.
W. F. C. NINDERMANN.	A. DRESSLER.	ALEXY.
H. H. ERICKSON.	H. H. KAACK.	

The Jeannette was crushed and sunk by the ice on the 12th of June, 1881, in latitude 77 deg. 15 min. north, longitude 155 deg., after having drifted twenty-two months in the tremendous pack-ice of this ocean. The entire thirty-three persons composing her officers and crew dragged three boats and provisions over the ice to latitude 76 deg. 38 min. north, longitude 150 deg. 30 min. east, where we landed upon a new island—Bennett Island—on the 29th of July. From thence we proceeded southward in boats, sometimes dragging over ice, until, the 10th of September, we reached Semenoffski Island, ninety miles northeast of this delta. We sailed from there in company on the 12th of September, but that same night we were separated in a gale of wind, and I have seen nothing since of the two other boats or their people. They were divided as follows:—

SECOND CUTTER.—Lieutenant Chipp, Mr. Dunbar, A. Sweetman, W. Sharvell, E. Star, H. D. Warren, A. P. Kuehne, and P. Johnson.

WHALE-BOAT.—Past Assistant Engineer Melville, Master Danenhower, Mr. Newcomb, J. Cole, J. H. Bartlett, H. Wilson, S. Lauderback, F. Mansen, Charles Tong Sing, Anequin, and H. W. Leach.

My boat, having weathered the gale, made the land on the morning of the 16th inst., and after trying to get in shore for two days, and being prevented by shoal water, we abandoned the boat, and waded to the beach, carrying our arms, provisions, and records, at a point about twelve miles to the north and east of this place. We had all suffered somewhat from cold, wet, and exposure, and three of our men were badly lamed; but having only four days' provisions left, reduced rations, we were forced to proceed to the southward. On Monday, September 19th, we left a pile of our effects near the beach, erecting a long pole, where will be found everything valuable—chronometer, ship's log-books for two years, tent, &c., which we were absolutely unable to carry. It took us forty-eight hours to make these twelve miles, owing to our disabled men, and these two huts seemed to me a good place to stop while I pushed forward the surgeon and Nindermann to get relief for us. But last night we shot two reindeer, which gives us abundance of food for the present, and we have seen so many more that anxiety for the future is relieved. As soon as our three sick men can walk, we shall resume our march for a settlement on the Lena River.

Saturday, Sept. 24—8 A. M.

Our three lame men being now able to walk, we are about to resume our journey, with two days' rations deer-meat and two days' rations pemmican and three pounds tea.

GEORGE W. DELONG,
Lieutenant Commanding.

COPY OF RECORD NO. 3.

[This record, and a rifle, were found in a hut by a Yakut hunter, and given to Mr. Melville, at Upper Bulun, on the 12th day of November, 1881.]

Monday, Sept. 26th, 1881.

Fourteen of the officers and men of the United States Arctic steamer Jeannette reached this place last evening, and are proceeding to the southward this morning. A more complete record will be found in a tinder case hung up in a hut fifteen miles further up the right bank of the larger stream.

GEORGE W. DELONG,

Lieutenant Commanding.

P. A. Surgeon J. M. AMBLER.	H. H. ERICKSON.	L. P. NOROS.
Mr. J. J. COLLINS.	AH SAM.	W. LEE.
A. GÓRTZ.	H. H. KAACK.	N. IVERSON.
W. F. C. NINDERMANN.	ALEXY.	G. H. BOYD.
A. DRESSLER.		

COPY OF RECORD NO. 4.

[This record was found in a hut by a Yakut hunter, and given to Mr. Melville, at Upper Bulun, on the 12th day of November, 1881.]

Saturday, Oct. 1st, 1881.

Fourteen of the officers and men of the United States Arctic steamer Jeannette reached this hut on Wednesday, September 28th, and, having been forced to wait for the river to freeze over, are proceeding to cross to the west side this A. M., on their journey to reach some settlement on the Lena river.

We have two days' provisions, but having been fortunate enough thus far to get game in our pressing needs, we have no fear for the future.

Our party are all well except one man, Erickson, whose toes have been amputated in consequence of frost bite. Other records will be found in several huts on the east side of this river, along which we have come from the northward.

GEORGE W. DELONG,

Lieutenant U. S. N., Commanding Expedition.

P. A. Surgeon AMBLER.	Mr. J. J. COLLINS.	G. H. BOYD.
W. F. C. NINDERMANN.	A. DRESSLER.	H. H. ERICKSON.
H. H. KAACK.	A. GORTZ.	N. IVERSON.
W. LEE.	AH SAM.	L. P. NOROS.
ALEXY.		

CHAPTER XII.

EXPERIENCES OF NINDERMANN, NOROS, AND LEACH.

IN Engineer Melville's narrative he refers to a letter, addressed to the American Minister at St. Petersburg, which Mr. Nindermann (who is a German) wrote at Bulun after he and Noros had arrived there in an exhausted condition. The following is a *verbatim* copy thereof:—

"BULUN, October 29—To the American Minister St Petersburg

Please inform the Secretary of U. S. Navy of the loss of the Jeannette

Arctic steamer Jeannette

Crused in the ice June 11th 1881 in lat 77 deg. 22 min. N., longitude 157 deg. 55 min. E or thareabout, saved three Boats, also from three to four mounths provisions, with sleds, travilled S. W to to reach the New Siberian Islands, travilled two weeks or thareabouts then sighted an Island, the Captain determined reach it, and landed in about two weeks on the southern end and planted the *Americken Flag* and called it Bennett Island, Lieutenant Chipp was sent on the west side to determin the size with a Boats crew, Ice Pilot Dinbar with the two Natives on the East side, returned in three days, remained one week on the Island, took to the boats and started South, made the New Siberian Islands and camped on a couple of them, set our course from the most Southern Island to strike the North side of Siberia, to enter one of the small rivers to the Leana, on our passage a gale of wind set in, a sea running, lost sight of the Boats, one in charge of Lieut Chipp, the other Engr Melville, know not what has become of them, our boat almost swamped carryed away the mast lost the sail, hove too under a drag one night and a day, shipping seas all the time pumps and bailers gowing Night and Day all hands feet frostbitten when the gale was over the Captain had lost the use of his *feat* and *hands* made the cost, struck one of the small rivers, not finding water enough to enter, the Ice making, beatting around for two days, the Captain determined to make the land, the boat struck two miles off shore the Captain made everybody that was able to stand on his feet to get over board, to lighten the boat and tow her in we towed her one mile, could not get her any further, took out the ship's papers and provisions, the Captain then had got the use of his hands and feat a little, in evening of the 25th of September. Names of boats crew Captain DeLong Surgeon Ambler Mr. Collins, W. T. C. Nindermann Louis P. Norris, H. H. Erickson, H. H. Kaack, G. W. Boyd, A. Gortz, A. Dressler, W. Lee, N. Iverson, Alexia, Ah Sam and one dog remained a few days on the seacoast on account of some of the mens feet being badly frost bitten, leaving behind the ships log and other articles, not being able to carry them, started to travel south with five days provisions. Erickson, walking on crutches a few days after made a sled to drag him, came to a hut on the 5th of October. On the morning of the 6th the Dockter cut off all his toes, the Captain asked me if I had strength to goo to one of the settlements with one of the men to get assistance, as he was gowing to stay by Erickson. While talking about it Erickson *Died,* we Bured him in the river the Captain said we will all go together name of place *Owtit Ary,* lat. 71 deg. 55 min. north, long. not known. Oct. 7th Eat our last Dog meat, started traville south with about one quart of Alkihall, and two tin cases of ships papers two rifles and little amunition, travilled until the 9th. Nothing to Eat, drank three ounces of Alkihall a day per man, the Captain and the rest of them got weak and gave out travilling he then sent me and L. P. Noros with three ounces of Alkihall and one rifle and 40 rounds of amunitions on ahead to a place called Kumak Surka. Distance about 12 twelve miles to find natives, if not finding any to traville south until we did, took us five days to walk to Kumak Surka, found two fish took one days rest started south again nothing to eat, travilled untill the 19th getting weeker every day gave up in dispair, sat down and rested, then walked one mile found two huts and a storehouse, where there was about fifteen pounds of *Blue moulded Fish* stoped three days to regain strenth, boath beaing to weak to travill. On the afternoon of the 23d or thareabouts a *native* came to the hut, we tryed to make him understand that there was eleven more men north, could not make him understand he took us too his camp whare thare was six more, also a lot of sleighs and raindeer they travilling at the time south, next morning broak camp came to a settlement on the 25th, called Ajakit there tryed again to make the people understand there was more people north, did not succeed, Ajakit is lat 70 deg. 55 min. north, long. not known as the chart is a coppy, sent for the govener to Bulun, came 27th he knew the ships name, and knew about Nordenchawl, but could not talk English, we tried to make him understand that the Captain was in a starving condition or probably dead, and that we wanted natives, Raindeer and food to get them, as I thought that we could make it in five or six days to save them from starvation but the Govoner made signs that he had to Telegraph to St. Petersberg, he then sent us on to *Bulun*. We stand in kneed of food and clothing at present our health is in a bad condition hoping to be well soon we remain your humble servants,

WILLIAM C. F. NINDERMANN,
LOUIS P. NOROS,
Seamen of the U. S. Navy, Steamer Jeannette."

The following are extracts from a letter which Mr. Noros wrote from Yakutsk, to his father who resides in Fall River, Massachusetts:—

"On the 4th of September we were frozen fast in pack ice, where we remained drifting north and west until the

THE LAST PARTING WITH DE LONG.

ship was crushed on June 11th, 1881. While being held fast in our icy cradle we had a good time hunting bears, seals, walrus, and other game. We frequently had face, nose, and ears frozen, but thought nothing of it, as we had got used to the climate.

After the ship went down we had a hundred days of hard dragging and sailing in open boats. On the night of September 13th we had a gale of wind, and the boats got separated. The boat that I was in was the captain's boat. We had fourteen men and dogs, and were loaded quite deep. When we reached the Siberian coast we could not land on the beach from boats. We had to wade through ice and water up to our waists. We were nearly all day carrying our things to shore, and it was dark before we got through. This was on September 17th. On the 19th we commenced our march. We traveled until October 6th, when one of our men died from frozen limbs. We had killed and eaten our last dog on that day.

On October 9th the captain sent Nindermann and myself on ahead to look for assistance and food, none of the party having had anything to eat for two days. We started without a particle of food. I had a pair of sealskin trousers. We cut pieces from these and chewed them until we were found by the natives. We were so weak we could hardly stand. I believe that if we had had to endure our sufferings for two days longer we would have shot ourselves. The natives took us to their camp and gave us plenty to eat and drink. The result was we were both quite sick for some time. We were taken to a village, and from there to Bulun.

At Bulun we tried to get a telegram sent, but could not make them understand. We supposed that we were the only two men alive out of the whole expedition. Then we heard of a boat's crew landing at one of the mouths of the Lena. The boat proved to be Melville's, and as soon as they learned of our arrival at Bulun they joined us at that place, so there were thirteen of us alive."

While at Irkutsk, Mr. Jackson, the *Herald* correspondent,

learned from Mr. Noros the following additional particulars respecting Lieutenant DeLong and his men:—

The party made land at a point near the northernmost branch of the Lena, but found it impossible to enter on account of shoals. DeLong therefore determined to land at a point whence they could see this northerly outlet, but more to the east. Two miles from the beach, the captain ordered those of the men who could walk to get out and drag the boat nearer in shore. The captain, the doctor, Erickson and Boyd (both disabled) stayed in the boat, which the others were then enabled to drag a mile further toward the land, when they, too, waded to the shore.

Collins had left the boat with the first lot and had made a fire on the shore. This was on or about the 16th of September, and the landing of articles was completed on the 17th. There the party stayed two days to recuperate, all the men being badly frost-bitten; the doctor alone was in comparatively good condition. Noros and Nindermann were the best conditioned among the men.

The journey south was then commenced, the burdens being equally distributed. The captain bore his own blanket and some records. The burdens borne by some of the others were heavy; some complained of taking them further, but the captain insisted. The party then traveled south four days. On the way two deer were shot by the Indian Alexai. The party sat down and had a good feed, DeLong's motto being, Noros says, to "feed well while they had it."

Noros thinks they made twenty miles in the first ten days. The four next days brought them to the extremity of a peninsula, and after some delay, waiting for the river to freeze, they crossed the river to the west bank on or about the 1st of October. The width of the river was there about five hundred yards. Before crossing they got another deer. The captain's intention was to make for the place called Sagasta on the map. Erickson died. His toes had been amputated by the doctor during the retreat. After crossing the river he one night pulled off his mittens, and one of his hands became frost-bitten and circulation could not be restored in it. He died, and was buried in the river.

Then it was that the captain decided to send Noros and Nindermann ahead. The food had been quite exhausted; the party was existing only on brandy. Noros thinks it was a Sunday when they left. The captain had held divine service, the men seated on the banks of the river. After service he called the two men and told them he wanted them to push on ahead, and that he would follow with his party.

"If you find game," were his last words, "then return to us; if you do not then go to Kumak Surka."

Noros thus describes the parting:—"The captain read divine service before we left. All the men shook hands with us, and most of them had tears in their eyes. Collins was the last. He simply said:—

'Noros, when you get to New York remember me.'

They seemed to have lost hope, but as we left they gave us three cheers. We told them we would do all that we could do, and that was the last we saw of them. Snow had fallen to a depth of a foot or a foot and a half."

The river at this place was about five hundred yards wide, and the place was near where the mountains on the western side ended. There was one spot which remained distinctly impressed upon his mind—namely, a high, conical, rocky island, which rose up out of the river, and which he called Ostava, or Stalboy. How he got the name is not quite clear. But the rock is a landmark in his memory, and it bore about east by north from the spot where they left the captain. The rock is just at the end of the mountains; the mountains commence with that rock.

After leaving this rock the two men traveled slowly and wearily. They sighted deer once, but could not get near them. They shot one grouse and caught an eel, which was all the food they had. They made a kind of tea from the bark of the Arctic willow, but often had only hot water to drink. They chewed and ate portions of their skin breeches, and the leather soles of their moccasins. About two days after leaving the captain they crossed the Lena to the east side, in the hope of finding game in the mountains, and it took them a very long time to cross the ice at that point.

The following is a copy of a letter written by Seaman Leach to his mother at Penobscot, Maine, after his arrival at Irkutsk:—

MY DEAR MOTHER,—Your welcome letter came to hand last night. I was at a party, enjoying myself as well as possible for me to do here, when one of the boys came running in and gave me nine letters from home. Oh, mother, you should have seen me dance around the room. The young ladies all thought I was crazy. They were about right. After nearly three years without hearing a single word from home, the news, when it did come, quite upset me. Well, I will try to give an account of myself. I will begin at the beginning.

After passing through Bering's Strait we stood north until we struck the ice. We ran into it and it closed around us. We had thirty-three of the best boys on board that ever walked a ship's deck. Poor fellows! only thirteen are left to tell the sad tale. After getting into the ice we made preparations to spend the winter, expecting to get out the following summer. We spent the winter very pleasantly—had theatricals Christmas and New Year. It was very cold, but we all enjoyed it tip-top. The winter passed, and so did the summer, without any signs of our being released; so we made up our minds to stay another winter. It passed quite pleasantly, although three months of the time we did not see the sun. It looked good when it did come up: I think it was worth waiting for.

We laid in the ice until June, when our ship (our home) was taken from us. Then our hardships began. Oh, mother, you can have no idea of what we went through. When I look back it seems more like a strange dream than a reality. But it is over now, and we that pulled through are safe. About eight days before we reached the coast we encountered a heavy gale, which nearly put an end to our sufferings.

When it commenced to blow the lieutenant put me at the helm. It was very cold, and the boat was nearly full of water all the time, in spite of the men's bailing for dear life. I sat at the helm about fourteen hours before the wind abated enough for me to be relieved. When the time came I rose up and fell flat into the bottom of the boat. My feet were frozen stiff, and my legs were chilled up to my body so badly that I think they could have been taken off without my feeling it.

When we got ashore I was in a tight fix. I could not walk, and was in much pain, and my feet had begun to putrefy. Bartlett, one of the men, took a knife and cut out the corrupt places, and cut about half of one of my great toes off, leaving about half an inch of the bone sticking out of the end. About a month ago I found a doctor who took it off. It troubles me to walk now, and I think that it will for some time.

Guess I have written enough about my trials; will tell you something about the people I find here in Irkutsk. The ladies here call me the savior—they have heard about the boat scrape. We are received by the best families in town. They seem to think it a feather in their caps to have the Americans call on them. I make myself as agreeable as possible. The life is not altogether crushed out of me if I am a little run down. By the way, they are going to form a search party, and I think it is my duty to join it and search for the poor boys that are left. I don't know yet whether I shall go or not. If I do you must not worry about me, for we shall not start before spring, and will get back next fall; so you see it will not be long to wait, and no risk to run, and besides you want to see your son do by another as you would have another do by him. Gracious! how I want to see the folks at home. Give my love to everybody, in town and out, keep the lion's share for yourself, and believe me, your loving son, HERBERT."

CHAPTER XIII.

YAKUTSK—TOWN AND PROVINCE.

YAKUTSK, or the 'city of the Yakuts' as the natives proudly call it, where the survivors of the expedition found the first comforts of civilized life after their long journey, is situated on the Lena River near latitude 62° north. It is the capital and chief town of the province of Yakutsk,—one of the six into which Eastern Siberia is divided-and a commercial center of the fur and ivory trade.

The region of the Upper Lena has been subject to the Russian power for 250 years. After crossing the Yenisei, the Cossack conquerors of Siberia advanced to the shores of Lake Baikal, and in 1620 attacked and partly defeated the populous and warlike nation of the Buriats. Then, turning northward to the Lena, they descended the river to the principal town of the Yakuts, where, in 1632, they founded the city of Yakutsk, and after considerable resistance made subject the powerful nation of the Yakuts.

The province of Yakutsk is the largest in Siberia, and covers an area of no less than a million and a half of square miles. The population, consisting almost wholly of natives, —Tunguses, Yakuts and Yukaghirs—is estimated at 235,000; making about one inhabitant to every seven square miles.

The Russian population of the province is about 7,000, and is confined almost entirely to the valley of the Lena, Yakutsk, and its neighborhood. In the most northern villages of Siberia their dwelling places consist of cabins, built of logs or planks from broken-up lighters, and having flat, turf-covered roofs. Such carvings and ornaments as are commonly found on the houses of well-to-do Russian peasants are here completely wanting.

Further south the villages are larger, and the houses of the Russians finer, with raised roofs and high gables richly ornamented with wood carvings. There is usually a church

SIBERIAN VILLAGE CHURCH.

painted in bright colors, and everything indicates a degree of prosperity. In the center of the house is a brick stove, and the walls of the rooms are white-washed or papered, and adorned with pictures according to the means and taste of the owner—portraits of the Imperial family, battle scenes, lithographs of the saints, and family photographs. Sacred pictures are placed in a corner, and before them hang small oil lamps or wax-candles which are lighted on festive occasions.

The sleeping place is formed of a bedstead near the roof, so large that it occupies a third of the room. The top of the stove is also used as a sleeping place at times. Food is

RUSSIAN PEASANT, WITH SAMOVAR.

cooked in large baking ovens. Fresh bread is baked every day, and even for the poor, a large tea urn (*samovar*) is an almost indispensable household article. The foreigner is certain to receive a hearty welcome when he crosses the threshold, and if he stays a short time, he will generally, whatever time of the day it be, find himself drinking a glass of tea with his host.

Along with the dwellings of the Russians, the tents of the natives, or "Asiatics," are often seen; and near them are generally a large number of dogs, which are used in summer for towing boats, and in winter for drawing sledges.

OSTYAK TENTS MADE OF BIRCH BARK.

Very little is known of the Yukaghirs, who roam over the northern portion of the tundra; their numbers are few, although at one time, as their legend says, there were more hearths of Yukaghirs on the banks of the Kolyma than stars in the sky. They were no doubt once a powerful race, and on the rivers Yana and Indigirka tumuli and ancient burial-places are pointed out containing, with the remains of the natives, bows, arrows, spears, and the magic drum.

The Tunguses wander over a larger area than any other tribe in Siberia, stretching through Manchuria across the district of the Amoor, and northeast and west to the sea of Okhotsk and to the Yenisei. Of the Tunguse family the Manchu is the most civilized, while in Siberia we have them in their extreme character of rude nomads, unlettered, and still pagan, or but imperfectly Christianized. The Tungusian approaches the Mongolian, the Ostjak, or the Eskimo, according as his residence is north or south; within the limit of the growth of trees or beyond it; on the champaign, the steppe, or the tundra. On the tundra the horse ceases to be his domestic animal, and the reindeer or the dog replace it. Hence we hear of three divisions of the Tunguse family, called by different names, according as they possess horses, reindeer, or dogs.

In the center of the province, occupying the valley of the Lena, roam the Yakuts. They are of middle height, and of a light copper color, with black hair, which the men cut short. They belong to the great Turk family, and as a race are good-tempered, orderly, hospitable, and capable of enduring great privation patiently; but they have not the independence of character which distinguishes their Tunguse neighbors. Some travelers see in them a strong resemblance to the North American Indians.

The winter dwelliugs of the Yakuts have doors of raw hides, and log or wicker walls calked with cow-dung, and flanked with banks of earth to the height of the windows. The latter are made of sheets of ice, kept in their place from the outside by a slanting pole, the lower end of which is fixed in the ground. They are rendered air-tight by pouring on water, which quickly freezes round the edges. The flat roof is covered with earth, and over the door, facing the east, the boards project, making a covered place in front. Under the same roof are the winter shelters for the cows and for the people, the former being the larger. The fireplace consists of a wicker frame plastered over with clay, room being left for a man to pass between the fireplace and the wall. The hearth is made of beaten earth, and on it there is at all times a blazing fire, and logs of larchwood throw up showers of sparks to the roof. Young calves, like children, are often brought into the house to the fire, whilst their mothers cast a contented look through the open door at the back of the fireplace. Behind the fireplace, too, are the sleeping-places of the people, which in the poorer dwellings consist only of a continuation of the straw laid in the cow-house.

In the winter they have but about five hours of day-light, which penetrates as best it can through the icy windows; and in the evening all the party sit round the fire on low stools, men and women smoking. The summer yourts of these people are formed of poles about 20 feet long, which are united at the top into a roomy cone, covered with pieces of bright yellow and perfectly flexible birch bark, which are not merely joined together, but are also handsomely worked along the seams with horsehair thread. The houses are not over-stocked with furniture, and the chief cooking-utensil is a large iron pot.

The Yakuts who inhabit the inclement region adjacent to the Frozen Ocean have neither horses nor oxen, but breed large numbers of dogs, which draw them to and fro on their fishing excursions. Even those living on the 62d parallel keep cattle under far greater difficulties than usual, for they have to make long journeys to collect hay, and do not always find enough. The cold prevents their breeding sheep, goats, or poultry. Nevertheless, cattle and hunting are their chief means of subsistence, for they do not in general cultivate the land, though in the gardens at Yakutsk are grown potatoes, cabbages, radishes, and turnips. Some products of Yakutsk industry are purchased by the Russians, particularly floor-cloths of white and colored felts, which are cut in strips and sewed together like mosaic. From the earliest times they have been able to procure and work for themselves metal. The language of the Yakuts, which is largely spoken by the Russians who live among them, is one of the principal means by which we are led to assume their Turkish origin, for Latham says their speech is intelligible at Constantinople, and their traditions (for literature they have none) bespeak a southern origin.

Strahlenberg calls these people pagans, but the latest

writers call them Christians; and the method of their conversion was, it is said, extraordinary; for the Russian priests not making much headway against their superstitious, an ukase was one day issued setting forth that the good and

NATIVE GIRLS OF YAKUTSK IN WINTER COSTUME.

loyal nation of the Yakuts were thought worthy to enter, and were consequently admitted into, the Russian Church, to become a part of the Czar's Christian family, and entitled to all the privileges of the rest of his children. Success attended the measure. The new Christians showed perfect sincerity in the adoption of their novel faith, and the Russian priests have established their sway over the Yakut race, though amongst the outlying portion a lingering belief in Shamanism still survives.

The town of Yakutsk has a population of about 5,000 persons, some of whom are political exiles. All the Russian inhabitants might well be considered exiles, for they are over 5,000 miles from St. Petersburg. The town presents a curious medley of dwellings, for there are seen the government buildings, the cathedral and churches, the wooden houses of the Russians, and also the less pretentious winter dwellings of the Yakuts, and even their summer yourts.

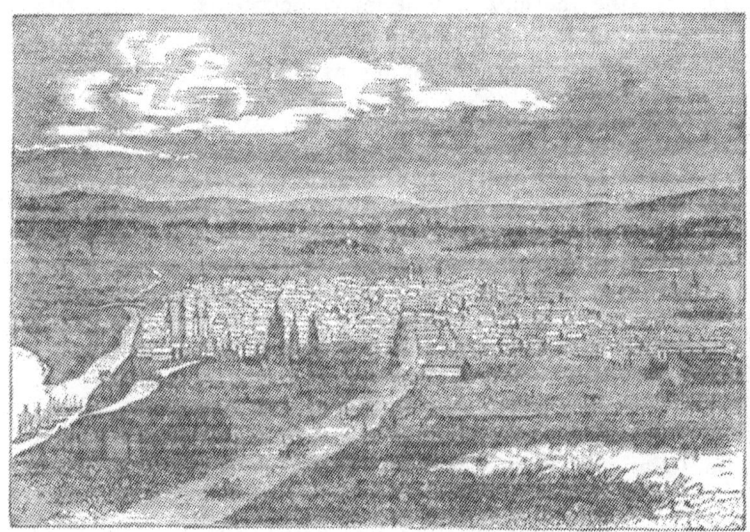

YAKUTSK IN OUR DAYS.

The cathedral is built of stone, and dedicated to St. Nicholas, and there are in the town some half-dozen churches in which parts, or all, of the service is performed in the Yakut language. The chief ecclesiastic is Dionysius, Bishop of Yakutsk and Viluisk, who has in his hyperborean diocese 49 churches and chapels, and one monastery containing a dozen monks.

According to Sir Edward Brewster the town of Yakutsk is near the Asiatic pole of cold—one of the two coldest places on the globe. The mean temperature of the air is 18.5 Fahrenheit. At times the cold reaches 70° below zero, and mercury is frozen for one-sixth of the year. A warm summer follows the cold winter; the ground is then thawed three feet deep, and though the crops rest on perpetually frozen strata, yet they produce from fifteen to forty-fold. Oxen here take the places of horses, and men and girls ride them astride. When used to draw sledges, the driver is perched on the back of one of the oxen.

So accustomed do the natives become to the cold, that even with the thermometer at many degrees below freezing point, the Yakut women, with bare arms, stand in the open-air markets, chatting and joking as pleasantly as in genial spring. In fact, the great cold is not thought a grievance in Siberia, for a man clothed in furs may sleep at night in an open sledge when the mercury freezes in the thermometer; and wrapped up in his pelisse, he can lie without inconvenience on the snow under a tent where the temperature of the air is 30° below zero.

John Ledyard, referred to in a former chapter, resided at Yakutsk in the winter of 1787, and was an attentive observer of whatever came under his notice. The following are extracts from the journal which he kept at Yakutsk:—

"The people in Yakutsk have no wells. They have tried them to a very great depth, but they freeze over—even in summer; consequently they have all their water from the river. But in winter they cannot bring water in its fluid state; it freezes on the way. It is, therefore, brought in large cakes of ice to their houses, and piled up in their yards. Milk is brought to market in the same way. A Yakuti came into our house to-day with a bag full of ice. 'What,' said I, 'has the man brought ice to sell in Siberia?' It was milk. Clear mercury exposed to the air is constantly frozen.

"In these severe frosts the air is condensed like a thick fog; the atmosphere itself is frozen; respiration is fatiguing; all exercise must be moderate as possible. In these seasons there is no chase; the animals submit themselves to hunger and security, and so does man. All nature groans beneath the vigorous winter.

"The Russians have been here 150 years, and the Yakuti Tartars have been under the Russian government ever since; yet they have made no alteration in their dress in general: but the Russians have conformed to the dress of the Yakuti. They appear to live together in peace and harmony, but the Yakuti hold no offices, civil or military.

"The Tartar is a man of nature, not of art. He is a lover of peace. No lawyer here perplexing natural rights of property. No wanton Helen, displaying fatal charms. No priest with his outrageous zeal has ever disturbed the peace. Never, I believe, did the Tartar speak ill of the Deity, or envy his fellow-creatures. He is contented to be what he is. Hospitable and humane, he is uniformly tranquil and cheerful, laconic in thought, word and action. Those that live with the Russians in their villages are above mediocrity as to riches, but discover the same indifference about accumulating more and for the concerns of to-morrow that a North American Indian does. If it happens that they profess the Russian religion, they treat it with strange indifference, not unthinkingly, but because they do not think at all.

"The house of the Russian is a scene of busy occupation, filled with furniture, provisions, women, children, dirt, and noise; that of the Tartar is as silent and as clean as a mosque. There is very little furniture, and that is rolled up and bound in parcels in a corner of the house.

"So strong is the propensity of the Russian to jealousy, that an ordinary Russian will be displeased if one even endeavors to gain the good-will of his dog. I affronted the commandant of this town very highly by permitting his dog to walk with me one afternoon. He expostulated with me very seriously. I live with a young Russian officer, with whom I came from Irkutsk. No circumstance has ever interrupted the harmony between us but his dogs. They have done it twice. A pretty little puppy he has came to me one day and jumped upon my knee. I patted his head and gave him some bread. The man flew at the dog in the utmost rage, and gave him a blow which broke his leg. I bid him beware how he disturbed my peace a third time by this rascally passion.

"I have observed among all nations that the women ornament themselves more than the men; that, wherever found, they are the same kind, civil, obliging, humane, tender beings; that they are ever inclined to be gay and cheerful, humorous and modest. They do not hesitate, like man, to perform a hospitable or generous action; not haughty, not arrogant, nor supercilious, but full of courtesy and fond of society; industrious, economical, ingenuous, more liable in general to err than man, but in general, also, more virtuous, and performing more good actions than he. I never addressed myself in the language of decency and friendship to a woman, whether civilized or savage, without receiving a decent and friendly answer. With man it has often been otherwise. In wandering over the barren plains of inhospitable Denmark, through honest Sweden, frozen Lapland, rude and churlish Finland, unprincipled Russia, and the wide-spread regions of the wandering Tartar, if hungry, dry, cold, wet, or sick, woman has ever been friendly to me, and uniformly so; and to add to this virtue, so worthy of the appellation of benevolence, these actions have been performed in so free and so kind a manner, that if I was dry I drank the sweet draught, and if hungry ate the coarse morsel, with a double relish."

The following are extracts from a letter which Lieutenant Danenhower wrote to his mother while in Yakutsk. It was dated December 30th, 1881, and published in the New York *Herald:*—

"The events of the last two and a half years are of course unknown to me, and it is with mingled feelings of doubt, hope, and fear that I write this letter. But I always hope for the best, and I am disposed to look upon the bright side. That sort of philosophy has carried me through very trying experiences during the past three years when there seemed to be a very forlorn hope for me.

"We are passing the time quietly, but impatiently. I will give you an idea of how we live. It is daylight here about eight A. M. We get up and have breakfast at a little hotel that is handy by. The forenoon I spend in reading a little, writing a little, and in attending to any business that I may happen to have on hand. About two P. M. General Tchernieff's sleigh arrives, and I go to dine with him; generally return about four P. M., and if I do not have visitors I take a nap and kill time as well as I can until nine P. M., when we have supper at the little hotel and then go to bed.

"As I have told you before, I have found nice people in every part of the world that I have visited, and this place is by no means an exception. Last evening, for example, we spent very pleasantly at the house of a Mr. Carrilkoff, an Irkutsk merchant, who entertained us very well. His wife is a charming lady, and it was very pleasant to see their three beautiful children. They have a fine piano, the first one we have seen since leaving San Francisco.

"I took our sick man, Jack Cole, with me to give him a little diversion. He behaved very well and the visit did him good. After my experience of the night before I was very glad to have him quiet yesterday. Some time after midnight I was awakened by a noise in my room. It was the 'old man' looking for a match. I took him to task sharply and sent him to bed. He went quietly, but after a little while I heard him go out; I waited five minutes, and, as he did not return, I awoke the Cossack and sent him to look for the 'old man' He returned without finding him; I immediately dressed and went to the office of the Police Master and had the town searched for him. I was afraid that he would lie down on the snow, as he did on one occasion in the mountains. He was brought back within an hour with his toes frozen. I immediately applied snow to them, and got the frost out of them, but he will probably suffer from chilblains for a long time. The next morning he was quiet and reasonable, and he begged me to have him well guarded, for at times he is out of his head. He is a very worthy man, nearly fifty years of age, and has been a very excellent man in his time. The great trouble at present is that he has to be idle, there being nothing for him to do but kill time.

"Yakutsk is a city of 5,000 inhabitants, and is situated on the west bank of the Lena River. It is the chief city in this part of Siberia, and is the residence of the Governor General Tchernieff. The houses are built of wood and are not painted. The streets are very wide, and each house has a large yard or court. The principal trade is in furs, and in summer a great deal of fresh meat is sent up the river. This is a very cold place. During nine months of the year snow and ice abound. In the winter the thermometer falls to 70 degrees below zero. Since our arrival it has been 68 degrees below, and to-day it is only 35 or thereabouts. In the summer the temperature rises as high as 95 degrees, but the nights are cold.

"There are many horses and cows in this vicinity. The natives of Yakutsk eat horse-meat, but the Russians eat beef and venison, potatoes, cabbage, and a few other vegetables. A few berries, wheat, and rye are grown in this vicinity. There are a few sheep and poultry also. The Russian Christmas is twelve days after ours. They have a great round of festivities during the Prasnik. In fact it has already commenced, and it is hard to get any work done. I went to the tailor's to get some clothes made and he refused to take any more work.

"Of course there is very little American news in this faraway place, but I have been able to pick up a few bits of it here and there. The death of Garfield is a topic often mentioned, and from the accounts here I learn that he was shot by 'Guiott,' on the train near Long Branch. A great deal of interest and sympathy is manifested by the Russians."

A WINTER JOURNEY.   153

On the 8th of January, 1882, Lieutenant Danenhower, Raymond L. Newcomb (Naturalist,) Herbert Leach, Henry Wilson, Frank Mansen, George Lauderback, Louis P. Noros, Jack Cole, the Chinaman Tong Sing, and the Indian Anequin, left Yakutsk, and started for Irkutsk, 2,790 versts, or more than 1,900 miles distant. They were accompanied by a Cossack guide, and traveled slowly in sledges called povvshkas, which could be partly or entirely covered, as the traveler chose.

CHAPTER XIV.

IRKUTSK.

IRKUTSK is the capital of Eastern Siberia, and also of the province of the same name. It was founded in 1680, and in 1879 had a population of 33,000. Geographically it is in latitude 52 deg. 40 min. north, and it is about 1,300 feet above the level of the sea. Although a cold place in winter, the climate is generally well spoken of; high winds and storms are less prevalent than in St. Petersburg and Moscow, and the fall of snow is not large. Earthquakes are not infrequent.

Much has been written in praise of Irkutsk by travelers coming from China or traveling eastward, and they have found it a cheerful restingplace after the fatigues of a long overland journey. In summer the city is approached from the west over a road lying near the cold and swiftly-flowing Angara, and the plains around are stocked with cattle. The town is built on a tongue of land formed by the confluence of the Angara and Uska-Kofka, and with its numerous churches, domes, and spires, looks extremely inviting. Handsome villas, nestling among the trees on the hills around, add not a little to the picturesqueness of the scene; and both in summer and winter the panorama of the city and its suburbs is one of much beauty.

Forty miles to the eastward of Irkutsk is the celebrated Lake Baikal, over 400 miles long, about 35 miles broad, and the largest body of fresh water in the world. It has nearly 200 tributaries, large and small, and only one outlet, the Angara, which discharges about one-tenth of the water that flows into the lake. No one knows what becomes of the remainder, but the natives believe there is an underground

LAKE BAIKAL IN WINTER.

THE VALLEY OF THE ANGARA. 157

channel to the sea. The lake is very deep, and in some places no bottom has been found at a depth of 2,000 feet.

Shortly after leaving Irkutsk, the eastward-bound traveler enters a wooded part of the Angara Valley, and as the road winds along it many points are passed presenting magnificent views. Afterwards the valley becomes more rugged, with deep ravines running up into the mountains. Beyond this the road has been cut along the edge of a cliff at a considerable height above the river, and about five miles before reaching the Baikal a scene is presented which will cause the traveler to pause and admire.

VIEW IN IRKUTSK.

The valley becomes wider, and the mountains rise abruptly to a much greater elevation. The Angara is here more than a mile wide, and its great volume of water is seen rolling down a steep incline, forming a rapid nearly four miles in length. At the head of this, in the center of the stream, a great mass of rock rises, held sacred by the followers of Shamanism, and where its victims used to be sacrificed by tossing them into the torrent below. Beyond is the broad expanse of the Baikal, extending about 50 miles to where its waves wash the foot of Amar Daban, whose summit, even in June, is usually covered with snow. The mighty torrent throwing up its jets of spray, the rugged rocks with their fringes of pendant birch overtopped by lofty pines, and the coloring on the mountains, produce a picture of extraordinary beauty and grandeur. A few miles further, and the Baikal is seen spreading out like a sea, and its waves are heard beating on the rocky shore.

In July, 1879, the city of Irkutsk was devastated by a terrible fire, from the effects of which it has not yet recovered. Mr. Henry Landsell, an English traveler, arrived at a hotel in Irkutsk just as the fire broke out, and has given a graphic description of what followed, in his book "Through Siberia," from which the following extracts are taken:—

"The waiter said he thought the fire would not come towards the hotel, as the wind blew from the opposite direction; but I was disinclined to wait and see, and so we bundled our things back into the tarantass, and told the yemstchiks, who fortunately had not left the yard, to put to their horses, and in a few minutes we were out in the street, witnesses of a sight that is not easy to describe. Men were running from all directions, not with the idle curiosity of a London crowd at a fire, but with the blanched faces and fear-stricken countenances of those who knew that the devastation might reach to them; they looked terribly in earnest—women screamed and children cried. The yemstchiks asked, 'Where should they go?' and my companion suggested that we should go out of the town, across the river. We soon put nearly a mile between us and the flames, and reached the bank of the Angara, where was a swinging ferry.

"Meanwhile the increased smoke in the distance showed that the fire was spreading, and the inhabitants of the small suburb called Glasgova, to which I had come, were looking on in front of their houses. Among the people I noticed a well-dressed person, whom I addressed, asking if she spoke English or French. She at once inquired who I was, and what I wanted. I replied that I was an English clergyman traveling, that I had just arrived in Irkutsk, had run away from the fire, and was seeking a lodging. She answered that there were no lodgings to be had in any of the few houses on that side of the river; 'but,' said she, 'pray come into my little house, where you are welcome to remain at least during the day.' I was only too glad to do so; and, seeing that there was a small yard adjoining, I asked permission to put therein our two vehicles, in which we might sleep until some better place could be found. We soon found that our hostess was of good family, and an exile, though not a political, but a criminal one. On arriving at Irkutsk, the Governor-General had shown her kindness in allowing her to remain in the city, where she partly supported herself by giving lessons, and was living for the summer in this quasi country-house with a young man whom she called her brother, her little girl she had brought from Russia, and a small servant whom she spoke of as 'ma petite femme de chambre.' There was one tolerably spacious dwelling-room in the house, and in this were sundry tokens of refinement brought from a better home. On the wall hung a photograph of herself, as a bride leaning on the arm of her husband in officer's uniform, whilst several other photographs and ornaments spoke also of a better past.

"The conflagration was increasing, and I offered to accompany Madame to her friends residing in the town, to see if we could be of use, whilst my interpreter stayed with the tarantasses and the little girl to guard the premises. We accordingly set out, accompanied by her maid. At the ferry we met a crowd of persons fleeing from the city, and carrying with them what was most valuable or most dear. An old lady tottering under a heavy load of valuable furs, piled on her head; a poor half-blind nun, hugging an ikon, evidently the most precious of her possessions; a delicate young lady in tears, with her kitten in her arms; and boys tugging along that first requisite of a Russian home, the brazen *samovar*. Terror was written on every countenance.

"Before long we came to the wide street in which were situated the best shops and warehouses, and where the fire was raging on either side and spreading. Those who were wise were bringing out their furniture, their account-books, and their treasures as fast as possible, and depositing them in the road and on vehicles, to be carried away. A curious medley these articles presented. Here were costly pier-glasses, glass chandeliers, and pictures such as one would hardly have expected to see in Siberia at all; whilst a little further on, perchance, were goods from a grocer's or provision merchant's shop, and all sorts of delicacies—such as sweets and tins of preserved fruit, to which they who would helped themselves; and working-men were seen tearing open the tins to taste, for the first time in their lives, slices of West India pine-apples or luscious peaches and apricots. Other prominent articles of salvage were huge family bottles of rye-brandy, some of which people hugged in their arms, as if for their life, whilst other bottles were standing about, or being drunk by those who carried them. The effects of this last proceeding soon became apparent in the grotesque and foolish antics of men in the incipient stage of drunkenness.

"In the street were all sorts of people—soldiers, officers, Cossacks, civilians, tradesmen, gentlemen, women, and children, rich and poor, young and old. Some were making themselves useful to their neighbors, and a few were looking idly on. At every door was placed a jug of clean water for those to drink who were thirsty, and it would have been well if nothing stronger had been taken. The fire brigade arrangements seemed to be in great confusion. There were some English engines in the town, but the Siberians had not practiced them in the time of prosperity, and the consequence was that the pipes had become dry and useless, and would not serve them in the day of adversity. The arrangements, too, for bringing water were of the clumsiest description. A river was flowing on either side of the city, but the firemen had no means of conducting the water by hose, but carried it in large barrels on wheels. Moreover, no one took command. Now and then one saw a hand-machine in use, about the size of a garden engine.

"It soon became apparent that Madame could not reach her friends, who lived on the other side of the city, and therefore we made our way back towards the ferry, calling here and there and offering help. One friend asked us to take away her little daughter, which we did, and her husband's revolver, which I carried, and a bottle of brandy—put into the arms of the *femme-de-chambre*. Thus laden, we walked towards the river, whilst on all hands men and women were pressing into their service every available worker for the removal of their goods. A religious procession likewise was formed by priests and people with banners, headed by an ikon, in the hope that the fire would be stayed.

BURNING OF IRKUTSK.

"It was evening before we reached our temporary lodgings, and as the day closed the workers grew tired, many were drunk, and others gave up in despair. The flames continued to spread till the darkness showed a line of fire and smoke estimated at no less than a mile and a half in length. It seemed as if nothing would escape. To add to the vividness of the scene, an alarm of church bells would suddenly clang out to intimate that help was wanted in the vicinity. Perhaps shortly afterwards the flames would be seen playing up the steeple and peeping out of the apertures and windows; then reaching the top, and presenting the strange spectacle of a tower on fire, with the flames visible only at the top, middle, and bottom. At last the whole would fall with a crash, and the sky be lit up with sparks and a lurid glare such as cannot be forgotten.

"Meanwhile the inhabitants continued to flee by thousands—the swinging ferry near us crossed and recrossed incessantly, bringing each time its sorrowful load, either bearing away their valuables, or going back to fetch others. Many of the people brought such of their goods as they could save to the banks and islands of the two rivers, and there took up their abode for the night in a condition compared with which ours was comfortable.

"We were supposed to *sleep* that night in the tarantass, but I rose continually to watch the progress of the fire, which towards morning abated, but only because it had burnt all that came in its way. About eleven o'clock the last houses standing on the opposite bank caught fire, and thus, in about four-and-twenty hours, three-fourths of the town were consumed."

Danenhower's party arrived at Irkutsk, January 30th, and were received in a most courteous manner, and told to consider themselves the guests of the Russian government. During their long stay they were lodged a portion of the time in the house of the private secretary of General Pedashenki, the vice-governor-general of the province, which was finely located on the suburban side of the Angara, and afforded a delightful view of the pretty city on the other side of the frozen river. The men had nearly recovered from the effects of their hardship, excepting Lieutenant Danenhower, whose eyes were in such a precarious condition that his physician forbade his traveling in winter, Mr. Newcomb, who was badly run down, and Jack Cole, the boatswain of the Jeannette, whose mind became unbalanced during the retreat to the coast.

Just about the time when Danenhower's party left Yakutsk to travel westward, another traveler, Mr. Jackson, special courier and correspondent of the New York *Herald,* started from Paris for Eastern Siberia, to meet the survivors of the Jeannette expedition, and thence to proceed to Yakutsk or to the mouth of the Lena, if advisable, to assist in the search for the missing men.

Mr. Jackson arrived at St. Petersburg on the evening of January 12th, which was the new year's eve of the Russians. At this city he received every attention and much assistance from General Ignatieff, Minister of the Interior, and from General Anutschin, Governor-General of Eastern Siberia, who was passing the winter in St. Petersburg. He was furnished with a crown pordorhosna, a document carried by all high officials traveling on Russian post-routes, and it gave him the right to demand horses at the stations in preference to the ordinary traveler. The following is a translation thereof:—

BY COMMAND OF HIS IMPERIAL MAJESTY THE EMPEROR
ALEXANDER ALEXANDROVICH,
Supreme Ruler of all the Rusaias,
&c., &c., &c.

From St. Petersburg to Irkutsk and return.   * * *
The Special Correspondent of the NEW YORK HERALD shall be given horses up to the number of five without delay, to be paid for according to the fixed tariff.

Given at St. Petersburg January 4th (Russian style), 1882.

For the Chief of the Chancellery of the Government of Irkutsk, [Seal.]
[Seal.] GOREW.

Mr. Jackson also received from the Governor-General an open letter, which read as follows:—

"The bearer of this, Mr. J. P. Jackson, leaves St. Petersburg for Eastern Siberia, his mission being to render assistance to the crew of the Polar exploration vessel, the steamer Jeannette, who have been wrecked in the Polar Sea. All local authorities of Eastern Siberia are therefore commanded to render all the assistance in their power, so far as the law permits, to Mr. Jackson, especially to facilitate him to a quick and undelayed journey to his destination and back, and to fulfill all his wishes, so far as they are lawful and may be assisted by the local authorities of the districts through which he passes.

St. Petersburg, January 4th, 1882.

The Governor-General of Eastern Siberia, member of the General staff, General Lieutenant,

Anutschin.

Countersigned, A. Ursaff, Member of the Imperial Council and Chief of the Chancellery of Travel."

Equipped with these documents, and accompanied by M. A. Larsen, of the *London News,* Mr. Jackson left St. Petersburg, January 19th, for Moscow. Thence he continued his journey by railroad to Orenburg. From this place the journey to Irkutsk was made in a sledge owned by the Governor-General, which had been placed at his service. It was well provided with furs, and drawn by four or five horses, which were changed at every post-station. More than 800 different horses were used on the journey, which extended over 2,500 miles.

The following are extracts from a letter which Mr. Jackson wrote to the New York *Herald* from Irkutsk, February 25th, 1882:—

"The long and weary journey across the Siberian wilds and wastes was finished at seven o'clock of the evening of the 23d of February (O. S.), and an hour later I was with Lieutenant Danenhower and the survivors of the Jeannette who were landed at the mouth of the Lena in boat No. 3. I hardly need say that these men were greatly pleased to receive letters and papers from home, and I will venture to assert that few of them could sleep that night until the early hours, for pleasure and excitement. Lieutenant Danenhower I found with his eyes bandaged and strictly forbidden by his doctor to use his sight, so I spent an hour and a half reading to him the messages of love sent to him by friends and relatives from the Western land.

The party have received a kindly welcome from the people of Irkutsk, and have been frequently invited to accept pleasant courtesies and hospitalities. Poor Jack Cole is carefully attended to by his comrades in turns, and a Cossack soldier watches by him night and day. When I met him he immediately embraced me, as he does all his friends, and said he was glad I had come, for he was just about to start out for the *Herald* office. Poor fellow! He lost his reason during the retreat from the crushed exploring vessel, and his mind is wandering far off. At first, after landing, he was inclined to be quarrelsome; then he began to invent mysterious machines, the last of which was a winking piano filled with boys and girls; but after my arrival he became possessed of the idea that he was in New York, and when he goes out (under safe conduct), he says he is going to the *Herald* office; and when he comes back from his daily ride he informs the lieutenant that he was not able to get his bearings straight. So Lieutenant Danenhower bids him be of good cheer, and tells him that he has the chart of the route in his pocket, and will bring him safely to port in good time.

In a darkened room of the house of M. Strekofski, I have spent the day in taking down a portion of Lieutenant Danenhower's narrative of the voyage of the ill-fated Jeannette. The lieutenant was not an eye-witness of all the events about which he speaks. Struck, about a year after the vessel left San Francisco, with an affection of the left eye, by which the right one was sympathetically affected, he was confined to his darkened berth for a period of six months, during which time he underwent thirteen operations, and for a year, until the time of the disaster, indeed, he was declared by the doctor as incapacitated for duty, and was thereby deprived of any active share in the labors in the Arctic. But while confined to his berth his companions relieved the tedium of his existence by telling him all that was going on in the little world above and around him, and when he was able to go on deck and on the ice he was an accurate observer of all that went on around him, and his marvellous memory enables him without notes to tell with exactitude every date, name, or event memorable in the history of the voyage.

Though deprived of his legitimate command, which was entrusted by Captain DeLong, before leaving the vessel, to Engineer Melville, he was permitted temporarily to assume the command of the boat during the severe gale that separated the three boats when so near to the land of the Lena's mouth, and all the men saved with him join in the assurance to me that without him they must inevitably have perished. His work, with his defective sight, during that memorable retreat, was grandly and nobly done.

The narrative of the retreat, through which he carried his boat safely to land, will be, I am sure, of surpassing interest."

LIEUTENANT DANENHOWER TELLING HIS STORY.

CHAPTER XV.

LIEUTENANT DANENHOWER'S NARRATIVE.

THE Jeannette left San Francisco on the 8th of July, 1879, with a full outfit for three years, with five commissioned officers of the navy, two civil scientists, and twenty-four of the ship's company. We arrived at Ounalaska on the 3d of August, after a long passage caused by head winds and the vessel being laden below her proper bearings. The Jeannette was perfectly seaworthy, having been thoroughly put in order at Mare Island before starting. After coaling ship at Ounalaska we proceeded to St. Michael's, Alaska, to meet our supply schooner, the Fanny A. Hyde. There we filled up with stores, got fur clothing, purchased forty dogs and engaged two American Indians—Anequin and Alexai—as hunters and dog-drivers, thus completing our complement of thirty-three. On the 25th of August we crossed Bering's Sea, in a very heavy gale, and though the ship was loaded very deeply she behaved admirably.

We visited St. Lawrence Bay in order to take in coal and the remaining supplies from the schooner, as well as to converse with the native Chukches and to get news of Nordenskiöld. We met about twenty natives, one of whom had learned a little English from American traders, and he told us that a steamer had passed south the previous June. The natives were ragged and dirty, and had no food to dispose of. We shot some wild fowl, and then we saw remains of vessels burned by the Shenandoah. Up the St. Lawrence Bay we found magnificent scenery. We sent off our last mail by the supply schooner, and on the 27th of August, seven P. M., we started north. Next day we passed through Bering's Strait.

We rounded East Cape about three of the afternoon of the 28th; it was then cloudy, no observations, running by dead reckoning. The East Cape loomed very bold and bluff. We could not see the Diomedes in the straits.

On the 29th I saw, from the crow's-nest, huts on the beach. We stood in and found a summer settlement. Captain De-Long and a party of officers started ashore in the whale-boat, but could not land owing to the surf breaking on iceward. Seeing the difficulty, the natives launched a *bidarah,* or large skin boat, very skilfully, and came off to the ship, bringing their chief with them. We had a long interview with them in the cabin, but as neither party could understand the other the results of the conversation were not great. They made us understand, however, by bending the elbow and saying "Schnapps" what they wanted, but the captain refused to listen to their request. Lieutenant Chipp then went ashore and succeeded in landing about midnight, and from an old woman from King's Island who could talk with our Indians, we learned that Nordenskiöld with the Vega had wintered to the north of them, and had passed east to Bering's Strait in the month of June. The next day we cruised along the coast to the westward. Met two other parties of natives, who came alongside, but took a look at us only.

On Sunday, August 31st, we fell in with some drift ice, and at daylight discovered a few huts on the beach. The drift ice extended about four miles off shore. Lieutenant Chipp, Ice-Pilot Dunbar and I, went ashore in the whale-boat to interview the natives. After a two hours' pull through the drift-pack, and seeing many seals, we reached the beach and found several carcasses of recently slain walrus. The natives seemed rather shy, and we had to look them up in their skin tents. There we found a sailor's trypot, and a cask marked "Centennial brand of whiskey,"—conclusive proof that the people were in occasional communication with American traders.

We met an intelligent young Chukche, who offered to show us the spot where the Vega had wintered. We took a

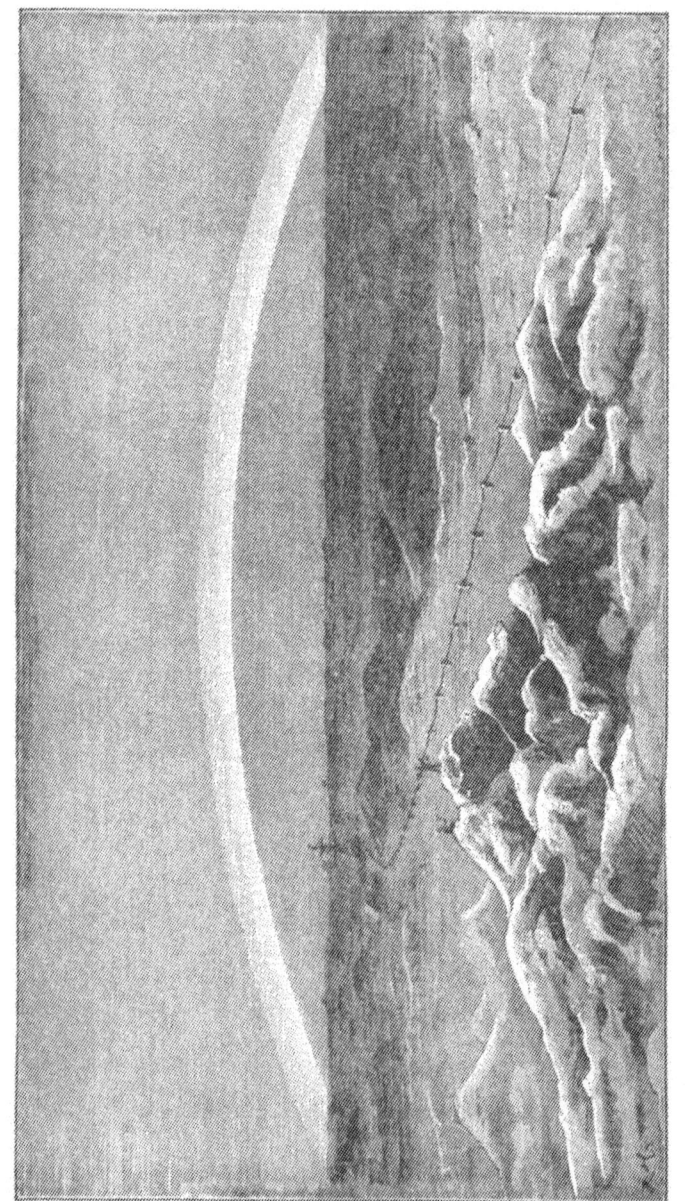

NORDENSKIOLD'S WINTER QUARTERS, KOLYUTSCHIN BAY.

tramp of several hours to the westward, and saw a bay about fifteen miles wide between the headlands, and there the natives told us the Vega had passed the winter. We found nothing there of any consequence. In the tents, however, we found tin cans marked "Stockholm," scraps of paper with soundings marked in Swedish, and some interesting pictures of Stockholm professional beauties. The natives indicated to us by signs that the steamer had passed safely out to the east. After purchasing some of the pictures and tin cans we returned to the ship.

During my absence the captain had got the sun at noon, and the latitude placed us about fifteen miles inland. Our astronomical positions were not reliable, owing to the state of the weather, but from them and the dead reckoning we felt assured that the coast is not correctly charted. The general appearance of the coast was fresh and pleasing. Off what we supposed to be Cape Serdze Kamen we saw a large heart-shaped rock, of which Mr. Collins made an elaborate sketch. There were several sugar-loaf mountains in sight.

Our walk to the Vega's winter quarters was over a mossy tundra; no signs of deer; the vegetation withered. The natives were hospitable, and one old Chukche dame pressed us to eat a dish of walrus blood, but we felt compelled to refuse the offer. The natives were stalwart and handsome; they lived in skin tents and were exceedingly dirty. They were well clad, and the chief wore a red calico gown as the distinguishing mark of his dignity. This was the last time most of us touched land for a period of more than two years.

About 4 P. M., August 31st, we stood to the northwest, shaping our course to the southeast cape of Wrangel Land, and then we felt that our Arctic cruise had actually commenced. We met considerable drift ice; the weather was stormy and misty. About sunrise, September 1st, we discerned an island which was taken to be Kolyutschin, in Kolyutschin Bay. Next day we met pack ice in floes of moderate size, turned to the northward and northeastward, and cruised along the Siberian pack, entering leads at times to examine them.

On the afternoon of September 4th a whaling bark bore down to us; we stopped engines and awaited her approach, but the weather became misty and she did not speak us. We had an Arctic mail on board at the time, and were disappointed at not being able to send letters home. We ran in several times and made fast to floe-pieces, to await clear weather. That afternoon, about 4, we saw an immense tree, with its roots, drifting by. Ice-pilot Dunbar, seeing it, said that in 1865, when the Shenandoah destroyed the whalers, he was at St. Lawrence Bay; and when, a few months later, he landed on Herald Island, he was greatly surprised to see masts and portions of the destroyed vessels drifting in that vicinity. This made me look out for a northwest drift. Then Herald Island loomed up in the clouds.

WHALERS STOPPED BY THE ICE.

On the 6th of September the captain judged that we had reached the lead between the Siberian and North American packs, and that this was a good place to enter. He took charge from the crow's-nest, and we entered the pack. We met with the young ice, and forced our way through it by ramming. This shook the ship very badly, but did not do her any damage; indeed, the ship stood the concussions handsomely. But at 4 P. M. we could proceed no further. We banked fires, secured the vessel with ice-anchors, and remained. That night was exceedingly cold. The ship was frozen in. At this time the ice was in pieces ranging from ten square yards to several acres in area, with small watercourses like veins running between them, but now quite frozen over. It remained quiet for a number of days, and we found ourselves in the middle of a large accumulation of floes about four miles across. We were then in about twenty fathoms of water, and had Herald Island in sight to the southward and westward, twenty-one miles distant by triangulation on a base line of 1,100 yards.

About the 15th of September, First Lieutenant Chipp, Ice-Pilot Dunbar, Engineer Melville, and the Indian, Alexai, started with a dog-sledge for Herald Island. They got within six miles of the beach, when they found open water before them, and were compelled to return. We found the ship drifting with the ice, and with so uncertain a base the captain would not send other persons to the island with boats. The general appearance of the ice at this time was uniform, with here and there almost snowless hummocks appearing above the surface, between which were pools whereon the men could skate. The deflorescence of salt was like velvet under the feet. From day to day we saw a looming of land to the southwest, and sometimes in the clouds. We soon found that the ice always took up the drift with the wind.

The ship at this time began to heel to starboard under the pressure, and inclined about twelve degrees. We unshipped the rudder, got up mast-head tackles on the port side, with lower blocks hooked to heavy ice-anchors about a hundred and fifty feet distant, and set them taut in order to keep the ship upright. The propeller was not triced up, but was turned so that the blades would be up and down the sternpost; the engines were tallowed, but not taken apart. When the ship commenced to heel, the local deviation of the compass increased in the ratio of one and a half degrees duration to one degree of list. This was owing to the vast amount of iron-work, and especially the canned goods, which had to be stowed in the after-hold and on the quarter-deck. All our compass observations had of course to be made on the ice

SKATING ON THE YOUNG ICE.

well clear of the ship. At this time and later on we noticed that the turning motion of the floe or change in azimuth of the ship's head was very slow; but the floe did have a cycloidal motion with the wind, and the resultant was in the northwest direction.

Our position was not an enviable one. At any moment the vessel was liable to be crushed like an egg-shell among this enormous mass of ice, the general thickness of which was from five to six feet, though some was over twenty where the floe-pieces had overrun and cemented together and turned topsy-turvy. Pressures were constantly felt. We heard distant thundering of the heavy masses, which threw up high ridges of young ice that looked like immense pieces of crushed sugar.

The month of October was quiet. We had had no equinoctial gales even in September. The cold was very bitter. Wrangel Land was in plain sight to south and west many times, and especially on the 28th and 29th of October, when we could see mountains and glaciers, which we identified on many occasions. Collins took sketches of them. The ship was drifting to and fro with the wind. Up to this time we saw a considerable number of seals and walrus, and got two bears. Two white whales were also seen, which were the only ones noticed during the whole cruise. Life on board was quiet but monotonous. We got many observations, especially from the stars. The nights were very clear, and suitable for artificial horizon work.

We began to find at this time, and by later experience became convinced, that Rear-Admiral John Rodgers was right when he said that the sextant, artificial horizon, and the lead were the most efficient and useful instruments in exploring Arctic waters, and that transits and zenith telescopes were not useful, because refined observations could not be obtained, and were not necessary in this region. The cold is so great as to affect the instrument, and it is almost impossible to keep the lens free of frost and vapor, thus making the refraction a very indefinite correction. Our experience in this pack was, that the state of the atmosphere was constantly changing; without a moment's notice the ice would sometimes open near the ship, and vast columns of vapor would rise whenever the difference of temperature between the air and water was great. The surface water was generally 29° Fahrenheit, the freezing point of salt water.

About the 6th of November the ice began to break up. We had previously observed considerable agitation about the full and change of the moon, and attributed it to tidal action. This was observed particularly when we were between Herald Island and Wrangel Land, and when the water was shoaled—that is, about fifteen fathoms—the ice began to break round the ship, and a regular stream of broken masses gradually encroached upon us. From aloft, the floe that had appeared so uniform a few weeks before was now tumbled about, and in a state of greater confusion than an old Turkish graveyard. Tracks began to radiate from the ship, and the noise and vibration of distant ramming were terrific, making even the dogs whine.

THE ICE IN MOTION.

November 3d was a calm, starlight night. I got good star observations, with Melville marking time, at eleven P. M. I was working them up, when a crack was heard, and we found that the floe had split, and that the ice on the port side had drifted off, leaving the ship lying in a half cradle on her starboard bilge. The water looked smooth and beautiful, and there was no noise save that of four dogs which had drifted off with the port ice. We had previously taken in the observatory, and had prepared for such an accident, but on the starboard side the steam-cutter and the men's outhouse had been left. We got the steam-cutter aboard, but left the outhouse standing.

And here let me mention an interesting fact. About sixteen months afterward, the Indian Anequin came in, in a state of great excitement for an Indian generally so stolid, and reported, "Me found two-man house!" He described it as a house large enough for two men, and when asked if he had been inside said, "No, me plenty 'fraid!" Judge of our surprise. Lieutenant Chipp immediately started with the Indian and others, and found the house at a distance of about three miles to the southeast. It proved to be the lost out-house, thus showing that the relative positions of the pieces in the vicinity were comparatively unchanged.

The next morning the half cradle on which the port side had rested could be seen about a thousand yards distant, and this immense lead was open, but of very limited length. The appearance of the ice can be likened to an immense cake as it comes from the oven, broken and cracked on the surface.

A few mornings later the drift ice came down upon us under the starboard bow, and wedged the ship off her cradle, and she went adrift in the gale. This was about eight A.M. She drifted all day until seven P.M., when she brought up on some young ice, and was frozen in solid again. It was dark, in the long night, and there was no chance of working the pack had it been good judgment to do so. We reckoned that she had drifted at least forty miles, with the ice in her immediate vicinity.

Previous to this time the ship had stood the pressure in the most remarkable manner. On one occasion I stood on the deck-house above a sharp tongue of ice that pressed the port side just abaft the fore chains and in the wake of the immense truss that had been strengthened by the urgent advice of Engineer-in-chief William H. Shock, on Mare Island. The fate of the Jeannette was then delicately balanced, and when I saw the immense tongue break and harmlessly underrun the ship, I gave heartfelt thanks to Shock's good judgment. She would groan from stem to stern; the cabin doors were often jammed so that we could not get out in case of emergency, and the heavy truss was imbedded three-quarters of an inch into the ceiling. The safety of the ship at that time was due entirely to the truss. The deck planking would start from the beams, showing the unpainted wood for more than half an inch. This, together with the sharp cracking of the ship's fastenings, like the report of a distant charge of rifles, would wake us at night. Each man kept his knapsack by him ready for an instant move, and preparations were made for leaving the ship with sleds and boats if necessary.

Several gales, the heaviest being about fifty miles an hour, occurred in the fall of 1879. The long night commenced about the 10th of November, and lasted till the 25th of January, 1880. On November 1st the winter routine commenced. At seven, call all hands and start fires in the galleys; at nine, breakfast; from eleven to one, guns given to all hands to hunt and for exercise on the ice; at three P. M., dinner; then galley fires put out to save coal; between seven and eight, tea, made from the Baxter boiler, which was used constantly to condense water, we having found that the floe ice was too salt for use, and the doctor insisted on using condensed water. This boiler was originally intended for the electric light, but it was found that we could not afford to run the light, so we used the coal in condensing water. Twenty-five pounds of coal per day was allowed for heating the cabin, twenty-five pounds for the forecastle, and ninety pounds for ship's galley for cooking purposes.

We lived on canned goods, with bear and seal twice a week, pork-and-beans and salt beef once a week; no rum or spirits, except on festive occasions, two or three times a year. The discipline of the ship was excellent, and during the whole twenty-one months in the pack there was but one punishment given, and that was for profanity. The crew were well quartered in berths, and were comparatively happy; had navigation class and theatricals. The health of all was excellent, and there was a special medical examination the first of every month.

Things went on in this fashion until the middle of January, when there were tremendous pressures, and the floes actually backed up into mounds under the strain, the ice being very tough and elastic. The heaviest strain came in the stem of the ship, in a longitudinal direction. There was also a heavy lateral strain, especially under the starboard main chains. About nine o'clock one morning a man went down into the fire-room on duty and found the floor-plates covered with water; he immediately reported the fact, and all pumps were started. The temperature was below 42 degrees Fahrenheit (the freezing point of mercury). Mr. Melville had great difficulty in getting up steam and starting the donkey pumps, but succeeded admirably, the men working with their feet and legs in ice-water, and everything frozen and freezing solid. It was found that the vessl leaked badly in the bows, and we supposed that the hooding of the planks had been started at the stem, and it was not until the last day, June 12th, 1881, that we discovered that the forefoot had been twisted to starboard.

The carpenter (Sweetman), with Nindermann, worked day and night, and (under the direction of Lieutenant Chipp) built a bulkhead forward of the foremast, which partially confined the water. Melville rigged an economical pump with the Baxter boiler, and the ship was pumped for nearly eighteen months. A windmill pump was also made for summer, but the winds were so light that it hardly paid. During the last few months the leak decreased, owing to the ship floating higher, and we had then only to pump once every half hour by hand. The experience of January 19th gave me great confidence in the ship's company, as it was a very severe test on the men. I was confined to my berth at the time, but knew everything that was going on, and the solid and effective work done was very gratifying.

As well as I can remember, about fifteen barrels of flour and some other dry provisions were damaged by this accident. Previous to this we had to throw away a large quantity of canned roast-beef marked "Erie brand," it having proved bad. The coldest weather occurred in February, 1880, being —58 degrees. There were also some great and remarkable changes of temperature in the course of the day.

About the middle of February we were found to be about fifty miles from the place where we had entered, and Herald Island was said to have been in sight during one day. During these five months we had drifted over an immense area, approaching and receding from the 180th meridian, but I do not think we crossed it at that time. We continued to drift in this uncertain manner. We noticed that the ship always took up a rapid drift with southeast winds, and a slow drift with northeast winds, owing, doubtless, to Wrangel Island being under our lee. Southwest winds were not frequent.

At times land was reported to the northeast, but nothing trustworthy. Some observers were constantly seeing land at all points of the compass, and many was the trip that the navigator and the ice-pilot had to make to the crow's-nest in vain. We were very much disappointed at not being able to shift for ourselves, and up to this time we had only demonstrated to our satisfaction that Dr. Peterman's theory in regard to Wrangel Land being a portion of Greenland was no longer tenable, for its insularity was evident, as subsequently proved.

March and April, 1880, were passed quietly, and we were surprised at not having any March gales. The geese and wild fowl that some of us expected to see on their spring migration, did not put in an appearance. One poor eider duck fell exhausted near the ship, and one of our sportsmen shot at it, and after administering chloroform it succumbed. There were some birds seen later in the season, moving to the westward, but they were not numerous. A great many mussel-shells and quantities of mud were often found on the ice, which indicated that it had been in contact with land or shoals. Our hunters ranged far and wide, and often brought in small pieces of wood—on one occasion a codfish head, and on another some stuff that was very much like whale-blubber, all of which had been found on the ice.

On May 3d, fresh southeast winds began, and the ship took up a rapid and uniform drift to the northwest. Now Mr. Collins began to predict, and told me several times, that these winds would continue till the early part or the middle of June, and would be followed by constant northwest winds for the balance of June. This prediction was fully realized, and in the month of June we actually drifted back over the May track. During July and August there was scarcely any wind, and the weather was misty and raw, it being the most unpleasant time of the year, the coldest weather not excepted. The damp and fog and cold struck chill to the bones, and we could not afford to heat the ship as we did in winter. The ice seemed to absorb all the heat from the sun during the melting period of the year.

The snow disappeared from the surface of the floe about the middle of June, and the best traveling period over the floe was considered to be between the middle of June and the middle of July. But this was a subject for constant discussion among the savans, among whom Mr. Dunbar was the most experienced, he having been an old traveler in the Baffin's Bay region. A considerable number of birds, principally phalaropes and guillemots, were shot and very much appreciated at dinner.

The surface of the floe-pieces was now of a hard, greenish blue, and flinty, being covered in many places with thaw-water. There were numerous cracks near the ship, but no leads that went in any definite direction, and there was no chance to move, for the ship was imbedded in the ice so firmly that a whole cargo of explosives would have been useless. Lieutenant Chipp, an experienced torpedo operator, made torpedoes and all the arrangements for taking advantage of the first opportunity to free the ship. But the opportunity never came.

Mr. Chipp was an accomplished electrician, and during the whole time in the ice he took up the subject recommended by the Smithsonian Institution to the Polaris Expedition—namely, observations of the disturbances of the galvanometer during auroras. He had wires laid out over the ice, and earth-plates in the water, and the galvanometer in the current, and obtained over two thousand observations during auroras, which he intended to turn over to a specialist for purposes of analysis and judgment. He always found disturbances of the needle coincident with the most brilliant auroras. He also ran the telephones, which, however, gave a great deal of trouble, owing to the wires being broken by the wind and the ice movements. Those on the ship of course were all right. During my sickness he also made observations of the eclipses of Jupiter's satellites, and got some excellent results for chronometer errors by using an improved ship's telescope mounted on a barrel. He afterward used the transit telescope similarly mounted. This was the best data for our chronometers, being far superior to lunar observations.

The summer weather was very bright and pleasant for about fifteen days in July, and when the thermometer was above 40 degrees Fahrenheit we called it a warm day; but the latter parts of July and August were particularly bad, being foggy and raw.

During the first year we got sufficient game for table use, and seal-skins for clothing for the men, but this necessitated a great deal of hunting, and there was a great scarcity of game in this region. The seal most frequently obtained was the species called by Lamont, the "floe rat," and averages about sixty pounds in weight, and thirty to forty pounds when dressed. The men generally made up the skins into boots and trousers. The meat was not pleasant to the taste, and it required the strongest philosophy to enable one to eat it at all. Walrus was scarce, the depth of water being a little too great for them, as they seldom inhabit depths of more than fifteen fathoms. We got six, however, which furnished excellent food for the dogs, and our Chinese cook was an adept in making walrus sausage for our *cuisine*.

Bear chases were frequent and exciting, and about fifteen animals were obtained the first year. Mr. Dunbar was the champion bear-slayer, and was always ready for a keen jump when game was reported. During the first winter a tremendous bear approached the ship about midnight, drove

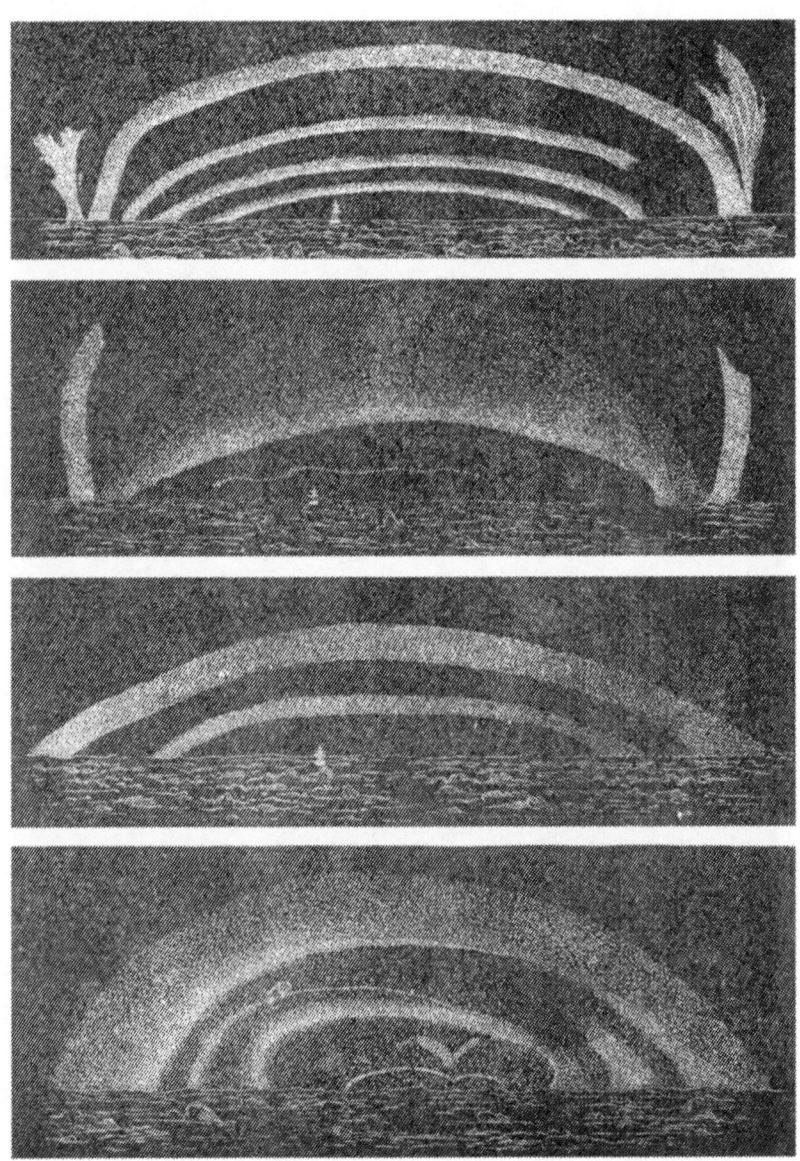

ARCTIC AURORAS.

the dogs in, and attempted to board us over the port gangplank. The alarm was given. Mr. Dunbar was on deck instantly, with rifle in hand, and shot the bear through the heart at ten paces. It was probably the biggest and most ferocious bear secured on the cruise, and he had been attracted by the quarters of his comrade that were triced up in the fore-rigging. A few foxes were seen, and their tracks quite frequently observed. They seemed to either accompany or follow the bears, like pilot-fish with the sharks, and jackals with their ferocious and stronger friends.

During the summer some of us used to take the skin boats or the dingy, and paddle among the cracks. On one occasion Captain DeLong was alone in the dingy, and was

A MUTUAL SURPRISE.

interviewed by a bear who suddenly approached out of the mist and stood watching him in the most dignified manner. The captain retreated in good order. During the summer it was very difficult to get bears, because they could take to the water so readily, and thus cut off their pursuers. During the misty times they were very bold, and on one occasion a she bear with two cubs approached the ship to within 400 yards of the starboard quarter. Fortunately, the dogs were on the port side and to windward, so they did not scent the bear. The greatest quietness prevailed, and a squad of about ten riflemen was immediately organized on the poop. I was watching the bears through a cabin air-port, and it was a very fine sight to see the mother and her two cubs approach the ship in a wondering and cautious manner. I could see better under the mist than the people on the poop. I heard the captain say:—

"Do any of you think it is over 250 yards?"

All seemed to agree and he said:—

"Aim at 250 yards, and wait for the word 'Fire!'"

Then succeeded a volley. The bears reeled and made several turns, and I thought that we had bagged all of them, but was astonished to see them get up and walk off in the most lively manner. Of course all the dogs took the alarm and pursued them to the first crack, which the bears calmly swam, across and thus escaped. But large drops of blood were seen, and the she-bear lay down once or twice as if wounded. In making her retreat she drove her cubs before her, and became impatient when they moved slowly. The bears had been hit, but the distance had been under-estimated and most of the shots had fallen short. This was not extraordinary, because it was very misty.

After this one year of experience in the ice we concluded that the general motion of the ice was due principally to the wind, and that the resultant of the winds was from the southeast. Some of us talked about the polar region being covered with an immense "ice cap," which seemed to have a slow, general movement in the direction of the hands of a watch, the direction of the drift, of course, being different in the different segments. The influence of Wrangel Island would be to impede the drift of the segment lying to the northward and eastward, and I imagined that there must be a constant strife between Wrangel Land and the solid phalanx of ice from the northeast. This polar ice cap we know throws off in its revolutions millions of acres every year through the gates of Robeson's Channel and between

Iceland and Greenland. A branch of the Gulf Stream attacks it from the Spitzbergen side, and its influence is felt as far as the North Cape of Asia. The general motion of this "cap" must be very slow, but the local motions of course depend upon the depth of the ocean and the vicinity of land, and near nature's outlets it is very rapid.

Melville gave me lots of food for reflection. He analyzed all data obtainable from the Hydrographic Office reports and Arctic literature, and marked on the circumpolar chart with arrows the currents as reported by various navigators as well as those mentioned in the theories of distinguished geographers. We constantly discussed the question, and both felt assured that if the ship could remain intact long enough, she would eventually drift out between Spitzbergen and Bear Island to Atlantic waters. A very high latitude would doubtless be attained, and would depend in a great measure on the influence of Franz Josef Land upon the motion of the pack. If the ship passed to the southeast of it, the local motion to the southwest might be very rapid by the pack impinging on those lands; and if passing to the northward, the pack would be deflected toward the Pole and a very high latitude would be obtained, supposing no polar continental land to exist. It is my opinion that had we entered the pack 200 miles to the eastward of where we did, we could have worked up near Prince Patrick Land; for Collinson found the deepest water over there to the eastward, and sounded with 133 fathoms without finding bottom.

Our smallest depth the first year's drift was seventeen fathoms, and the greatest depth not over sixty, the average being generally thirty, and the occan bottom usually uniform, with blue mud and in some cases shale,—something like round pieces of potato, cut thin and fried, and supposed to be meteoric specimens. We felt pretty sure that we would continue to drift to the northwest during the following year, but I was not sure what influence the peculiar coast line in the vicinity of the North Cape would exert, it being in the form of an elbow, and must therefore have great influence on the general motion of the pack.

From the fact that the spars of the Shenandoah's devastations drifted to Herald Island, and that the whaling bark Gratitude had been last seen drifting to the northwest in that vicinity, we augured that there must also be some northwest current; but we have no other evidence of a current except the formation of banks and shoals in the vicinity of Herald Island, which may be similar to the formation of the Grand Banks, by the ice bringing earthy matter there. The locality east-northeast of Wrangel Land may be regarded as the Arctic doldrums, as far as drift is concerned. We also considered the possibility of drifting down the western side of Wrangel Land, and then again perhaps once more being able to shift for ourselves.

The general health of the ship's company was excellent, and we looked forward coolly, but not without some anxiety, to the long night of the second winter, during which time we might at any instant be rendered homeless and at the mercy of the Arctic fiends.

THE CROW'S-NEST.

CHAPTER XVI.

LIEUTENANT DANENHOWER'S NARRATIVE
(CONTINUED.)

AT the beginning of September, 1880, the Jeannette was firmly imbedded in ice of about eight feet in thickness; but there were immense masses shoved under her keel, and the bows were lifted so that the keel was inclined about one degree, the ship at the same time heeling to starboard two degrees, and so firmly held in this gigantic vice that when the blacksmith struck his anvil in the fire-room, one could see the shrouds and stays vibrate, and they were not very taut. Our executive officer had slackened up the rigging during the first winter, and the contraction of wire rigging by the intense cold was of course very great. The ice was piled up under the main chains and as high as the planksheer. In the vicinity of the ship the ice was tumbled about in the greatest confusion, and traveling over it was almost an impossibility.

In the latter part of September, when the cracks froze over, came the best time for travel, but the outlook was poor. There was comparatively little snow, and what there was was constantly blown by the wind, and rendered salt by attrition on the surface of the ice, so that we could not use it for culinary purposes. The captain was very favorable to fall traveling, and he several times expressed himself to the effect that he would not abandon the ship while there was a pound of provisions left, and we generally understood that he would hold on a year longer, and probably start when the fall traveling commenced, a year later. We all considered that if our provisions held out long enough, if we were not attacked by scurvy, and if the ship was not crushed by the ice, we should eventually drift out after reaching the vicinity of Franz Josef Land, either north or south of it. The morale of the ship's company was excellent, yet we looked anxiously toward the long night of the second winter, which proved to be the most fearful part of our experience. The anxiety and mental strain on many of us were the greatest at that time. We were so completely at the mercy of the ice that the vessel might be crushed at any moment by the thundering agencies which we constantly heard.

In the month of September the ship was put in winter quarters for the second time. She was banked up with snow, the deck-house was put up for the use of the men, and the awning spread so that the spar-deck was completely housed over. Economy and retrenchment were the order of the day in fuel, provisions, and clothing. The old winter routine of meals, two hours' exercise, and so on, commenced on November 1st, and all was going well.

November and December were extremely cold, but we had no severe gales that I remember. The meteorological observations were taken every hour during the first year, but every two hours only during the second. They were very thorough, and Mr. Collins was very watchful to add something to the science to which he was so thoroughly devoted. During my sickness the captain and Mr. Chipp took the astronomical observations, but each officer in the ship had a round of duty as weather-observer and to assist Mr. Collins. There was a quartermaster on watch all the time, and steam was kept on the Baxter boiler for distilling purposes. To save coal, fires were put out in the galley at 3 P. M., being used only from seven A. M. till that hour.

The month of January, 1881, was remarkable for its changeable temperature, and as being warmer than the two previous months. About the middle of the month the wind set in from the southeast, and subsequently to that time the drift of the ship was uniformly to the northwest. The depth of the water began to increase toward the northwest, but would always decrease toward the southeast or southwest, as well as to the northeast. The vessel seemed to drift in a groove, which we called Melville's Canal, as he was the first to call attention to the fact. Mr. Chipp took the soundings every morning, and by long experience we could judge of the drift so accurately that his dead reckoning generally tallied with the observations. He adopted a scale by which 'slow' drift meant three nautical miles per day; 'moderate,' six miles; 'rapid,' nine miles; 'very rapid,' twelve miles. He always reckoned the direction and speed of the drift and placed the ship before making the observation. His judgment was excellent. He and the captain made frequent lunar observations for chronometer errors, but those of the eclipses of Jupiter's satellites were the best.

BEAR-HUNTING ON THE FLOE.

February was the coldest month; and the mean for the three months was only six degrees lower than that for the same months during the previous year. The soundings generally ran thirty-three, but one morning Mr. Dunbar sounded in forty-four; some called that place Dunbar Hole. We drifted over this spot once again at a later period. The absence of animal life prior to May was greater than during the previous year. All hands hunted every day, especially as the doctor wanted fresh meat for the Indian Alexai, who was said to have the scurvy, and suffered very greatly from abscesses on his leg. On May 1st, Dr. Ambler reported the physical condition of the crew rapidly deteriorating, and six or seven were placed on whiskey and quinine to tone them up. The weather at this time was good, and there were no spring gales. Of course when I say good, it is in an Arctic sense.

JEANNETTE ISLAND.

During the month of May, old man Dunbar was always in the crow's-nest, and got blind several times. The old gentleman was looking out sharp for land, and about the 16th of May he was the first to announce it in sight. You can imagine the excitement it caused, for we had not seen land for many months and had not set foot on it for nearly two years.

Jeannette Island, as the new land was called, was not landed on, but the astronomical position of it could be, and doubtless was, well established from the data obtained by Captain De Long. It was by triangulation, on the base established by observations on different days, the ship having drifted rapidly and giving a long base line, the extremities of which were established by artificial horizon and sextant observations. I was confined to my room at the time of the discovery, but every item of it was brought to me by Dunbar, Melville, and Chipp, and everything was so minutely described to me that I could almost see the land through the ship's side.

I understood Jeannette Island to be small and rocky. The southern end appeared high, and the land sloped down to a low point to the northward when the island was first seen, but subsequently mountains behind the low point were observed, and from this fact the island was adjudged to be more extensive than at first supposed. Sketches were made whenever the island was in sight, but it would have been foolish to have attempted a journey to it, for the drift of the ship was too rapid and the state of the ice so changeable.

A few days afterwards, Henrietta Island hove in sight, and appeared extensive. The drift of the ship seemed arrested by the northeast extremity of the island. Lieutenant Chipp was sick a-bed with what afterwards proved to be tin poisoning, and I was confined to my room with my eyes. So Mr. Melville had the good fortune to be the first to visit Henrietta Island, and he did his work admirably. When he left the ship the captain judged the island to be from twelve to fifteen miles distant, it appeared so plain, but he had not yet triangulated for it owing to the state of the weather.

The journey from the ship to Henrietta Island was one of the hardest on record. Melville had to travel over immense masses of broken ice that were constantly in motion, and in most cases the dogs were worse than useless. He landed in a state of exhaustion, took a short run on the island, and then ordered the men to turn in. He intended to sleep until ten o'clock the next morning, but was probably anxious, and when he turned out his watch said seven o'clock, but it was probably P. M. In his anxiety he had slept only an hour and a half or two hours. The men said that they felt as if they were just going to sleep. Feeling confident, however, that they had passed the twelve hours in their sleeping bags, he finished the examination of the island and started back to the ship, and was surprised on his return that he had gained twelve hours in time. This was not surprising, from the fact that during his visit to the island he did not see the sun but once, at which time Erickson said, 'The sun is west, sir, and it is morning with us.' So Mr. Melville, on his return, had a suspicion that his time was 'out.'

During this trip Mr. Dunbar broke down with snow blindness, and had to be carried back by the party to the ship. On the way to the island he went ahead to select the road, and worked so hard and used his eyes so much that he became thoroughly disabled. The old gentleman felt very badly, it being the first time in his long career that he had ever been physically unequal to the occasion. He begged Melville to leave him, his mortification was so great. But of course this was not done. The others bore the trip remarkably well. They had been picked out as the flower of the ship's company.

There was a mountain on the island that the men named after the captain's little daughter—'Mount Sylvie;' also another mountain which was called 'Mount Chipp;' two very bold headlands were called 'Bennett Headlands;' one bald cape was called 'Cape Melville,' in honor of one of the chief engineer's characteristics. There was a low, shingle beach cape extending to the northeast, that was called 'Point Dunbar.' All these names were given by the sailors who rambled over the island, and we have always called them by the names thus originally given them. At one time the land appeared so near to us that Machinist Lee said to me, 'Why, I can walk there and back, sir, before dinner.' On that day I was able to get on deck, and judged the land to be between twenty and thirty miles distant, and so I advised my friend not to try it.

Melville told me that he could not tell the distance he

traveled to within ten miles, but that the lowest possible estimate was eighteen, and the highest twenty-eight miles. You see, his journey back was on a different route, because the ship had drifted and had approached the island in the meantime. He gave me every detail of his trip with great minuteness. The island was bold and rocky, with a small number of birds, principally guillemots, and very little deer-moss on the place where he landed. But, of course, we do not know the possibilities of the extensive region to the southwest of the landing-point.

ARCTIC GLACIER.

The island was covered with an ice and snow cap, and the immense glacier near the landing-place was gigantic and magnificent. I think Melville got eighteen fathoms close to the island. No seal or walrus were seen, and no traces of bears on the island. No driftwood was seen.

Melville built a cairn, and buried a square, copper case containing copies of the *New York Herald* brought from New York by Mr. Collins, and a copper cylinder containing official documents,—the latter being a record of Captain DeLong's determination to stay by the ship to the last moment. He announced in them his determination to stand by the ship as long as possible, as he was in hopes of making a high latitude during the following summer. We were all very glad when Melville got back, for the ice had commenced to swing around the corner of Henrietta Island very rapidly, the land to the westward of Bennett Headlands coming out rapidly, and keeping Collins and Newcomb busily sketching as the view changed.

A SKETCH.

The ship continued drifting to the northwest rapidly until June 10th. During this time the ice in which she was imbedded began to crack, and the area of the piece was decreasing rapidly. We knew that the important moment was coming when the Jeannette would be liberated from this cyclopean vice, and that her future would be more hazardous than while in the monster's grip; for it was impossible to shape a course, and she would be momentarily liable to be crushed by the impact of the antagonistic floe-pieces, which sent immense masses of ice into the air, and among which the Jeannette would be like a glass toy-ship in a railroad collision.

About eleven P. M., June 10th, I was awakened by the ship's motion. It sounded as if she were sliding down hill, or off the launching-ways. I was frightened for an instant, but immediately recovered and jumped out of bed for my clothes. The ship had slid off her bed after the ice on the port side had opened with a loud crack. There she floated calmly on the surface of the beautiful blue water.

The Jeannette was finally released from her icy fetters after an imprisonment of twenty-one months—that is, almost the entire duration of our voyage—during which time we had been drifting with the pack. The important point of this drift is that we traversed an immense area of ocean, at times gyrating in almost perfect circles, and it can now safely be said that land does not exist in that area. Of course the depth and the character of the ocean-bed and the drift were also determined, as well as the animal life that exists in this part of the world; also the character of the ocean water, and many other facts of interest which were finished with the discovery of the two new islands.

At this time we had a feeling of pleasure and pride that our voyage had not been entirely in vain, and we felt sure that we could add considerable to the knowledge of this region of the Arctic; and if we could have got out safely without loss of life, the voyage would have been a grand success. Captain DeLong, in my opinion, entered the ice boldly and deliberately, with the intention of trying the most hazardous route to the Pole that has ever been contemplated. When spoken to on the subject, within a few days after we found ourselves imprisoned, I stated that to be my opinion, and that he had undertaken the most daring and magnificent venture on record.

To return to the Jeannette. She was floating idly, but,

of course, could not proceed, being hemmed in on all sides by almost limitless masses of ice in close contact, and having only a small pool in which she could bathe her sides. The starboard half of her old cradle remained, so she was hauled into it and secured with ice-anchors on the bow and quarter, to await her chance to escape. The rudder had been previously shipped, and the screw propeller had been found to be undamaged, so every preparation was made to move at a moment's notice. On June 11th Henrietta Island was seen for the last time, to the southeast of us.

I will now describe the supreme and final moments in the life of the Jeannette. At this period of the cruise I was able to spend one hour on deck, three times a day, for exercise, the last relapse of my left eye having taken place a month previous. I went on deck at one o'clock in the afternoon, and saw the hunters start out. The day was clear and beautiful, there was a light wind from the northeast, and in some quarters of the horizon it was misty and very much as in the trade-wind regions of the Pacific. A large party was sent out to get seals and guillemots, if possible. My hour was up, but I still lingered on the quarter-deck, for the ice on the port side, some twenty-five yards distant, had commenced to move toward us, and I was fascinated by the dangers of the situation.

The captain was on deck, and immediately hoisted the hunters' recall, which was a big, black cylinder, at the main truck. They began to come in, one by one, and the last ones were Bartlett and Anequin, who were dragging a seal with them. At the time of their arrival the ice was in contact with the port side of the ship, and she was heeled about twelve degrees to starboard, with port bilges heavily pressed. The two hunters approached on the port side, passed their guns to me, and came up by a rope's end that I had thrown to them. The pressure on the ship was terrible, and we knew that she must either lift and be thrown up bodily upon the ice, or be crushed. During the whole cruise, provisions, tents, and boats with sleds, were kept ready for immediate use, and at this time every step was taken for the impending catastrophe.

About three P.M., Machinist Lee reported the ice coming through the bunkers, and the captain immediately ordered, 'Lower away!'—men having been previously stationed at the boats' falls and some provisions put on the ice. Melville immediately contradicted the report, and the captain delayed the order. Thus the ship lay for two hours and a half, the pressure of the ice relaxing at times and the ship almost righting. Then again she would be hove over to twenty-three degrees, and we felt sure there was no longer any hope for her, for she would not lift. There was nothing in the world to be done to assist her at that time. We had to depend upon her shape. She floated much higher than when we entered the pack, and that led us to hope that she would lift easier in the nip; for the pressure of the ice would be below the point where her sides commenced to tumble home. On the starboard side, while she was heeling, the nip was felt on her timber heads, which were the weakest parts of the frame; but on the port side she was pressed below the turn of the bilge. Her fate was practically decided the moment we found she would not lift, and a large amount of provisions and clothing was then placed on the ice in readiness for the catastrophe.

One watch went to supper at half-past five, and the officers had bread and tea in the cabin at six. I was on the sick list, with eyes bandaged, but told the doctor that I could get the charts and instruments together and be of assistance. He said he would ask the captain. Each officer kept his knapsack in his room, and most of us thought it was time to have them on deck; but we would not make the move until ordered for fear of attracting the attention of the crew, who were at work on provisions and boats. While I was taking tea, I saw Dunbar bring his knapsack up and put it in the cabin. Feeling that the moment had arrived, I went for mine, and at the head of the ladder on my return the doctor said to me:—

'Dan, the order is to get knapsacks.'

It seems that he had stepped below and found water in the wardroom, which he reported to the captain, and the order was then given to abandon the ship. The national ensign was hoisted at the mizzen, and Captain DeLong was on the bridge directing the work.

Lieutenant Chipp was confined to his bed. I threw my knapsack over the starboard rail and returned for clothes, but on stepping into water, when half way down the wardroom ladder, I realized that the ship was filling rapidly. The doctor and I then carried Chipp's belongings out, and I was told to take charge of the medical stores, especially the liquor. The ship in this condition was like a broken basket, and only kept from sinking by the pressure of the ice, which at any moment might relax and let her go to the bottom.

The crew worked well, and Edward Star, seaman, especially distinguished himself. He was doing duty at the time as paymaster's yeoman, or 'Jack o' the Dust.' The order was given to get up more Remington ammunition, and he went into the magazine when the ship was filling rapidly and succeeded in getting two cases out. This man was in Lieutenant Chipp's boat afterward. We always thought him a Russian, but he spoke English very well and never would speak of his nationality; but during his dreams he talked in a language that was neither English, French, German, Swedish, Spanish nor Italian, and most of the men thought it was Russian. He was an excellent man and a giant in strength. The captain thought a great deal of him, for he served him faithfully in every responsible position.

When the order was given to abandon the ship her hold was full of water, and as she was heeling twenty-three degrees to starboard, at the time the water was on the lower side of the spar deck. We had a large quantity of provisions on the ice about a hundred yards from the ship, but Mr. Dunbar, who was alive to the occasion, advised the shifting of these to an adjacent and more favorable floe-piece. It

ABANDONING THE JEANNETTE.

took us till eleven P. M. to effect the removal. We also had three boats,—namely, the first cutter, second cutter and the whale-boat. As soon as Dr. Ambler had looked out for Chipp, he relieved me at my post, and I went to work with No. 3 sled party, which I had been detailed previously to command. The order was given to camp and get coffee; so we pitched our tent abreast of the whale-boat, and I set about fitting out for the retreat.

While waiting for coffee I walked over to the ship to take a final look at her, and found the captain, Boatswain Coles, and Carpenter Sweetman on the port side looking at her under-water body, which was hove well out of water. I observed that the ship's side between the foremast and smokestack had been buckled in by the pressure, and that the second whale-boat was hanging at the davits, and also that the steam-cutter was lying on the ice near by. Coles and Sweetman asked the captain if we could lower the second whale-boat, and the captain said 'No.' The three boats, however, were considered enough; and while journeying on the ice we afterward found Chipp's boat to be the favorite with all hands, because she was considered short and handy, with sufficient carrying capacity for eight men. I then suggested to the men to return to camp, for the captain doubtless wished to be left alone with the Jeannette in her last moments.

We three returned to the camp together, having to jump across numerous wide cracks and from piece to piece, and soon after the watch was set and the order given to turn in. Most of us obeyed the order promptly, and were just getting into our bags when we heard a crack, and a cry from some one in the captain's tent. The ice had cracked immediately under the captain's tent, and Erickson would have gone into the water but for the mackintosh blanket in which he and the others were lying—the weight of the others at the ends keeping the middle of it from falling through. The order was immediately given to shift to another floe-piece which Mr. Dunbar selected for us. This was about three hundred yards from the untenable ship. After about two hours' work we succeeded in shifting all our goods and our three boats to it. We then turned in.

About four o'clock I was awakened by Seaman Kuehne calling his relief, Fireman Eartlett, who was in our tent. Kuehne called to Bartlett that the ship was sinking, and the latter jumped to the tent door and saw the spars of the Jeannette after the hull was below the surface. We heard the crash, but those were the only two men who saw the vessel disappear. It was said that the ice first closed upon her, then relaxing allowing the wreck to sink; the yards caught across the ice and broke off, but being held by the lifts and braces were carried down; depth, thirty-eight fathoms, as I remember.

The next morning the captain and others visited the spot, and found only one cabin chair and a few pieces of wood,—all that remained of our old and good friend, the Jeannette, which for many months had endured the embrace of the Arctic monster.

CHAPTER XVII.

LIEUTENANT DANENHOWER'S NARRATIVE.
(CONTINUED.)

THE Jeannette sank about four o'clock on the morning of Monday, June 13th, 1881. Daylight found us encamped on the ice about four hundred yards from where the ship went down. We had slept late after the exhausting work of the previous night. The day was spent by us in arranging our effects, and in gaining rest, which was much needed. Many of us, indeed quite a quarter of the number, were incapacitated for active work by reason of severe cramps caused by tin-poisoning from tomato cans. Among the sick were Chipp, Kuehne, the Indian Alexai, Lauderback, and the cabin steward.

The doctor recommended delay until the sick party should have recovered; but the time was not wasted, and the rest of the crew began the work of dividing the clothing and stowing the sleds and boats. We had as provisions about 3,500 pounds of pemmican in tinned canisters of 45 pounds weight each, about 1,500 pounds of hard bread, and more tea than we needed. We had also some canned turkey and canned chicken, but these we disposed of in the first camp. We had a large quantity of Liebig's extract,—a most important element in our diet. We had a large quantity of alcohol, which was intended to serve as fuel for cooking during our retreat. We had plenty of ammunition, and a good equipment of rifles. The provisions were stowed on five sleds, each having a tier of alcohol cans in the middle, and on either side a tier of pemmican canisters. Another sled was loaded with bread and a limited quantity of sugar and coffee. The weights of the sleds, when loaded, were as follows:—

No. 1.—Ship-made sled, 1,500 pounds.
No. 2.—McClintock sled, 1,300 pounds.
No. 3.—McClintock sled, 1,200 pounds.
No. 4.—McClintock sled, 1,300 pounds.
No. 5.—McClintock sled, 1,300 pounds.
Total, 6,600 pounds.

We had three boats, mounted upon ship-made sleds, each of which consisted of two heavy oak runners, about twelve inches high and shod with whalebone, of about twelve feet in length, and having eight to ten cross-pieces made from whiskey-barrel staves. The weight of the first cutter, with sled and outfit, was 3,000 pounds; weight of second cutter, with sled and outfit, 2,300 pounds; weight of whale-boat, with sled, 2,500 pounds. Making a total of 7,800 pounds; or a grand total of sleds and boats of 15,400 pounds.

To draw these we had a working force, when the retreat commenced, of twenty-two men; and the dogs were employed, with two light St. Michael's sleds, to drag a large amount of stores that we had in excess of those permanently stowed upon the larger sleds. Each man had a knapsack stowed away in the boats; each knapsack contained one change of underclothing, one package of matches, one plug of tobacco, one spare pair of snow-goggles, and one spare pair of moccasins.

On the 16th of June, three days after the Jeannette had sunk, the captain called all hands and read an order to the effect that we would start at six P. M. on the following day, on our march south; that we would work during the night and sleep during the day, to avoid the intense light, which might cause snow blindness, the routine to be as follows:—

At half past five P. M. call all hands, have breakfast, and break camp at half past six; at twelve, midnight, stop one-half hour for dinner; at six P. M. stop for supper and sleep. Ration table during the march to be as follows:—

Breakfast (per man)—Four ounces pemmican, two biscuits, two ounces coffee, two-thirds ounce sugar.

Dinner—Eight ounces pemmican, one ounce Liebig, one-half ounce tea, two-thirds ounce sugar.

Supper—Four ounces pemmican, one-half ounce tea, two-thirds ounce sugar, two biscuits, one ounce of lime-juice.

This amounted to less than two pounds per man per diem. The party was divided into five tents.

No. 1—Captain DeLong, Mr. Collins, and five others.

No. 2—Lieutenant Chipp, Dunbar, and five others.

No. 3—Lieutenant Danenhower, Newcomb, and five others.

No. 4—Engineer Melville and five others.

No. 5—Dr. Ambler, Boatswain Cole, and five others.

The captain had also an office-tent, in which half of his men were berthed. The tents were nine feet long by six in width, and required very close stowage for seven men. Each tent had a fire-pot, a heavy galvanized-iron kettle, in which a copper kettle was arranged, having an alcohol-lamp beneath it with a circular asbestos wick ten inches in diameter. It also had a stewpan on top. A cook was detailed to each tent, with an assistant to provide snow and to draw provisions. Each tent had a Mackintosh blanket nine by six, upon which the men could lie at night. The sleeping-bags were made of deer-skin, covered with hairless seal-skin or cotton drilling. In our tent there were three such single bags and two double ones; but generally single bags were in the other tents. Ours had been designed by Mr. Dunbar in November, 1879, and were the only ones that did not require alteration after we got on the ice. Each boat was provided with an outfit of oars, a boat-box with suitable articles for repairing damages, and ammunition for the arms that had been detailed to each boat.

The order said that the course would be south 17 degrees east (magnetic), which was south (true). I may here state that the boat compasses were intentionally left behind, because the captain said he preferred the pocket prismatic compasses. We had six splendid Richie boat compasses, always kept in the Jeannette ready for instant use, but they were, as I said, left behind, much to our detriment at a later period. Each boat had been provided with a luff tackle, anchor, and grapnel. Of course the anchor and grapnel had to be left behind; but the whale-boat retained. the luff tackle, which proved extremely useful at a later date. The order of march was as follows:—

All hands, except a special detail of four men, were to advance the first cutter to the first black flag established by Ice-pilot Dunbar, who was to go ahead to select the best road; then the second cutter and the whale-boat and provision-sleds were to be brought up to the first station as rapidly as possible. While this was going on the special detail of four men, with St. Michael sleds, were to advance the extra provisions; and the sick, with the hospital sled, were also to move to the front.

We were ordered to sleep during the afternoon of June 17th, and on the anniversary of the battle of Bunker Hill we commenced our long retreat. Chipp was on the sick-list, and I, with my eyes constantly bandaged and covered, could only do light duty, —so the task of leading the working party fell to Melville, the captain directing. Each officer and man was provided with a harness, which consisted of a broad canvas strap, fashioned to go across the chest and over one shoulder, and which had to be attached to the sled by a lanyard.

At last the order was given to break camp. The order was obeyed with enthusiasm, and the drag rope of the first cutter was immediately manned, Melville, Dr. Ambler, myself and two other men stationing ourselves on either side of the boat with harness fast to the thwarts, and then our work commenced in terrible earnest. The snow was knee deep, the road very rough, and the ice full of fissures. Through the former our feet sank easily, soon wearying the best of us; over the fissures, if not too wide, we had to jump the boats, and we had to drag the sled over lumps of ice that would have taken a whole corps of engineers to level. But we advanced steadily, if slowly. We reached one of the black flags that had been planted by Ice-pilot Dunbar, but seeing that he had planted another one ahead of us we pushed on with the first cutter to reach that too. This goal reached, we found that we were a mile and a half from the starting place, and that it had taken us three hours to make the distance.

But we, in our enthusiasm, had gone too far. It appears that the captain had only intended that we should make a single short station on the first day, but the order had probably been misunderstood by Mr. Dunbar, whose only wish was that we should make as good progress as possible. So we had to return; but on our way back we found that the ice had shifted and that our original road had been entirely broken up, and so we had to leave our sled midway between the two flags and then go to the assistance of the rest. We soon found that we had been fortunate with the first cutter. During our absence the captain, with a special detail and dogs, had attempted to advance the second cutter and whaleboat. He had launched the whale-boat across a fissure, and had broken the sled in hauling her out. No. 1 sled, named the 'Sylvie,' had also been broken, as well as two others.

The ice was all in motion, and we had a very bad outlook, with our boats and sleds at various points on the road. Chipp had been ordered to advance with the hospital sled, with Kuehne and Alexai and three men to assist him. The sled was heavily laden, and the work was too severe for the first lieutenant in his weak state, and the result was that he fainted from sheer' exhaustion, requiring the services of the doctor to restore him.

On our first outward march, Machinist Walter Lee had fallen out of the ranks and rolled upon the ice in agony with cramps in the calves of his legs—a result, doubtless of his having worked for so many months on the iron plates of the fire room, oftentimes with wet feet. He was a large, heavy-bodied man, and the unusual task fell heavily upon him at first.

At six o'clock in the morning (we had been in the region

of the midnight sun since the early part of May) we had advanced the second cutter about three-quarters of a mile from the old camp; the whale-boat was about a hundred yards back of her. Several disabled sleds stood at intervals along the road, while the balance of our stock still remained in the spot where they had been placed before the Jeannette went down. It was a cold, foggy morning, and we were very much chagrined at our ineffective efforts. We had a cup of tea, then brought up everything in the rear of the position of the second cutter, and then camped down, leaving the first cutter about three-quarters of a mile in advance. Everybody voted this the hardest day's work he had ever done in his life.

For two days we stayed to repair damages, and we all concluded that the 'now or never' policy of progress was a very ineffectual one. It would have been better for us to have spent a few minutes in removing the ice obstacles out of our way, rather than to attempt to drag the sleds over them by brute force. I did not know much about sleds and just how much spread to give the runners, but fortunately Seaman Leach was from the State of Maine, and I depended on his judgment; and I may add that our boat sled never broke down once after he and Bartlett—an old mountaineer and Californian traveler—had secured it.

After two days we again made a start for the south. We made slow progress, about a mile or a mile and a half a day, over the rough and moving floe. It was terrible work for the men. They had to go over the road no less than thirteen times—seven times with loads and six times empty handed—thus walking twenty-six miles in making an advance of only two! The empty handed business was the worst.

On the 19th of June the captain called me into his tent and told me to go with the hospital sled because, he alleged, I could not see. I remonstrated, but without avail. I went back to my tent, naturally deeply mortified to know that thirty-three men were working for their lives and I was not allowed to help even at the cooking, although physically I

FIRST CAMP AFTER STARTING SOUTH.

was one of the strongest men of the party. That morning I started with the hospital sled, which was dragged by seven dogs, driven by Erickson, the doctor and I assisting over the hummocks. We advanced over rough moving ice with great difficulty about half a mile, and then set up the tent for the three invalids—Chipp, Lauderback, and Alexai—to await the coming up of the rest of the party. I myself would never go inside the hospital tent. Thus the survivors trudged along, the well heavily handicapped by the six or seven who furnished no motive power at all. Twenty-one men did all the work for the thirty-three.

At the end of the first week the captain found by observation that the drift had more than neutralized the way covered by our advance; that, in fact, we had lost twenty-seven miles by the drift to the northwest in excess of our march to the south. This, of course, was kept a profound secret.

By and by Lauderback and Alexai got well enough to work; and finally Mr. Chipp, after several ineffectual requests to be put on duty, was allowed to relieve Melville and take charge of the working party. Melville was put in charge of the road gang, which consisted of Lee and Seaman Johnson, with the dingy and the team of dogs. Their principal duty was to keep in position the blocks of ice that were used as temporary bridges to enable the sleds to pass safely over the fissures. We often came to wide water holes, which caused us much delay in ferrying over. The method of doing this was as follows:—

First, a large ice piece was found; on this the boats and sleds were placed, and then all the floating mass was drawn over by the men on the other side, who had transported themselves across by the little dingy or even on smaller ice floes. Some of these water spaces were as much as a hundred yards wide. These openings were not connected, and of course could not be used in the direction we wished to go. On many occasions the boats had to be launched and paddled across, and then hauled up again on the opposite side. Chipp took charge of this part of the work admirably, and the men were always glad to have him at their head. It was wonderful how he kept up.

As soon as the list was clear of sick the hospital tent was dispensed with, and I for many days walked after the whale-boat, but with Melville always watching me in jumping cracks and pulling me out when I fell in. I found it very difficult to judge of distances with one eye bandaged and the other covered with a dark goggle. Collins generally walked with me; Newcomb and Seaman Star followed other sledges, all of us suspended from work. Besides these the captain, Chipp, Melville, and the doctor added little or nothing to the motive power. Eight persons out of thirty-three, or twenty-five per cent. of the whole were thus, so to speak, not working their passage across the ice.

In the latter part of June the snow all melted and traveling was better, but the men had to wade through pools of thaw-water and their feet were constantly wet. Seaman Kaack's feet were covered with blood-blisters, but he never gave in. Nindermann and Bartlett were always the leading men in dragging the boats, each being stationed at the bow to slew them and to lift them over heavy obstructions. As the roads became better we were able to advance two sleds at a time, but we would often have to jump them from piece to piece in crossing leads. Jack Cole and Harry Warren were the leading men of one party, and Bartlett and Nindermann of the other. The number of times passed over the ground was now reduced to seven, and the advance was thus very much facilitated. Mr. Dunbar used to start out, with two or three flags on his shoulder, and pick out the best road, planting his flags here and there in prominent places. The old gentleman was very careful and efficient, though the captain would often take an entirely different road,—on several occasions insisting on ferrying the goods across after the ice had come together within fifty yards of us.

About the 12th of July we saw a 'whale back' that looked very much like a snow-covered island. There had been some slight changes in the course previous to this. I think it was changed to south (magnetic), which would be about south 17 (true), for there was about 17 degrees of easterly variation. The captain then shaped the course toward the point where land was thought to have been seen. At this time we began to see a heavy water sky to the south and southeast, and the ice to the southwest was more broken and in greater motion, making traveling very difficult. About July 20th we worked nearly twelve hours in advancing 1,000 yards over small pieces of ice constantly shifting. We could not float the boats. The land already mentioned appeared greatly distorted by atmospheric effects, and indeed, until within a few days of reaching it, a great many would not believe that it existed at all.

Our progress toward the land was very slow, but finally we could see the glaciers and water-courses upon it quite distinctly. We were shaping a course toward the northeast end of the island, the drift of the ice being along the east face. At times we were forced to remain idle in our camping-place, it being quite impossible either to move over the rough, broken ice, always in rapid motion, or to launch the boats. On the 24th of July we reached a point not more than two miles distant from the land, but the men were so exhausted that we had to camp. Next morning we found that we had drifted at least three miles to the southward and along the east side of the island.

July 27th was very foggy, and we were working our way through living masses of ice, when the mist lifted a little and an immense sugar-loaf towered above us. We had been swept in by the current, and now seemed to be our chance of reaching the ice-foot of the island, which was very narrow, rugged, and broken, being aground in nineteen fathoms of water. We finally got everything on one big floe-piece, and as we caromed on the ice-foot we made a rally and jumped everything upon the ice-clad beach. But before the last boats and sleds were hauled up the floe-piece drifted away, leaving them perched on the edge of the ice in a very dangerous position, and they had to be left there for some

218   THE JEANNETTE ARCTIC EXPEDITION.

hours. Then came the difficult work of getting the boats and sleds through the very rough and broken ice-fringe along shore.

About six P. M. we had succeeded in reaching some smooth pieces near the south cape, and there we camped down, each tent being on a separate piece of floe. There was a solid breakwater outside of us,— consequently we were not in any great danger, though the blocks we were on were sometimes in motion as the tide rose and fell. At this point the sides of

A LAND-SLIDE.

the island were very bold and steep, composed of trap-rock and a lava-like soil, very dry,—so much so that frequent land-slides were occurring all the time we were there. Mr. Collins and I took a walk over the rough ice and along the south point of the island in order to get a view of the south side. It appeared very rugged and trended off to the west-northwest. From a high hummock we saw land to the west-northwest.

About seven P. M. the captain mustered everybody on the island. It was so steep that we could hardly get a footing. He then unfurled the beautiful silk flag that had been made for him by Mrs. DeLong, and took possession of the island in the name of the President of the United States, and called it 'Bennett Island.' This was succeeded by hearty cheers, three times three, with a good American 'tiger.' There were millions of birds nesting in the cliffs, and their noise was almost deafening. I think one seal was seen, but no walrus, during our stay of nearly a week on the island. The south cape was called Cape Emma, after the captain's wife, and was in latitude 70 deg. 38 min. north, longitude 148 deg. 20 min. east.

The whaleboat was so long that in crossing hummocks the stern-post used often to receive heavy knocks and her garboards had been stove; indeed, she had been shaken up so badly that she was as limber as a basket and required repairs, as did the other boats. The captain and doctor thought, too, that the party needed rest and change of diet,—so the men were sent out to get birds and driftwood, so that we could economize on our alcohol. In a few hours they knocked down several hundred birds with sticks and stones. These were brought into camp and divided out. Their effect after being eaten was like that of young veal, and pretty nearly every one of the party was made sick, the doctor included. I used to eat half a peck of scurvy grass every day, and that kept me well. But we had finally to return to pemmican, and were very glad to do so after such a surfeit of birds.

Mr. Dunbar and the two Indians were sent up the east side of the island to explore. They were gone two days and reached the northeast point. They found the land on the east side was more promising than on the south. They found several grassy valleys, some old deer horns, some

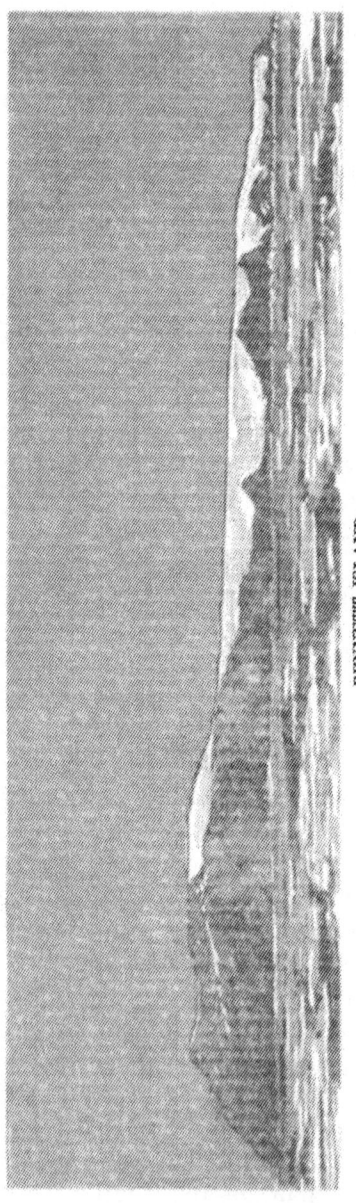

BENNETT ISLAND.

driftwood, and saw large numbers of birds. Lieutenant Chipp, with Mr. Collins and a boat's crew, explored the south and west sides, and promising reports came from them. A fair quality of lignite was found in several places. Mr. Melville experimented with it, and determined that it would be serviceable fuel for steaming purposes.

The tidal action at the island was very great, and quite remarkable for this part of the world. The ice outside of us was in constant motion, and seemed to be lifted regularly with the rise of the water. We had a tide-gauge set up, and it was observed every hour by Bartlett, Nindermann, and Lee. As I remember, the greatest rise and fall was about three feet; they were regular six hour tides. We were there near the time of full moon, and the 'vulgar establishment' was properly established. At Cape Emma the captain got a set of equal altitudes of the sun for chronometer error, but the weather was generally misty and unfavorable for such work. A box of geological specimens was obtained, and is now in my charge, it having been recovered from the captain's cache, near the mouth of the Lena. The doctor was very enthusiastic about certain amethysts, opals, and petrifactions that he had obtained; these are probably lost.

EXPLORING BENNETT ISLAND.

While on the island I observed that the sea to the south and west was freer from ice than that to the eastward, and that water-clouds to the northwest were very common; and it occurred to me that in good seasons a vessel could reach the island, which might form a good base for explorations further to the north.

CHAPTER XVIII.

LIEUTENANT DANENHOWER'S NARRATIVE.
(CONTINUED.)

WE left Bennett Island about August 4th. We were then fifty-three days out from the place where the Jeannette had sunk. We were fortunate enough in being able to launch our boats and to make better progress in the cracks between the floes. But we still had to keep our sleds for a short time longer. Some of the dogs rendered us very important services; but about half the number were now disabled by famine and weakness. We had forty originally, but about sixteen had died, or had been killed by the others during the two winters in the ice. After the stock of dog-food gave out, and owing to the scarcity of game, there were long periods of starvation for the poor brutes. Each man had a favorite animal, and would share his own rations with him; but this was not sufficient. At Bennett Island we still had, I think, twenty-three left, and the day before leaving eleven of the poorest of these were shot. We took the remaining twelve in the boats, but in passing close to big floe-pieces these gave us a great deal of trouble by jumping out and running away. Finally, Prince and Snoozer were the only two that had sense enough to remain by us.

For the next eighteen days we were working between floe-pieces, and sometimes making as much as ten miles a day on our course to the southwest. Several times a day we would have to haul the boats out, and make portages across the large floe-pieces that barred our progress. This was very severe work. We had at this time retained only the boat sleds, having left the provision sleds and all superfluous

WORKING SOUTH.

articles on a floe-piece about August 6th. We now worked during the day and slept during the night.

At Bennett Island the doctor, who belonged to my boat, had been transferred to the captain's, and Mr. Melville was placed in charge of mine—that is, the whale-boat. I was ordered to remain in the boat as a passenger, and to assist in emergencies. I always carried my own baggage, and assisted whenever possible. Dunbar was detailed with Chipp.

We made very good progress until about August 20th. On that day the leads were very open, and we thought we were all right. The wind was fresh and favorable; the first cutter and whale-boat, which followed closely, passed safely through great quantities of ice, but the second cutter was in the rear, and became jammed by the floe-pieces coming together very suddenly, and Chipp had to haul out and transport his boat about a mile in order to get her afloat again. In many cases a passage was obtained by prying the floe-pieces apart; but several times these sprang back, thus cutting off the advance of the second cutter. It was very hard and slow work, but much better than dragging the sleds over the ice.

The delay caused by getting Chipp's boat afloat was very fatal to us, for the wind shifted suddenly and we were forced to camp after waiting for him several hours. The ice jammed up during the night so that we had to remain there ten days without being able to move. Then land came in sight, and we seemed to be drifting along the north face of an island which the captain at first thought was New Siberia, but it was afterward found that we were drifting along the north coast of Thaddeoffsky. We drifted along this coast until August 28th, when, at last, we were again able to make a move. We called the place the Ten Day Camp. But we had used the delay in making repairs, and the food had been distributed per capita among the boats.

On the afternoon of the 29th we launched the boats again and worked in the pack for about two hours, when further progress was again barred by the ice. Finally, new connecting leads were found, and we proceeded to the southward and eastward for about five hours. Then we hauled up for the night on a small piece of floe-ice, which was drifting very rapidly to the southward and down the passage between New Siberia and Thaddeoffsky.

The next morning found us in navigable water, and with land about seven miles distant to the westward. Then we rounded the south point of Thaddeoffsky. We found the

THADDEOFFSKY ISLAND.

island to be composed of mud hills that were wearing away rapidly and forming shoals off the land. Beyond the low hills there was a wet, mossy tundra, upon which we camped for the night. All hands were then sent out hunting. Reindeer tracks and traces were numerous, but none were seen. Bartlett reported that he found footprints in the sand made by a civilized boot. The steward found a hut about two miles west of the camp, and a small piece of black bread, as well as a small tusk and a knee piece for a boat, fashioned from a deer horn. The next morning we proceeded west along the shore, the water being very shoal. We saw remains of several huts and quantities of driftwood. We also saw lots of ducks and wild fowl, and Newcomb succeeded in getting about six brace of ducks, which were very welcome. That night we tried to land, but after several ineffectual efforts gave up the attempt, as the water was too shoal for our boats.

The following is a detailed description of the boats, with lists of persons attached to each:—

FIRST CUTTER.—THE CAPTAIN'S BOAT.—Captain DeLong, Dr. Ambler, Mr. Collins, Nindermann, Erickson, Gortz, Noros, Dressler, Iverson, Kaack, Boyd, Lee, Ah Sam, Alexai.

Extreme length, 20 ft. 4 in,; breadth, 6 ft.; depth, 2 ft. 2 in., from top of gunwale to the top of keel; clinker built, copper fastened, inside lining; drew 28 inches loaded, and had the greatest carrying capacity of the three; fitted with mast and one shifting lug sail; pulls six oars, and was an excellent sea boat. She had a heavy oak keel piece to strengthen her in hauling over the ice, and it was retained after reaching the water. She was fitted with weather claws at Semenoffski Island, September 11th, by Nindermann.

SECOND CUTTER.—Lieutenant Chipp, Dunbar, Sweetman, Star, Warren, Kuehne, Johnson, Sharvell.

Extreme length, 16 ft. 3 in.; breadth, 5 ft. 1 in.; depth, 2 ft. 6 in., from top of gunwale to top of keel; clinker built, copper fastened, a very bad sea boat; she was carefully fitted with weather claws; had one dipping log sail and four oars. She had not sufficient carrying capacity for Chipp's allowance of provisions, so the captain had two extra tins of pemmican in his boat when we separated. This is an important fact, for Lieutenant Chipp must have run out of food very quickly.

14

228   THE JEANNETTE ARCTIC EXPEDITION.

WHALE-BOAT.—Engineer Melville, Lieutenant Danenhower, Newcomb, Cole, Leach, Mansen, Wilson, Bartlett, Lauderback, Charles Tong Sing, Anequin.

Extreme length, 25 ft. 4 in.; breadth, 5 ft. 6 in.; depth, 2 ft. 2 in. from top of gunwale to top of keel; clinker built, copper fastened, drawing about twenty-four inches when loaded, this being caused by the heavy oak keel piece, similar to those of the first and second cutters. She had one mast and one dipping log sail, and was fitted with weather claws about September 11th. The master boat-builder at

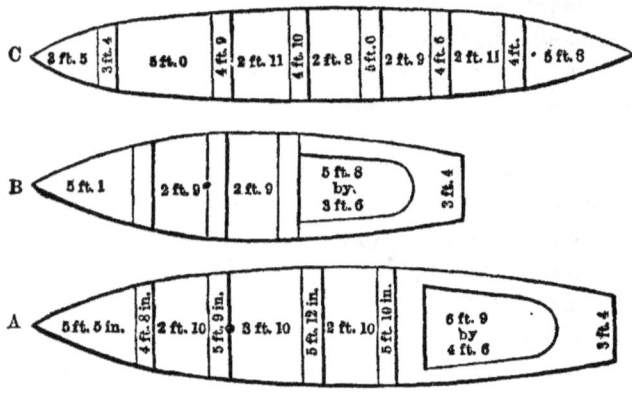

A—First Cutter. B—Second Cutter. C—Whale-Boat,

Mare Island told me that she was one of the best fastened boats that he had ever seen, and our experience proved it; for the racket she stood on the journey over the ice was almost incredible. The plans of the boats I got from Carpenter Sweetman at Kotelnoi Island, September 4th, 1881.

The captain decided to work along the shoal that lies between Thaddeoffsky and Koteloi Islands. There was a moderate wind from the eastward, and the captain tried to keep close in, in about four feet of water. The result was that the first cutter was constantly grounding, and then laboriously getting off again. We continued on our course to the southward, the captain's boat getting in breakers at one time and calling for our boat to pull him out. There was not much ice at the time, and it was decreasing. One day, about noon, we ran through a line of drift ice, and the whaleboat struck on a tongue that was under water. She began to fill rapidly, and we had to haul her out, but not before she was two-thirds full could we reach a suitable ice piece. The plug had been knocked out, but she had sustained no other damage. That afternoon we passed through a large water space several square miles in area, with a heavy sea running. We were steering dead before the wind, having to follow in the wake of the captain, and it was very difficult to keep from jibing.

About three P. M. the coxswain let her jibe, and she was brought by the lee by a heavy sea on the starboard quarter. The sheet was not slacked in time, and the boat was hove almost on her port beam ends. A heavy green sea swept over the whole port side and filled her to the thwarts; she staggered and commenced to settle, but every man with a baler in hand quickly relieved her, and she floated again. I was never frightened before in a boat, but it was a most dangerous and terrible situation. There was no chance for the captain or Chipp to have assisted us, and had another sea boarded us not a man of our party would have been saved.

The weather was very cold. Two hours afterward we met the ice, among which we made our way. Chipp's boat was still astern and in the water hole, and we were very anxious about his safety. The captain hauled up about seven P. M., and camped with us. The next day the gale was still blowing, and Chipp's boat still missing,—so about six P. M. the captain hoisted a black flag.

On the following day Bartlett reported that the ice was closing around us, and that if we did not move we would be shut in. Two hours afterward all outlets were closed. Land was also in sight at this time, being Kotelnoi Island. Erickson was the first to see Chipp's boat, and presently we saw two men making their way over the floe and jumping across the obstructions. It was Chipp, with Kuehne. His boat had been nearly swamped, and in a sinking condition he had reached a piece of ice and managed to haul up. Star was the only man with his boat at that time who could walk, the others requiring ten or fifteen minutes to get up circulation in their benumbed limbs. The captain had previously given written orders that in case of separation each boat should make the best of its way to Lena River, but he had recommended touching at Kotelnoi Island. Chipp had fortunately decided to follow these instructions, because he had not his allowance of food. We ourselves had been on half rations for some time. He had remained on the ice about

STOLBOVOI ISLAND.

twenty-four hours, and then got a chance to get under way. He told us that by making a portage of about two miles we could launch our boats and fetch the land. He sent his men to assist us, and after six or eight hours of terrible work we succeeded in getting our boat to the second cutter. That night we reached the southeast corner of Kotelnoi Island and camped on a low cape extending well out from the mountain and forming a beautiful bay.

HUNTING ON SEMENOFFSKI ISLAND.

This was September 6th, I think. We stayed there about thirty-six hours. Large parties were sent out hunting, as numerous deer tracks had been seen. Next morning we got under way again and worked along shore until about noon, when we had to make a long and laborious portage, during which Mr. Dunbar fell down exhausted and with palpitation of the heart. We continued until midnight, and then camped on a bleak, desolate spot. Next morning, September 7th, we shaped a course for the island of Stolbovoi from the south point of Kotelnoi, fifty-one miles distant to the southwest. We had fresh breezes the first day, and during the night got into a very bad place and came very near being smashed up by drift ice. We passed in sight of Stolbovoi; but it was not considered worth while to land on the barren island, which was, besides, too distant.

On the night of September 9th, we hauled up on a piece of ice off the north end of Semenoffski Island, and there slept. On September 10th, we rounded the north end of this island and came down the west shore, stopping to cook dinner and to examine the island. Having seen the tracks of deer going toward the south end of the island, the captain suggested that a party of hunters deploy across it and advance to the south in hopes of getting a deer. About ten of us went. I went along the beach with Kuehne and Johnson, Bartlett, Noros, Collins, and the Indians skirting the hills. We raised a doe and fawn running to the northward as fast as possible, they having previously seen the boats. Several shots were fired, and the doe fell under Noros' last shot. We hurled the body down a steep bluff to Chipp, who had it butchered, and the captain ordered all served out, having previously given orders for all hands to camp.

That evening the captain told Melville that he and many of his party were badly used up and must have rest and a full meal before proceeding. All these days—for the past twenty—we had been on very short allowance and had never had a full meal. Melville said that he and his party were in excellent condition and wanted to move on, and did not like losing time. The entire deer was served out and we had orders to remain till Monday morning, or about thirty-six hours. We had noticed that after two or three days of northeast winds it generally finished up with a heavy gale from that quarter, and it was thought we would be likely to get it on Monday or Tuesday. That evening Chipp came over and asked me to go out with him to get some ptarmigan if possible. We came upon a large covey, but could not get a shot. This was my last talk with Chipp. He was in better health than usual and was cheerful, but not altogether satisfied with the outlook.

On Monday morning, September 12th, we left Semenoffski Island, and stood to the southward along the west side of the island, lying to the south. About half-past eleven A. M. we ran through a lot of drift ice, following the first cutter. It was pretty close work, and our boat had to luff through between two big cakes of ice. The sheet was hauled aft in luffing, and the boat sided over against the lee piece, thereby knocking a hole in the starboard side. She filled rapidly, and we barely succeeded in making fast her bow to an adjacent cake of ice; there we put on a lead patch and remedied the damage. This was the last piece of ice that we saw. While repairs were going on I had a chat with Collins, who was as amiable as usual, and had some pleasant story to tell me. The doctor was also very affable, and asked particularly after my health and comfort.

We then started on a southwest course. The captain kept his boat almost right before the wind; it was very difficult to keep from jibing, and as the whale-boat was the faster sailer it was hard to keep in position. Our orders were to keep astern of the captain, within easy hail, and for Chipp to bring up the rear, he being second in command. The wind and sea increased very rapidly, and about five P. M. we were out of position about nine hundred yards off the weather quarter of the first cutter. Melville asked me if we could get in position safely, and I told him that by jibing twice and lowering the sail we could do so. He then told me to

FIRST CUTTER.   WHALE-BOAT.   SECOND CUTTER.

THE SEPARATION OF THE BOATS

take charge; so I jibed very carefully, ran down to the captain's wake and then jibed her again, each time having lowered the sail, and having gotten out two oars to keep up the headway before the sea while shifting the sail. I then had seaman Leach put at the helm, as he was the best helmsman in the boat. My eyes would not permit my taking the helm or I would have done so. We then ranged along the' weather side of the first cutter, had our sail close reefed, and to keep from running away from her had to take it in, thereby allowing the seas to board us.

About dusk the captain stood up in his boat and waved his hands as if to separate. This is what the men say; I did not see it. At the same time Chipp was said to be lowering his sail. Melville asked my advice, and I said we should steer with the wind and sea four points to the north quarter; that we could make good weather of it until dark, when we should heave to on account of the liability to meet young ice in the darkness. In the meantime I advised that we should prepare a good drag. He told me to go ahead and do it. So I ordered Cole and Mansen to take three hickory tent-poles, each about eight feet in length, lash them in a triangle, and lace a strong piece of cotton canvas across it,—then take the boat's painter, and make a span similar to the bellyband of a kite, and to the middle of this span make fast the luff tackle fall. On the lower end of each tent-pole there was a brass nib which, with the weight of the wet canvas and the bight of the rope, would, I said, probably make the drag heavy enough; if not we would send down the spare fire-pot and boat bucket to help it.

The gale was now at its full force, and the seas were running high and spiteful. Leach was steering admirably, but we had to keep four balers going all the time to prevent the boat from filling and sinking. The drag, having been completed, was placed forward of the mast in readiness for use. I had the drag rope coiled down clear for running. The men were very weary. There were only two seamen in the boat who would pull in a seaway, the others being inexperienced, except the helmsman. I had been watching the seas for a long time, and had noticed that they ran in threes, and that there was a short lull after the third and heaviest one. I had the men detailed as follows:—Wilson and Mansen at the oars, keeping them peaked high above the sea, Cole at the halyards to lower sail, Anequin and the steward to gather the sail, Bartlett to launch the drag, and Leach at the helm. I gave preparatory orders very carefully—at the words 'Lower away!' to put the helm hard-a-starboard, lower sail and give way with starboard oar, holding water with the port oar, if possible in the seaway.

I watched more than five minutes for my chance, for our lives depended on the success of that movement. At the proper moment I shouted 'Lower away!' and every man did his duty; the boat came round, gave a tremendous dive and she was then safe, head to sea. We eased the oars and launched the drag. It watched about three points on the port bow,—so I sent down the spare fire-pot and a bucket by putting loops, or what we call beckets, on the bales. Cole suggested sending down a painted bag with the mouth open. It filled with water, dragged, and was very effective. We then lay head to sea during the night. A number of the party turned in under the canvas. Melville was exhausted and had his legs badly swollen; so he turned in abreast the foremast, leaving me in charge.

Leach and Wilson steered with a paddle during the night, and I sat at their feet watching. The upper gudgeon of the rudder had been carried away, so we took the rudder on board. Our fresh water had been ruined by the seas that had boarded us, but late on the night before leaving the island Newcomb had brought in several ptarmigan, which had been dressed and put in our kettle, the other tents not caring to take their share. This proved excellent food for us the next day, as they were not too salt to be eaten.

At daylight, September 13th, there were no boats in sight, and the gale was still raging. About ten A. M. I noticed that a new sea was making and the old sea was more abeam.

SKILFUL SEAMANSHIP.

From this I judged that the wind had veered to the southeast and would grow lighter. About noon the water began to tumble in very badly on the port quarter; and the boat was down by the stern. We were thoroughly wet, and the sleeping gear was so water-soaked and swollen that it jammed between the thwarts and could not be shifted in trimming. I rigged the mackintosh on the port quarter, the stroke oarsman holding one corner and I the other for seven hours. This kept a great deal of water out of the boat and acted like a 'tarpaulin in the rigging' to keep her head to sea. At 4.40 P. M., per log, I called Melville and told him that it was time to get under way. The sea was very heavy, but was falling, and by standing west at first we could gradually haul up to south-southwest as the sea went down.

We got under way without getting a sea aboard and stood to the westward, and by eight P. M. were able to haul up to south-southwest, on which course we stood during the night. The second night was more comfortable, but still we were all very wet; but we were perfectly safe. I lay down for an hour abreast the foremast while Melville relieved me, but could not sleep, and soon returned to my old place.

CHAPTER XIX.

LIEUTENANT DANENHOWER'S NARRATIVE.
(CONTINUED.)

AT six o'clock on the morning of the 14th, I gave orders to prepare breakfast, and a few minutes later we were surprised by the boat taking ground in two feet of water. We backed off, and I recommended standing to the eastward. I had reckoned that when we rounded to we were about fifty miles off Barkin, our destination; that we had drifted at least fifteen miles to the southwest during the gale, and that we had run about twenty-five miles during the night, so that we were on the shoals north of Barkin. I said that if we stood to the west we would have no show; but that if we went east until deep water was reached, and then stood due south to the highlands of the coast, we would find plenty of water and a good landing place. Melville was of course in command, but he relied on my judgment, as he did in all emergencies.

Bartlett thought he saw a low beach with logs upon it. I told him to take another good look, and then he said he thought he was mistaken. It was only a smooth patch of water among the shoals. We noticed that the water was only brackish, and that there was a thin skim of young ice near us. We stood to the eastward, occasionally feeling our way south, but always touched the ground quickly when moving in that direction. I noticed there was a very strong easterly set here. The winds were light and southerly; we stood all night about east-southeast, and early next morning got nine fathoms. I then recommended steering due south, but Melville wanted to go southwest, because that was the captain's course; so I assented and shaped a southwest course, which we continued to steer until the morning of

September 17th. The winds were very light, and we often had to pull the boat. I was at the coxswain's feet conning the boat.

At daylight we got ten feet of water, and soon after saw a low beach. We made two attempts to land through the breakers, but could not get within a mile of the shore. The land trended north and south, and I said that we were evidently south of Barkin, and that if there was water enough we might fetch it that night from the southward, as we had a good breeze about east. With a view to finding the captain and Chipp we stood up the coast, hoping to reach Barkin before dark.

The condition of the party on this morning was very bad. Leach and Lauderback were disabled with swollen legs, the skin having broken in many places, and most of the others were badly off. We had been in the boat ninety-six hours and wet all the time. I had taken the precaution twice during that time to pull off my moccasins, to wring out my stockings and to rub my feet, in order to restore circulation. I advised the others to do the same, but the most of them unfortunately did not take the advice. I also beat the devil's tattoo almost all the time to keep up the circulation; so the next morning I was the best man in the party on my feet.

After going to the northward about thirty minutes we saw two low points of swamp land, and it was evident that we were at the mouth of a swamp river. We had a talk, and I advised getting ashore as quickly as possible and drying our things out. So we entered this river with a leading wind, the current being very strong. We got as much as five fathoms in the middle of the river, but it shoaled very rapidly on either side of mid-channel. It was four or five miles wide, but we could not get within a mile of either beach. I advised standing up the river until noon, and then to decide fully what we should do. When that time arrived I said we were probably in a swamp river, about thirty or forty miles south of Barkin; the wind was east, and if we turned back we would have to beat out, but would have the current in our favor; after getting clear of the point we could run up the coast with a fair wind. 'But,' I added, 'if a gale comes on we will be in the breakers.' Melville then decided to turn back and start for Barkin.

At this juncture Bartlett spoke up and said that he believed we were in the east branch of the Lena. Melville referred to me, and I said that it might be so, but that we should have higher land on our port hand if that were the case. The trend of the river corresponded pretty well with the coast outlet, and if we could find an island about thirty miles up stream it would, doubtless, prove that we were in that place. Bartlett said that he believed such a vast body of water could not be a swamp river; it was bigger than the Mississippi at its mouth. I still held to my belief that it was a swamp river, but said that it would be a good plan to try to make a landing before night.

So we stood up stream and were fortunate enough to make a landing at seven P. M., in what we found afterward the Tunguses call an *orasso,* or summer hunting hut. We had been 108 hours in the boat since leaving Semenoffski Island. The men immediately built a fire in the hut, and gathered round it before they had restored circulation by exercise. I knocked about outside and carried up my sleeping bag before supper, so my blood was in good circulation before I went near the fire. We had a cup of tea and a morsel of pemmican, having been on quarter rations since we separated. We went to sleep with our feet toward the fire, and several of the men passed the night in agony, as if millions of needles were piercing their limbs. Bartlett described it as the worst night he ever passed. I slept like a child and was very much refreshed next morning. We found fish bones, reindeer horns and human footprints; also a curiously fashioned wooden reindeer with a boy mounted on his back. We were very much delighted with our prospects of meeting natives.

Next morning we got under way about seven, steered up the river about two hours, and then could proceed no further. Bartlett started out to reconnoitre, but when he was a hundred yards distant I saw that he was limping; so I ran after him and sent him back. I went about half a mile and saw several swamp-like rivers coming from the northwest; then went back to the boat and told Melville he had better prepare tea while Mansen and I took a more extended scout. We went further, and Mansen used his eyes for me. I could see some high land about two miles off, and I asked Mansen to look well to see if he could get over to it, for I was sure deep water lay alongside of it. He thought he could trace a passage to it, all but in one small place; so we returned with that information. The land was about ten feet high and covered with good deer moss. We saw many deer-tracks, especially where they had come down to water at the river; we also saw another hut close by on a small flat.

We then went back to Melville, and soon after started out with the boat. We had splendid luck; we struck a passage and reached the deep water. We passed an island, and I began to think that Bartlett was right. We proceeded at least thirty miles that afternoon, and at dark we reached a point about sixty feet high, where we expected the river to turn due south. Here we pitched the tents and passed the night.

About four o'clock next morning Bartlett and I took a scout. We saw two large rivers to the northwest, and a broad river coming from the south. We thought we were at the right turning-point, but were not sure. At six I called Melville and the others and ordered tea cooked. The wind was fresh from the west and blowing right on the beach. We had breakfast, and then I took the well men and loaded the boat. We struck the tents at the last moment and assisted Melville and Leach into the boat, close-reefed the sail, and made every preparation for getting the boat off the lee shore. After some difficulty we succeeded in doing this, and ran close hauled on the starboard tack under close-reefed sail, standing about south-southwest under the lee of a mud-flat. I was at the helm, and Bartlett on the bows with sounding-pole. We saw seven reindeer among the hills, but did not stop to get at them. About eleven we saw two huts on the west bank and in a good situation for landing; so I recommended that we should get ashore and dry out everything.

It was Sunday, September 18th, and was the first real day of rest that we had taken for a long time. We found two very nice summer hunting dwellings, built with sloping sides and shaped like the frustrum of a pyramid, the sloping sides forming the cover for the occupants and the aperture at the top being the chimney. This was what the Russians call a *polotka* and the Tunguses an *orasso*. The sun was bright and beautiful. We opened out everything to dry and passed a delightful Sunday, being sure that rescue was not far off. Newcomb made a good warm jacket out of his sleeping bag. We also wrote a notice to the effect that the whale-boat had landed at this point, and stuck up a flag to mark the place of the record. There were lots of fish bones in the hut, some refuse fish, and a piece of black bread, all of which our Indian ate with avidity. There were also frames for nets and for drying fish.

At eight A. M., on Monday, September 19th, we got under way again and stood up the river. I was at the helm and Bartlett on the bows, and the crew, divided in two watches of four each, taking two-hour tricks at the oars. Melville was in the stern sheets in command of the boat. We stood south for two hours with light wind and oars. All was going well, and we were in strong hopes of reaching a settlement marked on the chart before night; but we soon began to be headed off by mud flats and sand banks. About one A. M. we were more than a mile from the west bank, which we were following because the village was marked as on that side. We then saw a point of land, and I proposed to go ashore to set up the prismatic compass and get some bearings, as well as to prepare dinner.

After two hours' work against a strong current we succeeded in reaching the shore, and the cook had set about getting fire when, to our surprise and delight, we saw three

FIRST MEETING WITH NATIVES.   243

natives coming around the point in three dug-out canoes and pulling with double paddles. We immediately manned our boat and went out to meet them, but they appeared shy and stood to the southward. We lay on our oars and held up some pemmican, and finally a handsome youth of about eighteen approached cautiously and took a piece. Then he called his two companions and they also came to us. We then induced them to go ashore with us to the old landing, where we built a fire and commenced preparing tea. One of the natives gave us a goose and a fish,—all they had at the time. Their boats were very neat and well fitted with nets.

I noticed that one of the strangers had a gray coat with a velvet collar, and when I pointed to it inquiringly he said 'Bulun.' Then I pointed to his knife, or *bohaktah,* as he called it, and he also said 'Bulun.' From this I imagined that Bulun was the name of the place where they had obtained them. We had a very joyous time drinking tea and eating goose, for we felt that we were safe. The natives showed us all their hunting gear, and we showed them the compass, the watch, and our rifles, much to their delight.

After eating they crossed themselves, shook hands, and said *'Pashee bah.'* They also showed us their crosses, which they kissed; and I was very glad to have in my possession a certian talisman which had been sent to me by a Catholic friend at San Francisco, with the message that it had been blessed by the priest and I would be sure to be safe if I wore it. I did not have much faith in this, however, but I showed it to the natives, and they kissed it devoutly.

It was the only article in the possession of the party, indeed, that indicated to the natives that we were Christians. You can imagine our feelings at meeting these people, for they were the first strangers whom we had seen for more than two years; and I never before felt so thankful to missionaries as I did on that day at finding that we were among Christian natives.

We indicated to the three natives that we wanted to sleep,

by making signs, and resting the head upon the hand and snoring. They understood us, and took us around the point where we had hauled our boats upon the sand beach, and then climbed a hill which was from sixty to seventy feet high. This was at the mouth of a small branch of the Lena, and we have since learned this to be on Cape Borchaya, said to be about eighty-five miles northwest of Cape Bykoffsky. There we found four houses and several storehouses, all deserted but one, which was in very good condition. There was a graveyard near by, with many crosses. We all lodged in the one house.

The natives were very kind to us; they hauled their nets and brought us fish, parts of which they roasted before the fire, giving us the most delicate morsels. Some of the fish we boiled, and altogether we had a very enjoyable meal. Then I noticed that Caranie (one of the natives) had gone away, leaving only the youth, whom we called Tomat, and the invalid, whom we called Theodore. From Caranie's absence I argued that there must be other natives near by, and that Caranie had gone to inform them of our presence.

Next morning, while the men were loading the boat, I took the compass and got some bearings of the sun for local time, direction of the wind, and general lay of the land. Previous to this I had interviewed Tomat, who drew a diagram on the sand showing the course of the river, and that the distance to Bulun was seven sleeps, which he indicated by snoring deeply when he pointed to each stopping-place. He appeared perfectly willing to go with us as pilot to Bulun.

On my return, Melville asked me to hurry up, as he wanted to get off. I was surprised, and asked where the other native was. Melville replied that he had left, having refused to go with us. I then asked him to wait a few minutes while I ran back to the house in order to try and induce them to come. Returning, I found the youth Tomat on the housetop looking very sad and bewildered. When I asked him to accompany us he replied, mournfully, 'Sok!

Sok! Sok!' which meant 'No! No!' and then tried to explain something which I could not understand, saying 'Kornado,' which I only afterward learned meant 'father.' I felt sorry for the youth, and gave him a colored silk handkerchief and one or two little things, and then went back to Melville.

We then started out on our own hook and tried to work south (that is toward Bulun) among the mud flats; but in this we were not successful. At five P. M. we had a consultation, and I urged that we must decide at once whether to remain out all night or go back. I recommended going back and forcing the natives to go with us. We had two Remingtons and a shot-gun, and I knew that it would be easy to carry our point. Bartlett had been sounding from the bow, so I asked him if he knew the way back. He said yes, and we started to return. We did quite well until dark, but then the wind shifted and began to blow a gale. It was a very bad situation for a boat in such shallow water. We were fortunate enough, however, to get under the lee of a mud bank, where we secured the boat, with three tent-poles driven into the mud and our line fast to them. Thus we rode all night. It was very cold, and some of the men got their feet and legs badly frostbitten. During the snow squalls of the evening before I had to give the helm to Leach, because my glass would constantly get covered with snow and I could not see.

At daylight I got Bartlett and Wilson to stand up in the boat and take a good look at the land. Bartlett said he could not recognize it, but Wilson was sure it was the place where we had first met the natives. Bartlett said that if we could weather a certain mud-flat we would have a fair way in; so we close reefed, I took the helm, and went to windward of the mud-flat. Then we ran in with a leading wind and landed. Newcomb shot some sea-gulls, and we breakfasted on them in order to save our few remaining pounds of pemmican. Wilson insisted that in less than half an hour he could go to the house where we had slept the night before. Most of us laughed at him, but I told him and Mansen to go and see, while I sent two men to reconnoitre in an opposite direction. Wilson and Mansen came back very soon. We were rejoiced to learn that they had seen the house.

We immediately recalled our scouts and embarked, rounded the point, and were received at the old place by the natives in the most cordial manner. They were headed by another native, an old man, who took off his cap, and said 'Drasti! Drasti!' at the same time shaking hands. He immediately took possession of Melville, who was very lame, and helped him up to the house. We unloaded the boat, and carried up the sleeping-gear. When the natives saw a couple of gulls that we were expecting to feed on, they threw them down in disgust, and immediately brought deer-meat to replace them. Veo Wassili, for that was the old man's name, proved to be our great friend; he willingly consented to pilot us to Bulun, and measured the boat's draught, thus showing that he was wide awake and knew what he was about. This old Tunguse, Wassili, or Wassili Koolgiak, or 'Cut-eared Wassili,' in his style and bearing always reminded me of the late Commodore Foxhall A. Parker. He was always dignified and kindly, and had a certain refinement of manner that was very remarkable.

We saw at once that Wassili was the man whom Caranie had gone to bring to us, and that was why the youth would not go with us until his father arrived. I got Wassili to draw a chart of the route we should take, and the following is a copy of it, with the way in which he proposed to pilot us and the points at which we should sleep. [See next page.]

We took a good rest, and were all ready to start next morning with Wassili. Bartlett and myself asked to go ahead, in order to send succor from Bulun and also to spread the news about the two other boats; but Melville preferred that we should all keep together, for he probably did not feel that we were out of the scrape ourselves yet.

On Wednesday morning, September 21st, Wassili, with two other natives, started with us, and pursued the same course that we had done on the previous forenoon to the southward and eastward among the mud-flats. He went ahead, and had his two men on the flanks constantly sounding with their paddles. Their boats, or *veatkas,* are about fifteen feet in length and twenty inches beam, modeled very much like a paper race-boat, and provided with a double paddle. The native faces the bow, pulling alternately with the right and left hand, the fulcrum of the lever being an imaginary point between the two hands. It is a very graceful and fascinating movement, and the natives make their

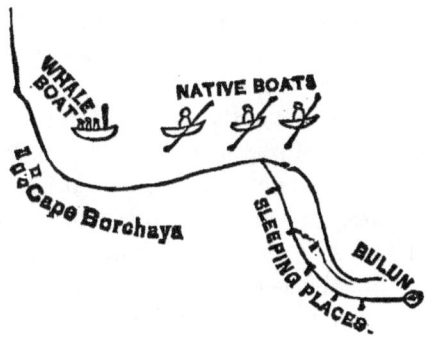

boats skim along very rapidly, sounding at each stroke when going in shoal water. Wassili found a channel among the mud-flats for our boats, which at this time drew about twenty-six inches. We worked all day to the southward and eastward, and about eight o'clock P. M. hauled out on a flat beach and camped for the night, Wassili giving us fish for supper. The weather was very cold and raw, with a strong breeze blowing, and our pilot was very anxious about the state of the river, fearing that we would be stopped by young ice at any moment.

The next morning the banks were fringed with young ice, but this we broke our way through and continued our course up the river. After the sun came out, the ice melted, and we worked all day through a labyrinth of small streams, passing several hunting-lodges. At night we slept in two houses on shore, and next morning we entered a large body of water which we thought was the main river. About noon we reached a point of land on which there was a deserted village of about six well-built houses and a number of storehouses. Wassili took us to a house and told us to *couche,* or eat. I noticed that one of the natives went away in his canoe. I then took a look at the village. The houses were in good repair, and there were numerous troughs for feeding dogs, and cooking utensils in them. The doors were not locked, but those of the storehouses were well secured with heavy iron padlocks of peculiar shape.

Things looked more promising now, and I felt sure that the winter occupants of these houses could not be far off. During this resting spell I examined Leach's and Lauderbach's feet and limbs. Leach's toes had turned black, and Lauderback's legs were in a fearful condition, being greatly swollen and having large patches of skin broken. We dressed them as well as we could with some pain-extractor that I happened to have along, and when that gave out we used grease from the boat-box.

In about an hour a boat appeared in sight, and a number of people disembarked and entered a house near us. A few minutes later, Wassili came and asked Melville and me to go with him. He conducted us to the house, where we shook hands with an old native named Spiridon, who had two very hard-looking women with him, each of whom had lost the left eye. They served tea to us, however, in china cups; also gave us some reindeer tallow, which they considered a great delicacy. Spiridon looked to me like a regular old pirate, and there was an air of mystery about the place that made me tell Melville I thought Spiridon was an old rascal, and that I was afraid to trust him. He gave us a large goose, however, that was dressed and stuffed with seven other geese, all boned, and this he said we must not eat until sleeping-time on the following day. He also said that we would leave next morning. Newcomb had seen a number of ptarmigan flying about the deserted houses, and had bagged a few of these beautiful birds, which were in their white winter plumage, feathered from beak to toe.

Then we started with a new pilot (Kapucan), a young man who lived with Spiridon. Old Wassili was quite exhausted, and he showed us his left elbow, where he had a severe gunshot wound, not yet healed. Caranie and Theodore still accompanied us, and the former proved to be a better pilot than the latter. We worked very hard that day until eight P. M., the men pulling all the time in one-hour tricks. I had the helm and Bartlett the sounding-pole. We camped for the night in a *palotka,* and when we got under way again next morning only four of us were able to load the boat and get her off the beach.

During the previous three days Leach and Lauderback had been working manfully at the oars whenever their turn came, although their limbs were in such a condition that they could not stand, and they had to be assisted to and from the boat. Melville and Bartlett were in a similar condition.

CHAPTER XX.

LIEUTENANT DANENHOWER'S NARRATIVE.
(CONTINUED.)

ABOUT noon we reached the village of Geemovialocke (which we afterwards found to be on Cape Bykoffsky), where we were received cordially by about twelve men, women, and children. Melville and I were taken to the house of a certain Nicolai Shagra, who was the chief.

A few minutes later in dashed a slight young man whom we at once saw was a Russian, and I thought he was a Cossack. His name was Efim Kopiloff, a Russian exile who lived in this village, and he proved very useful to us later on. At this time he could say 'Bravo!' which he thought meant good, and that was the only word we had in common; but in less than two weeks he taught me so much Russian that I could make myself fully understood to him in a mixture of Russian and Tunguse. We stayed at Nicolai's all night, and his wife gave us a fish supper, which we enjoyed heartily. We described as well as we could that three boats had been dispersed in a gale, and that we did not know where the other two boats were; also that we wanted to go to Bulun, which place he told us was fifteen days off.

I need now to give you some explanation why we were at Cape Bykoffsky, so far out of our course to Bulun. Old Wassili, we understood at the time, was bound first of all to deliver us to the care of his chief, Nicolai Shagra, and with him we eventually found ourselves. The reason why they did not take us to Bulun, as they promised, is not very clear, even to me. It was a very unfortunate time in the season. Young ice was making during the night and breaking up and thawing during the day. It was the transition period between navigation and sledding. Nicolai Shagra told us it would take fifteen days to reach Bulun, but I think that he meant that a delay of fifteen days would be necessary before we started—that is, to await the freezing of the river. The next morning it was stormy, and he told us that we could not go; but about nine o'clock he came in and began to rush us off, as if he really intended to send us to Bulun. He put sixty fish in our boat, and made signs for us to hurry up and embark. We did so, and he, with three others, went ahead to pilot us through the mud-flats. Efim was in the boat with us.

We worked up the river for about two hours, constantly getting aground, and, in the teeth of a fresh breeze, were making very slow progress. Before the village was out of sight, however the pilots turned around and waved us back. We up helm and went back to the village, where they had a sled ready to carry Melville back to the house. About four of us secured the boat, but Nicolai insisted on hauling her up, for he made signs that she would be smashed by the young ice if we did not do so. The natives then assisted us, and we hauled her high and dry up on the beach. The condition of the men that day was such that I was not sorry that we had turned back, because they were not up to a fifteen days' journey as represented by the natives. We were then taken to the house of a certain Gabrillo Pashin, where we remained all night.

Next morning Efim and Gabrillo came to me and made signs that they wished me to go with them. They took me to an empty house at the end of the village, where I found some old women engaged in cleaning up. They indicated that they wished us to occupy it; so I had it cleaned out and moved the whole party into it about noon. Melville mustered the party and told them that he and I were afraid that scurvy had appeared among us, that we must keep the house and ourselves very clean, keep cheerful, and we could probably get along very well until proper food arrived. He also told them that I should take charge of everything during his sickness.

The next morning all hands except Jack Cole, the Indian, and myself, were in a very bad condition, and we were the only persons who were able to get wood and water. Wilson was able to hobble about the house and prepare the fish, of which we were given eight per day—four in the morning and four in the evening. Yaphem lived with us; so that made twelve men with four fish, weighing about ten pounds, for breakfast, and the same amount for supper. We had no salt, but we had a little tea left. After a few days the natives gave us some decayed wild geese for a midday meal; they were 'pretty high,' as an Englishman would call them, but we managed to stomach them, for we were capable of eating almost anything. Efim also gave us some goose eggs.

Thus we lived for about a week. Then came an *orasnik,* or native feast-day, during which Efim took some of us out to make calls, when the natives presented us with fifteen other geese of a similar high character as the others. But our party improved in condition day by day; one by one reported himself as fit for duty, and in about a week's time Melville, too, was well enough to reassume charge informally. The natives were generous to us. I am not sure what their resources in fish were at the time; but I know they were not catching too many. One day I hauled the nets with Andruski Burgowansky; we drew seven nets and got only eleven *bulook*—a splendid fish, one of which he gave me as a present. There was a little deer-meat in the village at the time, but we were unable to get any.

One day we were surprised by the arrival of a Russian at the village. I have forgotten to tell you that on the night after we got back the young ice formed on the river, and that sledding commenced in our vicinity about a week later. This Russian was brought to our house, and I acted as interpreter as well as I could. Learning that he lived only nine or ten versts away, I asked him to take me home with him, as I wished to talk with him about our future movements and to learn the best route for getting to Bulun. To this he willingly consented, and at two in the afternoon we drove over to his house. With him and his wife, a Yakut woman, I spent the evening, and here I learned some news from the great world from which we had been so long absent. He told me that the Czar had been assassinated, that the Lena was still in the river, that Sibiriakoff was running some steamboats, and also that Austria and Prussia had been at war. He spoke of Count Bismarck, of Generals Skobeleff and Gourko, and the Turkish war, and of a great many other things besides. His wife presented me with some tobacco, about five pounds of salt, a small bag of rye flour, some sugar, and two bricks of tea. And here let me say that the native women were always very kind, in spite of their ugliness, and I would like to send up a large load of gay calicoes, bandanas, and other fineries for them if I could.

Next morning Kusmah Eremoff—for that was the name of this Russian exile—took me to the door and showed me a fine little reindeer which he had bought for us, and asked if it suited me. I told him it would be very welcome, and so it was immediately slaughtered. We had tea for breakfast, with fish, and fish pâtés which the good woman had made specially for me; and just before I left, Kusmah promised that on the following Sunday he would take me to Bulun with deer-teams. I asked him who else would go, and he said two other Russians. I asked how many Tunguses, and he said there would be none, because they were bad; and on all occasions he tried to indicate that there was something wrong with the Tunguses. I asked him to come over the following Wednesday to consult with Melville, and then I returned home with the provender. Our people were delighted with the change of diet. The deer, when dressed, weighed ninety-three pounds.

On Wednesday, Kusmah came over as he had promised Melville. We took him down to the boat and had it turned over for his inspection. We then retired to an empty house, where Melville, Kusmah, and I had a consultation, Kusmah said he could go to Bulun and return in five days. When asked if he could go quicker with or without me or Melville, he indicated that it made no difference. Melville decided that Kusmah had better go alone. Kusmah acquiesced, but on the following Friday we were surprised to learn that he was going to take Nicolai Shagra with him. I have not mentioned that the second day after our return to the village, Nicolai came to us and wanted a written paper from us, which he promised to forward to Bulun at the earliest opportunity. I wrote a paper in English and French, which Wilson put into Swedish, and Lauderback into German; and all four versions of this document, together with a picture of the ship and a drawing of the American flag, were sewed up in oil-skin and given to Nicolai, who handed them to his wife, and that good woman put them in her cupboard for safe keeping. They were never forwarded. Subsequently, Melville and I prepared despatches for the Minister at St. Petersburg, for the Secretary of the Navy, and for Mr. James Gordon Bennett; but Melville sent nothing by Kusmah.

The day after we arrived it was decided that I should go to Bulun, as I was in the best physical condition and the most available person. For more than two weeks my projected trip was talked about by us and by the men. I was to bring back food and deer sleds for the whole party, and also to take the despatches which we had prepared. After my return from Kusmah's house, however, Melville decided that Kusmah should go alone, and as he promised to be back in five days he decided not to send any despatches by him, but to take them himself. He seemed to think that Kusmah ought to get there and back quicker if he went alone, and was very much disappointed when he learned that Nicolai Shagra went with him.

This man Kusmah was a robber, who had been exiled there and was dependent upon the natives in a great measure. He could not leave his home without official permission; but he took the responsibility in this emergency, and evidently had to have somebody to back him and to assist him as a witness, and he therefore, very naturally, took with him the chief of the natives, though he first proposed to take me. He said that it made no difference in time if one should accompany him.

The next morning I told Melville that before Kusmah left he should be particularly enjoined to spread the news of the two missing boats among the natives everywhere he went, and I said I would like to run over to his house to give him those orders. Melville consented. I went down to Nicolai Shagra's to get a dog team, and while there Spiridon hove in sight with a fine team of nine dogs. I immediately took possession of him and his team, and drove over to Kusmah's house, where I had a long interview, during which I went over the charts with him again. On this occasion he told me positively that Barkin was only fifty versts northeast of his house, and I immediately determined to go there to seek for traces of the missing boats. I went back to Melville and told him what I wanted to do. He did not assent to the proposal at first, but finally agreed. While at Kusmah's I wrote a line to my brother in Washington, and gave it to Kusmah to mail at Bulun. My eye would not permit writing much.

I took my rifle and sleeping bag, put them on Spiridon's sled, and pointed toward his village. He seemed very much astonished, but finally obeyed, and started homeward. On reaching his house I had a consultation with him and Caranie, and tried to get them to consent to take me to Barkin next morning. But they said that the *boos-byral*—that is, posh-ice—would prevent them from going, and that it was impossible to go there at that time of the year. We then had supper, after which I hunted up old Cut-eared Wassili, and he consented to take me to Kahoomah, which Kapucan said was to the northwest of us. If I could not go to Barkin, I was glad at any rate to go to the northwest to search in that quarter and to spread the news.

The next morning Wassili, Kapucan, and I started with

twelve dogs for Kahoomah. We first went down a little river to the southeast, and the young ice broke in many places, letting the dogs and sled into the shallow water. I was surprised at the southeast course, for Kapucan had told me that Kahoomah was to the northwest. After thinking a few moments I concluded that Kahoomah must be the Tunguse name for Kusmah, and that surmise proved to be correct. They took me back to Kusmah's house, where they had another talk, and then agreed to try to take me to Barkin. I set up the compass, and Kusmah pointed to the northeast, saying that Barkin was only fifty versts distant in that direction, but that we would have to go first to the southeast and then swing round to the northward.

We had to wait all night for another sled from our village. It came next morning, and then we started to the southeast. About eleven o'clock we came to a big river running north, and I noticed that old Wassili looked up the stream very anxiously and thoughtfully. I set up the compass, and when the needle came to rest the natives sung out with delight and surprise, 'Tahrahoo,' and pointed toward the south end of the needle. I insisted, however, on going north, but the old man said it was impossible, on account of *boos-byral* or posh-ice. I then decided to let him follow his intentions and see what they were.

About four P. M., after having traveled over a region covered with driftwood, we reached a small hut situated near a bold headland, and the island that they call Tahrahoo was about three miles off shore. They said they would take me there the next morning. At this time another sled hove in sight; it was driven by an old man named Dimitrius, who had been sent after us by Kusmah, with a kettle and a teapot for me. Wassili and I went upon the hill about sunset, and had a good view of the river and the adjacent island. He indicated that the steamer Lena had entered there, and that there might be some signs of boats on the adjacent islands; but I told him that I wanted to go round the headland and to the northward. But both old men insisted that this would be impossible.

The next morning, to satisfy me, they started toward the island, the two old men and myself going in advance, to test the young ice. About a mile off shore the ice was black and treacherous, and so unsafe that the old men refused to go any further. So we had to turn back and return from a fruitless search. It demonstrated, however, that what the natives said was true—that the ice was not strong enough for traveling. The second night we slept at Kusmah's, and then returned to Geemovialocke.

At the end of five days Kusmah had not returned, and it was not until October 29th that he put in an appearance, after an absence of thirteen days. On his way back, at Kumak Surka, he had, however, met with the two men of the captain's party, Noros and Nindermann, who had written a brief statement about the condition of the captain's party. They gave it to Kusmah, and he hastened to bring it to us. He told us that the men were to have reached Bulun the previous day (October 28th); so Melville immediately started with old Wassili and dog teams, to find the men and learn the position of the captain's party and carry food to them. He gave me orders, which he afterward put in writing, to take charge of the party and get it to Bulun as soon as possible.

On November 1st, the Bulun commandant, a Cossack, named Gregory Miketereff Baishoff, came to us with a good supply of bread, deer-meat, and tea. He handed me a long document addressed to the American Minister at St. Petersburg, and signed by Noros and Nindermann. It contained some details of the captain's position, but was not definite enough to allow me to start immediately to their relief. Besides, I knew that Kumak Surka was nearer to Bulun than to us, and that Melville, after seeing the men, could get to the captain much quicker than we could; so I immediately despatched the document to Melville, by special courier James H. Bartlett, fireman, who was the best man of the party at that time. The commandant at the same time had the foresight to appoint a rendezvous at which he and I should meet Melville on his way north. He also sent a letter to a subordinate, ordering him to equip Melville for the journey. This man was a non-commissioned officer of Cossacks, and he acted with great intelligence and good judgment. He was a tall, fine-looking man, with black side whiskers, forty-two years of age.

Bartlett started that night with a deer team, and was likely to get to Bulun only a few hours after Melville, because the latter had taken the dog road, which was 240 versts long, while the deer road was only eighty versts across country. The commandant had come by the deer road, thus missing Melville. I told the commandant that he must get us to Bulun as soon as possible, but he was rather non-committal, and would not state a definite time for starting.

That night I slept uneasily and was awake by four o'clock next morning. Efim was up, and I asked him where he was going. He said that he was going with the commandant to Arrhue, the village where Spiridon and Wassili lived. I told him to tell the commandant to come to me immediately. I thought I would try a high-handed game with this Cossack commandant, and it worked admirably. He came to me about five A. M., in uniform, and I told him that if he did not get us clothed and started by daylight next morning I would report him to General Tchernieff and have him punished; but that if he did well and got us ready he would be handsomely rewarded. He accepted the situation gravely and said 'Karascho,' which meant 'all right.' I invited him to sleep with us the next night; and the next morning, at daylight, fourteen dog teams, with about two hundred dogs, were assembled at our village, and the natives brought us an ample supply of skin clothing. This was Thursday, November 3d.

We started for Bulun, and on Saturday met Melville at Kumak Surka Serai, which is the first deer station. I had a long consultation with him, and he told me that there was no possible hope for the captain's party, but that he and the two natives were going to the spot where Noros and Nindermann had left him, and also to the Arctic Ocean to look for relics. He told me, further, that he had left written orders at Bulun for me to proceed to Yakutsk with the whole party. I will here state that his orders to me were given by virtue of a written order from Lieutenant DeLong which placed him in command of my boat, and all persons embarked in the boat were made subject to Melville's orders and directions. This I knew to be unlawful; but, as the captain was the highest naval authority at the time, I had nothing to do but to obey. And so I had accepted duty under Melville from the time of the separation, because I considered that it was my duty, under the circumstances, to do so.

We arrived at Bulun on Sunday, and the commandant informed me that we must remain until the following Saturday. I found written orders from Melville telling me to proceed to Yakutsk with the whole party as soon as possible, and there await his arrival; but he told me verbally at Kumak Surka Serai to leave Bartlett at Bulun.

As transportation further south could be provided for only six of the party, I took the five weakest men and started for Verkhoyansk, leaving the other six to follow when Melville should return. I left written orders with Bartlett to start a search party out for Melville in case he did not return by November 20th. The resources of Bulun were very limited, it being only a village of about twenty houses; and our presence there made fearful inroads on their winter stock. We traveled by deer sled to Verkhoyansk, a distance of 900 versts. Thence to Yakutsk by means of deer, oxen, and horses, a distance of 960 versts, reaching the latter place December 17th, 1881, where we were well taken care of by General Tchernieff, the governor. About December 30th, Melville arrived at Yakutsk, and soon afterward the other six men came on. On New Year's day the thirteen survivors of the Jeannette were all present at Yakutsk. The most of us were in good condition, but my left eye was completely disabled, and the right one was suffering by sympathy. One man was insane and had to be kept under restraint, and Leach was disabled slightly with frozen feet.

Melville started north from Yakutsk January 27th, taking with him Bartlett and Nindermann—Nindermann because he was one of the men who had last seen the captain, and Bartlett because he had picked up a little Russian and could get along first rate with the natives. Most of the men would have been worse than useless, because they could not have made themselves understood, and would have had to be waited on by the natives.

At Yakutsk, Melville received the first despatch from the Secretary of the Navy, which ordered him to send the sick and frozen to a milder climate. So he ordered me to proceed with the whole party to Irkutsk, and thence to the Atlantic seaboard. At Irkutsk I received despatches from the department ordering me to remain and continue the search, but I was quite unable to do so. After the long excitement of our life in the north my eyes began to trouble me more and more, and having got cold in them during the sledge journey from Yakutsk to Irkutsk, I was compelled to seek professional advice. The two oculists whom I consulted told me that my left eye was ruined, and should be taken out to prevent the right one from being constantly affected; that I should not read or write, and should not leave here until the right eye was in a better condition. The reports of the oculists about my right eye were at first very encouraging, and that was why I proposed to the department to charter the steamer Lena, in order to make a spring search for Chipp. I also asked for two officers to be sent to assist, thinking that if my right eye broke down there would then be somebody here to take my place.

Melville told me every detail of his trip of twenty-three days from Bulun. He says he has traced the captain's party as far as a summer hunting station called Sisteranek, on the west bank of the Lena, and that the party must be somewhere between that station and Bulcour, neither of which places is marked on the ordinary map. They had been two days without food when Noros and Nindermann left them, and the region is devoid of game and inhabitants. The men had insufficient clothing, and there is no reasonable hope.

I think Chipp's boat swamped during the gale, for she nearly did so on a previous occasion, and was a very bad sea boat. If he succeeded in reaching the coast he had less food than the other boats, and his chances of life were therefore worse than the captain's party. If his boat swamped she would probably come to the surface, after the bodies floated out; she had not sufficient weight in her to keep her down. The specific gravity of pemmican is nearly that of water, and we found that some of the canisters, which probably contained air space, would actually float. The sleeping bags, when water soaked, would be the heaviest weight in the boat, and these were probably thrown overboard in the gale. The northeast winds continued two days after the gale, and Chipp's boat may have drifted ashore near the mouth of the Olenek, if not carried to the northeast as the driftwood seems to be—that is, to the New Siberian Islands."

16

CHAPTER XXI.

LIEUTENANT DE LONG'S LOG-BOOK.

DURING the time when Lieutenant Danenhower was relieved from duty as navigator of the Jeannette, on account of his eyes, the log of the ship was kept by the commander of the expedition. Lieutenant DeLong always made his entries with two dates, that is, he did not advance one day on crossing the 180th meridian to east longitude, because he expected to drift back again to west longitude, as he had often done before. He always clung to the idea that he would experience a northeast drift, sooner or later, and re-cross that meridian.

The log-books of the Jeannette were taken to the Siberian coast by Lieutenant DeLong, and were left, with other articles, near the beach when he started south, September 19th. They were recovered by Mr. Melville, November 14th, and Lieutenant Danenhower brought them home. The following are extracts from the log-book, kept by Lieutenant DeLong, commencing with the discovery of Jeannette Island, and continuing to the end; the last entry, Saturday, June 11th, was made with a lead pencil:—

LOG OF THE UNITED STATES ARCTIC STEAMER JEANNETTE, BE-
SET AND DRIFTING IN THE PACK-ICE ABOUT FIVE
HUNDRED MILES NORTH-WEST OF HERALD
ISLAND, ARCTIC OCEAN.

TUESDAY, May 17, 1881.—Latitude by observation at noon, north 76 deg. 43 min. 20 sec.; longitude by chronometer from afternoon observations, east 161 deg. 53 min. 45 sec.; sounded in forty-three fathoms; muddy bottom; a slight drift northwest being indicated by the lead line; weather dull and gloomy in the forenoon; close, bright and pleasant in the afternoon. At seven P. M. land was sighted from aloft by William Dunbar, ice-pilot, and bearing south 78 deg. 45 min. west (magnetic) or north 83 deg. 15 min. west true. It appears to be an island, and such portion of it as is visible is of this shape:—

=S. 78° 45′ W. (mag.)

But owing to fog hanging partly over it and partly to the northward of it no certainty is felt that this is all of it. It is also visible from the deck, but no estimate can be made of its distance.

As no such land is laid down upon any chart in our possession, belief that we have made a discovery is permissible.

This is the first land of any kind seen by the ship since March 24th, 1880, at which date we saw for the last time the north side of "Wrangel Land."

WEDNESDAY, May 18, 1881.—Latitude north 76 deg. 43 min. 38 sec., longitude east 161 deg. 42 min. 30 sec.

The land sighted yesterday remains visible all day, but with greater clearness. We are now able to determine its shape with greater exactness, and it is as below, roughly sketched:—

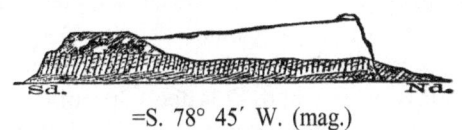

=S. 78° 45′ W. (mag.)

The clouds of yesterday, or fog-bank as then called, having disappeared from the upper part of the island, we are able to see apparent rocky cliffs with a snow-covered slope extending back to the westward from them and terminating in a conical mass like a volcano-top.

THURSDAY, May 19, 1881.—Latitude 76 deg. 44 min. 50 sec. north, longitude 161 deg. 30 min. 45 sec. east.

Crew engaged in digging down through the ice on the port side of the stem in an effort to reach the forefoot. The ice was first bored to a depth of ten feet two inches without getting to the bottom of it; next a hole was dug four feet in depth and from the bottom of this hole a drilling was made to a depth of ten feet two inches; still not reaching the bottom of the ice at fourteen feet two inches; but water now came oozing in to fill up the space dug, and further effort was not made. It is fair to assume that the thickness is of more than one floe, and that the water flows in between the blocks as they lie one above the other.

An opening occurred in the ice about five hundred yards to the eastward of the ship and partially closed at ten P. M., the ship receiving several slight shocks as the edges of the ice came together.

The island remains in plain view all day, and at times, after six P. M., a very strong appearance of higher land beyond and to the westward is seen, seemingly connected by a snowy slope with what we have called an island.

FRIDAY, May 20.—The island remains in plain view all day, though nothing can be seen of the high land beyond, the strong appearance of which is noted in yesterday's log.

The center of the island now bears west (true), but as no observations could be obtained to-day its position and distance cannot be determined by the change of bearing.

SATURDAY, May 21.—Latitude north 76 deg. 52 min. 22 sec., longitude east 161 deg. 7 min. 45 sec. The point of the island which on the 16th inst. bore north 83 deg. 15 min. west (true) to-day bears south 75 deg. 30 min. west (true), from which change of bearing it is computed that the island is now twenty-four and three-fifths miles distant. The position of the observed point is therefore latitude 76 deg. 47 min. 28 sec. north, longitude 159 deg. 20 min. 45 sec.

From measurement made by a sextant it is found that the island as seen to-day subtends an angle of 2 deg. 10 min.

WEDNESDAY, May 25.—Latitude north 77 deg. 16 min. 3 sec., longitude east 159 deg. 33 min. 30 sec.

At eight A. M. the ice was found to have opened in numerous long lanes, some connected and some single, extending generally in north-northwest and south-southeast direction. By making occasional portages boats were able to go several miles from the vessel, but for the ship herself there were no ice-openings of sufficient magnitude.

The strong appearance of land mentioned on the 19th inst. proves to have been land in fact, and for reasons similar to those herein set forth (in the remarks of the 17th inst.) it may be recorded as another discovery. The second land is an island of which the position and present distance are yet to be determined. The following bearings were taken:—

Ship's head, S. 14 deg. W. (true).

Eastern end of island first seen on 17th, S. 17 deg. W. (true).

Nearest end of island seen to-day, S. 69 deg. 30 min. W. (true).

The following sextant angles were taken from the crow's-nest:—

Island first seen subtends an angle of 2 deg. 42 min.

Island first seen has au altitude of 0 deg. 16 min.

Island seen to-day subtends an angle of 3 deg. 35 min.

Island seen to-day has an altitude of 0 deg. 10 min.

Interval between two islands, 49 deg. 55 min.

TUESDAY, May 31.—No observations. Crew engaged in digging a trench round the vessel, and after four P. M. in getting up provisions, etc., in readiness for a sledge party directed to leave the ship to-morrow morning.

WEDNESDAY, June 1.—No observations. At nine A. M. a party consisting of Passed Assistant Engineer G. W. Melville, Mr. William Dunbar, W. F. C. Nindermann (seaman), H. H. Erickson (seaman), J. H. Bartlett (first class fireman), and Walter Sharvell (coal-hearer), started to make an attempt to land upon the island discovered by us on the 25th ult. and which bears southwest half-west (true) at an estimated distance of twelve miles. They carried with them the light dingy, secured upon a sled drawn by fifteen dogs, and provisions for seven days, besides knapsacks and sleeping-bags and arms.

All hands assembled on the ice to witness the departure, and cheers were exchanged as the sled moved off. At six P. M. the traveling party could be seen from aloft at about five miles distant from the ship.

THURSDAY, June 2.—Latitude 77 deg. 16 min. 25 sec. north. During the forenoon the traveling party was in sight from aloft, seemingly more than half way to the island.

SATURDAY, June 4.—Latitude 77 deg. 12 min. 55 sec. north, longitude 158 deg. 11 min. 45 sec. east. From the cracked appearance of the ice around the stern it would seem that the ship is endeavoring to rise from her ice dock. To facilitate her rising and to relieve the strain upon the keel under the propeller the men were engaged forenoon and afternoon in digging away the ice under the counters and in the neighbourhood of the propeller well. The said ice is of flinty hardness and clings so closely to the ship as to show the grain of the wood and to tear out the oakum, visible where the ship's rising has left open spaces.

Bearings of the island toward which the traveling party was sent: South end S. 52 deg. W. (true). North end S. 61 deg. W. (true).

SUNDAY, June 5.—No observations. At eleven A. M. started a fire on the ice ahead of the ship, adding tar and oakum to make a black smoke as a signal of our location to the absent traveling party. At four P. M., the weather being foggy, fired a charge from the brass gun and one from a whale-gun as a similar signal. Carpenters pushed repairs to steam cutter.

MONDAY, June 6.—No observations. At ten A. M. called all hands to muster and read the act for the government of the navy. The commanding officer then inspected the ship. At 1.30 P. M. divine service was read in the cabin. At six A. M. sighted the traveling party making their way back to the ship; sent the starboard watch out to assist them in. At nine A. M. the sled arrived alongside, drawn by the dogs and accompanied by Nindermann, Erickson, and Bartlett. Mr. William Dunbar, ice-pilot, was brought in by this party, having been disabled by snow-blindness. At twenty minutes of ten A. M. Engineer Melville and Walter Sharvell, coal-heaver, with all remaining traveling gear, arrived on board.

The party landed on the island at half-past five P. M. on Friday, June 3d, hoisted our national ensign and took possession of our discoveries in the name of the United States of America.

The island discovered on May 17th has been named and will hereafter be known as Jeannette Island. It is situated in latitude 76 deg. 47 min. north and longitude 158 deg. 56 min. east.

The island discovered on May 25th and landed upon as above stated has been named and will hereafter be known as Henrietta Island. It is situated in latitude 77 deg. 8 min. north and longitude 157 deg. 43 min. east.

TUESDAY, June 7, 1881.—Latitude 77 deg. 11 min. 10 sec. north; longitude, no observations.

In anticipation of our floe breaking up and our being launched into the confusion raging about us, hoisted the steam cutter, brought aboard the kayaks and oomiaks, and removed from the ice such of our belongings as could not be secured at a few moments' notice.

WEDNESDAY, June 8.—No observations. So thick was the fog until 10 A. M. that our position with reference to Henrietta Island could not be determined, but at that hour the fog cleared away, and the island was sighted right ahead and at a distance of about four miles. As indicated yesterday, we were being drifted across the north face.

The large openings near us have closed, and the general appearance of the ice to west and northwest is that of an immense field broken up in many places by the large piles of broken floe-pieces, but, with no water spaces.

Considerable water-sky is visible to the south and southwest, and several unconnected lanes of water are to be seen in those directions. The ice, having passed the obstruction caused by Henrietta Island, has closed up again and resumed its accustomed drift to the northwest.

FRIDAY, June 10.—Latitude N. 77 deg. 14 min. 20 sec., longitude E. 156 deg. 7 min. 30 sec.

The following bearings were taken of Henrietta Island at twenty minutes past five P. M.:

Ship's head S. 13 30 W. true.
S. W. point of island S. 59 24 E.
Second cliff S. 64 30 E.
Blackhead S. 66 30 E.

At eleven P. M. the ship received several severe jars. At half-past eleven the ice, eighty yards to the westward, opened to a width of ten feet, and after several shocks from the ice, the ship was found to have risen an inch forward. At midnight there was considerable motion to our surrounding floe, and strong indications of a breaking up of the ice alongside the ship.

SATURDAY, June 11.—Latitude 77 deg. 13 min. 45 sec. north, longitude 155 deg. 46 min. 30 sec. east.

At ten minutes past 12 A. M. the ice suddenly opened alongside and the ship righted to an even keel. Called all hands at once and brought on the few remaining things on the ice. The ship settled down to her proper bearings nearly, the draught being 8 feet 11 inches forward and 12 feet 5 inches aft. A large block of ice could be seen remaining under the keel. At the first alarm the gate in the watertight bulkhead forward was closed, but the amount of water coming into the ship was found to decrease—a small stream trickling aft being all that could be seen.

There being many large spaces of water near us, and the ice having a generally broken-up appearance, it was concluded to ship the rudder to be ready for an emergency involving the moving of the ship. After some trouble in removing accumulations of ice around the gudgeons, the rudder was shipped, and everything cleared away for making sail.

As well as could be judged by looking down through the water under the counters there was no injury whatever to the afterbody of the ship. As soon as possible a bow line and a quarter line had been got out and the ship secured temporarily to the ice, which remained on the starboard side, as nearly in the same berth as she could be placed. By looking down through the water alongside the stern on the port side one of the iron straps near her forefoot was seen to be sprung off, but otherwise no damage could be detected. It was assumed by me that the heavy ice, which all along bore heavily against the stern, had held the plank ends open on the garboards, and that as soon as the ship was able to move from this heavy ice the wood ends came together again, closing much of the opening and reducing the leak. The water line or rather water level being below the berth deck, no difficulty was anticipated in keeping the ship afloat and navigating her to some port should she ever be liberated from the pack-ice of the Arctic Ocean.

Sounded in thirty-three fathoms, bottom mud, rapid drift to north-northwest.

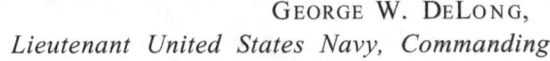

GEORGE W. DELONG,
Lieutenant United States Navy, Commanding.

CHAPTER XXII.

A ROLL OF HONOR.

VERKHOYANSK, situated on the Yana River, eastward from the Lena, is the name of one of the villages which the men of the Jeannette passed through on their circuitous journey from Bulun to Yakutsk, and it is also the name of one of the districts into which the province of Yakutsk is divided. The following are extracts from a translation of the report made by the Ispravnik (chief man) of this district to the Governor of Yakutsk, respecting the arrival and reception of the strangers:—

"By searching for the strangers all the natives have done all they had in their power to do. Mr. Ipatieff (aid to the ispravnik) knew about the natives, and which of them had done more than the others. Those who did the most were named respectively as follows:—The overlooker from Gigansky Uluf, Gregory Baishoff, who took the found strangers to Bulun, showing them the way and giving them all necessary provisions; and Ipatieff had heard from the strangers how much Gregory Baishoff had done for them. Candidate Constantine Mohoploff was the man who took the two saved sailors to Bulun from Bulcour, and accompanied Mr. Melville on all his searching to find the missing members of the expedition and helped Mr. Melville very much. Then the overlooker from Ywo Katurlinsky Nasleg, Wassili Bobrowsky, who brought the eleven strangers who were on Cape Borkai to the Cape Bykoffsky, and who gave them fresh provisions to the people from his own stores. He guided Mr. Melville to Simatsky Nasleg, on the Lena, through the wilderness. Then the two exiles, one of them Kusmah Eremoff, from Gigansky Uluf, and Efim Kopiloff, from Ust-Lena.

These two people were the first to bring all necessary assistance to the saved strangers. Eremoff volunteered to drive to Bulun to give news about the found people.

The man Nicolai Diakonoff, in whose hut, on Cape Bykoffsky, the strangers were living, gave the people bad fish and rotten geese. Then he did not go to Bulun as soon as Mr. Melville told him to go. Through a person who knows the English language has Mr. Melville told the ispravnik about those people who showed the most hospitality to him and his sailors. The first, Kusmah Eremoff. He gave to Mr. Melville all the provisions in his poor house. He went without assistance to Bulun to give information where Mr. Melville and the saved people were living, and that they could not come further because they were so weak.

Another man, Wassili Bobrowsky, has served Mr. Melville as pilot from the mouth of the Lena to the habitation of Nicolai Diakonoff, and has done all, refusing to take anything for his assistance. More than that, he gave to Mr. Melville and his sailors, fishes, sleds and dogs, and was very careful to keep Mr. Melville well and to save him. The third man, Efim Kopiloff, gave all that was necessary without requiring pay for it, and as soon as all the fishes were eaten he gave his geese, whereby he was running the risk of hunger himself in the spring time.

The two Yakuts who found Nindermann and Noros have to be rewarded too. Nindermann and Noros would have been dead from hunger if Ivan Androsoff and Constantine Mohoploff had not found them Constantine Mohoploff was all the time with Mr. Melville, giving him provisions. Mr. Melville said that without his assistance he could not have made the journey from Bulun in twenty-three days when searching for the people. Nicolai Diakonoff ought not to be rewarded, because he did not give the help which he could have done. Of the overlooker from Gigansky Uluf, Baishoff, Mr. Melville says he cannot reward him enough, and wanted to speak himself about him to the general.

I have the honor to explain all that I have written above

to Your Excellency, as well as I have to inform you about five hundred (500) roubles expended in provisions and clothes for the thirteen (13) saved strangers, and will send to you afterward a special account about this. From the missing people we as yet have not any news; but I have ordered all the inhabitants to do all in their power to find all they can, if only the bodies. If they find the bodies they have to be careful to do all they can to keep them, and also anything belonging to the strangers."

A copy of the ispravnik's report having been sent to Lieutenant Danenhower by General Pedoshenko for examination, he returned it with a communication in part as follows:—

"As you have invited my attention to this report and have requested my opinion relative to the merits of the people who helped us, I would respectfully submit the following statements:—

First— The man named Wassili Bobrowsky rendered the most important services. He is known among the natives and by me as Wassili Koolgiak, which means Cut-eared Wassili. This man may be identified by a gunshot wound near the left elbow. The moment we met him we felt safe, for he gave us food and immediately consented to pilot us to Bulun, at the same time measuring how much water the boat required, and thereby showing that he knew what he was about. He took us to Nicolai Diakonoff, whom we un-understood to be his superior. At a subsequent time he brought us fish and took me on a journey to the mouth of the river in search of the two missing boats, and also took Mr. Melville on his journey to Bulun. He was always kind and good to us, and it is not only my opinion but also that of the others that we owe more gratitude to him than to any one else.

Second—The exile Kusmah Eremoff I will recommend as second in the order of merit. He found us accidentally and agreed to take me to his house, where he gave me more than one-half of his small stock of provisions and volunteered to carry me to Bulun on the following Sunday. I

WINTER RESIDENCE OF THE RUSSIAN EXILE.

THE GENEROUS EXILE.   275

told him to come over to us in three days to consult with Mr. Melville. He came, and Mr. Melville decided that Kusmall should go without me. He went to Bulun, and on his way back he met, at Kumak Surka, the two sailors from the captain's party, and brought us the first intelligence of them. Before his first visit the natives gave us scarcely enough food, being only eight fish per day and some decayed geese. He gave us salt, flour, tobacco in small quantities, and also bought a deer, which he gave me on my first visit to carry back to the men. He threatened the natives, and made them bring us more fish than we could eat. He lived only ten versts from us, and said that Nicolai Diakonoff should have informed him of our presence, and he could have taken us to Bulun before the river froze over. Kusmah Eremoff acted boldly and well. He is more or less dependent on the natives, but was not afraid to threaten them, by which he made them give us enough food.

Third—I will call attention to the prompt and intelligent action of the Commandant, Gregory Mikatereff Baishoff, at Bulun. He sent word by Kusmah that he would come to us on a certain day. He arrived at the fixed time and with an ample supply of provisions. He brought with him a long document that had been addressed by the two sailors of the captain's party to the American Minister at St. Petersburg. The two sailors could not make themselves understood, so the commandant brought the paper to us. I immediately despatched it by courier to Mr. Melville, who was then on his way to Bulun. He going by the dog road had missed seeing the commandant, who came by the deer road. The latter had the foresight to send by the same courier a written order to his subordinate to equip Mr. Melville, and also appointed Kumak Surka as a rendezvous.

At all subsequent times the commandant of Bulun provided for us in a very practical and efficient manner, and I do not hesitate to say that he is the most intelligent and best balanced man that I met north of Yakutsk. His position being a very subordinate one, it required great force of character and good judgment in controlling the natives and getting from them everything that we needed without an equivalent. His task was a difficult one, and he did admirably.

Fourth—The two men, Ivan Androsoff and Constantine Mohoploff, are deserving of high reward for the rescue of the two sailors at Bulcour.

Fifth—The exile, Efim Kopiloff, lived in our house and rendered us important services. Before I left the village I had him and all the natives render their accounts of all food furnished. Efim was a very good man, and we, one and all, would be very glad to see him rewarded.

Sixth—In regard to the three fishermen whom we first met, I would state that they attempted to run away because they were afraid of us. We induced the youth, whom we called Tomat, to approach, offered him something to eat, and then the other two approached. They gave us a goose and one fish—all they had at the time. They took us to a hut, where we passed the night. The next morning they would not go with us, but seemed very much agitated and sorry to have us go alone. We could not understand them at the time, but afterward learned they had sent for old Wassili and wanted us to wait. These three fishermen, as well as the assistants of Ivan Androsoff, in my opinion, should be suitably rewarded through their chiefs.

In conclusion I would respectfully state that we received good treatment from the authorities at Verkhoyansk, and that we are especially indebted to Governor-General G. Tchernieff for the kind and fatherly treatment we received at his hands. The moment he was informed of our presence in Siberia he adopted the most prompt and efficient means of relief, and I am safe in saying that we all regard him as our best friend in Siberia."

The whale-boat which carried Melville's party safely to the Delta, was subsequently given to the generous exile, Kusmah Eremoff, for services rendered.

CHAPTER XXIII.

MR. NEWCOMB'S NARRATIVE.

AFTER the final arrangements were completed, our voyage to the frozen North was commenced on Tuesday, July 8th, on which day, at ten minutes past four o'clock P. M., the Jeannette slowly steamed away from San Francisco. The harbor was lively with yachts, tugs, and other craft, many of which accompanied us to the "Gate." The high parts of the city were thick with interested spectators. The fort at the "Gate," made so golden by the beautiful sun, saluted us as we passed. Soon the captain's wife bade us good-bye, and the yacht Frolic left us amid cheers, and we stood out into the broad Pacific.

Our voyage was without interest until nearing the Aleutian Islands. Ougalgan Island was the first to strike my attention. Strange, wild, grand scenery burst upon our gaze as the fog lifted on the afternoon of the 1st of August. We were at anchor, and the boat was sent ashore to look over the island. I was the first man to land, and as I jumped on the rocky beach between the jagged headlands a scene of indescribable beauty surrounded me. Thousands of birds were in the air and screaming discordantly, for I was invading their nesting-place: glaucous-winged gulls, tufted and Arctic puffins, guillemots, auks and murres.

I can never forget the scene. On the right arose great mountains, clad with snow; on the left another mountain, a volcano, was seen, from the top of which a thin stream of blue smoke was slowly curling. Not a vestige of life save the birds and myself. A great upheaval of nature marked these Aleutian Islands. Central Pacific Railroad scenery

278   THE JEANNETTE ARCTIC EXPEDITION.

is nowhere, for these islands combine the picturesqueness of the Alleghanies with the vastness of the Sierra Nevadas. The islands generally are delightfully green. Flowers are found in many varieties. One little kind was much like my own New England buttercup of the meadows dear at home. To the naturalist this is a great field.

GLAUCOUS-WINGED GULLS.

We made Ounalaska on the 2d of August; a lovely locality, with much of interest. We soon left, and after a short trip reached St. Michael's, Alaska. Here we got our dogs and skin clothes and two Indians. Leaving here, we stood across Bering Sea for St. Lawrence Bay, Siberia. Many birds here; among them the lovely Aleutian tern and Sabines gull—both rare.

From this place we started on the evening of August 27th for the North, and entering the Arctic Ocean on the 29th, we anchored at five P. M. off Serdze Kamen. The captain, with Chipp, Collins and Dunbar, took a boat for the shore, but pack-ice prevented their landing.

On the 31st, at Kolyutschin Bay, Mr. Chipp and Mr. Danenhower found traces of Nordenskiöld—pictures, coins, and coat-buttons. I shot a number of herring (Siberian variety of *Argentatus*) and glaucous-winged gulls, and saw numerous seals (the "floe-rats" of Lamont, *Phoca fœtida*). In the afternoon of this day we left for Wrangel Land, through loose ice which floated from one to ten feet out of water.

After some days, on Thursday, September 4th, at six P. M., we sighted Herald Island. Among the creatures seen I enumerate walrus, seals, and bears, and of the birds there were phalaropes in small flocks of six, ten, or twelve. These graceful little creatures were very unsuspicious, swimming quite near and in circles, as is their habit when feeding. They ride very buoyantly in the water, and are so interesting that I could watch them for hours. Then there were murres and guillemots, beautiful kittiwake gulls, some burgomasters (these last very shy), and the lovely ivory gull, in both adult and immature plumage. Its immature white, spotted with black, is very pretty, but the pure whiteness of the adult, with the coal-black feet and legs, makes a very pretty picture. This species, afterward very common, was always very tame.

The men were at this time enjoying themselves with football and skating on the new ice, which was at this time from four to six inches thick. Their skates were made on board for the occasion. Having read and heard much of the ferocious polar bear, I can never forget my feelings as upon one occasion Mr. Collins and I approached two large ones which we discovered. In my journal I find this note:—

"I thought they were going to show fight as they came toward us, then stood defiantly awaiting our approach. Loading our rifles we walked toward them, cocking our pieces, but when within some four hundred yards one of them turned and left. We got about one hundred yards nearer, when the remaining bear turned and started off, shaking his head ominously. We immediately let go a shot each, which made him jump and start off quicker, we in hot pursuit. But he and his companion soon distanced us. At first I thought it was going to be a fight for life between us, but when I saw them turn and run my only sensations were those of disgust and disappointment. I measured the footprints of one of these bears and found them to average 18 inches. This day I saw a raven, the first since leaving Ounalaska; and Mr. Collins saw a hawk, and from his description I think it was the Iceland falcon. This bird, I regret to say, I did not once see during my stay in the Arctic, and my disappointment is great, as I hoped to add further knowledge of its habitat."

The first seal, a young "floe-rat," was shot by one of the Indians, when with Mr. Chipp on his sled trip toward Herald Island. After skinning this seal the Indian cut small pieces off each hind foot to "give good luck; more seal; kill um." Then taking the bladder and gall, he dropped them carefully into the water to "make um more seal."

The first bears killed were taken on the 17th of September by Mr. Chipp and Mr. Dunbar. Mr. Collins photographed them in fine style. On this day I got seven beautiful young gulls. These birds were attracted by the killing of the bears, and as they invariably came from the leeward I believe it was the scent of blood, and not by sight, that they were drawn around. I have seen birds on the Banks of Newfoundland attracted similarly, and always in those cases from leeward.

Among my notes I find the following:—"This morning a singular phenomenon occurred. Seaman Mansen described it as follows:—'This night, or early morning, I went aft to look at the compass; going forward again, I noticed a dull red ball of fire on the port bow. It had an oscillating, horizontal motion. In size it looked as big as the moon when full. It lasted for a few minutes, then suddenly disappeared; caused much surprise and discussion among the sailors and others. Mr. Collins called it an electric gaseous formation.' A similar phenomenon was afterward seen by Seaman Dressler, who said this one exploded. He went out where he thought it had fallen, but failed to find any pieces."

During this time numbers of seal and walrus were seen. One of the Indians and myself got two walrus; both had fine tusks. These creatures were dozing on the edge of the ice and partly in the water close beside each other. They were both mortally hurt with the first bullets. The

WALRUS.

blood spurted out some two feet into the air from each bullet-hole. After the first fire we sprang forward within three feet and fired five more bullets, finishing them. Their combined weight was some 3,600 pounds. The Indian bared one arm, pushed it down the throat of the one he shot, and, pulling it out, wiped the fresh blood on his forehead, after this applying some snow on the place. This, he said, was for "good luck," and "because his father taught it him." Thirty dogs, with a number of the men, dragged my walrus over the ice, some three miles, to the ship.

Snowshoe-traveling on the ice became quite the rage about November 10th, and many were the tumbles got by all. Our snow-shoes were those used by the natives about Norton Sound and upon the Yukon. By the 14th of October, the observatory being put up, telephone communication with the ship, distant some one hundred yards, was established.

One day soon after this I got two small gulls. They came along near a lead where I was sitting, and when within range I fired, tumbling one down into the water; the other turned and I got it. They proved to be Ross' gulls (*Rodostistua rosea*), an exceedingly rare species, very buoyant and graceful on the wing, beautiful pearl-blue on the backs, vermilion feet and legs, and lovely tea-rose on the breasts and under parts; the rosy tint being scarcely a color, yet blending in exquisite harmony with the pearl-blue of the upper parts. They were in full feather. I afterward got three more in adult and immature plumage. This species is the loveliest I ever saw. I saw more birds, seals, and walrus this first autumn than at any subsequent time. Of course, I except our stay at Bennett Island, where there were thousands of murres, guillemots, and gulls breeding.

During the last of October and in November light snow fell at intervals, and as it packed hard improved the walking; also on newly-made ice, after the rime had formed, traveling was very pleasant. I made frequent excursions over the ice in quest of specimens, and though the birds were leaving, I gathered much of interest. The ice this first fall jammed and smashed a good deal. My notes of November 7th state:—

"Ice is in motion as yesterday, cracking fearfully. The pressure is very great. Great pieces are pushed about like toys. The floe upheaves and gives way in a manner one would believe impossible. The ship is all right now, but for how long no one knows. Have gun and knapsack ready to leave at a moment's notice for—God knows where."

Some beautiful solar halos were seen about this time, and the aurora was very fine. "To-night, November 10th, the finest I ever saw. Six arches intersected by cirrus clouds near the horizon and extended from west-northwest to east, covering almost half the heavens. Through this the stars were twinkling beautifully. Wonderfully grand! Some perpendicular rays near horizon, the whole display full of majestic power. With the booming and cracking of the ice, it formed an incident to be remembered. One could almost feel the electricity. Lights required twenty-four hours through. Soon the sun will leave us."

ICE PRESSURE.

On the night of November 13th a sound was heard as if of ice relaxing its pressure. A look outside showed an opening on our port, forming an extensive and increasing lead, with quite a current. All hands turned out and stood by for a call. The ship was in a peculiar position—open water over the rail port side and gang-plank out on the starboard. She was supposed to be held by a tongue of ice under her, forward.

Herald Island and Wrangel Land were both in sight at this time. In two days the young ice on our port was strong enough to walk on,—so we were held at times, getting heavily nipped, until the morning of November 24th, when we broke away from one floe-piece and drifted in a perilous manner. One heavy "nip" on the Jeannette, listing her to nine degrees, made her creak and groan like some leviathan in death agonies; weather thick; no land visible. In the evening, the ice being quiet, we got some tea. A general feeling of thankfulness was apparent on the faces of all. The only perceptible effects of this severe handling were about the joiner-work and a hole stove in the bulwarks on the port side. During these heavy nips and scenes of commotion the dogs, some forty in number, often broke out in choruses of howls most unearthly.

On Christmas Day all hands, fore and aft, enjoyed a good dinner, with a bill of fare for the cabin mess. The men came aft dressed for the occasion. They offered seasonable greetings, and then returned to the "deck house," where an impromptu entertainment of singing, dancing, and so on was given, and enjoyed by all.

New Year's Day was a pleasant one, being ushered in by the ringing of the ship's bell and cheers. In the evening a nice entertainment was given by the men. A programme of the dinner, which I have saved, reads thus:—

SOUP.
Julienne.
FISH.
Spiced salmon.
MEATS.
Arctic turkey (roast seal). Cold ham.
VEGETABLES.
Canned green peas. Succotash.
Macaroni, with cheese and tomatoes.
DESSERT.
English canned plum pudding, with cold sauce.
Mince pie.
Muscat dates, figs, almonds, filberts, English walnuts, raisins, mixed candy from France direct by the ship.

NEW-YEAR'S FESTIVITIES.

WINES.
Pale sherry.
BEER.
London stout.
French chocolate and coffee.
"Hard tack."
Cigars.
ARCTIC STEAMER JEANNETTE, Dec. 25, 1879.
Beset in the pack, 72 degrees north latitude.

The programme of the entertainment was as follows:—

THE CELEBRATED JEANNETTE MINSTRELS.
PROGRAMME.
PART FIRST.

Overture	by	Orchestra
Ella Ree	by	Mr. Sweetman
Shoo Fly	by	H. Wilson
Kitty Wells	by	Edward Star
Mignonette	by	H. Warren
Finale	by	Company

Intermission.

PART SECOND.

The world-renowned Anequin, of the Great Northwest, in his original comicalities.
The great Dressler in his favorite accordion solo.
Mr. John Cole, our favorite clog and jig dancer.
Wilson as the great Captain Schmidt, of the Dutch Hussars.
Violin solo by George Kuehne, Ole Bull's great rival.
Intermission.

PART THIRD

concludes the performance with the side-splitting farce of

MONEY MAKES THE MARE GO.
Characters.

Mr. Keen Sage	George W. Boyd
Miss Keen Sage	W. Sharvell
Charles Tilden (a promising young man, in love with Miss Sage)	H. W. Leach
Julius Goodasgold	H. D. Warren

Costumer, A. Gortz.
Property Man, W. Nindermann.

NEW YEAR'S, 1881.

Thus opened the year, soon to prove eventful. The number of birds shot by all hands during 1879 was 215; many more might have been taken, but, like Josh Billings' crow, we did not "hanker arter" them, nor had we learned to value them for fresh food, as was afterward the case. Our first season for collecting was short; still we could enumerate specimens ornithological, botanical, ethnological, osteological and alcoholic, which looked well as a nucleus. As the days began to lengthen the cold began to strengthen. Our coldest weather for this year was in February, when the spirit thermometer indicated—57.8 Fahrenheit. Very little wind, as a rule, with these low temperatures.

One day, soon after New Year's, I was out walking with one of the Indians. Noticing the new moon, he stopped, faced it, and blowing out his breath he spoke to it, invoking success in hunting. The moon, he said, was the "Tyune," or ruler of deer, bears, seals, and walrus. The Indian told me this particular manner of invoking good-will was a secret handed down to him by his father, who got it from a very old Indian for a wolf-skin.

The Jeannette was under pressure off and on all winter, and on the 19th of January, in consequence of a crack which made right under her forefoot, she sprung a leak. "The men are at the pumps constantly night and day. I took a spell myself. The ship at this time, by estimate of the carpenter, is leaking between 2,500 and 3,000 strokes per hour. Unless the pressure ceases it is only a question of time how soon we have to abandon the Jeannette. The Siberian coast is some two hundred miles south by compass. A long, tough journey; but a will to work has helped many a man through a tight place, and, I trust, will yet help us. The quivering of the ship indicates the pressure yet upon her."

On the 21st a steam-pump was rigged forward. "This greatly relieves the men, who are working splendidly." From the date of this accident until her being crushed—a period of some eighteen months—pumping was kept up night and day. "Yesterday evening (January 20th) one of the Indians made an offering of some tobacco to the moon for the safety of the ship." The effects of the cold at this time when out on the ice was to freeze the moccasin soles and mittens while on feet and hands. Nose-guards were worn by many. After walking perhaps an hour or so, a feeling as of lump in the stomach from indigestion would be experienced." Under date of January 24th I wrote: "Ice now about ship is bulged and pushed under her from ten to eighteen feet thick in accumulative masses." For the 25th I find: "The sun was seen to-day for a brief period after an absence of seventy-one days. Wrangel Land is visible."

As an illustration showing the danger always attendant upon going any distance from the ship I quote: "February 16th.—Off with one of the Indians to the northwest; some twelve miles; found only old tracks of bears. When about half a mile from the ship, on our way back, we found that where we walked over solid ice in going out there was now a lead or lane of water some forty feet in width. This looked serious, as it was in old heavy ice and increasing.

"After taking a smoke we struck off east some three-quarters of a mile, where we found it much narrower, and succeeded in jumping from piece to piece, and thus crossing safely to the floe in which the Jeannette was fast, soon reaching the vessel, and very glad to get out of an awkward situation." Lest some reader may think the above sensational, I would say that the wind, though light, was against us, daylight short, the water widening, and a temperature —45 degrees Fahrenheit. The exception to the rule occurred next day when, at a temperature of—33 degrees Fahrenheit, a gale of wind sprang up, blowing some forty-five miles per hour in squalls, with thick, blinding snow which one could not face.

On the morning of February 1st, one of the Indians shot a fine white fox; we were some fifty miles northwest of Herald Island, and nearly as much from Wrangel Land at the time. This animal is decidedly a rover. On the morning of the 2d a large bear made us a visit, walking up the gang-plank with evident intentions of coming on board. The dogs had come in ahead of him and were huddled together on deck, barking furiously. Bruin paid for his temerity with his life, for Mr. Dunbar came out with his rifle and soon dispatched him. Though we received other numerous visits from these huge creatures, none were so bold as he. They would commonly make off at sight, though when cornered showed fight at the dogs.

On the 22d of February the ship was dressed with bunting and presented a very gay appearance. American ensigns at the fore and main, and the American yachting ensign at the mizzen. Our soundings at this season averaged about thirty-three fathoms, with a mud bottom. "The returning light shows the effect of its absence in the bleached appearance of all. I notice the cold renders the finger-nails brittle. Measurements beside a recent crack show the floe to be about ten feet in thickness. This is ice made this winter." A series of measurements taken after this made the average thickness eight feet.

Among the peculiarities of some of the walrus which I saw, I would mention the difference in size and length of the tusks,—the left tusk being the longest, the upper teeth much more worn than the lower, and in one skull a singular one-sided development of lower jaw. I believe it has been considered doubtful if the walrus is carnivorous. Without attempting any discussion I would say, I have taken pieces of skin with hair attached from the stomach of one shot by the Indian Alexai. This skin was from a young bearded seal (*Phoca barbata*). Four bears were the most seen together. During the month of April I took a small sparrow and a small bird (*Budytes flava*), stragglers from shore. May 1st saw the first gull—a kittiwake. It was rather distant. During the first part of this month I shot some murres (*U. Brunnichii*) and guillemots (*U. grylle*), and saw others. "All the birds go west. I think there must be land in that direction where they go to nest."

By the middle of May one could at midnight see to read in the cabin without lamp or candle. More bears were taken this spring than at any other time. I got a fine old fellow with a beautiful coat. On the 1st of June dredging was begun. This day's haul contained some asterias, and one small bivalve. Though the number of birds daily increases they are not yet plenty. The seals are now beginning to sun themselves on the ice, but they are very shy. The ice now

MORE FRESH MEAT.

wastes perceptibly every day. Under date of June 20th I find written: "To-day I collected nine mosquitoes." These were the first entomological specimens collected after we entered the Arctic Circle, though subsequently I got one fly and a spider. During June and July I took Ross', ivory and kittiwake gulls, jagers, murres, guillemots and phalaropes.

On the Fourth of July, 1880, the ship was again dressed with flags. In June we had some brief showers, and also in July and August. In June the dogs at times sought the shade of the ship to sleep. Some beautiful asterias were obtained by the dredge this month. I have saved sketches and notes for future study. On July 25th a bearded seal was shot by the Indian Anequin. This, the only one taken, was a fine specimen. The skin made excellent soles for our moccasins, and the meat was quite eatable. The stomach contained worms, which were very much like the *ascaris lumbricoides* of man. On the last day of the month Mr. Collins added a fine jager, species *Buffonii,* to the collection.

On the afternoon of August 3d a smoky haze with a strong smoky smell was very apparent. Its cause I must leave the reader to conjecture. In August, Mr. Chipp shot two sandpipers (*A. maculata*); these proved an interesting addition to our collection. Fish were never plenty, but a small species of cod (*G. gracillis*), some six inches long, was frequently seen during the brief summer season.

During this month I often noticed patches of snow sometimes blood-red, at other times nearer a brown; and, by viewing these deposits from different points, one could readily see exquisite shades of blue, green, purple, and crimson. These deposits were nearly always on old floe. I had not the chance to study it which I desired, but I think it was algæ, the same as or allied with *Pamella nivalis.*

During the first part of September a small flight of phalaropes (*P. fulicarius*) occurred. They seldom stopped, but moved in small flocks of six or eight in a general direction from northeast to southwest. In consequence of the wasting away of the ice, particularly where cracks had been, lanes of water were formed. The lanes connected with the ocean by holes, but were on the average only three feet deep, with the ice between this water and the ocean proper. I often paddled a kayak about these lanes, sometimes several miles, taking the gun with me. Surface ponds, in extent sometimes of several acres, also formed; to paddle about these was quite enjoyable; then, too, the possibility of picking up a specimen added to the interest. Though ice had formed over pond-holes, it was not strong enough to bear a man until about September 6th. Among the things found on the ice this season were pieces of wood and parts of trees, both birch and fir, and parts of two skeletons of good-sized codfish. These last evidently had been caught much farther south by seals, and drifted on the ice up to the latitudes where they were found.

Throughout the summer much of the time the men were hunting, and thus we had seal at least once a week for dinner—sometimes eatable, often not, but best when roasted and eaten cold. Both bear and seal, in the absence of other fresh meat, will pass, but are not very desirable. None of the bears taken by us came up to the weights I have seen mentioned by other Arctic voyagers. The heaviest one obtained by us weighed as shot $943\tfrac{1}{2}$ pounds, and was a fat one. In measurements they were about the same.

CHAPTER XXIV.

MR. NEWCOMB'S NARRATIVE.
(CONTINUED).

DURING the summer of 1880 the ice had been comparatively quiet, but by October it was grinding, smashing, and piling up in many places in a manner fatal to any ship caught by it. The mercury fell to—45 degrees by the middle of this month, and the snow would give a metallic ring at each footfall, loud enough to interfere with ordinary conversation. Standing near some of these conflicts between grinding floes, one first would realize the pressure by

CONFLICT OF THE FLOES.

the humming, buzzing sound; then a pulsation is felt. Something must give. Bang goes the ice right under foot, with a report like a big gun. Although you are watching, it startles you. It upheaves, lifts you with it, and you must step back to a safer place. I have often taken these rides. There is a wonderful fascination about it.

On November 10th the sun was seen by refraction; on the 11th it left us. The temperature this month varied a good deal, falling to—33° the first week and rising the last of the month to +8°. Whenever the ice opened the temperature would rise by reason of the amount of heat liberated. The lowest temperatures were during clear weather. Several meteors were observed this month. These were of much interest to Mr. Collins, and were he with us he would have something to say about them in his usual entertaining manner. Appetites and sleep were not so good this second winter. During December the ship was shaken up off and on, and much heavy jamming of ice occurred.

On Christmas Eve the men gave another very nice entertainment in the deck-house, buttonhole bouquets and all. These bouquets (I have nine of them before me as I write) were made of pink and green paper, and handed us by Seaman Johnson with one of his pleasant smiles. Poor fellow, he is now missing! A good man and a tiptop seaman. Of those who on that night contributed for our amusement nine are among the missing. I append a programme of the entertainment:—

JEANNETTE'S MINSTREL TROUPE.

PROGRAMME.

PART FIRST.

Overture	Company
The Slave	Mr. Sweetman
Nelly Gray	H. Wilson
What Should Make You Sad?	G. W. Boyd
The Spanish Cavalier	E. Star
Our Boys	H. Warren

PART SECOND.

The great "Ah Sam" and "Tong Sing" in their wonderful tragic performances.
Accordeon solo by the celebrated artist Herr Dressler.
Mr. Henry Wilson
in his serio-comic songs.
Alexai and Anequin still on the *rôle*.

Violin Solo	G. Kuehne
Magic Lantern Views	Mr. Sweetman

FAC-SIMILE OF THE LAST JEANNETTE ENTERTAINMENT PROGRAMME.

Jeannette Minstrels Theatre
S.W. Corner of the galley and the Bowery where the Star once in a lifetime of Wrangell Land comes may be seen every night

New Years Night 1881
— Programme —

The Jeannette Minstrels by the Company
written by one ourselves

Prologue — — — — — — — — Boyd
Song — Cries of trouble in Peasant Costumes — H Warren
Song — — — — — — — — — A Seaman
Characters etc — by the Indians Anegnen and Alexai

— Intermission —

Overture — — — — — — — In the orchestra
Song — — Poor and broken down — — — — Boyd
Jig — — — by the Gentlemen — — — Mr Cole
Song — "in costume Champagne Charlie" — — — Wilson

Tableaut.

Watching a dead marine; Neptune; Vulcan; throwing mercury. The planet Mars, Jacking an observation; Signalling made; pilot; Is that a Bear I see!; Playing for high stake; Beau Jocko; Chinese characters & ditches in costume, Singing & acting by the Cork & Steward

Kithing on the Violin, Selection from Daughter of the Regiment.

To conclude with the Screaming Farce
The Irish Schoolmaster

School master	Characters	– – – –	Jack Bartlett
Head pupils	– – – –	– – – –	H. Warren
	Leader of Orchestra		
	G. Ritchie and E. Starr		

Performance to commence at 8.30 P.M.
Sledges may be ordered at 10 P.M.
Tickets at the popular price of 000

N.B. The best of Liquors (Adams' also) may be had at Lee's Distillery, within a few steps of the Theatre.

To conclude with the popular play,
"THE SIAMESE TWINS."
Characters.

Professor	G. W. Boyd
Agent (in love with the Professor's daughter)	H. W. Leach
Professor's Daughter	W. Sharvell
The Twins	P. E. Johnson and H. Warren

FINALE.
"The Star Spangled Banner."
Given by all hands.

CHRISTMAS EVE, 1880.

Friday evening, December 31st, another and the last entertainment was given by the boys forward. One of the original programmes is subjoined. [See fac-simile.] Before the fun commenced a poem by Mr. Collins, which he had written for the occasion, was recited. It will now be read with a melancholy interest:—

A PROLOGUE.

On the lone icebound sea we gather here
To greet the dawning of another year.
The past is full of memories: we recall
   Thoughts, words and deeds, bright forms and faces,
  Hopes, blessings, yea, and loved ones' fond embraces;
And parting prayers, up offered for us all,
By lips from hearts to each of us endear'd,
To guard us on the course we've northward steer'd.

Now though for merriment we all unite
And make the deck-house ring with joy to-night,
At intermission, 'twixt the dance and song,
  How quickly our fleet thoughts will wing
  To distant lands and scenes, to bring
A mystic spell upon each darling throng
Of festive friends, who wondering ask each other,
"How fares our absent one—son, husband, brother?"

And dearer hearts, that beat with tenderest throb,
E'en now may yearn for us, and many a sob
May echo in a loneliness as drear as ours;
  For where stern fate the golden link hath riven,
  And hearts from hearts beloved afar are driven,
A common cloud o'er all the parted lowers;

A PROLOGUE.

As if a pitying heaven would so decree
That parted souls should feel in unity.

   *   *   *   *

But while we thus may sentimentalize
In manner p'raps the opposite of wise,
Mirth will demand the passing moments, too.
 And though our efforts here may fail to reach
 The heights of comedy, yet will they teach
Our audience that the bound Jeannette's good crew,
For Arctic dangers and the floe's worst jam
Don't care a single continental damn.

Some one remarks, "We have no coal for steaming:"
Why, no, but surely, if I am not dreaming,
I see quite near me—a small pile, 'tis true,
 But, gentlemen, no better Cole,* 'tis said
 E'er came aboard. What's more than this, he's red—
Ready, I mean, to do his duty, too;
And though his weight is heavy round New York,
In earlier days 'twas found not far from Cork.

And not since Adam sinn'd e'er lived a man
Who lov'd the Arctic like our Nindermann.†
Who can be found among our crew that ran a
 Risk on the ice like his, as sou'westward floating
 Upon the floe piece—most unpleasant boating?
But I suspect a buxom squaw named Hannah
Was very much the reason, if not cause,
Why William so admires the Esquimaux.

Again regretting that the much lov'd sex
Can't grace our festival, or light our decks
With eyes far brighter than the night queen's lanterns,—
 We're not so badly off, though, as you think,
 For Fortune, that our spirits might not sink,
Has sent a substitute along, and Sweetman turns
Up in our midst, his jolly visage beaming
With smiles and lips whence pleasantry is streaming.

Here, too, you'll find among us, as you see,
The stalwart, bold machinist man called Lee,
Whose hand is ready, like magician's wand,
 To turn an engine shaft or shape a pin,
 Or put a piece upon a pot of tin.

---

*Jack Cole, the Irish boatswain.
†Nindermann was with Tyson on the great 1,500 mile drift when separated from the Polaris.

No better hand e'er crossed the herring pond
Since Tubal Cain first hammered into form
Iron, for use in battle or in storm.

Now also mark that individual there,
Whose father must have been a Bartlett *père*.
Sweetness alone could such a youth produce.
   Come, don't be modest, lift your head up higher, man;
   Every one knows that you're our first class fireman,
Who puts his leisure to the best of use,
By thinking out full many a thing, worth mention
If I was talking up the history of invention.

And now, my friends, I think not much you'll marvel
If I refer to Lauderback and Sharvell—
Two youths who in the fire-room's gloomy deep,
   At temperature too high for e'en lost souls,
   Keep feeding hungry furnaces with coals,
And faithfully their six hours' vigil keep.
Perhaps they cheat old Time, and—this between us—
Tell to each other stories about Venus.

Ah, yes, my introduction would be void
Of interest if I had forgotten Boyd,
The youngest of our number, on whose head
   The weight of years, and all the sad belongings
   Of hopes expired and unrequited belongings
Have never pressed down heavier than lead.
To him is given the future with its bubbles,
Its sad successes and its merry troubles.

"All hands on deck!" pipes up my boatswain's whistle,
And I sincerely trust, my friends, that this'll
Be for our sailor lads the only call
   To summon them to duties hard and serious
   Before we leave this region most mysterious,
To face the rolling sea and treacherous squall
I've noticed often that when making sail,
Our boys care little for a breeze or gale.

There's Erickson, as tough as well-tanned leather,
Worth any common three men rolled together;
And Wilson, too, a very blithesome fellow,
   Who handles rope or rifle like a sailor,
   And needle like a first-class Broadway tailor.
Then, with a voice at once low, sweet and mellow,
Comes one—with boat or iron bar a wrestler;
Cooks for our mess in style—we call him Dressler.

A PROLOGUE.

I think that, too, I see, and not so far
Off either, quite a brilliant looking Star;
And what I say is really most surprising,
    He never seems to set; so keep your eyes on
    The Star that never sinks below horizon—
Indeed, he looks to me as always rising.
I'm dazzled also and my pulse is dancing
From studying up that jolly fellow, Mansen.

Mansen, you know, was once caught in a queer snap
By stepping unawares into a bear-trap;
But accidents like this will sometimes ruffle
    Even the most smoothly-running stream of life,
    Just like a little quarrel with one's wife;
And whether stuff of deerskin or of duffel
The moral points—if e'er you get your pants in
A trap don't have you're legs in it, like Mansen.

Now, here's another of us. If you want a tune he
Can play it like an artist; call on Kuehne.
Or if life's tension you would be relaxin'
    We can supply without the least delay—
    By giving us a fortnight's notice, any way—
Amusement really that's worth the axin'.
All this may seem to you a stupid riddle,
But not so puzzling as to learn the fiddle.

If Adam and his mate had had but one son
'Tis certain they d have named the youngster Johnson.
And he'd have died some forty centuries back,
    Being then, on that account, to us no use.
    We have, however, from the land of spruce
And Norway pine, a dapper little Jack,
To help us in our work, to haul and steer
And celebrate with us the good New Year.

If we could only tell what is before us
How well we'd know the fortune stored for Noros,
Who, like Chief Justice of the Common Pleas,
    Looks calmly at all dangers of the ocean.
    But I've thought sometimes—have, in fact, a notion
That Noros, when he looks so much at ease,
Is in reality but calmly thinking
About the girls at home—now stop your winking.

What would we do if Destiny most dire
Had robbed us of a man we all admire,
And sent us cruising round this icy place

Without companionship of our friend Nelse?
Or sent along with us, well—some one else?
We ne'er had known stout Iverson's bluff face—
A man above most others; you can put your
Last dollar on him as an Arctic butcher.

Another thought—it's contemplation hurts,
What would we do, boys, if we hadn't Gortz?
Our drink would lose all taste, our meat all relish;
   Our laughter would be silent, and our bones
   Would give occasion for a thousand groans;
In fact, the situation would be hellish.
But luck stood by us; Gortz is here, and willing
Even to fetch water up when Lee's distilling.

And now before I lose all power of speech,
Oh let me say a little about Leach,
Whose very smile would make sour apples mellow,
   And raise sweet blossoms on a topsail yard;
   But ah, kind friends, keep still, be on your guard.
A giant form I see—who is that fellow?
Gracious! I thought it was some monster foreign,
But really 'tis our messmate, gallant Warren.

Before belaying, just a look to leeward
Reveals the constellation, cook and steward;
And yet another peep along our decks. See!
   That's very like a face I've seen elsewhere,—
   Yes, at St. Michael's, when we anchored there.
That is our hunter, which his name's Alexai,
And with him, like a lady loved by many,
Is our young sylph-like friend, Queen Annie.*

On the 5th of February the sun was seen, and a most cheering appearance it had. About this time our drift northwest was rapid. The snow had drifted about the ship so much that fifty or sixty yards away but little more than the boat's smoke-stack and spars were to be seen. In my notes I find these items: "Our floe has been much reduced by recent cracks. It looks as if the Jeannette was in her last dock. Some people have said to me there is little danger in the Arctic. They were evidently not posted. A ship in the pack is 'under fire' all the time."

---

* Queen Annie was the nickname for Anequin, the Indian hunter.

THE JEANNETTE.

During the early spring of 1881 nothing especial occurred. The first bird (*U. grylle*) was seen April 6th, and more birds were seen this April than during the corresponding month of last year. Among them were no new species.

The Arctic is very shoal in these parts. From the 21st to the 23d of this month we shoaled our water 21 fathoms, giving but 18 or 20 fathoms where we had been getting 35 to 40. This was the most sudden shoaling we ever experienced.

A VISION OF HOME.

I suppose the reader will smile if I say that many a delightful repast I sat down to in my dreams. Such, however, was the case, and the most provoking part was to wake up finding it only a dream. Visions of pie—pumpkin pie, the particular weakness of a New England Yankee—always occupied an aggravatingly prominent place. Life under such circumstances as ours was well calculated to make a person sleep with "one eye and an ear open."

On the 16th of May, 1881, about seven P. M., seaman Erickson came in the cabin and reported to the captain, saying: "Captain, Mr. Chipp reports land in sight on the starboard beam." This news made us all glad. Notwithstanding the proximity of land would probably cause the floe to crack more dangerously, I could not overcome the sense of security which the sight caused me to feel. This land bore N. 83 deg. 15 min. W. (true) from the ship. Our position at the time was 76 deg. 43 min. N., and 161 deg. 54 min. E. On the 18th, I could see the land from the floe-level. Previous to this I had seen it only from aloft. This land was afterward named Jeannette Island. As illustrating the rapidity of our drift at this time, I mention the bearing of this island from the ship on the 20th. It was S. 78 deg. 30 min. W. It was much more plainly seen this day than before. This island was not landed upon.

On the 24th more land was seen. This afterward was named Henrietta Island. Both islands were in sight this evening. On the morning of May 31st, a party, consisting of Mr. Melville, Mr. Dunbar, with Bartlett, Nindermann, Erickson and Sharvell, left for the last new land. I was to go, but, being taken suddenly ill, was unable to do so. This illness was caused by eating canned tomatoes—probably lead poisoning. A number of the crew were similarly affected. Mr. Chipp was thus troubled when the island party left the ship. This party took with them a sled and fifteen dogs, with boat, tent, rifles and provisions. They had a hard time getting to the shore.

The party returned on the 4th of June, having landed, planted the Stars and Stripes, and taken possession. Three points were named. The first, Bennett Headlands, are bold and rocky. They form very secure nesting-places for multitudes of guillemots and murres. A number of guillemots (*U. grylle*) were shot by Sharvell, and Bartlett saw numbers of eggs, but in inaccessible places. The next place was Cape Melville, so named by the men. Between Bennett Headlands and Cape Melville was Point Dunbar. Near here a cairn was built, and some papers, suitably enclosed, buried beneath.

This island is from 2,500 to 3,000 feet high, barren and rocky, with one large and some smaller glaciers on the northern and eastern sides. The jacket of snow and ice spread over the high parts was from fifty to one hundred and fifty feet in thickness. Botanical specimens embrace two little mosses, two pretty lichens, and one of grass. Cape Melville is 1,200 feet high. Soundings off here were had in eighteen fathoms, with bold water. Point Dunbar is 600 feet in height. The ice near the land passes northwest, in heavy motion all the time.

The number of guillemots about at this time was much increased. These birds often circled about the ship with evident curiosity. On the morning the sled party left for the island I got a fine adult-plumaged snow-bunting (*P . nivalis*). I had seen this species before, but this was the first one taken. Every day, while near Henrietta Island, I noticed the guillemots going off in the morning toward the northeast, apparently to feed, and returning in the evening. This I afterward found to be the case, as the stomachs of all those I shot were full of food, crustaceans, and recognizable parts of small fish like *G. gracilis*. I afterward saw this bird (*U. grylle*) dive, and come up with a live fish of this species in its beak. It proceeded to kill the fish by beating it on the water and shaking it. I did not see it swallow the fish, as, becoming suddenly frightened, the bird flew away.

Soon after the return of the island party the ice about the ship cracked in a lively manner, and on the 9th she was afloat. In consequence of the open water about and the proximity of land, the shooting improved, and I at times got very good sport. The fresh food thus obtained was very desirable. On the 11th the ice was comparatively quiet. The ship lay alongside the floe with ice-anchors out.

On the 12th the ice came together, the ship was heavily nipped, and careened to 16 degrees; but the pressure relaxing, she righted again. All hands were on the alert for duty. Between five and six P. M. the pressure was heavy, raising the ship by the bow and settling her by the stern. She again heeled to starboard, and the ship showed the pressure, groaning and shaking in the ice-king's grasp. The humming sound throughout the vessel, with the cracking of deck seams and the dancing of the whole upper works, was a sad evidence of the situation. I can never forget the manner in which the gang ladders leading to the bridge jumped from their chucks, and danced on the deck like drumsticks on the head of a drum. In the midst of this wild scene a crash was heard. A man came up from below and said:—

"The ice is coming through the coal bunkers."

The old Jeannette was doomed. She had fought a good fight, as her battered sides showed, but this last hug was too much for her. After the smash, no sound save the silent rush of water. This silence, after the unearthly humming, was the saddest part of all. She had been stabbed in her vitals and was settling fast. The men worked with a will; everybody did; life hung in the balance. Seaman Star, noble fellow, stood below with the water up to his waist, passing out provisions until ordered out by the captain. To-day I know not where he is. The Jeannette contained many such men in her crew. Good seamen all. But 'silence and oblivion, like the waves, have rolled over them, and none can tell the story of their end.'

After getting boats and provisions on the ice, about midnight, camp was pitched, a watch set and the tired party turned in, soon to be turned out again by the opening of the ice under the sleepers in the captain's tent. All hands helped shift to a safer place, and about 1.30 A. M., June 12th, turned in again. At this time the Jeannette was heeled over, so the yard-arms were against the ice and starboard rail under water. 'About twenty minutes before the watch from our tent was called, I heard a noise which must have been the ship as she went down. I looked out soon after and she was gone, her requiem being the melancholy howl of a single dog. Only a few floating articles marked the place. Insignificant as the Jeannette was in comparison to the ice, her disappearance made a great change in the scene. During her existence there was always something animated to turn to and look at, but now all is a dreary blank.' I have seen far heavier grinding than that which crushed the Jeannette, but the ship is not yet built that can stand such hugging.

CHAPTER XXV.

MR. NEWCOMB'S NARRATIVE.
(CONTINUED).

NEXT morning our camp presented the appearance of a family who had broken up housekeeping in a hurry, as in fact we had. But excellent spirits prevailed. One of the sailors handed some stuffed decoys of mine to the cook for the captain's party. He commenced plucking the feathers before finding out the joke.

Our life for the next week was spent in getting ready for our retreat. Much of the time was spent in sewing, and some droll looking but very sensible costumes were completed. Our tents were numbered, and over the door of ours was the word 'Welcome.' The boats and provision sleds were named. The first cutter was named the Jeannette, and bore a beautiful silk ensign. The second cutter, Mr. Chipp's boat, was named Hiram; and Mr. Danenhower's boat was named Rosy. Our sleds were named Sylvie, Etta L., Lizzie, and Maud. One other bore the motto, '*In hoc signo vinces.*'

In consequence of the stronger light during the day, it was decided to march nights and sleep daytime. This was accordingly done and proved a good thing; and many a comfortable sleep I enjoyed after a hard night's work, either dragging with the men, or afterward with pick and shovel building roads.

The ice during the first of our tramp was very bad,—often one or two miles being all we could make in a night's work, and during the first week we drifted back twenty-four miles. From this time until I reached the Tunguse settlement I hardly knew what dry feet were, and often was wet through, —clothing, sleeping gear and all. During the march over

ON THE RETREAT.

the ice I saw a number of gulls (*B. rosea*), but was not able to secure any.

Our Fourth of July this year was passed in hard work, but we were all glad to be able to do it. On the 9th I first saw the land, which afterward was landed on and named Bennett Island. By July 16th most of the floe was old ice, the younger having disappeared both by breaking up and thawing. The proportion of water to ice had much increased. Occasionally a seal was shot by Mr. Collins and Mr. Dunbar, and on the 20th Mr. Collins shot a

A SUCCESSFUL HUNTER.

walrus which was afterwards secured by Mr. Dunbar in a very plucky manner. The fresh meat was very acceptable, and the blubber made good fuel. The boiled skin was not unlike tough tripe or, better yet, pig's feet, and with vinegar I think would be very good. As we journeyed toward land the number of birds increased, among them kittiwake and ivory gulls, guillemots (*U. grylle*) and (*U. Brunichii*). The gulls (*R. tridactyla*) were most numerous.

The ice July 24th was very lively, moving in circles as if the pack was being jammed and pushed by the land. On the 26th, at intervals when the fog lifted, I could with a glass see the gulls sitting on the cliffs. Light showers this evening, with the ice churning in every direction. Soundings to-day in thirteen fathoms; murres and guillemots were much more numerous, being often seen with food in their beaks flying toward the shore. A good deal of fog prevailed at this time.

On Friday, July 29th, after dinner, the fog suddenly lifted, disclosing the high cliffs of the land close at hand. This is

ANNEXATION OF BENNETT ISLAND.

a magnificent, though desolate, land of rushing torrents, glaciers and huge, impregnable, rocky fastnesses. After lively work we reached grounded ice near the southeast part of the island. Here were high basaltic crags of indescribable grandeur. The birds at this place were in great numbers, the rocks being whitened with their manure. They were coming and going all the time, day and night, cackling, chattering and laughing like parrots. With all this was a buzzing sound, as if from an enormous swarm of bees.

These birds were *U. Brunichii*. *U. grylle* were very common, but scatter more when nesting.

Our camp at this time was within fifty or sixty yards of the shore on the grounded ice. This evening after supper all hands were called, and headed by the captain, who carried the American ensign, marched ashore. After all were gathered about, the captain said:—

"The land we have been working for so long is a new discovery. I take possession of it in the name of the President of the United States, and name this land Bennett Island. I call for three cheers."

They were given. Then the captain, turning to Mr. Chipp, said:—

"Mr. Chipp, give all hands all the liberty you can on American soil."

I took a short ramble. The next day I went off with gun and note-book. Sunshine and fog, with light southerly airs. I noticed a rapid current by the shore here, with a tidefall of some two feet. The tidal observations were conducted near camp, beside a big rock, which, from its shape, was christened the 'rudder.'

My walk was past this rock to try and reach the places where the murres and guillemots were. I climbed up some twelve hundred feet over very treacherous disintegrated rocks. I found the birds in all stages, from the nestling to two-thirds grown. The murres sat in long rows like the citizens of 'Cranberry Centre' at 'town meeting,' and were very noisy. The guillemots nest very prettily. Fancy some pinnacled rocks of a rich, warm brown cropping out from a mountain side, on top of these small patches of short, beautiful green vegetation, and you have the spot. Place a coal black bird with white wing patches and bright red feet on this green cushion, silently watching the intruder, and the picture is complete, unless you can fancy a pure white gull flying past, and its voice echoing from crag to crag.

My ascent of this place was comparatively easy, though

the way was steep; but the descent was a difficult and dangerous one. I had in many places to dig places for my feet with my hands, and then by burying my sheath-knife to the hilt in this very insecure holding ground, let myself down. In one place I lost my grip and down I went some twenty feet, fortunately bringing up unharmed save torn clothes and hands. In another place when half way down a voice sung out, 'Look out, sir!' I did so, and saw an avalanche of huge rocks and earth coming for me. Seeing a chance of safety behind an out-cropping crag, I hastily availed myself of it, but barely in time, as these missiles of death hurtled down. My companion said he never expected to get out of it alive. That and many other narrow shaves I have since weathered, but my companion of that day is gone. Sharvell was a good fellow, always in excellent spirits, and contributed much toward the welfare of our camp life.

The next day the men by throwing stones got 125 murres, which were very acceptable as fresh food. Two days after this I shot forty-one more, shooting from a wild, dangerous place some seven hundred feet above the sea. It seemed as if the vibration of the report must cause the disintegrated rocks to fall. The 1st of August I took another tramp of some seven or eight miles, and visited the most extensive breeding ground I have ever seen of any bird. There were gulls, murres, and guillemots in thousands, and at the report of my gun they came out into the air so thickly as to darken the sun and almost make me think the walls of rocks were falling. Their noise drowned conversation. Kittiwakes were the most common. I got within six or eight feet of some on their nests without their offering to leave. I fairly envied these beautiful creatures their cosy home. The land here sloped at an angle of some fifty degrees, from which rugged rocks cropped out, and above which they towered, high trap ledges with red lichen in masses.

One place I passed that was most interesting. It was a rising valley, which receded gradually from the seashore. A fine stream of water was here, clear and cold. About half way up this valley a mass of pinnacled rocks arose like some great castle of old. Probably mine was the first human foot ever there, and as I stood looking I almost expected to see some gigantic knight appear and ask how or by what right I dared invade his realm. The results of this trip were some eggs and birds, and a nice lot of scurvy grass. This last added relish to our food.

CAIRN ON BENNETT ISLAND.

During the night of August 3d a heavy land slide occurred. Great rocks hurled themselves down the mountain side, and, bounding off into the air, struck the water below, lashing it into foam and sending the spray fifty feet into the air. A cairn was built by Mr. Dunbar and some of the sailors on the southern side of the island. A paddle was stuck on top of it. It is situated about one hundred feet above sea level.

On Saturday, August 6th, in the forenoon, we left this place and started south in our boats. In consequence of the

314   THE JEANNETTE ARCTIC EXPEDITION.

shaking up which the boats got while being hauled over the ice, they leaked badly. Pumping and baling had to be done about every fifteen or twenty minutes. This was kept up until we, in the whale-boat, reached the Tunguse village. On August 16th, Mr. Collins called my attention to land at the southwest. Some birds and seals were seen, also an occasional walrus and bearded seal. Soundings were had in nineteen fathoms. On the 17th there was more water in sight than I had seen for two years. On the 20th the land was very plain, and the ice packed as if jammed by some-

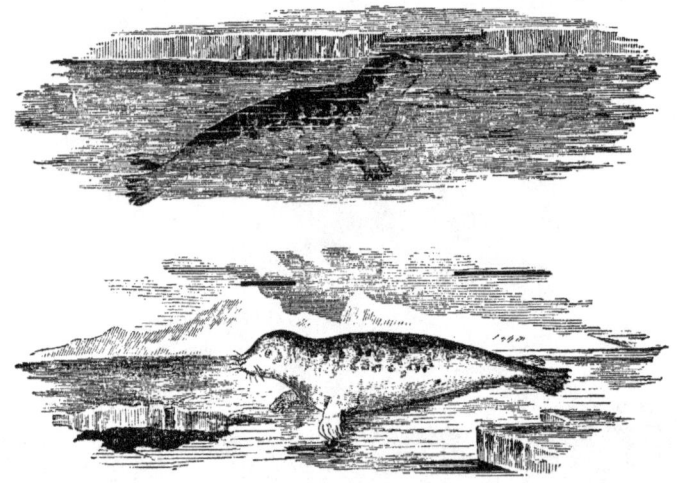

SEAL AND SEAL-HOLE.

thing. This packing afterward caused us to be delayed ten days. From this trying situation we were released on Tuesday, August 30th. On the evening of this day we made a landing on Thaddeus Island, one of the Liakhof group.

After eating my scanty supper of pemmican I started out, gun in hand, for a walk. I saw the long tailed duck (*H. glacialis*) in large flocks, also some eiders; but *glacialis* was the most common species I noticed while among these islands. I also saw fresh tracks of reindeer and foxes, and two bones (*tibia* and *fibula*) of a mammoth. These I

LAND-SLIDE AT BENNETT ISLAND.

shouldered and carried back to camp. They were all I could carry with my gun, three ducks (*H. glacialis*) and twelve sanderling (*C. arenaria*).

On September 4th we had to haul out of a bad pocket and over the ice about two miles. Launching again we, after a wet passage, reached a shoal about southeast of Kotelnoi Island. Found plenty of driftwood,—so pitched camp and partially dried our clothing. I got some birds here, eider

ARCTIC DUCKS.

ducks, gulls, and paiaropes, which came in handy for food. No seals were seen. The flora of Bennett Island, Thaddeus and Kotelnoi are much the same. Kotelnoi on its southeastern part is moderately high, with a small beach in places. While passing along the shore would be seen at intervals a large white owl (*Nyctea nivea*), sitting silent and alone.

After leaving Kotelnoi, on the night of September 7th, we experienced a severe gale, several times shipping very heavy seas, one of which all hands thought would swamp us. Seaman Leach did noble work that night, so did seaman Wilson. The night was very dark, and the danger of our position was, owing to the floating pieces of ice, much increased. We had to bale for our lives. To have struck one of these ice pieces would have been death. Our escape was miraculous, as we were running very rapidly.

On Saturday forenoon, September 10th, we landed on Semenoffski Island, got some food and fresh water, and, after dinner, pushed off, some of the party, with rifles, proceeding overland to the southern end of the island. Two reindeer were started, one of which being shot we again landed and remained until Monday forenoon. I shot some gulls, one goose, two golden plover and ten ptarmigan. Previous to this, and between Thaddeus and Kotelnoi, I shot some twenty ducks, all of which were excellent eating.

Leaving Semenoffski on the 12th, we ran south, stopping beside an ice piece at noon for dinner. After this we stood on until about four P. M., when, in attempting to run between two pieces of ice, our boat stove a hole in her starboard bilge. Shoving a rag into it we ran for the captain's boat, told him we were in a sinking condition, and hauled alongside an ice piece, pulled out, and, after nailing a piece of wood over the place, filled away for the main land of Siberia, distant perhaps one hundred miles.

The wind and sea increased toward night, and at dark we lost sight of the first and second cutters. Those two boats contained twenty-two men. Two of them—Noros and Nindermann—I have seen since, but the others I never saw after that night. During the night it blew a gale with a terrible sea. We had to lay 'hove to' with a drag out for twenty hours. Everybody did his utmost, but it seemed as if every moment would be our last. Starting again next afternoon we ran before a heavy sea; but though wet, made very good weather. Many of us were about used up with badly swollen feet. No chance to cook anything owing to tossing of the boat.

ON LAND ONCE MORE.

On Friday, September 16th, after a very hard day amid shoals and bad tide-rips, we succeeded in finding a dilapidated hut on one of the mouths of the Lena River. We were wet through, and so stiff as to be scarcely able to walk. But we were ashore again on the big land, and that was enough. Our water gave out about two days before this, thus thirst was added to our hunger; but after getting into the river we got plenty of this necessary article, and no nectar that I ever quaffed tasted like it.

I have had the pleasure of stopping at numerous good hotels since the Friday night above referred to, but not one of them seemed as luxurious as did that old hut, and our meal of pemmican on that night.

CHAPTER XXVI.

MR. NEWCOMB'S NARRATIVE.
(CONTINUED.)

SOME of us hobbled around and gathered fire wood, after which, beside a good fire, we discussed the comfort of the situation and obtained a little sleep. We remained here till the next forenoon when, about 11 o'clock, we got things into our boat and started up the river. While here we saw numbers of geese and ducks, but I was so lame I could not get round to shoot any of them. We were very much in need of fresh food, but could not, under the circumstances, procure it, though we afterwards got some ducks and a few gulls. The geese were in flocks together as if about ready to migrate, and there were also some swans on the sand spits as we passed along.

On September 19th we turned out before sunrise, and after eating our frugal meal of pemmican we continued up the river. After working all the forenoon we stopped and got a little dinner, landing on a point where we found signs of very recent occupation. Just after this, about one P. M., while Mr. Danenhower was taking some compass observations, three objects were descried or seen appearing around the left bank of the same river. These soon proved to be human beings—the first natives seen outside of our crew for over two years. They were a little afraid of us at first, and would not land, stopping in their canoes or *veatkas;* but by making signs to them we induced them to come ashore, after which we gave them a little pemmican to eat as an evidence of our good will; but they would not touch it until I had tasted it and showed them that it was good. I also showed them various other things that I had, and gave

SIGHTING THE FIRST NATIVES.

them some little buttons. We then made signs to them that we were very hungry, and they brought us a small piece of reindeer, one old goose, and a fish, which was all the provision that they had with them at that time. There being plenty of drift-wood on the shores of the river, we soon got a fire going and a stew under way.

While our stew was in process of cooking we showed the natives our rifles, and shot them off once or twice to show them what they were. I also charged my shot-gun, a breech-loader, and fired at a piece of wood, and they were very much interested to see the manner in which the small shot were distributed; they seemed to think that it would kill a duck very nicely. The manner of loading was the subject of much discussion. They handled this gun almost reverently.

Perhaps a short description of these natives will not be out of place. As soon as they came near so that we could hail them, they bared their heads, bowed, and devoutly crossed themselves. In stature they were small, complexion dark and swarthy, with straight black hair. They had very good features, and were of comparatively happy dispositions. Their names, as we afterward learned, were Theodore, Tomat, and Caranie. Tomat was a young fellow and quite a dandy; his clothing seemed to fit neater than that of the others. He had some ornaments about him, including tobacco pouches and a fancy pipe, and little copper ornaments for holding up his leggings; and knee-pads made of loon-skin, which he afterwards told me were of use to protect the knees when crawling over the ground after game. This idea I would recommend to sportsmen.

Without waiting for our stew to get as thoroughly cooked as some perhaps would have liked it, we arranged some logs in a semi-circle and sat down without formality. This meal, the first fresh food which we had tasted for a long time, was indeed good, and though the goose was very tough, we rapidly devoured it, and soon the pot was empty.

I showed our new-found friends some photographs which

I had, and they seemed much interested in them. They appeared not to understand how they were made, and evidently took them for pictures of saints, as they crossed themselves at sight of each one. They were, in reality, photographs of friends at home.

After we had concluded our meal we, by signs, induced the natives to pilot us up the river, and they conducted us to a point where five huts and a grave-yard were located. This place proved to be a small summer hunting station, and we subsequently discovered that our friends were Tunguses. We hauled up for the night, and the natives set their nets and caught some fish which they gave us.

These nets, by the way, are worth describing. They are made of horse-hair, with stones fastened to little hoops of wood for sinkers, and also to keep the net from coming in contact with the rough bottom. They are set like a gill net, anchored at each end, and floated on the surface by means of rolls of birch bark. I afterwards procured one of the same kind of nets, but did not find it necessary to use it.

We stayed at this place until the next morning, enjoying an excellent fish stew, although it was made without seasoning, and we had no bread. The natives partook of it with us. They were very devout in rising and crossing themselves, and shaking hands with and thanking us after the meal, and they seemed to regard us as a race of beings superior to themselves. One of them was very poorly clad, his boots were full of holes, and wet straw in the bottom of them took the place of stockings. His feet appeared to have been severely frozen at some previous time of life. I gave the poor fellow a pair of stockings, for which he seemed to be very grateful. His way of using them was quite amusing, for he pulled off his boots, put on the stockings, and then seemed to consider his foot-gear complete. He appeared not to know the correct use of such things.

I had at this place the pleasure of smoking a native pipe with Russian tobacco, and at their earnest solicitations I took snuff with the natives. This snuff was of a very good quality; they seemed to prize it highly, and kept it in small ingeniously-constructed wooden boxes.

Their pipes are rather long, and the stem is made of two pieces of wood, which can be taken apart and cleansed, lashed together by a thong of leather or fish skin. The bowls are cast of brass or lead, or whittled out of deer horn, and hold a thimbleful of tobacco, or only enough for a few whiffs. They have flints and steel for lighting, which are not only less expensive than matches, but surer in wet or windy weather. They carry the flint and steel in a small bag with "punk" or tinder, and the tobacco in another small bag, both of which are suspended at the side by a belt and leathern thong. Their knives are of iron, home made, or obtained from traders further south. They carry them in the boot-leg or lashed to the outside of the thigh in a fancifully-carved and highly ornamented wooden sheath, sometimes stained red or blue. Their moccasins and trousers are snug and very neatly made. Their caps in shape resemble hoods, and though designed for service are still quite ornamental, particularly those made of fox-legs for the children.

On Tuesday, September 20th, after making what proved to be a fruitless attempt to induce these natives to pilot us on our journey, we started without them; but after a bad day and stormy night we turned back on the succeeding morning, and were fortunate in finding the collection of huts which we had left, and also the natives, whose number had increased by the arrival of an old man who proved to be friendly and a person of good sense. It was a most fortunate meeting for us, as we were then on very short rations with only a few days' more food; and the fish which they gave us (I got twelve for a small match-box) proved very welcome indeed.

We started from this place again, September 22d, accompanied by the old Tunguse, of whom I have just spoken (whose name I afterwards learned was Bushielle Koolgiak), and two of the others, Theodore and Caranie. On the

24th we reached a place now known as Spiridon's Village, where we waited a while, and a native was sent away to bring further assistance and some more food. While here I got a few ptarmigan. Spiridon gave our party five geese, packed one inside the other, and all of them boned; and he also gave me a pair of moccasins, which were very handy as my old ones were much worn and too small.

In consequence of the last two days' paddling, Bushielle's left arm, which had been previously hit by a bullet at the elbow, gave out, and prevented his going any further; and so we took another man in his place and pushed on for the Tunguse village of Geemovialocke, which we reached on the forenoon of Monday, September 26th. A number of men paddled out to meet us before we lauded. Among them we noticed one who proved afterward to be a Russian exile, named Efim Kopiloff, and a very good-hearted fellow he was. Through his assistance we procured numbers of fish and geese. Quite a party, including men, women, and children, assembled on shore to meet us, and most droll-looking people they were. The women were short, and almost all of them very homely; but they had good-natured faces, and afterwards proved to be very good friends to us. They assisted in pulling up our boat, making signs that if we did not do so it would become injured, as the river would soon freeze. Then they brought sleds and dragged some of our men who were unable to walk to the hut of the commandant of the place, whose name we afterwards learned was Nicolai Shagra. Here we got a good supper, the first for a long time. After this we had a real good smoke of Russian tobacco, and a lot of tea with sugar,—something which we had not tasted for a long time. We were also given as a special delicacy, a little dried reindeer meat with a little fat cut up in small lumps; it was very palatable. Besides this, they also cooked another mess of fish for us, thinking that we might not have enough without it.

Two huts were subsequently assigned to us, and we enjoyed the first comfortable night's rest we had had for a long period. We were not anxious about breaking ice, or having to turn out to shift our tent. We had not seen any of our comrades since the gale of separation, but we one and all devoutly hoped that they were as well off that night as we were. The next morning we were assigned another house to live in, and we moved our goods and chattels and went to housekeeping. We stayed in this house a few days, when the native who loaned it signified that he desired to occupy it, and he pointed out to us another one which he had repaired especially for us. Accordingly we moved into it, and it was our headquarters during the remainder of our stay in this village.

This hut or *balogan**, typical of those seen in this village and some distance further south, was some six and a-half or seven feet high, and twelve feet square inside, with a fireplace backing up in front of the door, which was a small one, opening out, and in cold weather covered with skins to keep in the warmth. These huts have also outer wings made like a log cabin, in which are kept fuel, and various articles of domestic use. The walls of the living apartments are of logs placed vertically, with a flat roof laid on big log rafters, and outside of this is a sodding of grass and weeds. The windows are made of blocks of ice cut when six or seven inches thick, and renewed as often as melted through by the inside heat. The head of the hut abreast the fire is the post of honor. As a rule, the men eat first, being waited on by the women; or, if the women eat at the same time, it is at a separate table.

The routine of our life at this time consisted in collecting and splitting drift-wood; preparing our fish and birds, many of which were much decomposed but nevertheless very welcome; sewing; some letter-writing; keeping our journals, and regaining as much as possible our lost strength; also in caring for those who had been badly injured by frost and exposure.

---

*A balogan is an inhabited native hut.

The natives had once a week what they called a *prosnik*—a sort of feast, which is, I think, of religious origin. The people are under the control of the Russian Church, and in each of their huts I noticed a little religious emblem, placed, as a rule, at the head of the hut in the left hand corner. To these prosniks all in the village were invited, and generally came. The little entertainment consisted of drinking tea, and eating bits of reindeer meat, fat, goose eggs, and choice bits of fish; but they ate and drank sparingly, seeming to realize that the supply would become exhausted if used too freely. I must confess that some of the bits which they considered choice, I did not.

Their manner of preparing and drinking tea is perhaps worthy of note. They use two little chyniks, or copper kettles. One of them will hold a quart; in this they put the tea. The other will hold two quarts; in this they boil the water, and then pour it on to the tea, being careful not to boil the tea,—only steeping it. The mistress of the house then serves the tea to those partaking of it, who are seated on stools or other improvised seats around an unpainted pine table. Sugar is never put in the tea, but they nibble it sparingly and then sip the tea. I saw no milk in this village.

Their tea is the article known in Siberia as brick tea, being, I think, of an inferior quality to that in use in our country, and much inferior to the famous caravan tea found in other parts of Siberia and in use in some parts of Russia.

Large, heavy German silver or brass ear-rings seem to be highly prized by the native women, as also are brass buttons, calicoes and cotton handkerchiefs of bright colors, cotton cloth known as Turkey red, and black and green cotton velvets. The undergarments of both males and females of all ages are of calico or colored cotton. The outer clothing is of deerskin, with the hair taken off in the summer; and in the winter with the hair on. In moderately cold weather the clothing is worn with the hair inside, but in extreme cold weather the hair is outside. The soles of their moccasins are of deerskin. They use blankets and bags made of fish skin, and, when walking on slippery ice, over-shoes of the same material, which give quite a secure footing. They seemed not to be acquainted with seal-skin, and prized small pieces which I gave them very highly.

The natives at this settlement occupy themselves in fishing and hunting. Men and women attend the nets, and the women are often seen bringing in the fish, drawing water and cutting wood, and repairing fish-nets, dog-harnesses, and such things. Some of the women are very skillful sewers, and set a great value on thimbles and steel needles. They make the clothing, including moccasins. The men hunt with flint-lock rifles of small bore, and also use bows and arrows for killing geese, which they do at the time of year when these birds are moulting.

On the 27th of September we started to leave these people, under the guidance of one native and the Russian exile whom I have mentioned before; but, owing to bad weather and shoal water, we were obliged to turn back and seek again their kindness and hospitality. A few days before this we had light snows, which indicated that winter was near at hand. On the 28th the river was frozen nearly across.

One day early in October another Russian exile, Kusmah Eremoff, made his appearance in the village. I discovered him and took him to our hut, that Lieutenant Danenhower and Mr. Melville might see him. They made arrangements for him to go to Bulun to communicate with the authorities there. This man was absent much longer than anticipated. The result of this trip was that he brought back information that the Commandant of Bulun would be at our village in a few days, and also a brief note from Nindermann and Noros announcing that the first cutter party had landed; that Nindermann and Noros had reached Bulun; that the captain's party was in need of clothing and assistance, and so had sent these two men on in advance.

Kusmah brought with him forty pounds of black bread, about three pounds of very poor unsalted butter, some salt which we very much needed, about twelve ounces of sugar, some tobacco, and some dry black bread cut in small pieces, from the Pope at Bulun, with a note which was translated to us, and which stated that this bread and tobacco was for "the gentlemen who were traveling around the world." This was during the latter part of October—about the 28th. Previous to this Lieutenant Danenhower had made search, with the help of some of the natives, for traces of the two missing boats and crews, but without success.

OUR DEPARTURE FROM GEEMOVIALOCKE.

Mr. Melville, after receiving this information, started on Sunday, the 30th, with Bushelle Koolgiak, for Bulun, to do what he could for the other wrecked people and for us, leaving Danenhower to follow with the rest of the party as soon as he could.

On Tuesday Nov. 1st the commandant from Bulun arrived. He brought a letter from Nindermann and Noros, which was directed to the Minister Resident at St. Petersburg. This letter Danenhower immediately sent by fireman James H. Bartlett to Mr. Melville at Bulun. Lieutenant Danenhower explained our situation to the commandant, and the result was, that after some parley, on Thursday, Nov. 3d, we started on eleven dog sleds for Bulun, under the charge of the commandant who had collected from the natives for our use supplies of comfortable fur clothing, including moccasins, hoods, and mittens.

CHAPTER XXVII.

MR. NEWCOMB'S NARRATIVE.
(CONTINUED)

WE traveled by dogs as far as Kumak Surka, and from that place to Bulun we traveled by deer. At Kumak Surka we met Mr. Melville, who was now on his way north with some supplies to render what assistance he could to the captain's party. He took old Bushielle back with him.

Bidding good-bye to Melville at this place, we started on and arrived at Bulun on Sunday, Nov. 6th, about six o'clock, A.M., after a very rough journey, chilled through and hungry. We had often been obliged to run beside the sleds to keep from freezing. I attended service in the forenoon at the Russian church.

Bulun is the northernmost Russian settlement in Siberia. It is a trading station on the right bank of the Lena River. It consists of one church, a lot of log houses plastered outside with mud, and a trading store with store-houses. Everything here in the way of food and clothing is very expensive. Sugar is fifty cents a pound; cotton handkerchiefs fifty cents each. Even fuel is scarce, though coal is said to be found in this vicinity. While here some knives, handkerchiefs, and calico for towels were furnished us; also some leaf tobacco.

Owing to the lack of accommodations for our whole party traveling together from Bulun, we divided. Part of us with Lieutenant Danenhower left here for Werchoiansk, on the Yana River, by deer sleds, on Saturday evening, November 12th, accompanied by five natives to drive our deer. The distance was 900 versts, or about 600 miles.

Crossing over very rough and badly jammed up ice in the

river, we came to a *povarnia,* where we stopped for the night, some fifteen versts from Bulun. The povarnia is a rough log hut, with benches around the sides of the interior, upon which you lay your deer-skins to sleep on; in the middle is a raised fire-place, with a hole—or sometimes a chimney, made of wood and plastered with mud—for the smoke to pass out. They are uninhabited, and are kept in repair by

GOOD-BYE TO BULUN.

the travelers who pass through the country, and are found scattered all over Siberia. Although we were now traveling by post road, still it was a very crooked, rough, and uneven route, being in most places only a little foot-path like a cow-path in our pastures at home. Our sleds often came to grief by reason of contact with stumps of trees, or being overturned against the ice. The natives display much skill in repairing their sleds, which are lashed together and not nailed, and made of soft wood. In traveling long distances they carry spare runners to repair accidents.

On Sunday, Nov. 13th, after considerable delay in catching the reindeer, which was done by lassooing them among the woods where they had been allowed to go to browse, we resumed our journey. After traveling all day and crossing some mountains where the snow blew fiercely in our faces, (some of the party were lashed fast to their sleds) and making about seventy versts, we stopped for the night at a rude povarnia, full of cracks and holes. In the morning we started again. On the next day Mr. Danenhower shot a fine young reindeer which proved an important acquisition to our larder. The next night we lost our road, after traveling nearly one hundred versts, and had much difficulty in finding it again. We were very tired when we reached a povarnia, and after a meal of deer meat and black bread we turned in to sleep.

On Friday, November 18th, we made sixty versts, and reached a *stansea,* where we found people living, and where we procured a change of diet. A stansea differs from a povarnia insomuch as it is more substantially built of logs, and occupied. This stansea was a place of two houses, with a yard and fences made of small trees. Here were a number of cows, small, scrubby little animals; their milk was very nice indeed. We obtained a lot of frozen milk to take along with us. I saw five white horses and one bull at this place.

On the next day, about noon, we started again, and after a very cold ride of sixty versts reached a balogan, or native hut, where comfortable quarters awaited us. A fine-looking young Russian, an exile, occupied this place, and I exchanged with him a seal ring for new mittens and a fine pair of moccasins. The next day, Sunday, we made only a short run of forty versts over very good roads, reaching before dark a small povarnia where we stopped for the night. On Monday we started off in a snow storm, but it stopped about noon, at which time we halted for some hot tea at a balogan where were a number of cows and several horses—one with a saddle and bridle on which looked very nice indeed, although the saddle was much different from those in use at home.

On the 24th we made but a short run, as our road lay over mountains which were steep and rocky—so much so that we had to walk in many places, our drivers leading the deer. Along this part of our journey I noticed, in different places, small bow traps set for catching lemming. These lemming are used for food, and the skins are also utilized.

On the forenoon of Sunday, November 27th, after a tedious ride, we reached the town of Werchoiansk (or Verkhoyansk) and were taken to a house where we were received by an official in uniform and side arms. Our clothing was kindly cared for, and we were furnished with tea and pastry, and afterward with Russian cigarettes. We were then conducted to a room where were several beds. These beds, after our long absence, were to us indeed a novel sight.

The house in which we were quartered was a very comfortable-looking one-story structure, plastered inside and out, and warmed by a clay oven. There were five apartments on one floor, and a small cellar. The windows were of very poor patched glass, with small panes and heavy sashes. The outer windows, for such there were, were slabs of ice, and women came in each morning to scrape off the rime which daily formed on the inside of them. The cooking was done at a fire-place built up of clay and wood, over which was plastered more clay, rendering it fire-proof. A similar kind of fire-place, though not as well finished, had been common for some time along the road as we approached the town.

A supply of excellent tobacco, pipes, and cigarette-paper was furnished to us, and I *saw* some cigars, but did not smoke them. Here I met for the first time the famous Russian *vodka,* which is not unlike new rum. Here we also enjoyed the luxury of sitting down to a table to eat, and of using knives, forks, and spoons in a civilized manner; and it seemed very pleasant after our rough experiences. We succeeded, also, in getting some clothing for a portion of our party.

Immediately upon arising the morning after our arrival we were served with tea and sweet bread; this is an established Russian custom, with which I subsequently became familiar. Samovars were in use here, superseding the little copper chyniks of the Tunguses further north. The samovars are the famous tea-urns of Russia. And here I will say that in no part of the world have I tasted tea so delicious in flavor as that found in Russia; and I quite believe, what has often been said, that tea transported by ship loses much of its aroma.

This village is inhabited largely by exiles, and it consists of some sixty or seventy scattered dwellings and other buildings, including a school-house and a church. The ispravnik, or local governor, is a civil officer. A number of Cossack soldiers quartered here are under the control of another officer who is called the commandant. I met a number of political exiles living in the village, and they were fine, intelligent men, in the prime of life. One of them read and spoke French fluently, and some English, and several others spoke French. I have since found these exiles to be among the better classes of the people living in Siberia to-day—intelligent and capable men and women.

The country on our last day's ride toward this place looked more settled than further north, and numerous hay-stacks showed the presence of cattle, of which I saw some twenty or thirty; but tillage was not yet seen. In the village, chunky, long-haired horses and funny little wooden sleighs were in use; but bells are not allowed on the horses excepting on the roads outside the limits of the town.

On Wednesday, November 30th, between 9 and 10 o'clock, we left Werchoiansk for Yakutsk, with one Cossack, two Tunguses, and horses and sleds. Just before leaving, I was invited to the houses of the doctor and the ispravnik, where I had ice-cream, cigarettes, port wine and champagne; also a *cigar,* which was something to be remembered as one of the events of my life, for it was a long time before I got another.

I noticed that the Cossacks and Tunguses had very fine teeth—all of them. This, I think, is largely due to the black bread which they eat, and also to the absence of acids or sweet things, except in very limited quantities.

Our provisions were carried on five pack-horses. The weather at this time was pretty cold, being from twenty-five to thirty degrees below zero, Fahrenheit.

After traveling about thirty versts, we stopped at the best povarnia I had yet seen. A good fire had been prepared by the man in charge of the pack-horses, who arrived before us, and some hot tea was soon served. After this we continued on until night, when we stopped again for sleep. The condition of our party at this time was such that we could not travel both day and night, but were obliged to stop for sleep and rest.

On Sunday, December 4th, we started off before dawn, with three teams of deer and three sleds drawn by horses. After various accidents and stoppages, and winding around some really fine mountain scenery, with lofty woods, over very bad, rough, tussocky ground, we reached a stansea where we found quarters for the night. In our day's journey we had crossed the Arctic Circle. How many things had happened since we last crossed it in 1879! Thirty-three hearts were then buoyed with hopes for the future, or hopes of what the future might bring. Of that number twenty were now dead or missing. Time had made many changes, and who could tell what had happened at home?

On December 6th we traveled by deer over very rough roads, stopping once for tea and to warm our benumbed bodies. Pushing on again, we passed a fine-looking Pole going into exile. We traveled until nearly midnight, reaching a stansea to find it occupied by a Russian trader and other travelers, who had been at Yakutsk and were on their way to a settlement on the Kolyma River. His principal stock seemed to be vodka, with some calicoes, thread, needles, etc. He was accompanied by an elderly woman, and by his wife, a younger person, whom he had recently married, and

338   THE JEANNETTE ARCTIC EXPEDITION.

she treated us very hospitably. In the morning our friends left for their destination, and we soon moved on south, never, probably, to meet again in this world.

Shortly after this, in crossing a river, we broke through the ice, wetting things, throwing us off the sleds, and breaking one of them all to pieces. Afterward we reached a stansea in a beautiful little valley among the mountains. The scenery at this place was the finest I had yet seen in Siberia—rugged, inaccessible peaks clad with snow.

DOWN GRADE.

On Friday, December 9th, we crossed a range of mountains, and descended a pass in a manner worth describing. After toiling up the rugged ascent we reached a ridge, and, on looking over the other side, found a very steep and dangerous-looking place to be traversed; but our drivers went to work so systematically that confidence was soon restored.

The eight sleds were lashed together in a gang, and the deer, twenty-four in number, were fastened to these sleds behind. One of our party, Seaman Leach, who was unable to walk owing to frosted feet, sat in the center of this body of sleds, and at a given signal, with a native at each side to steer, the whole raft was pushed over down the hill. It disappeared amid a cloud of snow-dust around the corner of a projecting ledge, and reached the bottom in safety, much to my relief.

After this our party descended individually, rolling and tumbling, but bringing up without injury. Lieutenant Danenhower and myself started to walk down, but our feet slipped out from under us and down we went, finally bringing up at the bottom all right. This was one of the wildest parts of our journey. Over this road, by a side passage, with the use of pack-horses and by reindeer, are transported all the provisions which come to supply the town of Werchoiansk and other northern settlements on this line of travel.

After getting our teams into order, we pushed on down the mountains, traversing river beds now frozen, and reached a wretched povarnia late at night, tired, cold, and hungry.

This country in the summer time, or when the thawing season commences, must be about impassable, as washed-out banks, and stumps and logs, showed the force of the water which rushed down these mountain gullies in warm weather. To the geologist, and also to the naturalist, this country presents a very rich field.

On Sunday, December 11th, I met with a series of accidents, being thrown off my sled four times, smashing one sled beyond repair, and breaking another one four times. The last accident was just at night, when, in passing around a steep place, we were thrown, with one traveler who was ahead, with sleds and deer, down a gully some twenty feet, in a promiscuous heap at the bottom. During the day we passed three trains of 113 pack-horses, loaded with stores and bound for the settlements on the Kolyma River.

I paid a brief visit to one of three skin huts of some wandering Tunguses, whom I noticed in traveling along. These people are in stature and appearance like other settlers farther north. Their habitations are made of poles lashed together and covered with deer-skins with the hair removed. Fire was made on the ground in the center, and the smoke was allowed to escape through a hole at the top of the tent. Door-ways with flaps of skin were at each side, but one had to stoop and crawl in when desiring to enter. They had numerous fine-looking reindeer, with some dogs and sleds, scattered around their habitations. There were some twenty

REINDEER TONGUSES' SUMMER TENT.

men, women and children, old and young. They were the first of these wandering Tunguses that I ever saw, and like most of the others were not backward about begging, and particularly for tobacco. They extended their hands, and said in the most beseeching manner, "Tebac! tebac!"

Late on the night of Monday, December 12th, we reached a stansea called Ouldan, and routed out the inhabitants thereof, including fleas, multitudes of cockroaches, and other vermin, and obtained a little rest. The next morning we started off with five sleds—three with horses attached, and two harnessed to bulls. The sleds in use here were similar in shape to the deer sleds which we had been using, but broader, and those which the horses dragged were rude apologies for sleighs. These horses were driven with reins, and harnessed very primitively. The shafts were lashed to the runners, and had plenty of room to play, thereby relieving the animal of much jolting over the rough roads. The bulls were harnessed with a sort of yoke-collar in two parts, one of which went under and the other over the neck, and fastened by lines on the forward ends of the shafts. The driver of these animals sits on the back of one of them, almost over the hind legs, or on a sled; he carries a stick, but cannot make them travel very fast.

The next day we got horses for us all, and very good ones they were. As we continued on, the country improved in appearance, and a number of Yakut dwellings or farms were passed. We were fortunate in getting a quantity of frozen milk and some very fair crushed butter at a stansea, and we met the wife of a trader traveling from Yakutsk to Werchoiansk with supplies—a very agreeable person, who served us nice tea and cigarettes.

The next day we stopped off at a house where I saw some calico quilts—evidences of civilization not before noticed. The roads continued to improve, and the natives we met wore less skin clothing and more of cloth than those farther north. It was evident, also, that the steppes which we were passing over had been tilled between the towns.

At the stations where we stopped I observed how the cooking was done. Thin barley porridge was made in a large kettle, by a woman who used a wooden stick some three feet long, with a button six inches in diameter on the end; she stirred the porridge by twirling the stick dexterously between her hands. The fire-places were the same as those of the Tunguses and Yakuts, but considerably larger and better made. The habitations of the people were also larger, partitioned off, and the logs were squared up, and in some instances dovetailed very nicely. In one of these houses which we entered I noticed a dead horse on the floor, and was led to inquire his age on account of the worn appearance of his teeth. I was informed that he was twenty years old when killed, and was now going to be used for food.

The whips used by the people of these parts when driving horses are funny-looking affairs, being a combination of whip and curry-comb. The handle is some two feet long, with a leathern thong or lash, and has a looped strap by which the whip can hang suspended from the arm. A small, very dull blade is inserted in the handle, which the drivers use in cold weather for scraping off the rime and clearing the frozen moisture away from the nostrils of their horses while on the road. Another peculiarity which I noticed was that the drivers always whipped their horses when they came to a hill, running them up-hill and walking them down-hill quite often. We traveled with three horses abreast, and I must confess it was at times exciting to see them start on a tight run up-hill. They did this in fine style, and were evidently trained to it.

On Saturday, December 17th, we started in the early morning from the stansea where we had lodged, for Yakutsk.

CHAPTER XXVIII.

MR. NEWCOMB'S NARRATIVE.
(CONTINUED.)

OUR road, as we approached the city, lay on the Lena River, and, as I saw the church spires rising in the distance, it seemed as if I was approaching the Mecca of my hopes.

Yakutsk is situated on the right side of the river on rising ground. It is a place of some four thousand inhabitants, and the seat of government of Upper Siberia. On our arrival we were taken to the office of the Chief of Police, whose name was Carpuf. He was a dapper little man of some thirty-two or three years, and very kind and attentive during our stay in Yakutsk. When we first went into his office Mr. Danenhower inquired if there was any one there who could speak French. Upon this, a man stepped forward whose name was Bobokoff, and through him Mr. Danenhower told the Lieutenant of Police that he wished to see the Governor-General, and also who we were.

After this we were taken to a large house which was for the accommodation of Russian army officers when traveling that way. Our apartments consisted of two large rooms comfortably heated, with chairs and some pictures and flowers, and they proved quite a luxury to us. A hanging lamp to burn kerosene (the first one I had seen in this country) was suspended from the ceiling. We were waited upon by the Ispravnik, the Lieutenant of Police, and Captain Groenbek of the steamer Lena, and the next day received a call from Governor-General Tchernieff.

After this, arrangements were made for us to obtain our meals at an eating-house across the street from where we lived, and the next day we got some cheap shirts and stockings, and comfortable baths. Thus we were quite well provided for again. We also, a few days later, got other clothing, including boots, new mittens, caps, etc. Mr. Danenhower had received some funds through the Russian authorities, and a little spending money was given to each one of us.

We went out shopping several times, and whenever any of our party appeared on the street, numbers of people were attracted to take a look. In one instance three of us went into a store to get some caps. These stores are near the market place—in fact they form a part of the general bazaar of the city—and a number of people were about at their different vocations. Soon after we got into the store people began to come in until the store was crowded, and the street outside was literally blocked with people as we passed out. They were Yakuts and Cossacks, and were so numerous that I had to push them aside to get into the sleigh to ride back to our house. They had assembled to see the Americans,—probably the first (at all events the first party of many) who had ever visited that country.

We occupied the time a few days before Christmas in writing, and on Saturday, December 24th, our party gave a supper at the hotel to some of our Yakutsk acquaintances. This proved a sociable affair, and passed off pleasantly.

The next day, Sunday, was Christmas. On this day we had our photographs taken, and then a number of our party went visiting, and were very hospitably entertained. The people were warm-hearted, and always appeared glad to see us.

On Wednesday, December 28th, four of our party and a gentleman who resides in Yakutsk took a drive of some twelve versts, to a village occupied by five or six hundred unmarried males and females. They are a very peculiar race of people, made up of all the different nationalities, and of a singular religious belief. Many of them are exiles, and all of them are very thrifty, working at different vocations. Their houses were generally very tidy-looking, and one of them, the home of a dyer, was scrupulously clean. They raise some cattle, sheep, and swine, and also an excellent quality of wheat; I have eaten bread made from some of it, and can attest its goodness. They also raise barley, oats, potatoes, and onions. A few strawberries occasionally ripen, but the summer is short. The people neither drink liquors or smoke, nor do they eat any meat.

The fire engines of Yakutsk consist of a number of barrels mounted on wheels. When starting out for fires in cold weather the water in the barrels is heated, because, if it were not, before they could dip it out with their long-handled bailers and throw it on to the fire by means of buckets, it would all freeze solid.

After our arrival at Yakutsk the temperature became colder than it had been on our journey thither. Much moisture was in the air, and in the early morning it looked almost like falling snow.

One day I went to see an old structure,—a sort of retreat or fortress some 250 years old, which was used by the Yakuts when at war with the Russians. It was built log-cabin fashion, some 500 feet long, with towers perched at both ends. These towers were some thirty feet square and sixty or seventy feet high. The logs, on the outside, were full of bullet holes made during the attacks of the Russians. Though the fortress was generally dilapidated, many of the logs were sound.

On the evening of December 29th I paid a visit to the family of a Russian merchant, and for the first time in two and one-half years heard piano music. The next day, accompanied by Captain Groenbek, I visited the steamer Lena, which was hauled up at this place for the winter. This noted steamer came around the northern coast of Europe and Asia with Nordenskiöld's ship, the Vega, and afterward ascended the Lena River under command of Captain Johannesen. She plies on the river, but draws rather too much water to be a success. She is a nice little screw vessel, built of Bessemer steel, schooner-rigged, and about 100 tons burthen.

On December 30th, Mr. Melville surprised us by putting in an appearance. On the next day the remainder of the whale-boat party arrived, with Noros and Nindermann, and the thirteen survivors of the expedition were united again.

On New Year's day our party kept open house, American fashion, and all hands seemed to enjoy themselves. On the Russian Christmas, which occurs twelve days later than our own, I attended services at two of the churches—of which there are some ten or twelve in the city. Christmas with the Russians is a day of much rejoicing. All the churches were illuminated, outside and in, with candles; and the music of the bells (which, hung several together, are rung by means of lines fastened to the clappers,) kept the air filled with—discord, I should probably say. The religion is that of the Greek Catholic Church. Numerous priests, in robes covered with tinsel, read, chant, and exhort the people, who are gathered before the altar or some one of the numerous devotional shrines, some standing, others kneeling, and all frequently bowing and crossing themselves. Great importance attaches itself to rank. The governor, in full uniform, stands nearest the altar, and alone; then other military officers and prominent citizens. The soldiers stand in a body together. The poorer classes, some of them arrayed in fashions long since departed, make up the balance of the congregation, and stand mostly in the rear.

RUSSIAN PRIEST.

Soon after this our party, consisting of Lieutenant Danenhower, eight seamen, and myself, left Yakutsk for Irkutsk. Mr. Melville with Bartlett and Nindermann remained to

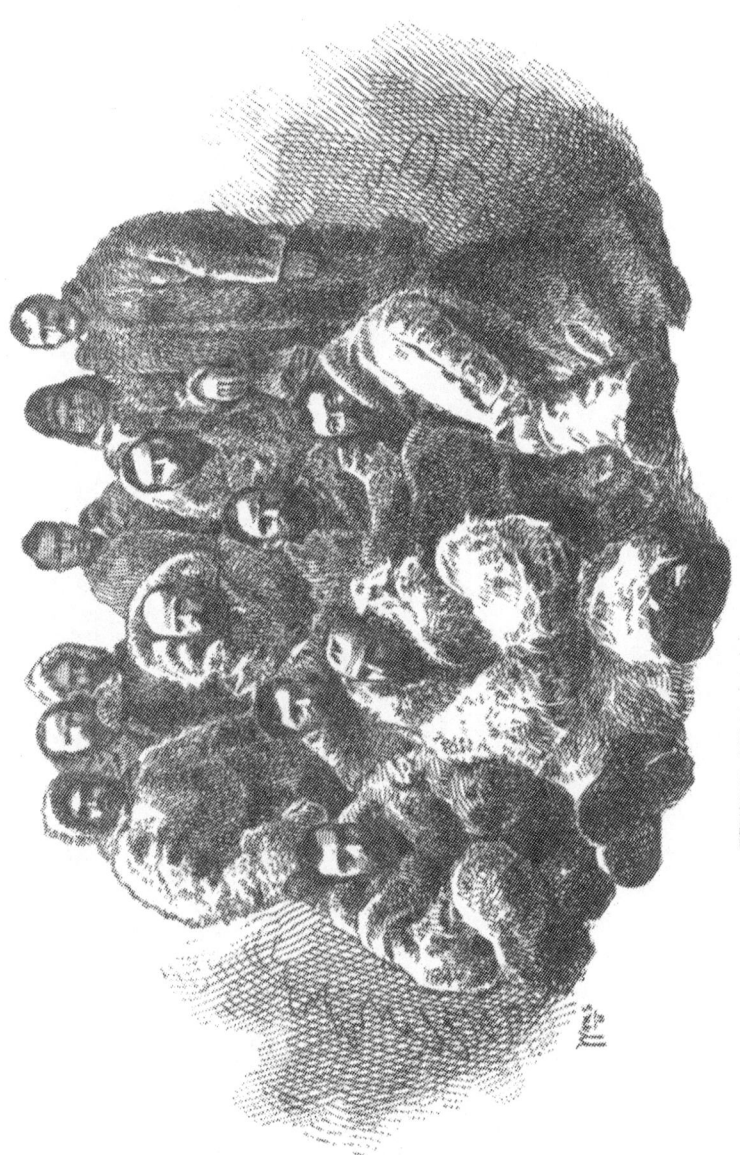

NEWCOMB. NOROS. WILSON. TONG SING. ANEQUIN. LEACH.
MELVILLE. DANENHOWER.
LAUDERBACK. BARTLETT. COLES. NINDERMANN. MANSEN.
THE SURVIVORS OF THE EXPEDITION AT YAKUTSK.

prosecute further search for the missing members of the Jeannette's crew. We reached Irkutsk after twenty-one days' journey over some 1,900 miles of cold, rough country, passing on the way through the villages of Larinsk and Vitimsk.

At Larinsk I saw a gang of some fifty conscripts, all young men. They were going to "jine the army," and were in charge of a squad of Cossacks, who sang a sort of chorus in place of drum and fife as they marched along. The rear was brought up by weeping women and children. The principal stores in this place (there were but two or three) were dram-shops. Vodka, or Russian rum, was the liquor mostly sold; next in demand were a cheap native wine, and a kind of beer called *pevo*. In many houses a beverage made from black bread and called *quas* is used. The vodka is detestable, though when spiced it often finds its way among the upper classes. The wine, or *molifka,* is sometimes good, though intoxicating. Pevo and quas are very good indeed, and wholesome, safe beverages.

Our next stopping place was Vitimsk. Here are situated the works of the "River Steamship Company;" the manager was Mr. Lee, an Englishman, and a hearty welcome met us at his hands. We remained here over night, and next day pushed on in two detachments for Irkutsk. Mr. Lee built three new *povoshkas* or sleds for us, working his men all night that we might not be delayed; furthermore, he would accept nothing for his labors. Thus equipped, with parting salutes to our friends, we moved away towards Irkutsk.

We were met on the outskirts of Irkutsk by a Cossack soldier who looked at our pordorhosna or road pass, after which we were escorted to the residence of M. Strikosky, secretary to the Lieutenant-Governor. Lieutenant Danenhower with his detachment of the party had arrived before us. As I walked up the steps a gentleman came forward and with a pleasant smile said:—"These are the rest of the Jeannette party; how do you do?" "Oh!" I said, "you speak English, don't you? Who are you?" at the same time we shook hands heartily. "Are you an American?" I continued. "Yes, I am Dr. Ledyard from California; and you?" "Oh, I'm Newcomb, bug-hunter of the party." After a few other remarks I went into the house and found hot tea with lemons, sugar, and cake, all of which were nicely served by servants. Thus we were in civilized ways again, and with a good deal of "style," too.

Irkutsk, before the fire of 1878, must have been a very pretty city, situated as it is near pleasant rivers and surrounded by well-wooded hills. The streets are wide, but the sidewalks are poor. Churches are numerous; some new and others dating back years before the fire. There are three hotels and several eating houses. Dekos Hotel is the leading one. Here can be had good food, excellent tea, fair coffee, and first-rate wines and cigars. The stores were numerous and well filled with goods, fancy articles, such as confections, French notions, cosmetics, perfumes, and cigarettes being most plenty. Business in these articles must be good, as there are many feast days in the church when these articles are much used. French fashions prevail among all (dressed) ladies. Ball costumes were some of them very elegant, but a ready-made flannel shirt I could not find in town.

The theatre is quite a pretty place, with parquette, three rows of boxes, and gallery. It seemed the custom to leave your box and promenade in the corridors—both ladies and gentlemen—and to visit the lunch room, where wines and liquors of all kinds, with hot tea, cakes, pastry, and cigarettes were freely indulged in. The performances were very good, embracing tragedy and comedy à la mode. Of course the language is Russian. There is also a hall where entertainments by a local musical society are given. These are truly enjoyable, having the characteristic Russian lunch room attached, where champagne and other nice wines are taken by both ladies and gentlemen.

Irkutsk contains two market places or bazaars—large open

squares, with long rows of stands and small booths where new and second-hand articles, food for man and beast, clothing, house-keeping utensils, etc. were to be found. The dealers, men and women, were a shrewd set. One feature of trade here and elsewhere in Russia is detestable. I refer to "beating down" the price of an article. It is a practice regularly indulged in. In purchasing trunks here, for our journey further, I effected a discount of more than twelve dollars from the first price. Dealers, I am told, expect to be asked to sell goods for less than the price first asked. Then, too, for the same articles, the difference in prices asked at stores on the main street and by dealers at the bazaar often was a good deal.

At Irkutsk telegraph communication commences. Over two thousand miles beyond this place we first heard rumors of the assassination of the American President Garfield and the Czar. How this information was transmitted so far beyond the wires, and so nearly correct, must be left to the reader to conjecture. At this place, after the lapse of nearly two and a half years, I first received tidings from my family, first by cable, and later from eighteen letters brought by Mr. Jackson, London correspondent of the New York *Herald*. This gentleman was sent by Mr. Bennett to gather all information possible about the Jeannette and the fate of her crew. He was accompanied by Mr. A. Larsen, artist of the Illustrated London News. The reader can perhaps imagine the pleasure it was to us to meet these gentlemen, and to hear our mother tongue again from other lips than those with which we had for so long been associated. In this place, however, I must not fail to mention a gentleman who spoke English very fairly. I refer to Count Ahlefeldt Laurvigen. His kind thoughtfulness will keep thoughts of him green in our memories for many a day to come.

After interviewing the party and gathering all possible news and sketches of our movements, and making necessary preparations, Mr. Jackson and Mr. Larsen, with Seaman

Noros and a Cossack servant, and three large povoshkas, whirled out of the yard of Dekos Hotel amid cheers. They were bound for Yakutsk, some 1900 miles further north, to do what they could towards rescuing our missing comrades. Seaman Noros went with Mr. Jackson by permission of the Secretary of the Navy, and also at his own desire. This man, one of the two who started south from DeLong's party for assistance, after the terrible hardships endured with Nindermann on that fearful tramp was again "facing the music." Nindermann was at this time with Mr. Melville and Bartlett similarly engaged. These examples I mention to show the stuff of which our boys were made.

CHAPTER XXIX,

MR. NEWCOMB'S NARRATIVE.
(CONTINUED.)

THE next night, March 13th, Lieutenant Danenhower with Mr. Cole, our steward, and myself bade good-bye to our Irkutsk friends and started towards home, following the first detachment, which, I have omitted to state, left Irkutsk the evening before the departure of Jackson and Larsen. We journeyed on, sometimes on runners, then on wheels, the snow having already begun to disappear. We got as far as Nijni Ujinsk and then waited to meet the officers sent out by government for our assistance and relief. After some delay (the roads were very bad) those gentlemen, Lieutenant Harber and Master Schurtze, U. S. N., arrived with letters. Thus, after more than two and one-half years, I was talking with real live Americans, fresh from home.

As Lieutenant Harber was clothed with the authority to employ those of our party who were of use and available, despatches were sent to Seaman Leach, who, with our first detachment, had reached Krosnayarsk. Every member of our party had previously volunteered his services to the department for a continuation of the search for the missing, and Leach's party willingly returned. They left Krosnayarsk about the time we left Nijni Ujinsk, and we met them and said good-bye on the road. We, as ordered, kept on towards home. They pushed on for Irkutsk, where they met Lieutenant Harber and Master Schurtze, and subsequently went north with them.

Continuing our journey, we passed through several minor towns to Krosnayarsk, where we spent a part of a day and night. Pushing forward again we reached Tomsk, the capital of Western Siberia, about the first of April. We called on the governor, visited several stores, two photograph saloons, and the market. We laid in fresh meat and other road supplies. The meat which was frozen, was cut up with a *topore,* or axe, on a dirty block of wood. This block was surrounded by gaunt, hungry dogs, and as soon as the market man stepped aside they jumped on to the block, snapped up every morsel left and licked the grease with their tongues. To see cigarette stumps and dogs on the meat block of an American market would be surprising; yet it was customary here.

Tomsk, like most Siberian towns, lies near a river and in a valley. I could readily see how invading forces on the hills surrounding would have these places completely at their mercy. Tomsk looks pretty from the east, but the roads

CRADLE-HOLES.

are full of cradle-holes; the worst I ever saw. Even in the streets of the city these things are common. No American community would begin to tolerate them. The city is irregularly divided by a small river, and has a dilapidated appearance, as does the average Siberian city or town—government buildings and churches excepted.

The governor of Tomsk, when I was there, was a young man of perhaps thirty-five years; he appeared smart and to have an eye for business. He treated us courteously, and transacted the business of our road passes very promptly. The improved appearance of most of the stansea or stations in Western Siberia over those of Eastern Siberia are evidences of a more energetic administration.

Tomsk is a post and telegraph station. The inhabitants show the Jewish characteristics to a considerable extent, many of the tradespeople being of this class. The stores, though containing many varieties of goods, were not as spacious or of as good architecture as are seen at Irkutsk.

Owing to the fact that very many of the buildings in Siberian towns are of wood, and also because the fire departments are very poor and inefficient, fires are generally disastrous and extensive. Such was the case in 1878 at Irkutsk, and Krosnayarsk, Tomsk, and Omsk have been similarly visited.

The country surrounding Tomsk was fairly wooded, but from what I could see it was young soft wood; the first growth apparently having been cut off. About the commonest bird is the magpie. In weather when the snow is dry and granulated from extreme cold, these birds take a snow bath as a hen sifts dirt among her feathers; they use both wings and seem to enjoy it much. I saw one perched on a pig's back, possibly performing an act of charity by relieving piggy of other and less welcome guests.

We left Tomsk April 4th, and after making 156 versts stopped for the night. The roads between Tomsk and Omsk were much better than we had traveled over coming from Krosnayarsk. On the morning of April 7th our leading *yemstchik* or driver had his nose frozen. "March winds and April showers" (conspicuous by their absence) were not bringing forth May flowers very numerously at this time with us. In fact, it was smart winter weather with heavy drifts of snow, often ten feet deep, so that on entering and leaving stations our sleds were higher than the eaves of the dwellings.

The women of Siberia crochet and knit very skillfully, and

I was fortunate enough to secure some beautiful shawls and table covers. The shawls were made from cashmere wool, the yarn having been spun in the country by hand. I also saw some very pretty netted bed-covers with figures marked in with Berlin worsteds very tastefully. The love of ornaments is universal. Among the Tunguses the women were inveterate beggars, especially for small pieces of scarlet flannel—part of a pair of woolen drawers of mine.

The population of most Siberian towns increases considerably in the autumn. Petropaulofsky, a small town of some 1,100 inhabitants, between Omsk and Orenburg, swells its numbers in the fall to 17,000 by the arrival of natives with goods for trade and barter. The business of the place consists of raising horses, and exporting tar, sheepskins, hides and furs, which are sent to Russia.

SPINNING.

After leaving Omsk we traveled across the Kirghesian steppes, a generally level country, evidently producing some hay and grain, but at the time covered with snow. On these steppes I saw numerous droves of horses grubbing an existence. There must be good pasturage here a part of the year to support so much stock. The inhabitants, particularly the men, wear a surprisingly small amount of clothing. They have a cap or big hood of sheep-skin tanned with the hair on, and coats of the same material with long sleeves; and over this, in severe weather, a big deer-skin or some other skin garment is worn. The under garments are of cheap, bright-colored cotton, with pants of shoddy gray, and foot gear made of plaited straw, skins, or leather, according to the wealth of the owner.

On the 8th of April I slept on a feather bed for the first time in nearly three years. April 9th opened Easter Sunday with solid winter weather. Easter is a day of much interest to Russians. After the Lenten season fasting is in order. On the forenoon of this day we were invited by the keeper of a stansea to partake of refreshments with him. We enjoyed excellently cooked roast goose, ham, and little pig, with bread, sweet cakes, tea, and vodka, or rum. The children gave us some music, and with exchange of best wishes, and some coppers for the little folks, we pushed on.

The snow was about gone when we arrived at Throisky, April 15th; children were running about barefooted, and numbers of men, women, and children were sitting about in sunny spots and on the ground sunning themselves. I saw one party of "fellers and gals" who were being entertained by the music of an accordion. Fifteen or twenty curious and much interested spectators gathered about me as I sat writing on the steps of the station.

On the ceiling of the rooms where we slept that night the proprietor painted a black cross. I asked what it was for; and our courier said it was supposed to keep the devil away, and was an old custom in some parts of Russia.

In Throisky we saw numerous Kirghese men and women. The latter wore very pretty white caps trimmed with gold bands and real or imitation jewels; also finger rings of silver with red carnelian stones. Their boots were made of black and bright-colored red and green leather, fancy stitched. Their dresses were of a variegated rainbow-hued silk and wool fabric, open at the throat. These people are Mahommedans. Bright, gay colors, with even glaring contrasts, seem to be the taste of most of the women in the humbler classes.

We left Throisky April 17th, and about 2 P. M. reached a stansea where a peasant wedding-party was assembled. They danced, sung, and feasted a good deal, and many of them, both men and women, were "feeling good" from drinking vodka.

358   THE JEANNETTE ARCTIC EXPEDITION.

At this time we were traveling with tarantass, and on the 18th reached a river where we were ferried over in dug-out canoes. Our vehicle was taken across in two canoes placed

A RUSSIAN WEDDING.

side by side, each canoe holding two of the wheels. After this we journeyed on until night, when it began to rain. Just before stopping for the night we got a capsize down an embankment into a ditch. The horses started to run, but were held by the driver, while a friendly tree stump near at hand kept us from a bad accident. When we capsized Lieutenant Danenhower came down on top of me, and as we were confined by the apron of the vehicle and by the pillows and baggage, I was nearly smothered. After getting another wagon we started ahead again amid half a gale of wind and rain, glad to get off so easily.

On the 20th we capsized three times, crossed numerous creeks, ferried a river, and came to a halt after a run of 89 versts only. The weather was by this time getting spring-like, being breezy, with heavy roads and swollen streams. Our progress was necessarily slow, averaging but

A SIBERIAN TARANTASS.

seven or eight versts an hour. The country was hilly, with rocks, ledges, and a very few scattered, stunted bushes, and an occasional tree. The grass was beginning to show some green. The roads through the villages were a foot deep with mud, and geese and hogs were wallowing in it. On the 21st I saw oxen yoked together for draft purposes.

On the 22d we passed the town of Osk and the Ural River at night, reaching a stansea at the foot of the Ural Mountains, on the western side. The Ural River is a winding stream, with steep, high earth banks in many places. Our road on the afternoon of the 22d, lay along one side of this river, and I obtained fine views. I noticed but little timber in its vicinity. I saw numerous flocks of ducks, easy of access, and should say good shooting might be had. Hawks and eagles were very plenty. I saw, also, a flock of teal, and noticed that they started and flew off, apparently much frightened. They crossed the road, but not soon enough to escape a large hawk which darted among them, seized one, and bore it off over the river bank. Our driver stopped his team, jumped off, gave chase, and made the hawk drop the teal. Both birds flew off for some 300 yards in different directions, when the hawk turned, overtook and recaptured his prey, and carried it away to devour at leisure.

A good deal of the country just before entering the mountains on the western side is about level, or gently undulating, with numerous pond-holes, excellent for both snipe and duck. I saw three Kirghese hunters riding horseback. One of them had some ducks. Two of them had flintlocks, and one had a single-barreled percussion gun.

In this country I often saw, situated by themselves, and on the outskirts of Cossack villages, some dome-shaped huts. These were either the temporary abodes of Cossacks tending horses and camels at pasture, or else the homes of Kirghese. They were constructed of light, portable crossed frames, and covered (except a hole at the top for air and smoke) with a thick, heavy felting cloth outside, and with straw matting about the walls inside. They were comfortable dwellings, besides being cheap, and easy to keep in repair and move about.

On the morning of April 23d we started early, and after a hard, tedious day, over rough roads, winding about through narrow, rocky defiles, past some pretty bits of scenery, and others that were bare and inhospitable, we reached, at nine P.M., a stansea which, though yet in the mountains, was only 120 versts from the railroad. Yakutsk and Irkutsk had each been at different times the "Mecca" of my hopes; now it was Orenburg and the iron horse.

Owing to the scarcity of wood and its value for other purposes in this section, a fuel is made from the manure of horses and cattle. It contains much straw, and is pressed, dried, and cut up into pieces like peat. It makes excellent fuel, and burns without any disagreeable odor.

April 24th opened cold and cloudy, with a light breeze, spits of snow, and rain. The roads were very heavy, and we traveled this day by both runners and wheels. On the next morning, at 8:45 A.M., we reached Orenburg, and found

AT ORENBURG.

quarters at the Hotel Europansky. This hotel and its proprietor I can recommend as very nice. After dinner we drove to the depot, saw the locomotives and cars, conversed with the station-master, and arranged for our passage to Moscow. The passenger cars are in compartments, with accommodations not to be compared to our Pullman or Wagner cars. They are mounted on six wheels and steel side-springs. The locomotives use wood for fuel, and are of German manufacture on the lines on which I have traveled.

Orenburg is, in my mind, a very interesting place, and before the last heavy conflagration must have been a fine city. I saw in the public square a circus, which looked natural. Telegrams, letters, and some drafts for money (last but not least) awaited us here. The stores were well filled with many kinds of goods. The Tartar bazaars were very interesting places, containing many fancy articles, such as caps, slippers and boots, beautifully embroidered with silk and tinsel; also, perfumes, rugs, and droll-looking, rainbow-hued silk and wool robes. Peddlers came to us at the hotel with different articles. They had beautiful rings of diamonds and turquoise, necklaces of amethysts and Siberian crystals, pearls, topazes, and rubies in pins and ear-rings, and not mounted. Also jewel-boxes in malachite and lapis lazuli, with other varieties of native stone, carved to represent fruit and flowers. I fortunately obtained some of these lovely things, and brought them safely home.

We left Orenburg at 9:30 P. M., April 26th, for Moscow. When the train arrives at a station a man in uniform strikes quickly and several times a bell hung on the depot near the mail box. The train is started by the same man, who announces the departure by striking the bell. At every station numbers of Cossacks with sidearms are seen, doing police duty.

The country we now went through was level, and good for grazing, with some woods, pond-holes, and streams. Numerous flocks of plover, snipe, and ducks started up as the train proceeded. The sensation of being bowled along in cars after my varied experiences of two and one-half years was very novel, and I felt for the first time as if I was really going home. The conductors and porters were quiet, civil, and attentive.

The first city of importance after leaving Orenburg is Samarah, the capital of this portion of Russia. Crossing the Volga for the first time, just before noon, we arrived at this place in time for dinner at the station, and had an excellent meal of cabbage soup, fish, cutlets, and vegetables. While we were eating, a gentleman of fine appearance came into the restaurant and spoke to some military officers; he then came up to our table and inquired if we were the Jeannette party. On being answered affirmatively, he introduced himself as the governor of Samarah, chatted a few minutes, took a glass of wine, and then, after inviting us to call on him in his car, and shaking hands, he withdrew. Meantime some twelve or fifteen gentlemen had gathered around us, and during the remainder of the time we were at dinner our little party was the center of attraction.

The Volga at this place is about a mile in width. The ice was nearly gone when I saw it, near the last of April, and there were numbers of row-boats with two or three men in each busy fishing. The banks of the river were in places much overflowed. I also saw a dozen steamers, some with steam up; part of them were fore-and-aft rigged, and all of them side-wheeled.

We were passing along the Volga all the afternoon, and in one place crossed it over a fine bridge nearly a mile long. This bridge was of iron, and rested on fourteen stone piers some sixty feet above the river, in which at this place was considerable running ice.

On the 28th of April I saw a number of farmers busy ploughing and harrowing. Three horses working abreast drew a pair of wheels to which the plough was attached. The ploughs were of wood and the ploughshares were faced with iron. The harrows were drawn by one horse, but one man guided two teams. A dozen or more teams might be seen at once on a fine, rich-looking level or gently undulating field. Similar scenes were noticed for miles over a country reminding me of our Western prairies.

Here and there was a town, village, or hamlet. Numerous small streams furnished a good supply of water. The cultivated fields were divided by lines of turf, in consequence of the absence of rocks for walls or wood for fences. The embankments of the railroad were kept from washing out by the same means, and also by willow branches fastened down with cross pieces on wooden pins. Many horses, cattle, and sheep, with some hogs, were eating the young grass. Banks of snow five to ten feet deep and sometimes 200 feet long, attested the severity of the winter.

We arrived at Moscow at nine A. M., April 29th, and found nice quarters at Slavanski Bazaar. The hum of the city sounded natural. Moscow is a fine old city, with many scenes of interest; her cathedral, churches, and old palaces, the Kremlin, the big bell, the chapel of John the Terrible, the gates of the city, the maiden monastery where a sister of

GREAT BELL OF MOSCOW.

Peter the Great was confined, and a foundling hospital being among them. I attended one very interesting wedding in this city, and then bidding good-bye to Moscow and to some very pleasant American residents there, we continued our journey.

We reached St. Petersburg about May 1st, and through the efforts of the correspondent of the New York *Herald,* we were provided with delightful quarters on the English Quay fronting the Neva River. The emperor and empress having expressed a wish to see us, we went to Gatcheua by special train and were taken in the carriages of royalty to the palace where, after waiting some time and viewing many objects of interest, we were ushered into a smaller apartment, there meeting the emperor and empress, both of whom spoke English. Concluding our interview and shaking hands we withdrew, and after being shown through the palace and meeting a number of notables, we were driven to the station and returned to St. Petersburg. In the evening we attended a banquet given in our honor.

We remained in this city eight days waiting for instructions from home. Among other interesting attentions which we received I remember with pleasure the banquet given us by the chargé d'affaires, Mr. Hoffman.

St. Petersburg contains many sights for the traveler, and the European tourist who fails to visit this city loses much of interest which is not to be seen elsewhere. Among the sights are the fortress where are kept a number of important prisoners; the cathedral with the tombs of the dead emperors; the hermitage; and St. Isaac's Cathedral with its beautiful mosaic pictures and columns of malachite and lapis lazuli. This cathedral is 350 feet from the floor to the interior of the dome. On a clear day and with a glass one can get good views of Cronstadt, some eighteen versts away.

We left St. Petersburg on the yacht of the admiral of the port, and after a pleasant passage and lunch arrived off Cronstadt, where we paid our respects to the admiral, and then with good-byes all around we put to sea. As we passed out of the dock the naval band played the "Star-Spangled Banner" and "America." We steamed away, night shut down, and we were off for Hull, England. After a comfortable passage of six days we arrived at the port, where we were pleasantly received by English naval officers and our consul, Mr. Howard.

Crossing from Hull overland we arrived at Liverpool, and were met by Consul Packard of that port, Consul Shaw of Manchester, and others. A delightful banquet was given here by Consul Packard, upon which occasion I had the pleasure of meeting the mayor and other citizens.

Leaving Liverpool on the White Star steamer "Celtic," we reached New York where friends soon surrounded us, and we were "home again from a foreign shore."

In conclusion, I would advise travelers who may be looking for an interesting locality to visit, to try Russia and a trip across the Ural Mountains into Siberia, traveling by rail, steamboat, and horses. There is much of fine natural scenery. In the summer the weather is delightful. Plenty of good, wholesome food may be obtained, and the expenses need not be heavy. With these concluding remarks I leave the reader.

EUROPE AND ASIA—BOUNDARY LINE.

CHAPTER XXX.

DELONG'S FATE DISCOVERED—THE GRAVE ON THE LENA.

AFTER making the necessary preparations for a systematic search for his missing comrades of both boats, Mr. Melville left Yakutsk, January 27th, and proceeded to Verkhoyansk. He was accompanied by Bartlett and Nindermann; Captain Guenbeck of the steamer Lena; Efim Koploff the exile; Peter Kolenkin, a Cossack sergeant; Constantine Buhokoff; and a native Yakut and his wife as porter and cook.

At Verkhoyansk the ispravnik of the district joined the party, which started north February 11th, and reached Bulun on the 17th. On the 22d, Melville started for Bykoff Cape to procure dog-teams for the search parties and a supply of fish as food, and also to pay some small bills contracted by the whale-boat party while sojourning there. The snow was very deep, and the weather most of the time was terribly stormy. Among those who joined him as dog-drivers were Tomat Constantine and Wassili (or Bushiclle) Koolgiak.

On the 25th the remainder of the search party, with provision trains, started for Mot Vai, the central rendezvous for the search parties at the start, situated about 200 versts north of Bulun.

Mr. Melville rejoined his companions on the 9th of March, at Cath Carta, and on the 12th wrote a letter from this place to the Secretary of the Navy, in part as follows:—

"I arrived at Bykoff Cape on the 24th of February, and was detained there until March 6th by continuous bad weather—the worst I have ever seen. The seven dog teams I sent to carry the transport party returned after an absence of fifteen days, having lost their way in the storm. Six of their dogs died of exhaustion, and the drivers were terribly frost-bitten in face, feet, and hands, refusing to again venture out until the weather became settled.

As soon as I get sufficient fish on hand, and three teams of dogs selected, the three search parties will set out and the search actively commence."

Mr. Melville also wrote a letter to the New York *Herald,* from Cath Carta, March 13th, as follows:—"The place from which I now write, Cath Carta, is a collection of four mud hunting huts, on one of the many branches of the Lena, about fifty versts south of Usterda, where the last of DeLong's records were found. I selected this point as the nearest place to pick up the trail, and as it is nearly due south of Usterda, it is in his line of march. It is the only place in this vicinity that has a collection of four huts, two of which we occupy—six men in a house eight feet by fifteen. Both are too low for a man to stand upright in. The other two contain our stores of fish and other supplies. I have three of our people of the Jeannette, and three other persons hired at Yakutsk. We have, besides, a Yakut man and wife as cook and wood and water or ice carrier; also a general hand—a Russian exile—making nine people in all. I have hired dog teams by the month; also dog drivers. I have all the teams in the country carrying fish; and as soon as I get sufficient fish to feed ourselves and our dogs, we will scour the country between the Olenek and Yana.

To-morrow myself and Nindermann, with two interpreters and dog sleds, will go to Usterda and Sisteraneck to pick up DeLong's trail where I lost it last December. I feel very confident of finding DeLong's people and records, but fear that Chipp never reached the coast. His boat was very short and the sea very heavy, and although he was the best seaman on the Jeannette, I fear the weather was too much for the boat—not for the man.

The weather has been the worst I have ever seen. Any

number of the (native) people have been lost and frozen during the last month. On our journey here from Bykoff Cape, where I went to get fish and dogs, we came across two families who had taken refuge in an old hut. They had been exposed to the storm for eight days. Food had given out, and three of their children—aged eight, five, and three years, respectively—were frozen to death. We gave them fish and tea, and our teams on their return to Bykoff will carry them through.

The weather is now more settled, and I can get to work right away, but the snow is very deep. It covers everything. You can sledge right over the houses without knowing of their whereabouts except by the chimneys or smoke. The snow does not leave the ground by melting from heat of the sun, except on very high ground. The water from the south comes down the river in floods long before the Arctic summer sets in, and covers nearly all the country where our search lies. You may, therefore, imagine some of the difficulties we may have in finding our missing comrades.

When I got into Bykoff last September not one man was well in the boat. Not more than two were able to walk, and then only for a short distance. The ice in the river was thick enough to stop any boat worked by strong, vigorous men, yet not strong enough to walk upon. During the month of October the river freezes and breaks up again half a dozen times. Long before I got to Bulun to see Nindermann and Noros I fear my comrades' troubles were over. I did all I could in the circumstances to get my people up the river and relief to DeLong. I lost no time by going to Yakutsk or in getting my party there, as all my travel was done in the dead of winter when work could not be done at the delta, and it was necessary to get supplies for the spring and summer, all of which come from Yakutsk. It was necessary for me to get to the end of telegraph communication, and I was in Yakutsk a week before an answer to my telegram of two months before was received. However, now that we are on the ground we will use

ALL DEAD! 369

our best endeavours to complete our work to the general satisfaction.

I am anxious to finish up our work here. Our eyes are almost blind from the smoke of our huts. There are no chimneys, only holes in the roof, and I can barely see what I have written. The Prefect of Verkhoyansk, who accompanied us to this place, returns home and will carry our mail; and as there are no means of getting letters through to Yakutsk, except by special courier, before the river breaks up, you may not hear from me until fall."

THE RIFLE IN THE SNOW.

Eleven days after the above letter was written Mr. Melville forwarded from the Lena Delta to Yakutsk, by special courier, the following message:—

"I have found Lieutenant DeLong and his party; all dead. All the books and papers have also been found. I remain to continue the search for the party under Lieutenant Chipp."

On the same day, March 24th, Mr. Melville wrote to the Secretary of the Navy as follows:—

"I have the honor of informing you of my successful search for the party of Lieutenant DeLong, with its books, records, &c., &c. After several unsuccessful attempts to follow DeLong's track from the northward, I tried the retracing of Nindermann's track from the southward; and after visiting every point of land projecting into the great bay at the junction of the Lena branches, from Mot Vai, around from the west, to a point bearing E.N.E., and forming one of the banks of the River Kugoasastak, on ascending the bank, I found where a large fire had been made, and Nindermann recognized it as the river down which he came. I turned the point to go north, and about one thousand yards from the point I noticed the points of four poles lashed together and projecting two feet out of the snow drift, under the bank. I dropped from the sled, and on going up to the poles saw the muzzle of a Remington rifle standing eight inches out of the snow, and the gun strap hitched over the poles.

I set the natives digging out the bank, and Nindermann and myself commenced to search the bank and high ground. I walked south, Nindermann walking north. I had gone about five hundred yards, when I saw the camp kettle standing out of the snow and, close by, three bodies partially buried in snow. I examined them, and found them to be Lieutenant DeLong, Dr. Ambler, and Ah Sam, the cook.

I found DeLong's note book alongside of him, a copy of which please find enclosed, dating from October 1st, when at Usterda, until the end. Under the poles were found the books, records, &c., and two men. The rest of the people lie between the place where DeLong was found and the wreck of a flat-boat, a distance of 500 yards. The snow bank will have to be dug out. It has a base of thirty feet and a height of twenty feet, with a natural slope.

The point on which the people lie, although high, is covered with driftwood,—evidence that it is flooded during some

THE DISCOVERY OF DE LONG AND PARTY.

season of the year. Therefore, I will convey the people to a proper place on the bank of the Lena, and have them interred. In the meantime I will prosecute the search for the second cutter with all diligence, as the weather may permit. The weather has been so bad that we have been able to travel but one day in four, but hope for better weather as spring advances."

The first cutter party, when it reached land, consisted of fourteen persons. Nindermann and Noros escaped the fate of their comrades; Erickson and Alexai, who died first, were buried in the river; and the remaining ten—DeLong, Ambler, Collins, Lee, Gortz, Dressler, Kaack, Iverson, Boyd, and Ah Sam—were carried about thirty miles to the southwest from where they were found, to the top of a hill of solid rock 300 feet high, and laid at rest by their devoted shipmates and sympathizing natives.

TOMB OF THE LOST EXPLORERS.

The tomb or mausoleum in which the bodies were deposited was constructed of the lumber of a broken-up flat-boat. First a cross was made from timbers one foot square, hewn out of logs which had drifted down the river, and erected on the crest of the hill. It was twenty-two feet high and the cross-beam was twelve feet long. Around this cross was built a box twenty-two feet long, six feet wide, and two feet deep, located exactly on a north and south line. After the bodies had been placed in the box it was covered with plank. A ridge-pole sixteen feet long was then framed into the cross five feet above the top of the box, and its ends were supported by timbers sloping outward. A roof was then formed by placing timbers side by side against the ridge-poles and ends. The whole outside was then covered with stones, and when completed it resembled a pyramidal mound of stones surmounted by a cross.

Before the cross was erected members of the search-party engraved upon it an inscription, as follows:—

IN
MEMORY
OF 12
OF THE
OFFICERS
AND
MEN
OF
THE ARCTIC STEAMER "JEANNETTE,"
WHO DIED OF STARVATION
IN THE LENA DELTA, OCTOBER, 1881.
LIEUTENANT
G. W. DE LONG.
DR. J. M. AMBLER.
J. J. COLLINS.
W. LEE.
A. GORTZ.
A. DRESSLER
H. H. ERICKSON.
G. W. BOYD.
N. IVERSON.
H. H. KAACK.
ALEXAI.
AH SAM.

Arrangements were subsequently made at Yakutsk to

have the entire cairn covered with a deep layer of earth, to prevent the possibility of the sun thawing the bodies therein. General Tchernieff also caused a Russian inscription to be prepared to be placed on the tomb, and directed that every care should be taken to preserve the tomb and the monument in good condition. Standing as they do on an eminence, they are conspicuous objects, and may be seen at a distance of twenty miles.

In a letter to the New York *Herald* written from the Lena Delta, April 12th, Mr. W. H. Gilder, who, strange enough, had appeared on the scene under circumstances hereafter related, gave the following particulars of the finding and burial of "Our Lost Explorers":—

"Melville's search party first started from the supply depot at Cath Carta to follow Nindermann's route from Usterda to Mot Vai, and afterward from Mot Vai back to Usterda. They stopped at the place where Nindermann and Noros passed the first day after they left DeLong, feeling sure that the others had not got much farther. There they found the wreck, and following along the bank they came upon a rifle barrel hung upon four poles sticking up out of the snow.

"They set the natives digging on each side of the sticks, and they soon came upon two bodies under eight feet of snow. While these men were digging toward the east, Melville went on along the bank, twenty feet above the river, to find a place to take bearings. He then saw a camp-kettle and the remains of a fire about a thousand yards from the tent, and, approaching, nearly stumbled upon DeLong's hand sticking out of the snow about thirty feet from the edge of the bank. Here, under about a foot of snow, they found the bodies of DeLong and Ambler about three feet apart, and Ah Sam lying at their feet, all partially covered by pieces of tent and a few pieces of blanket. All the others except Alexai were found at the place where the tent was pitched. Lee and Kaack were close by in a cleft in the bank toward the west. Two boxes of records, with the medicine chest and a flag on a staff, were beside the tent.

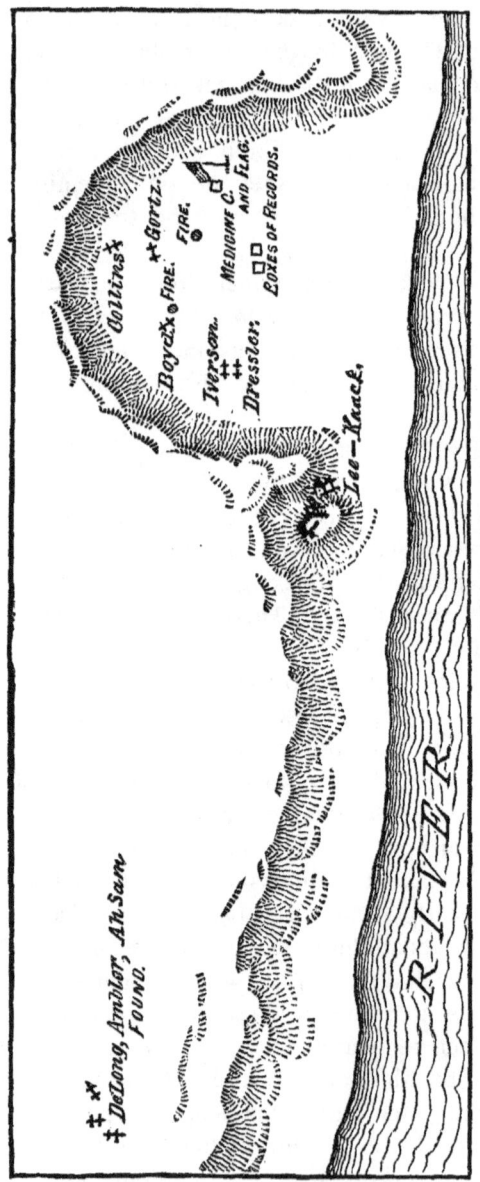

PLAN OF THE LAST CAMPING PLACE.

"None of the dead had boots. Their feet were covered with rags, tied on. In the pockets of all were pieces of burnt skin and of the clothing which they had been eating. The hands of all were more or less burned, and it looked as if when dying they had crawled into the fire, Boyd lying over the fire and his clothing being burned through to the skin, which was not burned. Collins's face was covered with a cloth."

The tent had been pitched in a deep gorge in the river bank. The bodies of Gortz and Boyd were the first two found. Iverson and Dressler were lying side by side just outside of where the

A STRANGE INCIDENT. 375

half-tent shelter had hung from the ridge-pole. Mr. Collins was further in the rear on the inside of the tent. Lee and Kaack were not found until after it was ascertained by reading DeLong's diary that they had been carried "around the corner out of sight;" then, by sounding through the snow, their missing bodies were found in a cleft in the bank.

Lieutenant DeLong's pocket journal and pencil lay on the ground beside him. It seemed apparent that he and his two companions had died the day that the last entry was made. In the camp kettle near by were some Arctic willows of which they had made tea.

"The place where the bodies of DeLong's party were found," wrote Mr. Jackson, "is fifteen miles northeast of the island of Stolboy, the prominent pillar-like rock in the Lena, where the river branches east to Bykoff. DeLong had all along imagined that Stolboy was a myth, and supposed he had passed it long before. He was bewildered by the maze of rivers flowing and intermingling on the delta proper, and in his own weak condition had put the distances accomplished longer than they really were.

"Fate seemed against him. Had he landed thirty miles farther west he would have struck a village of natives who reside north of Bulun all winter. He also passed by within twenty versts of a hut where twenty reindeer carcasses were hanging for the winter food. He had, unfortunately, no shotgun, from its having been left by his orders on the ice when the Jeannette went down, and though deer were rare, there was no lack of ptarmigan. On the day Noros and Nindermann were sent away by DeLong a large flock of 200 ptarmigan settled within a quarter of a mile of the party, but none were shot. With a single shotgun in Alexai's hands all might have been saved. The season was too late for deer.

"A strange incident, also, came to my knowledge at Geemovialocke. It seems that some Tunguse natives, traveling from the north to Bykoff, saw the footprints of the party two days old and picked up the Remington which DeLong had left in a hut half way from the landing place to the bluff. The natives were frightened, and thought that the footprints were those of smugglers or robbers, and left the ground without following. On arriving at Geemovialocke they heard of the presence of the Melville party and the loss of the captain's party, and they, fearing to be punished for not following the footsteps, kept their information to themselves for some weeks, until too late.

"DeLong made mistakes in endeavoring to secure the safety of his own private logs, which were bulky, as well as the scientific instruments and other useless impedimenta—a heavy burden for the men. These could have been left in the cache near the place where they landed, but they had to be borne by the men through all the days of their weary march. These things filled one entire dog sled when found near the bluff. After Noros and Nindermann left, the party did not make more than eighteen miles from October 9th to the 30th.

"DeLong's last effort was to carry his private logs and charts up from the place under the bluff, where Mr. Collins and the others died, and where they would have been swept away by the spring floods, to the top of the bluff where he and the doctor and Ah Sam perished. But he only succeeded in carrying the chart case up. Even before Noros and Nindermann left, DeLong was very weak. He used to walk ten minutes and then lie down to rest, saying to the men:—

"'Don't mind me; go on as far as you can. I will follow.'

"During his wanderings on the delta DeLong built a large bonfire as high as thirty feet every night, the last one being a few hundred yards from the bluff where they all perished, in the hopes of attracting the attention of parties who, he kept saying, would certainly be out looking for him. But the fires blazed in vain. There was not a human being at the time of their death within a hundred miles. Melville's party at Geemovialocke were about this distance away."

In the instructions which Mr. Melville as commander of the whale-boat party received from Lieutenant DeLong before leaving Bennett Island for the coast of Siberia, he was ordered, in case of separation from his superior officers, to ascend the Lena without delay to a Russian settlement. In attempting to carry out this order, Melville and his men, after entering a branch of the Lena River, were glad to place themselves in charge of natives, who undertook to pilot them to Bulun, the nearest Russian village. On the way thither the formation of new ice in the river compelled them to halt at a Tunguse village. It was the transition period between navigation and sledding, and the natives said they would have to remain there fifteen days till the river was sufficiently frozen.

At this time the physical condition of the men was such that Danenhower was not sorry they were obliged to halt, and Melville, Bartlett, Leach, and Lauderback had to be assisted to and from the boat. All felt the effects of exposure or frost-bites, and symptoms of scurvy appeared. Lieutenant Danenhower says in his narrative, that on the third morning after their arrival at this village all hands except Jack Cole, the Indian, and himself, were in a very bad condition. Melville was so disabled while in this settlement that for some time he gave the charge of everything to Danenhower.

On the 16th of October an exile named Kusmah Eremoff started for Bulun, and he told Melville he would be back in five days. He was a capable and energetic man, and Danenhower says he acted boldly and well. But he did not get back to Geemovialocke till the evening of October 29th, when he brought Nindermann's letter, which was the first intimation Melville had of DeLong's distress. Up to this time he had had no reason for supposing that his comrades were not at least as well off as his own party; and if he had known on arriving that they were in trouble, "it would," says Lieutenant Danenhower, "have been impossible to make a search north of the village. The natives positively refused to go, and we were wholly dependent upon them for food." The ineffectual search made by Danenhower shows that at that season travel was impracticable, owing to the weakness of the ice; and the condition of Melville and his men was another reason why no search could have been made.

As shown by DeLong's last diary, all of his party but three were dead on the 30th of October. This was the day when Melville started for Bulun, and during his subsequent search trip, which occupied twelve days, he could not, under any circumstances, have found any of the party alive. Doubtless his own experiences on the trip convinced him that all were dead.

CHAPTER XXXI.

LIEUTENANT DE LONG'S DIARY.

THE pathetic story of the wanderings, hardships, and intense sufferings of the members of the first cutter party, form the time when they landed on the Lean delta down to October 1st, as recorded by Lieutenant DeLong, has been given in Chapter XI. The sequel to this story was written by DeLong in his note-book, which was found beside his dead body, and covers a period extending from October 1st to the end.

Lieutenant DeLong's diary closes without any reference to himself, Dr. Ambler, or Ah Sam. The bodies of these three were found by Melville, lying under the snow near each other, and partially covered by pieces of the tent and pieces of blanket. It is probable that they did not long survive the last of their comrades, Mr. Collins, who died October 30th. The deaths of all the others had been previously recorded. The melancholy record is as follows:—

SATURDAY, October 1st,—111th day, and a new month.— Called all hands as soon as the cook announced boiling water, and at 6.45 had our breakfast, half a pound of deer-meat and tea. Sent Nindermann and Alexai to examine the main river, other men to collect wood. The doctor resumed the cutting away of poor Erickson's toes this morning. No doubt it will have to continue until his feet are gone, unless death ensues or we get to some settlement. Only one toe left now. Weather clear, light northeast airs, barometer 30.15 at 6.05. Temperature eighteen degrees at 7.30. Nindermann and Alexai were seen to have crossed, and I immediately sent men to carry our load over. Left the following record:—

[See Record No. 4, on page 129.]

At 8.30 made the final trip and got our sick man over in safety. From there we proceeded until 11.20, dragging our man on the sled. Halted for dinner—half pound of meat and tea. At 1 went ahead again until 5.05. Actually under way 8.30 to 9.15, 9.30 to 10.20, 10.30 to 11.20, 1 to 1.40, 1.50 to 2.10, 2.20 to 2.40, 3 to 3.25, 3.35 to 4, 4.15 to 4.35, 4.45 to 5.05. At 8 P. M. crawled into our blankets.

SUNDAY, October 2d.—I think we all slept fairly well until midnight, but from that time forward it was so cold and uncomfortable that sleep was out of the question. At 4.30 we were all out and in front of the fire, daylight just appearing. Erickson kept talking in his sleep all night, and effectually kept those awake who were not already awakened by the cold. Breakfast at 5 A. M.—half pound of meat and tea. Bright, cloudless morning, light northern airs; barometer 30.30 at 5.32; temperature at 6, thirty-five degrees. At 7 went ahead, following the frozen water whenever we could find it, and at 9.20 I felt quite sure we had gone some distance on the main river. I think our gait was at least two miles an hour and our time under way 2h. 40m. I calculate our forenoon work at least six miles, 7 to 7.35, 7.45 to 8.05, 8.15 to 8.30, 8.40 to 8.50, 9.20 to 9.40, 9.50 to 10.12, 10.22 to 10.40, 10.55 to 11.15. Dinner, 1 to 1.30, 1.40 to 2, 2.15 to 2.35, 2.45 to 3, 3.20 to 3.40, 3.50 to 4.05, 4.15 to 4.20. Camp. Total, 5h. 15m.

Two miles an hour distance make good ten to twelve miles, and where are we? I think it the beginning of the Lena River at last. Sagaster has been to us a myth. We saw two old huts at a distance, and this was all; but they were out of our road and the day not half gone. Kept on the ice all the way, and, therefore, think we were over water; but the stream was so narrow and so crooked that it never could have been a navigable stream. My chart is simply useless. I must go on plodding to the southward, trusting in God to guide me to some settlement, for I have long since realized that we are powerless to help ourselves. A bright, calm, beautiful day brought sunshine to cheer us up. An icy road, and one day's rations yet. Boats frozen, of course, and hauled up. No hut in sight, and we halt on a bluff to spend a cold and comfortless night. Supper—half pound meat and tea. Built a rousing fire. Built a log bed. Set a watch, two hours each, to keep fire going and get supper. Then we stood by for a second cold and wretched night. There was so much wind we had to put up our tent halves for a screen and sit shivering in our half blankets.

MONDAY, October 3d, 1881,—113th day.—It was so fearfully cold and wretched that I served out tea to all hands, and on this we managed to struggle along until 5 A.M., when we ate our last deer-meat and had more tea. Our morning food now consists of four-fourteenths of a pound of pemmican each, and a half-starved dog. May God again incline unto our aid! How much farther we have to go before making a shelter or settlement, He only knows. Brisk winds, barometer 30.23 at 1.50 temperature. Erickson seems failing. He is weak and powerless, and the moment he closes his eyes talks, mostly in Danish, German and English. No one can sleep, even though our other surroundings permitted. For some cause my watch stopped at 10.45 last night while one of the men on watch had it. I set it as near as I could by guessing, and we must run by that until I can do better. Sun rose yesterday morning at 6.40 by the watch when running all right. 7.05 to 7.40, 7.50 to 8.20, 8.30 to 9, 9.15 to 9.35, 9.50 to 10.10, 10.25 to 10.40, 11. Back. 11.20, 11.30, 11.40, 11.50. Dinner. 35, 30, 30, 20, 20, 20; total, 155—2 hours 35 minutes, say five miles.

Our force means work. I put as above five miles. Some time and distance were lost by crossing the river upon seeing numerous fox-traps. A man's track was also seen in the snow, bound south, and we followed it until it crossed the river to the west bank again. Here we were obliged to go back again in our tracks, for the river was open in places and we could not follow the man's track direct. Another of the dozen shoals that infest the river swung us off to the eastward, too, and I hastened to get on the west bank again, reaching there at ten minutes to twelve for dinner—our last four-fourteenths of a pound of pemmican.

At forty minutes past one got under way again and made a long spurt until twenty minutes past two. While at the other side of the river Alexai said he saw a hut, and during our dinner camp he said he again saw a hut. Under our circumstances my desire was to get to it as speedily as possible. As Alexai points out, it was on the left bank of the river of which we were now on the right side, looking south, but a sand bank gave us excellent walking for a mile or two

A TIME OF TROUBLE.

until we took to the river and got across it diagonally. Here, at twenty minutes past two, I called a halt, and Alexia mounted the bluff to take a look again. He now announced he saw a second hut, about one and a quarter miles back from the coast, the other hut being about the same distance south and on the edge of the bluff. The heavy dragging across the country of a sick man on a sled made me incline to the hut on the shore, since, as the distance was about the same, we could get over the ice in one-third of the time. Nindermann, who climbed the bluff, saw that the object inland was a hut; was not so confident of the one on the shore. Alexai, however, was quite positive, and not seeing very well myself, I unfortunately took his eyes as best and ordered an advance along the river to the southward.

Away we went, Nindermann and Alexai leading and had progressed about a mile when, plash, in I went through the ice up to my shoulders before my knapsack brought me up. While I was crawling out, in went Gortz to his neck about fifty yards behind me; and behind him, in went Mr. Collins to his waist. Here was a time. The moment we came out of the water we were one sheet of ice, and danger of frost-bite was imminent. Along we hobbled, however, until we reached, at 3.45, about the point on which the hut was seen. Here Nindermann climbed the bluff, followed by the doctor. At first the cry was, "All right; come ahead"; but no sooner were we well up, than Nindermann shouted, "There is no hut here."

To my dismay and alarm nothing but a large mound of earth was to be seen, which, from its regular shape and singular position, would seem to have been built artificially for a beacon. So sure was Nindermann that it was a hut that he went all round it looking for a door, and then climbed on top to look for a hole in the roof. But of no avail. It was nothing but a mound of earth. Sick at heart, I ordered a camp to be made in a hole in the bluff face, and soon before a roaring fire we were drying and burning our clothes, while the cold wind ate into our backs.

And now for supper nothing remained but the dog. I therefore ordered him killed and dressed by Iverson, and soon after a stew was made of such parts as could not be carried, of which everybody except the doctor and myself eagerly partook. To us two it was a nauseating mess, and

—but why go on with such a disagreeable subject. I had the remainder weighed, and I am quite sure we had twenty-seven pounds. The animal was fat, and as he had been fed on pemmican, presumably clean; but, immediately upon halting, I sent Alexai off with his gun inland toward the hut, to determine whether that was a myth like our present one. He returned about dark, certain that it was a large hut, for he had been inside of it, and had found some deer-meat scraps and bones.

For a moment I was tempted to start everybody for it, but Alexai was by no means sure he could find it in the dark, and if we lost our way we would be worse off than before. We accordingly prepared to make the best of it where we were. We three wet people were burning and steaming before the fire. Collins and Gortz had taken some alcohol, but I could not get it down. Cold weather, with a raw northwest wind impossible to avoid or screen, our future was a wretched, dreary night. Erickson soon became delirious, and his talking was a horrible accompaniment to the wretchedness of our surroundings. Warm we could not get, and getting dry seemed out of the question. Every one seemed dazed and stupified, and I feared some of us would perish during the night.

How cold it was I don't know, as my last thermometer was broken by my many falls upon the ice; but I think it must have been below zero. A watch was set to keep the fire going, and we huddled around it, and thus our third night without sleep was passed. If Alexai had not wrapped his sealskin around me, and sat alongside of me to keep me warm by the heat of his body, I think I should have frozen to death. As it was, I steamed and shivered and shook. Erickson's groans and rambling talk rang out on the night air, and such a dreary, wretched night I hope I shall never again see.

Tuesday, October 4th,—114th day.—At the first approach of daylight we all began to move around and the cook was set to work making tea. The doctor now made the unpleasant discovery that Erickson had got his gloves off during the night, and that now his hands were frozen. Men were at once set at work rubbing them, and by 6 A. M. had so far restored circulation as to risk moving the man. Each one had

"SUCH A DREARY, WRETCHED NIGHT."

hastily swallowed a cup of tea and got his load in readiness. Erickson was quite unconscious, and we lashed him on the sled. A southwest gale was blowing and the sensation of cold was intense. But at 6 A. M. we started, made a forced march of it, and at 8 A. M. had got the sick man and ourselves, thank God, under cover of a hut large enough to hold us. Here we at once made a fire and for the first time since Saturday morning last got warm.

The doctor at once examined Erickson and found him very low and feeble. He was quite unconscious, and under the shock of last night's exposure was sinking very fast. Fears were entertained that he might not last many hours, and I therefore called upon every one to join me in reading the prayers for a sick person before we sought any rest for ourselves. This was done in a quiet and reverent manner, though I fear my broken utterances made but little of the service audible. Then, setting a watch, we all, except Alexai, lay down to sleep. At 10 A. M. Alexai went off to hunt, but returned at noon wet, having broken through the ice and fallen in the river. At 6 P. M. we roused up, and I considered it necessary to think of some food for my party. Half a pound of dog meat was fried for each person, and a cup of tea given, and that constituted our day's food; but we were so grateful that we were not exposed to the merciless southwest gale that tore around us, that we did not mind short rations.

WEDNESDAY, October 5th,—115th day.—The cook commences at 7.30 to get tea made from yesterday's tea-leaves. Nothing to serve out until evening. Half a pound of dog meat per day is our food until some relief is afforded us. Alexai went off hunting again at nine, and I set the men gathering light sticks enough to make a flooring for the house; for the frozen ground thawing under everybody, kept them damp and wet and robbed them of much sleep. Southwest gale continues. Barometer, 30.12 at 2.40. Mortification has set in in Erickson's leg, and he is sinking. Amputation would be of no use, as he would probably die under the operation. He is partially conscious. At twelve Alexai came back, having seen nothing. He crossed the river this time, but unable longer to face the cold gale was obliged to return. I am of opinion we are on Titary Island, on its eastern side, and about twenty-five miles from Kumak Surka, which I take to be a settlement. This is the last hope for us. Sagaster has long since faded away. The hut in which we are is quite new, and clearly not the astronomical station made on my chart. In fact, the hut is not finished, having no door and no porch. It may be intended for a summer hut, though the numerous fox-traps would lead me to suppose that it would occasionally be visited at other times.

Upon this last chance, and another sun, rest all our hopes of escape, for I can see nothing more to be done. As soon as the gale abates I shall send Nindermann and another man to make a forced march to Kumak Surka for relief. At six P. M. served out half pound of dog meat and second-hand tea and then went to sleep.

THURSDAY, Oct. 6th—116th day.—Called all hands at 7:30. Had a cup of third-hand tea, with half an ounce of alcohol in it. Everybody very weak. Gale moderating somewhat. Sent Alexai out to hunt. Shall start Nindermann and Noros at noon to make the forced march to Kumak Surka. At 8:45 our messmate, Erickson, departed this life. Addressed a few words of cheer and comfort to the men. Alexai came back

BURIAL OF ERICKSON.

empty-handed—too much drifting snow. What in God's name is going to become of us? Fourteen pounds of dog meat left and twenty-five miles to a possible settlement.

As to burying Erickson, I cannot dig a grave, for the ground is frozen and we have nothing to dig with. There is nothing to do but bury him in the river. Sewed him up in the flaps of the tent and covered him with my flag. Got ten men ready, and with half an ounce of alcohol we will try to make out to bury him, but we are all so weak I do not see how we are going to travel. At 12:40 read the burial service and carried our departed shipmate to the river, where a hole having been cut in the ice he was buried, three volleys from our Remingtons being fired over him as a funeral honor. A board was prepared with this cut on it:—

"In memory of H. H. Erickson, October 6, 1881. U. S. S. Jeannette." And this will be stuck in the river bank almost over his grave.

His clothing was divided up among his messmates. Iverson has his Bible and a lock of his hair. Supper at five P. M., half a pound of dog meat and tea.

FRIDAY, Oct. 7th—117th day.—Breakfast, consisting of our last half pound of dog meat and tea. Our last grain of tea was put in the kettle this morning, and we are now about to undertake our journey of twenty-five miles with some old tea leaves and two quarts of alcohol. However, I trust in God, and I believe that He who has fed us thus far will not suffer us to die of want now. Commenced preparation for departure at ten minutes past seven. One Winchester rifle being out of order, is, with 161 rounds of ammunition, left behind. We have with us two Remingtons and 243 rounds of ammunition. Left the following record in the hut:—

"FRIDAY, Oct. 7th, 1881.—The undermentioned officers and men of the late United States steamer Jeannette are leaving here this morning to make a forced march to Kumak Surka or some other settlement on the Lena River. We reached here Tuesday, October 4th, with a disabled comrade, H. H. Erickson, seaman, who died yesterday morning and was buried in the river at noon.

"His death resulted from frost bite and exhaustion due to consequent exposure.

"The rest of us are well, but have no provisions left, having eaten our last this morning."

Under way by 8:30 and proceeded until 11:20, by which time we had made about three miles. Here we were all pretty well done up, and seemed to be wandering in a labyrinth. A large lump of wood swept in by an eddy seemed to be a likely place to get hot water, and I halted the party for dinner—one ounce of alcohol in a pot of tea. Then went ahead and soon struck what seemed like the main river again. Here four of us broke through the ice in trying to cross, and, fearing frost-bite, I had a fire built on the west bank to dry us up. Sent Alexai off, meanwhile, to look for food, directing him not to go far or stay long; but at 1:30 he had not returned, nor was he in sight. Light southwest breeze, foggy. Mountains in sight to southward. At 5:30 Alexai returned with one ptarmigan, of which we made soup, and with half an ounce of alcohol had our supper. Then crawled under our blankets for a sleep. Light west breeze, full moon, starlight, not very cold. Alexai saw the river a mile wide, with no ice in it.

SATURDAY, Oct. 8th—118th day.—Called all hands at half-past five. Breakfast, one ounce of alcohol in a pint of hot water.

Doctor's Note.—Alcohol proves of great advantage. Keeps off craving for food, preventing gnawing at stomach and has kept up the strength of the men, as given—three ounces per day, as estimated, and in accordance with Dr. Ambler's experiments.

Went ahead until half-past ten. One ounce alcohol. Half-past six to half-past ten, five miles struck Big Biver at 11:30. Ahead again. Snow banks. Met small river, have to turn back. Halt at five; only made advance one mile more. Hard luck. Snow. South-southwest wind, cold. Camp. But little wood. Half an ounce of alcohol.

SUNDAY, Oct. 9th—119th day.—All hands at 4:30. One

ounce of alcohol. Read divine service. Send Nindermann and Noros ahead for relief. They carry their blankets, one rifle, forty rounds of ammunition and two ounces of alcohol. Orders to keep the west bank of river until they reach a settlement. They started at seven. Cheered them. Under way at eight. Crossed the creek. Broke through the ice. All wet up to knees. Stopped and built fires. Dried clothes. Under way again at 10:30. Lee breaking down. At one struck river bank. Halt for dinner; one ounce alcohol. Alexai shot three ptarmigan. Made soup. We are following Nindermann's track, although he is long since out of sight. Under way at 3:30. High bluff. Ice moving rapidly to northward in the river. Halt at 4:40 on coming to wood. Find canal boat. Lay our heads in it and go to sleep. Half ounce alcohol. Supper.

MONDAY, Oct. 10th—120th day.—Last half ounce of alcohol at 5:30. At 6:30 sent Alexai off to look for ptarmigan. Eat deer skin scraps. Yesterday morning ate my deer skin foot nips. Light southeast wind. Air not very cold. Under way at eight. In crossing creek three of us got wet. Built fire and dried out. Ahead again until eleven; used up. Built fire; made a drink out of the tea leaves from alcohol bottle. On again at noon. Fresh south-southwest wind. Drifting snow. Very hard going. Lee begging to be left. Some little beach and then long stretches of high bank. Ptarmigan tracks plentiful. Following Nindermann's track. At three halted, used up. Crawled into a hole in the bank. Collected wood and built a fire. Alexai away in quest of game. Nothing for supper except a spoonful of glycerine. All hands weak and feeble, but cheerful. God help us.

TUESDAY, Oct. 11th—121st day—Southwest gale, with snow. Unable to move. No game. Teaspoonful of glycerine and hot water for food. No more wood in our vicinity.

WEDNESDAY, Oct. 12th—122d day.—Breakfast, last spoonful of glycerine and hot water. For dinner we had a couple of handsful of Arctic willow in a pot of water, and drank the infusion. Everybody getting weaker and weaker. Hardly strength to get firewood. Southwest gale, with snow.

THURSDAY, Oct. 13th—123d day.—Willow tea. Strong southwest winds. No news from Nindermann. We are in the hands of God, and unless He relents are lost. We cannot move against the wind, and staying here means starvation. After noon went ahead for a mile, crossing either another river or a wind in the big one. After crossing missed Lee. Went down in a hole in the bank and camped. Sent back for Lee. He had laid down, and was waiting to die. All united in saying the Lord's Prayer and Creed. After supper strong gale of wind. Horrible night.

FRIDAY, Oct. 14th—124th day.—Breakfast, willow tea. Dinner, half tea, spoonful sweet oil and willow tea. Alexai shot one ptarmigan. Had soup. Southwest wind moderating.

SATURDAY, Oct. 15th—125th day.—Breakfast, willow tea and two old boots. Conclude to move at sunrise. Alexai broken down; also Lee. Came to an empty grain raft. Halt and camp. Signs of smoke at twilight to southward.

SUNDAY, Oct. 16th—126th day.—Alexai broken down. Divine service.

MONDAY, Oct. 17th—127th day.—Alexai dying. Doctor baptised him. Read prayers for sick. Mr. Collins' birthday, forty years old. About sunset Alexai died. Exhaustion from starvation. Covered him with ensign and laid him in the crib.

TUESDAY, Oct. 18th—128th day.—Calm and mild. Snow falling. Buried Alexai in the afternoon. Laid him on the ice of the river and covered him over with slabs of ice.

WEDNESDAY, Oct. 19th—129th day.—Cutting up tent to make foot gear. Doctor went ahead to find new camp. Shifted by dark.

THURSDAY, Oct. 20th—130th day.—Bright and sunny, but very cold. Lee and Kaack done up.

FRIDAY, Oct. 21st—131st day.—Kaack was found dead

about midnight between the doctor and myself. Lee died about noon. Read prayers for sick when we found he was going.

SATURDAY, Oct. 22d—132d day.—Too weak to carry the bodies of Lee and Kaack out on the ice. The doctor, Collins and myself carried them around the corner out of sight. Then my eye closed up.

SUNDAY, Oct. 23d,—133d day.—Everybody pretty weak. Slept or rested to-day, and then managed to get enough wood in before dark. Read part of divine service. Suffering in our feet. No foot gear.

MONDAY, Oct. 24th—134th day.—A hard night.

TUESDAY, Oct. 25th—135th day.

WEDNESDAY, Oct. 26th—136th day.

THURSDAY, Oct. 27th—137th day.—Iverson broken down.

FRIDAY, Oct. 28th—138th day.—Iverson died during early morning.

SATURDAY, Oct. 29th—139th day.—Dressler died during the night.

SUNDAY, Oct. 30th—140th day.—Boyd and Gortz died during the night. Mr. Collins dying.

DE LONG'S DIARY.

With reeling brain and stiffening limbs, that bleak October morn,
Our brave commander knelt, while we, his comrades, all forlorn,
Hugged close the fire of faggots piled against the icy wall,
And snow and ice around us beat, and clothed us like a pall.

Close, aye, within the very flame we grouped in our despair,
For God had surely left the lonely crew to perish there!
But in our breasts a rebel cry sunk softened with a tear,
When brave DeLong spoke low of home and wives and children dear.

His book and pencil in his hands, he essayed, with a smile,
To mark the closing record of our wanderings;—many a mile
Of frozen sea we'd trudged across, and many a league of snow,
And now, on Tit Ary's icy isle, we faced at last our foe.

LIEUTENANT DE LONG'S DIARY.

The fire in front, Death at our backs, we calmly waited there,
To know the worst, and trust in God, who always answers prayer.
Our chief's numb fingers slowly moved across the log-book leaf,
While Erickson lay dying, and we crouched dumb with grief.

No word from Kumak Surka came, where Nindermann had gone,
His footprints mocked us in the snow on that October morn,—
That Sabbath still and silent, as we shrunk with bated breath,
Each sheeted in an icy shroud—all holding tryst with Death.

Then Erickson, brave Erickson, at last gave up the fight;—
He was buried in the river in the fierce Siberian night,—
The Arctic wind his requiem, the Arctic wave his pall,—
Then to our meager fire we crept, where gloom fell o'er us all.

Oh, God! those days that followed! What half-way hopes and fears!
What earnest prayers and unheard groans, and melting hearts and tears!
What hunger keen, and faces blanched! what howling Polar wind,
That pierced the marrow, mocked at fire, and almost made us blind.

Alexai, our stout hunter, who had breasted many a storm,
To give his messmates food and fire, their freezing limbs to warm
The sturdy oak lay felled at last before the scythe-like frost;
He, too, within the Lena lies, by its strong current tost.

Then others, tired of battling cold and hunger, drooped and died,
Nor strength had we to bury them—they lay there by our side;
But surely Christ the Saviour who within a manger lay,
Took pity on us, desolate, that bleak October day.

For on us dawned a quietude, a holy soothing calm,
And keen and cutting Arctic winds breathed voices like a psalm;
The sounding of the river running north beneath the ice,
Seemed whisperings of angels on the shores of Paradise.

Then pain and hunger left us—left us all our weary aches,
And our forebodings sad of home for wife and children's sakes.
Iversen and Dressler silent! Boyd—and Gortz, too,—speak my friend,
—'Tis the Sabbath—Collins—dying * * * * and the log was at an end.

New York Star.

CHAPTER XXXII.

NEW SEARCHERS IN THE FIELD.

(BERRY, HUNT, AND GILDER—HARBER AND SCHEUTZE.)

AFTER attending to the burial of Lieutenant DeLong and his men and completing their tomb, the three parties separated to search the delta for Lieutenant Chipp. Melville went to the northwest, Bartlett to the northeast, and Nindermann took the center. The sea-coast of the delta was examined from Olenek River on the west to Yana River on the east, but no traces were found of the second cutter or her crew. The search was extensive, but could not be made very thorough, owing to the depth of the snowdrifts.

After examining the delta, Melville and his reunited party proceeded to Verhoyansk. From this place they started for Yakutsk on sleds, but after going 120 miles they were obliged to take to horseback. At the deer station of Kengurach, on the northern side of the Verhoyansk mountains, they were obliged to halt, as it was impossible for the horses to pass the snowdrifts, which were from ten to twenty feet deep. While waiting for the snow to melt they were joined by three American travelers—Mr. Jackson, the *Herald* correspondent, and Lieutenant Berry and Ensign Hunt of the Jeannette search steamer Rodgers.

Some account of Mr. Jackson's journey to Irkutsk, where he met Danenhower's party, has already been given. Subsequently he proceeded to Yakutsk, accompanied by Mr. Noros, and started north, March 29th, to join in the search. On reaching Aldan River, he met a courier carrying dispatches from W. H. Gilder, Pay Clerk of the steamer Rodgers, to

TRAVELERS FROM THE EAST AND THE WEST. 395

General Tchernieff, and heard the startling news that the Rodgers had been burned at her winter-harbor in St. Lawrence Bay. The courier had accompanied Mr. Gilder from Nischni (or Nijni) Kolymsk, on the Kolyma River, to Verhoyansk, where they arrived March 28th; and from this place Gilder, hearing of the loss of the Jeannette, had started north, March 29th, hoping to fall in with Melville's party. Subsequently he returned south, and proceeded to Yakutsk.

Continuing his journey to the delta, Mr. Jackson visited Geemovialocke, and the bluff where Lieutenant DeLong and his party perished, and also their tomb. He followed the track of Nindermann and Noros to Bulun, and thence proceeded to Verhoyansk, where he learned that Lieutenant Berry and Ensign Hunt, of the Rodgers, had lately arrived there and gone south on horseback; they had brought news of additional disaster—the loss of Mr. Putnam, one of the most talented officers of the Rodgers expedition, who had been carried out to sea on floating ice.

Mr. Jackson overtook Berry and Hunt below Verhoyansk, and traveled with them to Kengurach, where they joined Melville, as previously stated.

After waiting a few days longer for the snow to melt, they all started on together. On reaching Aldan River they learned that Mr. Gilder had arrived there ten days before, and had been caught on the northern shore of the river when the ice broke up, and for seven days his party had to live (on a narrow piece of land which is frequently covered with water) on the flesh of one of their horses. He had for a traveling companion at this time Constantine Buhokoff (who was conveying papers from Melville to Yakutsk), and in order to save his own dispatches and those from Melville, the boxes containing them were placed in the trunk of a tree. The water rose thirty feet in a few hours.

The party consisting of Melville, Bartlett, Nindermann, Berry, Hunt, Jackson, and Noros finally reached Yakutsk, June 8th, in safety, losing, however, on their journey ten reindeer and eight horses, which were left on the roadside exhausted. One horse, too, was lost in crossing the quicksands of the Lena near the city.

On reaching Yakutsk, Mr. Melville learned that Lieutenant Giles B. Harber and Master W. H. Scheutze—two naval officers who had been sent out by the Secretary of the Navy to search for Lieutenant Chipp—had arrived at Vitimsk, a town at the junction of the Lena and Vitim rivers. These gentlemen left New York early in February by steamer, and proceeded via London and Paris to St. Petersburg, where they arrived February 20th. Here they consulted with Mr. Hoffman, General Ignatieff, the Governor-general of Siberia, and other officials, all of whom were particularly kind and anxious to render assistance. Special traveling passes and very valuable charts and books were furnished them.

At Moscow the travelers were cordially received by the French Consul, who entertained them at dinner, introduced them to the governor, and saw them started on their journey.

On their way to Irkutsk, at Nijni Ujinsk, Messrs. Harber and Scheutze met Lieutenant Danenhower's party going home; and by permission of Secretary Hunt, Leach, Wilson, Mansen, Lauderback, and Anequin cheerfully turned back with Harber and Scheutze to assist them in the search for Chipp. Mr. Noros had previously gone back with Mr. Jackson.

It was supposed that the steamer Lena would be chartered for the use of the search-party, as her owner, Mr. Sibiriakoff, had kindly tendered her to Mr. Bennett for that purpose; but on arriving at Irkutsk, Lieutenant Harber found that she had been sold, and that her new owner demanded an exorbitant price for her use during the summer. He accordingly chartered (subject, however, to inspection) another steamer, the General Simlinikoff, which was then lying in the Vitim River, some distance above Vitimsk.

Meantime Mr. Scheutze and four of the seamen had gone on to Vitimsk; and Mr. Harber, with Mr. Mansen and an interpreter, started from Irkutsk, April 13th, to rejoin them. The snow had gone from the ground and the rivers were breaking up, so that the roads were nearly impassable. Three hundred and fifty versts were traveled in post-wagons, over 900 versts in sleds (much of the latter being through mud and water), and nearly 250 versts were made on horseback. "Just as we had crossed a river by swimming our horses," says Harber, "and when the opposite bank was reached, a wonderful noise from up the river caused the natives to hasten up the river bank with horses and parcels, and at once the river rose some six feet in three minutes, and the river itself was filled with immense masses of ice in which no boat could live."

Vitimsk was finally reached, April 28th. Mr. Scheutze had seen the steamer and reported unfavorably respecting it. The same day Harber went on to Viska, where he learned that it would be nearly impossible to get to Voronzofsky where the steamer was; it was 110 versts distant through an uninhabited country, and the river, the only route to the place, was no longer safe. "I concluded," says Harber, "to wait at Viska until the river broke up, and in the meantime to have two dories built. I also found a boat fifty feet long and nearly ten feet beam, which could readily be made into a schooner sufficiently large and strong to do work along the coast outside of the delta. I accordingly purchased it and commenced repairing it."

Finally, towards the last of May, Harber and Scheutze reached Voronzofsky, and navigated the steamer to Viska. "During the trip down the river," says Harber, writing from Viska, June 11th, "I inspected the hull and engines and measured the amount of wood she burned. The result was, we found her quite unfit for our purpose and I declined to accept her. Too large a surface was exposed to the action of the waves, and she burned so much fuel that we would have to return frequently for wood. We were detained here, but now all is ready, and we leave at once with our boats. I still hope to reach the delta by July 1st. I go prepared to search the delta, and from the Olenek to the Yana, should it seem advisable."

While on his way down the Lena in his schooner, Harber, without knowing it at the time, passed, in the night, the steamer Constantine, aboard of which were Melville, Nindermann, Noros, Berry, and Jackson, who had started for home. Ensign Hunt and Mr. Bartlett remained at Yakutsk, both of them having volunteered to assist Harber. The northern search party started from Yakutsk for the Delta near the close of June.

The homeward journey of the returning explorers was, says Melville, one fair voyage filled with friendly God speeds from all quarters. At St. Petersburg they were received by the Emperor of Russia. On arriving at Berlin, Nindermann took time to visit his birthplace, on the Isle of Rugen, in the Baltic Sea, off the northern coast of Prussia. He was met outside his native village by a bevy of rustic maidens with flowers and wreaths, and had a joyful reception. The whole place was in holiday attire during his two days' stay.

The Cunard steamer Parthia, from Liverpool, brought the party over the last section of their long journey; and they arrived at New York, Melville's native city, September 13th, just one year from the day when the three boats carrying the Jeannette castaways were separated off the Siberian coast. When they left the steamer's deck, it was to meet "the warmest, the simplest, the grandest reception ever witnessed in New York Bay." They were taken to the city on the steam yacht, Ocean Gem, and disembarked amid a great display of enthusiasm from the assembled multitude, Melville was welcomed to the city by Lieutenant Jacques, in behalf of the Secretary of the Navy and the Commander of the Port. Subsequently he received distinguished honors from the officials and citizens of New York, Philadelphia, and other places, in all of which Nindermann and Noros shared.

BURNING OF THE RODGERS.

CHAPTER XXXIII.

BERRY'S SEARCH EXPEDITION—CONTINUED.

(BURNING OF THE RODGERS—AN ICE-FLOE TRAGEDY.)

AFTER cruising in the Arctic waters in search of the Jeannette during the summer of 1881, the United States steamer Rodgers arrived at St. Lawrence Bay, on the northeastern coast of Siberia, as stated in Chapter IV. Preparations for spending the winter in this harbor were immediately begun, but, owing to continued bad weather, Lieutenant Berry was prevented from building a small house on shore and transferring thither a large part of his provisions and supplies as he intended to have done.

On the 20th of November, Ensign Hunt started up the coast with a team of nine dogs intending to visit Camp Hunt, as Master Putnam's winter-quarters on Eteelan Island was named. This island is located about twenty miles west of Cape Serdze, near the native village of Tiapka, a little east of Nordenskiöld's winter quarters, and about 150 miles from St. Lawrence Bay. After going some distance Mr. Hunt was compelled to turn back, owing to severe storms, and he went on board the ship November 29th, leaving his dogs on shore. These dogs were the only ones of the expedition which survived the disaster which soon overtook the crew. Up to this time everything had gone well, and all the men were in good health and spirits.

At about nine o'clock on the morning of November 30th the startling cry of "Fire!" was heard, and smoke was seen issuing from the fore-hold, apparently from under the donkey boiler room. The crew were immediately called to quarters, and the hatches were closed to prevent the air from reaching the flames. Fires were burning under the donkey boiler to heat the ship, and the steam pump was quickly connected thereto. The deck force-pump was also immediately utilized. Two streams of water were soon playing, but owing to the dense smoke it was for some time impossible to get them directed on the fire. The main engine was also quickly put in working order; and when, as the fire spread, it became necessary to abandon the donkey boiler, the pumps were connected with and worked from the main boiler without any break in the flow of water.

The fire was in the lower hold, and the place was so closely filled with stores that it was next to impossible to get any water on it; and the dense smoke prevented the men from going into the hold. So much smoke escaped that the hosemen had to be frequently relieved, and the fireman at the donkey boiler had to quit his post.

As the vessel was lying head to the wind with a fresh breeze, hawsers were made fast to the chains, the chains were shipped, and the ship was brought round stern to the wind to prevent, if possible, the fire from spreading aft. The steam pipe running from the main boiler to the main windlass was broken, two sections of hose were fitted to the pipe, and steam was forced into the hold. This seemed to stay the fire, but it was only for a moment; the hose was melted by the intense heat, and smoke began to rush into the fire room and coal bunkers. The officers and crew worked bravely and unremittingly, but the fire continued to increase, and in the afternoon it became apparent that all efforts to save the ship would be unavailing.

About four P.M. Lieutenant Berry gave orders to make sail and run the ship on to the beach, where he hoped by scuttling her to save a supply of provisions. The chains were buoyed by the upper topsail yards, and the hawsers were cut. Lower topsails, foresail, jib, and spanker were set, and the ship was headed for the beach; but the wind failed, the ship was drifted by the ice and tide, and ran aground before reaching the desired position. A hawser was made fast to a kedge anchor and this was thrown overboard. The valves of the outward delivery were then opened to flood and sink the ship, and from six to eight feet of water rushed into the fore room; but as the ship was aground by the stern the water did not reach the fire. The ship at this time lay about 500 feet from the shore, surrounded by slush ice twenty inches thick; this ice was too soft to allow a man to walk upon it, and yet too thick and heavy to row boats through.

Meantime attention had been turned to the saving of stores. Some of the men had been taken from the force-pump, and had been working hard in attempting to get up provisions and clothing, but with little success owing to the smoke and a collection of carbonic acid gas below decks. Holes were cut through the deck, and some powder from the magazine and oil from the sail-room were passed aft to the quarter deck. All hands worked with almost superhuman strength.

At nine P. M. a boat was launched, but the ice was so heavy that it could not be forced thirty feet from the ship. A native skin boat was next tried, and two men succeeded in reaching the beach carrying the end of a line. A larger rope was then hauled ashore and made fast to a piece of driftwood.

At ten o'clock the flames had spread so far aft that it was resolved to abandon the ship. The boats were accordingly loaded with such articles as had been secured, and the crews got into them and began warping them to land. This proved to be very hard work, as the ice was rapidly thickening. The sailors had to get on the gunwales and rock the boats from side to side, which loosened the ice and enabled them to work along a few inches at a time. At last it became impossible to move the two rear boats, and their crews, after fastening them to the warping line and cutting the line adrift from the ship, were transferred to the other boats. The two rear boats were hauled ashore by the men after they landed.

The Rodgers was abandoned at a quarter to twelve o'clock

on the night of November 30th, and when the boats reached land it was two o'clock A. M. of December 1st. It had taken two hours and a quarter to get them from the ship to the land.

By this time the fire had enveloped the whole ship, and Lieutenant Berry and his companions stood on shore and watched their good ship burn. "It was a calm, still night—such a night as is seen during an Arctic winter only—the stars glistening and the moon shining brightly on the frozen waters and the snow-clad hills, and the flames from the doomed ship giving a crimson tint to the atmosphere." Suddenly, greatly to their surprise and sorrow, the ship began to move from her position and to drift away with the tide and ice. The ship had failed to fill with water enough to sink, and the burning of the hawser released her from the anchor.

With her rigging and sails on fire the burning ship presented a grand sight as she drifted up the bay. The national pennant was observed floating proudly from the main truck, above the flames. Subsequently the magazine exploded; and the ship was last seen on the morning of December 2d, still burning. The origin of the fire could not be determined, but it was most probably caused by the heat from the donkey boiler charring and firing the deck underneath.

The situation and prospects of the party at this time were anything but pleasant. They were turned adrift in a desolate country at the beginning of winter with but little food and clothing, and with no possibility of being rescued for many months. They had thus far had but little intercourse with the natives of the coast, but it was evident that upon them, to a great extent, they would have to depend for shelter and food during the long winter before them.

No one had thought of eating while fighting the fire, and when they landed all were too fatigued to prepare a meal or even a shelter. They tried to get some rest and sleep, wrapped in their blankets, but were so cold that occasionally some were obliged to get up and run to keep up the ciroulation.

In the morning boats were launched (the ice having drifted away from the shore) and headed for Noonamoo, the native village at North Head, but the ice again closed in and the crews had to turn back. The boats were hauled upon the beach and a camp was formed of overturned boats, sails and tents, and all found shelter from a violent snow-storm which had set in. Half a pound of pemmican and some bread were served out to each man for the day's rations.

Next morning, December 2d, a party of natives (two of whom were visiting the ship when the fire broke out) arrived at the camp with sledges drawn by dogs, and invited the shipwrecked people to their village. The invitation was gratefully accepted, and, after the storm had abated, all the party (excepting a detachment left behind to take care of the boats and other property) started for Noonamoo, about seven miles distant, escorted by the natives, whose sledges had been loaded with provisions. They arrived at Noonamoo after a most fatiguing tramp over hills and through snow from two to four feet deep, and were distributed among the eleven huts or habitations which constituted the settlement. Here they were speedily introduced to walrus and blubber as an article of food, and settled down to a long winter's siege, adapting themselves to the customs and requirements of savage life among the Chukches.

A few days later a party was sent to the camp on the beach, and, as the ice had drifted away from the shore, the boats were launched, loaded with the remaining stores, and taken around to the village, where they were hauled up for the winter. A barter trade with the natives was now commenced, and soon all the men were comfortably clad. Everyone was compelled to live on native food, the provisions saved from the ship being kept as a reserve.

It soon became evident that the supply of walrus meat in the village was insufficient for so large a population, and as people from other villages had invited some of the men to come and live with them, a new distribution was decided on. The officers and crew were divided into four parties, one of which remained at Noonamoo, while the others were conducted by the natives to three other villages along the coast, within a radius of twenty miles. William Grace, a member of one of the parties who migrated to another village, describes his reception, and some of his subsequent experiences, as follows:—

"After much difficulty in getting over the snow, we arrived at Ak-kun-neer at night, December 10th, cold, hungry, and exhausted. On stopping at the entrance of the hut, our conductor would not allow us to go in, but shouted in a loud voice, 'Atkeen' (no good). He then said to some one inside the hut, 'Wiki wiki pennena' (give me a lighted stick), and a woman came out with a lighted stick in her hand. The man seized it and shook it in our faces, over our clothes and the sledge, and then exclaimed 'Namaikee' (good). We were then permitted to enter, and were stripped of all our clothing in the outer compartment of the hut. On coming into the interior, we were given some frozen walrus meat, a few roots, somewhat resembling parsnips, and also a small piece of frozen, rotten seal flesh.

"After eating, I was surrounded by a group of natives, who came into the hut to see the white man. They examined my body, feet, and hands, and also every portion of my clothing, which was hanging up. The woman of the hut put an amulet made of seal-gut, with a large bead at the end, around my wrist. When I made signs as to its meaning, they replied, 'Namalkee' (no die). I slept on the ground that night, with a deerskin under me and over me. The vermin which covered my body and covering prevented my sleeping all night."

Near the close of the year Lieutenant Berry, leaving Master Waring in command, started with the only remaining team of dogs to visit Putnam's camp. At this time the upper limb of the sun was seen above the horizon for only two hours at a time, and then sank into the sea, and twenty-two hours of darkness followed.

In due time, through native sources, the news of the burning of the Rodgers had reached Camp Hunt, and Mr. Putnam at once resolved to carry supplies to his distressed shipmates. He hired three natives (one of whom was named Ehr Ehren) to accompany him, and started south with four loaded sledges. At Inchnan (25 miles from East Cape) he met Lieutenant Berry, who was on his way to Putnam's camp, and received instructions to continue his trip, and to bring Ensign Hunt and Engineer Zane back with him.

On the 4th of January Mr. Putnam and his party reached the village at North Head, delivered his provisions, and remained several days for his dogs to recuperate. Among the most acceptable articles which he brought to his comrades, was a quantity of books and magazines.

Master Putnam started to return to Camp Hunt, January 10th, accompanied by Hunt, Zane, Castillo, and the three natives. Mr. Putnam drove his own team of nine dogs, and Mr. Hunt rode on the sled beside him. Dr. Castillo rode with Ehr Ehren, Mr. Zane rode with a native named Nortuna, and the third native rode alone. They had not proceeded far when Putnam's sled broke down, and, although it was repaired, Hunt was obliged to ride with the third native. Subsequent events are described by the *Herald* correspondent as follows:—

"Toward noon the sky became overcast. A wind sprang up from the northward, and soon increased to a terrific gale, filling the air so thickly with snow that it became impossible to see the route, and consequently the natives lost their way. They kept on, however, making the dogs face the gale until six P. M., when the natives deemed it expedient to camp where they were for the night. The air was so thick with the drifting snow that the lead dogs could not be seen by the drivers. This was a night of severe suffering to the travelers, who sat on their sleds trying to obtain a little sleep, excepting when they were compelled to move about to get warm.

"In the morning it moderated a little, and they decided to return to St. Lawrence Bay, and wait until the weather became more suitable for traveling. The storm increased in violence all the time, but as the wind was now behind, they had no trouble and the bay was reached in safety. There being no dog food at the village at North Head, it became necessary to go to the south side. The bay was crossed safely, and they arrived on the southern shore about one and a half miles from the village of Nutapinwin—their destination.

"All the heavy gales during this season of the year were from the northward and westward. Just before getting to the village, it was necessary to make a sharp turn to the right, and go in the teeth of the gale for about two hundred yards. The order in which the sleds were proceeding was as follows:—Castillo and Ehr Ehren, Putnam, Zane and Nortuna, and Hunt and a native came last and were some distance behind.

"All proceeded along well until they made the turn to face the gale, when Putnam, not having the ability to control dogs so well as the natives, (it is difficult to force the dogs to go to windward in a severe storm,) or probably not knowing of the abrupt deviation from his course, as he could not see the other sleds turn, probably kept straight on. Zane, being familiar with the locality, recognized some landmarks when near the village, but Putnam could not recognize the marks, as this was his first visit to the place.

"About this time Zane overtook Putnam, and when their sleds were abreast remarked, 'Well, Put, it seems that we are all right after all.' Putnam answered, 'I hope so.' They were the last words he was ever heard to utter, and that was the last seen of him. His sled fell a little behind. The natives made the turn with some difficulty, but Putnam missed it, partly owing to his being unable to see them. It is thought that as the wind was quartering he was sitting on his sled back to the wind, which, being very strong, gradually edged his sled out of the track toward the ice, which was but a short distance off. However, he got on the ice, and the supposition is that after going some distance out he became aware of his mistake, and, not being able to see which way to go, and his shouts not being heard in such a violent gale, he camped to wait for fair weather, knowing that a search would be made for him as soon as he was missed.

"On reaching the village, in about five minutes after speaking with Putnam, Mr. Zane went immediately into a house, as he was almost frozen. It was soon discovered that Putnam was missing, and, thinking he had made some mistake, a native started down to the beach to look for him; and when Hunt came along on his sled he found Nortuna yelling with all his might, but thinking this noise was to guide him, kept on to the village. Here he ascertained that it was Putnam he was seeking. Hunt went in and inquired of Zane if Putnam had arrived; this was the first intimation Zane had of the unfortunate occurrence.

"Both then started for the beach to assist in the search; they were both now thoroughly alarmed, for they could appreciate the danger of being lost in such a storm. They offered every inducement, entreated, and ordered the natives to hitch up the dogs and hunt for the unfortunate man, but they would neither hitch up their dogs nor allow them to use their own dogs, saying that the gale was too heavy, they could not see, and that probably next day would be fine, and then all would go out and hunt. All threats proved unavailing, nothing could be done but to wait for the morrow. The gale was increasing in violence every moment. After going down to the beach it was impossible to get back to the houses, the wind blew so strong in the face. During the night the heavy wind detached the ice from shore, and carried it to sea."

Next morning, at daylight, they again went on the search. Hunt and Zane started along the beach, and natives taking various other directions to look for him. The wind had gone down some, but it was still blowing so hard as to make traveling very difficult. The morning was clear, however, and a considerable distance could be seen. Hunt and Zane gazed on the place which the night before had been one sheet of ice, and saw that it was now clear water with no ice in sight. They walked along the beach about a mile until they came to a bluff which they knew it would have been impossible to pass on a sled, and satisfied themselves that he was

GOING FOR PUTNAM.

not on the beach. It was almost certain that he had camped on the ice and been carried to sea with it. The only chance for his safety seemed to be that the wind would spring up from the southward and drive the ice in shore, or that it would become calm and allow the new ice to form between the old and the shore, so that the unfortunate man could walk over it.

The next day, 13th, Hunt and Zane with the three natives

started for North Head to notify Mr. Waring of the sad affair. After crossing the bay they met Waring and told him of the calamity. He told them to proceed to Camp Hunt in obedience to the orders of Lieutenant Berry, and set out himself on a search along the coast. The same afternoon he received a note from Seaman Cahill, one of the men stationed at the village at South Head, stating that Putnam had been seen on that morning on an ice floe about three miles from the shore. The natives would not launch their skin boats on account of the intervening thin ice, although Mr. Cahill offered large rewards to induce them to do so.

Late in the afternoon of the following day, 14th, word was received that Putnam had been seen from a village six miles south of South Head, on the ice eight miles from shore, and that the natives were making preparations to rescue him. Waring pushed on to the village, reaching it that night through a heavy wind and snow-storm blowing hard off shore. It was here ascertained that on the preceding day an attempt had been made by four men of the Rodgers crew, assisted by two natives, to rescue Putnam; but after proceeding nearly three miles they were forced to return, the boat having been cut through in so many places that they were barely able to keep her afloat until shore was reached.

Another severe off-shore storm was now raging, and the unfortunate man was lost sight of. The natives were confident that the ice floe would be driven inside of a point some distance down the coast, and preparations were immediately made to go down to the point as soon as the weather would permit. There was trouble in procuring dogs to travel, because the natives at both North and South Head were afraid, on account of some previous difficulty with the natives at Indian Point, to go down the coast or to allow their dogs to go, saying they would be killed. At last, however, a team was scraped up from four villages, ranging over a space of thirty or forty miles.

It was the 17th before another start could be made. The day opened stormy, but soon moderated, and the search continued with one native and a team of eight dogs. The coast was skirted to the sixth settlement, about thirty miles, but no news was heard; the off-shore wind had driven the heavy ice to sea. The next day, not being able to get dogs to continue the journey, Waring was compelled to return to the village next to South Head.

Natives were now dispatched along the coast, offering great rewards for the rescue of Putnam or for his body if he were dead. Another heavy gale set in, making traveling impossible. On the 22d a southeast gale brought the ice in shore again, but it was found that the sea had crushed it up into small pieces, no heavy floes being anywhere in sight. Men from down the coast brought no news. The case appeared almost hopeless now, as all of the floes must have broken up during the five days' gale.

On the 26th, Waring heard a rumor that some dogs had come on shore from the ice. For two days he was prevented by storms from proceeding; but on the 29th, though intensely cold, he started down the coast to identify the dogs. He arrived at Lauren, thirty miles down the coast, in the evening, and found three of Putnam's dogs there. Several dogs came ashore, but the natives could catch only three. They said that all came ashore without harness.

After being weather-bound for three days Waring started down the coast, February 2d, and searched the whole coast as far as Plover Bay. He communicated with several natives who spoke good English, and they were satisfied that Putnam had never come near the shore.

At Engwort (sixty miles from South Head) another dog, with a pistol-shot wound in his neck, had come ashore ten days previously and was recognized as belonging to Putnam's team. This dog—like all the others—was very thin and emaciated, covered with ice, and had every appearance of having been long in the water. Putnam had probably shot this dog, intending to use it for food, but he had succeeded in escaping. In all six dogs, out of his team of nine, came ashore.

Mr. Waring got back to his village after searching for his lost comrade for over a month. At Plover Bay and Marcus Bay he left letters for the officers of any whalers which might come there, informing them of the condition of the wrecked crew, and urging them to hasten to their assistance.

It is known that Mr. Putnam was alive on the third day after being carried out to sea, but how much longer he survived can only be conjectured. All this time the temperature was from 20 to 40 degrees below zero, and he had no protection from the piercing winds aside from his very warm clothing. He probably killed one or more of his dogs for food, and so did not die of starvation. The floe which he was on doubtless broke into fragments during one of the gales, and he was drowned. The circumstances of his death were sad and most lamentable. He was one of the most promising officers of the expedition.

CHAPTER XXXIV.

LIFE AMONG THE CHUKCHES.

THE natives of Northeastern Siberia are called Chukches, and their coast extends from Chaun Bay on the Arctic Ocean, around the Chukches Peninsula to the Anadyr River. Westward of Chaun Bay the coast as far as the Gulf of Obi (about 100 degrees of longitude) is uninhabited, although Russian samovies and native encampments are found on the rivers at some distance from their mouths.

The Chukches are divided into two principal branches speaking the same language, and belonging to the same race, but differing considerably in their mode of life. One division consists of reindeer nomads, who wander about with their herds, and live by raising reindeer and by trade—carrying on a traffic between the savages in the northernmost parts of America, and the Russian fur-dealers in Siberia.

The other division are the Coast Chukches who do not own reindeer, but have dogs, and live in fixed, but easily movable and frequently moved tents along the coast of Northeastern Siberia. They have also settled along the shore of Bering Sea, and some of an inferior race, nearly allied to the Esquimaux living there, have adopted their language and modes of life.

It was among the Coast Chukches that the Rodgers crew found shelter and sustenance during their five months' residence on the treeless shores adjoining St. Lawrence Bay. During this period they were received as friends, and at times when food was scarce families would go hungry that their guests might not suffer. The struggle to get food began as soon as they were fairly settled down for the winter. Everybody had to go hunting. Those who lived with poor huntsmen fared worse than the others, and had frequently to depend on themselves or go hungry. Ensign Stoney was quartered with a poor hunter, and did most of the hunting for the entire family; but the head of the house generally accompanied him and looked out for his safety like a faithful slave. If the ice was suspicious looking, he would go ahead with a long pole.

CHUKCHE COUNTRY HARES.

Sometimes hunting was done several miles out on the ice, and then perhaps a large seal would have to be dragged home through snow two or three feet deep. Ducks and rabbits were frequently captured. Deer were scarce and seen only a long distance inland. When hunting had to be suspended during a long spell of bad weather, there would be almost a famine in the villages. Small quantities of the ship's provision were dealt out once a month.

The Chukches are a hardy race, but exceedingly indolent when want of food does not force them to exertion. There were but few natives in the settlement who did not own a rifle, obtained from whalers. The men, during their hunt-

CHUKCHE WOMAN ANGLING.

ing excursions, pass whole days in a cold of 30 to 40 degrees below zero, out upon the ice, without protection and without carrying with them food or fuel. Women nearly naked often, during severe cold, leave for awhile the inner tent where the train-oil lamp maintains a heat that is at times oppressive. Both men and women wear snow-shoes during the winter, and will not willingly undertake any long walks in loose snow without them. The children nearly always make a pleasing impression, by their healthy appearance and their friendly and becoming behavior.

In early winter, before the ice is too thick, the women fish along the shore. Each fisherwoman is accompanied by a man, who cuts a hole in the ice with an iron-shod spear, and skims out the loose ice with an ice-sieve. Stooping down at the hole, she endeavors to attract the fish by means of a peculiarly wonderful clattering cry, and when a fish is seen in the water, a line with a baited hook of bone, iron, or copper, is thrown down. One of these fisherwomen might possibly have saved the lives of DeLong's party, had she been with them.

During the winter Mr. Stoney visited some Reindeer Chukches seventy miles inland, and saw several herds of reindeer, but did not get any as he could not pay for them. Lieutenant Palander, of the Vega, gives the following account of a visit to Reindeer Chukches made by him in 1879:—

"The camp consisted of two tents, one of which was unoccupied. The other was occupied by a Chukche and his wife, and another young couple who were visiting there. About fifty reindeer were pasturing on an eminence some distance off, but proposals to purchase some were declined, although bread, tobacco, rum, and even guns were offered in exchange.

"In the afternoon we were invited into the tent, where we passed an hour in their sleeping chamber. On our entrance the seal-oil lamp was lighted. Our hostess endeavored to make our stay in the tent as agreeable as possible; she rolled together reindeer skins for pillows, and made ready for us a place where, stretched at full length, we might enjoy much needed repose. In the outer tent the other women prepared supper, which consisted of boiled seal's flesh. After the meal was partaken of, our host divested himself of all his clothing, the trousers excepted. Our hostess let her *pesk* fall down from the shoulders, so that the whole upper part of her body became bare, and as they appeared to be sleepy, we retired to the other tent, where it was anything but warm.

THE STAROST OF THE REINDEER CHUKCHES.

"Next morning when we came out of the tent, we saw all the reindeer advancing in a compact troop. At the head was an old reindeer with large horns, that went forward to his master, who had in the meantime gone to meet the herd, and bade him good-morning by gently rubbing his nose against his master's hands. While this was going on the other reindeer stood drawn up in well-ordered ranks, like the crew in divisions on board a man-of-war. The owner then went forward and saluted every reindeer; they were allowed to stroke his hands with their noses. He on his part took every reindeer by the horn and examined it in the most careful way. After the inspection was ended, at a sign given by the master the whole herd wheeled round and returned in closed ranks, with the old reindeer in front, to their pasture."

According to Nordenskiöld there is not among the Coast Chukches any recognized chiefs nor any trace of social organization. Among the Reindeer Chukches living in the interior there appears to be a sort of chieftainship, and there are men who can show commissions from the Russian authorities. Such a person was Wassili Menka, the starost of the Reindeer Chukches, "a little dark man with a pretty worn appearance, clad in a white variegated 'pesk' of white reindeer skin, under which a blue flannel shirt was visible." He carried to Yakutsk a letter from Nordenskiöld, and the King of Sweden rewarded him with a gold medal.

CHUKCHE TENT FRAME.

The Chukches do not dwell in snow huts nor in wooden houses, because lumber is not found on the coast, and wooden houses are unsuitable for the reindeer nomad. They live summer and winter in tents of a peculiar construction not used by any other race. In shape they are oval, with conical tops, and resemble inverted basins. To make the tent warm it is double, the outer envelope enclosing an inner tent or sleeping chamber.

The outer tent consists of walrus skins sewed together and stretched over wooden ribs, which are carefully bound together by thongs of skin. The ribs rest on posts driven into the ground, or on tripods of drift-wood, which are steadied by seal skin sacks filled with sand or stones suspended from the middle of them. The frame and covering are anchored to the ground by means of twisted walrus hide rope fastened to stones which serve as tent pins, and sometimes a heavy stone is suspended from the top of the tent roof. The ribs are also supported by cross stays. Snow or earth is banked up around the outside of the tent.

THE CHUKCHE DWELLING.

The inner tent is used as a sleeping chamber, where all the family and their visitors pass the night. It is surrounded by reindeer skins, and is sometimes further covered with a layer of grass. The floor consists of a walrus skin stretched over a foundation of twigs and straw. At night the floor is covered with a carpet of seal skins which is taken away during the day. At night lamps of seal oil with wicks of dried moss are kept constantly burning, and keep the place uncomfortably warm for civilized people. The space between the tents is partitioned off by curtains. The entrance is a hole, with a skin hung before it for a door.

Inside the dwelling are stored all the effects of the one or more families who occupy it. Dogs are admitted to the outer space, and puppies are often received inside. Food is cooked in a pot suspended over a fire, and the smoke, or part of it, escapes through a hole in the roof.

The Coast Chukches are not only heathens, but appear also to have no conception of a Supreme Being. They are, however, superstitious, and have medicine-men, termed "ianglans," who exert much influence over them. Some of the exploits of these medicine-men are described by Messrs. Grace and Bruch, of the Rodgers crew, as follows:—

INTERIOR OF CHUKCHE TENT.

"A hunting party previous to setting out from the village sends for the ianglan. He brings with him a drum made of seal-gut, stretched on wood or bone hoops for heads, the body or sides being thick walrus hide. Upon entering the interior of the hut all lights are extinguished, and silence reigns for a brief space. Suddenly the stillness is broken by the ianglan breaking into a low, monotonous wail, which gradually rises into a loud, prolonged screech, the drum being beaten all the time, until the cunning knave, completely exhausted, falls to the ground, and pretends to go into a kind of trance. During such condition he is supposed to be in close communion with the spirits. Recovering from his pretended stupor, he tells his audience the spirits say that the hunters will kill seal, or walrus, or catch fish, as the weather prognostications, which these knaves study well, are almost a sure guide to the results of the hunt.

"On the 12th of March natives returned from East Cape and reported open water in that direction, and the ice going north. Two natives had been out sledging catching seals, and got carried out on the ice to sea, and had not been heard of. There was great excitement at At-kun-keer, owing to the fact that the natives who had been lost on the ice belonged to families there. The natives assembled in one of the huts and commenced the ceremonies of mourning by sending for the medicine-man who lived at Yandangie. He soon arrived, and opened the services by swallowing a large portion of raw walrus meat. He then began beating his tom-tom with a stick, and kept up a noise for six or seven hours resembling the bellowing of a calf. One of the men lost had a wife. She was sent for, and sat down on the floor of the hut. The medicine-man tied a seal rope around her head, and tied a large club to the end of it. He made her lay down on the floor, and proceeded to lift her up and down for nearly half an hour, exclaiming at the same time, 'Hi yang,' 'Hi yang;' 'Men namalkee' (no die, by and by come back). These ceremonies were repeated the following day and night.

"Early in the morning of the 14th, sledges coming from Yandangie were seen. Upon arrival their occupants proved to be the natives who had been carried away on the ice. The medicine-man then got a drum made of sealskin, with tails attached, beating it with his hands and making noises like a crow. Some dried grass was burnt, and the ashes shaken over the men, and they were allowed to enter their huts. They had killed a seal for subsistence during their stay on the ice."

Mr. Grace was at the village of Yandangie one night, and lodged in a hut where a young girl was sick. "I noticed," he says, "about nine P.M. that she was very sick, and that her breathing was very difficult. I looked at her, and told her people, 'Makee' (go die). As I said this two or three of them rushed over towards her with knives, and cut off some of her hair, her beads, and amulets (made of seal-gut with beads intertwined), at the same time calling her name and shaking her by the arms. But the poor girl was past hearing, and soon expired. They gathered her clothing, beads, bags containing needles and deer sinews, and placed the whole upon her breast. Then her boots were drawn on, and the ianglan and the neighbors were sent for.

"As soon as the whole of the invited guests had arrived, the ianglan tied the end of a long coil of sealskin rope around the head of the girl; the other end he fastened to a stick resembling a crutch in form. The father of the girl then commenced asking questions, and at each query the rope was lifted up, causing the girl's head to be raised from off the ground. This performance lasted three hours, during which time there was not a sound heard in the hut. At the expiration of the period, food was partaken of by all present, after which the ianglan, producing some seal-gut rope, proceeded to lash the corpse, tying the arms close to the body, and the legs with the feet pointing outward. A sledge was then prepared on the outside, and the girl's father taking a knife, cut a slit in the side of the hut, as a passageway for the removal of the corpse. The dead are not allowed to be carried through the ordinary entrance, as the natives say, 'Should that happen, the spirit will find its way home again.' The body being placed on the sledge, the relatives proceeded to pull it, and another sledge with provisions, toward a high range of hills distant some fifty miles inland."

Subsequently the body was visited to see if some walrus meat left with it had been eaten by crows—which is considered a favorable omen. At a second visit, the body was covered with snow.

Lieutenant Berry, after leaving St. Lawrence Bay as previously stated, proceeded to Camp Hunt, and on arriving there he directed Mr. Gilder to travel overland to Irkutsk and send home by telegraph the news of the loss of the Rodgers and the condition of her crew. Mr. Gilder started on his long journey January 7th; some account thereof will be given hereafter.

On the 10th of February, Lieutenant Berry and Ensign Hunt, with a team of thirteen dogs and accompanied by Ehr Ehren, who had a team of his own, started from Camp Hunt to make a journey westward along the coast in search of the Jeannette crew. On arriving at Nschni Kolymsk, March 25th, Berry heard of the loss of the Jeannette and sent back to Camp Hunt particulars thereof by Ehr Ehren. He also announced his intention of joining the searchers on the Lena, and directed Waring to return home by the first vessel. His meeting with Melville has been already described.

After the departure of his superiors Engineer Zane took charge of Camp Hunt. There was plenty of provisions and books, and also of Chukche visitors, but the long winter was a monotonous one for white men. The natives were friendly and had free access to the house, but they staid so long that it became advisable to send all of them away excepting some of the older ones at 4 P.M., which was the supper hour. Midnight was generally the time for turning in, and breakfast was eaten at ten o'clock in the morning.

Towards spring Dr. Jones and Petersen, with natives and two dog-teams carrying provisions, started for St. Lawrence Bay. Zane and Melms remained to take charge of the house, and during the absence of their companions they had quite an exciting adventure.

One day three strangers came to the house, and were well treated and given presents. Towards night all the natives excepting the strangers and two others were sent away; they were allowed to stay, and something to eat was given them after supper. While Melms was washing the dishes, Zane sat with his elbows on the table reading a book. The five natives were standing around, but as it was supposed that they were getting ready to go no attention was paid to them. Suddenly three of them seized Zane's arms and held them firmly on the table, and the other two secured Melms, so that he could offer no resistance.

One of the men, named Rochilon, who could speak English, then said that they wanted rum, and intended to have it, but did not want to take anything else or to kill any one. The 'rum' referred to was pure alcohol intended for use in stoves while traveling. He then moved the leg of the stove, which stood on the trap-door of the cellar, raised the door, and filled an empty oil-can and a bottle with alcohol stored in the cellar, and tied them on to a sled.

Rochilon then took down Zane's skin clothing and demanded that he should put it on and accompany them to Tiapka and stay there all night,—believing, no doubt, that Zane would follow them with a rifle if set at liberty. When Zane refused to comply, Rochilon flourished a knife, and declared that unless he went with them he would be killed.

MAN AND WOMAN OF TIAPKA.

As Zane still objected to go, believing they would not harm him, Rochilon took all the fire-arms in the house, and tied them on the sleds. He told Zane that they would be left at Tiapka; and when all was ready for a start, the sailors were released, and the natives ran to their sleds and hurried away as fast as their dogs could travel. Zane appeared very angry, but was much amused, and could not refrain from telling them to put some water in the "rum" before drinking it.

The guns were left at Tapika according to promise, and brought back by other natives. A knife which had been carried off with the alcohol was also sent back, showing that rum was what they wanted.

After this little difficulty, a new agreement was made with the Tapika people. The old men were to be allowed free access to the house, and no more stealing was to be done. The contract was honorably kept, and things went on smoothly. The sled party returned March 25th.

Camp Hunt was abandoned May 5th, and its garrison retreated southward, traveling by dog-sleds. North Head was reached May 10th, and on approaching South Head they were overjoyed at seeing a steamer anchored there.

It has already been stated that Waring, while looking for Putnam, left letters at Plover Bay and Marcus Bay, directed to the captain of any whaler which might arrive. Captain Owens, of the steam whaler, North Star, of New Bedford, got one of these letters and immediately started to rescue the men. He forced his ship through the ice opposite St. Lawrence Bay, reaching there May 8th, and fastened his ship to the outer edge of the ice, so as not to be carried to the northward by the large floes of ice floating by.

On the 9th of May, some natives who first saw the vessel informed Waring of her approach. The news caused great excitement among the Rodgers crew, and when the North Star came into the bay next day, they almost cried for joy. Some went on board the whaler immediately, but it was not until the evening of May 14th that all were on the ship. The boats, rifles, ammunition, trade goods, and many other smaller articles were distributed among the natives according to the services they had rendered. The skin boat in which a line was carried ashore from the burning ship, was brought home as a relic. Captain Owens extended to the rescued men the hospitality of his ship, and offered to convey them to St. Michaels, Sitka, or San Francisco. All of them felt grateful for his kindness and prompt action in coming to their relief.

When tidings of the loss of the Rodgers came to the United States by telegraph from Irkutsk, the Secretary of the Navy arranged to send a steamer to pick up the crew. The Corwn, commanded by Lieutenant M. A. Healey, was selected for the service, and sailed from San Francisco April 24th.

The Corwin arrived off the south entrance of St. Lawrence Bay on the morning of May 14th, and there spoke the whaler Hunter, whose captain confirmed the story of the burning of the Rodgers, and said that the North Star had come to rescue the crew. Lieutenant Healey pressed onward through the ice, and before midnight was in the bay. A steamer lying close to the land near South Head was spoken, and proved to be the North Star; she had just taken the last of the Rodgers crew aboard, and was ready to sail for Ounalaska. The party were immediately transferred to the Corwin, which started on her return early on the morning of May 15th.

The Corwin arrived at San Francisco, June 23d, after a quick and pleasant passage via Sitka and Wrangel.

The North Star was a new ship just arrived from New Bedford, Mass., via Cape Horn. After leaving the Corwin she went north, and was crushed by the ice June 25th. The crew escaped to the U. S. signal station at Point Barrow, and were there cared for by Lieutenant Ray.

CHAPTER XXXV.

GILDER'S TRAVELS IN SIBERIA.

EARLY in January, 1881, Mr. W. H. Gilder, an experienced Arctic overland traveler, and the special correspondent of the New York *Herald* accompanying Berry's search expedition, left the extreme northeastern coast of Siberia to carry to Irkutsk, and from thence to send home by telegraph, tidings of the burning of the Rodgers. His mission was an important one, for on its successful and prompt execution depended in a large degree the early rescue of the Rodgers crew. The following condensed account of his journey to Sredne Kolymsk, is compiled from his letters to the *Herald*.

"The sun was above the horizon less than two hours a day at the time I left Eeteetlan for the Kolyma River, on my way to the telegraph station in Eastern Siberia. This gave very short days and very long nights, which is one of the inconveniences of winter journeys within the Arctic circle.

The natives here, also, have a very inconvenient habit of starting long before daylight, even when they have only a short distance to go and could easily accomplish it by daylight. They will do this also when daylight is followed by a bright moon, and the mornings are as dark as Egypt. They have no idea of time, and often mistake the northern light for approaching sunrise. There seems to be some one up and moving around in camp at any hour of the day or night.

The day of Captain Berry's arrival at Eeteetlan, there also came from Nishni Kolymsk a Russian named Wanker, who agreed to take me to that city for the sum of fifty rubles. I did not like the fellow's appearance. His eyes were too close together, and then he had a general hang-dog look that would give him away in the company of saints. He could talk fluently with Constantine, though, and advised me to take him along to drive my dogs and as an interpreter. The interpreting was all well enough as far as they were concerned, and the only difficulty was in understanding Constantine or making him understand me.

Knowing I had to be for several months among the Russians, I thought that by gaining the start by a few words before I came plump into their country I would acquire an advantage; so I asked Constantine what the Russians said for "yes" "They say 'yes'," he replied. This was easy enough to remember, so I went to the next word. "What do they say for no?" I asked. "Why, they say 'no'." This seemed a most remarkable coincidence, but certainly convenient, so I went on to something harder.

"What does a Russian man say when he is hungry and wants something to eat?"

"Oh, sir, he says he wants something to eat."

This was a little more than I could stand, and I immediately took a recess. I saw that the poor fellow had no idea how he spoke what little English he knew. He did not translate it from one language to the other, but had merely learned as a parrot would learn, only with greater fluency, for he seemed to have the well known facility of the Russians in acquiring foreign languages, having in two months and a half on shipboard learned sufficient to be of considerable use there, as well as to our party on shore.

En route Constantine drove my sled, but we went very slowly, for the dogs I had were hastily bought after I had made up my mind to this trip, and proved a sorry lot. Constantine always examined the dogs as an expert, and had a way of running his hand along the dog's back-bone, and if it did not cut his finger he pronounced it a fine dog.

The second night of our journey we halted at the village of Ynedlin, near which the Vega wintered. We were entertained at the house of the chief, the largest house I had yet seen. The sleeping portion, the *yorónger,* was about thirty feet long by twelve wide and seven feet high. It was here that Wanker promised to meet me the night of my arrival, and hurry me on to Nishni Kolymsk without any delay *en route,* merely expressing his fear that I could not stand the cold and rapid traveling. I was forced to remain at this house four nights, partially detained by stormy weather and with the hope that Wanker might forget himself and actually keep his appointment within a day or two. It was fortunate for me that the house was such a pleasant one, since I had to remain there so long.

No matter how early you may awaken in the morning, you will always find the mistress of the household already up— that is, her position changed from reclining to sitting, and as soon as she observes that you are really awake, she hands you a few small pieces of meat. Then she goes into the adjoining apartment, and after fifteen or twenty minutes of pounding and chopping returns with the breakfast A large, flat, wooden tray is placed on the floor, and the landlady, dropping off her clothes, takes her position at one end,—a position inelegantly but accurately described as "squatting." The family and their guests gather around the board on either side, lying flat on their stomachs with their heads toward the breakfast and their feet out, so that a bird's-eye view of the table and guests would look something like an immense beetle.

The first course is some frozen weeds mixed with sea oil and eaten with small portions of fresh blubber, which the lady of the house cuts with a large chopping knife. The next course is walrus meat. This is also cut up by the presiding lady, and is served with no stinting hand. At this portion of the meal the one who can swallow the largest piece without chewing has the advantage. After this joint comes a large piece of walrus hide, which has a small portion of blubber attached to it, and the hair still on the outside. This hide is about an inch thick and very tough, so that it is absolutely impossible to chew it, or rather to affect it by chewing. Even the dogs will chew perhaps for half a day upon a small piece of walrus hide hanging from a bag of meat, and fail to detach it. This is, therefore, cut into very small pieces by the hostess, and finishes the meal. It is really the most palatable dish of the meal, and furnishes something for the stomach to act upon that generally occupies its attention till the following meal; but it is astonishing how easily a meat diet is digested.

There are usually two meals a day in a well provided Chukche's household—the breakfast just described and dinner, which comes on late in the evening. The dinner is almost identical in form with the breakfast, except that there is most always some hot cooked meat that follows the course of walrus hide. Some times the second course at breakfast or dinner may be frozen seal or reindeer meat, but the first and third courses are invariable unless changed by force of circumstances beyond the control of the householder. Besides those two meals there is always a similar service to any guest who may arrive during the day from a distance, and all present share his luncheon with him, and not unfrequently beat him out unless he watches closely and keeps himself well provided.

The evening after dinner is often devoted to games. They do not play chess or billiards, but we used to see who could walk the furthest on his hands, with his body held horizontally from the hips, or upon his knees, while his feet were held in his hands behind him. Or perhaps the lights were extinguished and some one played upon the drum or yarar, and sang or chanted a most lugubrious melody, increasing in volume from an almost imperceptible sound into the loudest noise possible, accompanying the drum with a howl like a bear at bay, the most frightful noise he could make; and it did sound prodigious in the dark. During this time the landlord would occasionally shout 'Ay-hék, ay-hék,' which seemed to inspire the drummer to renewed exertion. The drum is a wooden hoop over which is tightly drawn a thin membrane from the skin of the reindeer. It has a handle on one side, and is beaten with a small strip of whalebone. This drumming never ceases from the moment the lights are out until the concert is over, which is generally after about two hours and a half.

We had a concert the first night at Ynedlin, and during the performance I heard Constantine breathing heavily and gasping, and occasionally breaking out into groans and tears. This attracted the attention of the performer, who stopped and asked if he were sick. He groaned a 'Yes,' and I thought I would have to resort to my medical stores, consisting of pills and bandages; but I did not know which to use, for upon inquiry it transpired that he had only a broken heart. He wanted to return to Tiapka, the village near Eeteetlan, where was an old woman named At-túng-er, who had grown up children and grandchildren, and with whom he, a lad of nineteen years, had fallen in love. When asked what he was grieving for, he said 'At-túng-er;' and after that I felt relieved, for I did not believe he would die of his broken heart. During the entire journey this same scene was repeated every time the yarar was brought out, and as soon as the lights were restored he appeared just as cheerful as if nothing disagreeable had ever occurred to him.

There were two girls about fifteen years of age in this household, one the daughter of my host and the other some relation, but I could never make out exactly what. The old man often tried to explain it to me by using the fingers of one hand, which he named, and showed that Tay-tin-con-ne was the same relation to his daughter, Mám-mak, that his thumb was to his middle finger; but there is where I always fell out. I never could satisfy myself as to the kinship of his fingers. Occasionally during the day or evening these girls used to dance, taking their places side by side as if on the stage for a double clog, and, accompanying themselves with guttural sounds that it is impossible to describe, executed in unison fantastic contortions and gyrations somewhat similar to the Indians of North America.

Their costume was the usual evening dress of the country, and consisted simply of a string of beads around the neck and a narrow breechcloth of sealskin. This was an accomplishment which, I found, had been acquired by all the children along the coast, and such entertainments were not rare.

On the 13th of January I moved to the next village, starting in the dark at three o'clock in the morning, and arriving at our destination before noon. There were two other sleds beside mine, which belonged to a man from Onman, who had with him his wife and son, a young man of about twenty-two years, with yellow hair and light hazel eyes, the first blonde I had seen with these people. I afterward saw another, a woman, but they are very rare.

Here, too, I had to wait four days, looking for Wanker or clear weather. These houses along the coast are all so many hotels for the accommodation of those traveling to and fro. The natives pay nothing for their entertainment or for feeding their dogs, but they expect much from any white strangers who may happen to pass their way. If the native traveler has tobacco or beads, and his host wants some, he gives it to him; but that is not paying for his board and lodging. He would do the same if he received nothing in return.

While at Peelkan, the second station, I saw many natives who were returning from a trip to East Cape. They told me that Wanker did not intend to come along for some time yet, that he was trading along the coast. This was discouraging, and I determined to proceed to Kolyutschin village as soon as possible and get along as well as I could. I knew I could easily find people going from one village to another until I reached Wankarem, but from there to North Cape was a long stretch without villages. There was, however, an old man who came to Peelkan on his way back to his house at Wankarem, who said he would take me on from there. He wanted me to give him some biscuit to eat, as his teeth were not equal to the contest with frozen walrus meat, and when he showed me the teeth I agreed with him.

It was a long journey across the mouth of the bay to Kolyutschin Island, and my dogs were not equal to the emergency; so when night came on I halted and built a snow house. The natives who had started with us reached the village that night, and were much alarmed for our safety when they found we did not get in during the night. Their anxiety was increased when the following day brought a snowstorm which shut out the island from view, and left us as they supposed without anything to guide us.

When we started in the morning I cautioned Constantine to keep faithfully in the tracks of the sleds that preceded us, as they were but faintly discernible under the falling snow. He told me his leader was a good one and knew how to keep the road. For a while I trusted the dog's instinct, but when I found the wind upon my back instead of nearly directly in front of me, as it should have been, I began to doubt it, and asked Constantine where Kolyutschin Island was. He pointed straight ahead as I expected; but I had taken the bearing of the island by my pocket compass when we halted the night before, and on again regarding it I showed my driver that we were going almost exactly in the opposite direction.

I then took charge of the course myself, and after about an hour heard the barking and quarreling of dogs in a team. I could not see them, but shouted, and soon two sleds came up that had been sent out to look for us. They seemed glad to have found us, and said they had been worried all night thinking we were wandering around on the ice. I told them, however, that we were comfortably housed and that I knew where Kolyutschin lay, at the same time pointing in the proper direction. Then I showed them my compass, and as the island happened to be just magnetic north of us it appeared all the more wonderful to them. They imagined that it always pointed in the direction you wanted to go.

While we were at Kolyutschin, Wanker came up, being

only eleven days behind, and I felt greatly relieved when I saw him. We subsequently moved to Wankarem and proceeded on our journey with greater celerity than before, but not fast enough to satisfy one who felt so entirely dependent upon one man, and he thoroughly unreliable and bad. All along the route the natives, when an opportunity offered, cautioned me against him, and said he meant no good by me. They begged me to return to Eeteetlan and offered to

CAPE NORTH.

take me there. The only thing I was afraid of was that Wanker would get up in the night and run off with his team, leaving me high and dry on the beach.

From Wankarem to North Cape the weather was intensely cold, and the whole party, native and white (for there were three natives' sleds with us), suffered from frost bites, though not of a serious nature. We found plenty of drift wood at several points along the coast, and halted to make tea and cook some meat. This I found took the raw edge off the cold, and made traveling and sleeping without shelter much more endurable. From North Cape to Oogarkin there were villages at intervals of from five to thirty miles. From

Oogarkin to Erktreen, a native village of nineteen houses, near Cape Chelagskoi, there were no houses, and we slept three nights on the snow. Drift wood was plentiful, and in ordinary weather camping out would not have been as disagreeable as might be supposed.

We found several people at Eumatk, near Oogarkin, who were on their way to Nishni Kolymsk, and on the morning of February 8, eight sleds, drawn by ninety-three dogs, started. It was a brilliant sight, or would have been, if you could have seen it; but the start was at four o'clock in the morning, about three hours and a half before daylight. Some of the sleds had gaudy calico storm coats thrown over them, and the harness of several teams was trimmed with red. One man had several small bells attached to his harness, but I never heard a sound from them, and doubt that they had tongues. I believe they were dumb bells, and intended solely for ornament.

It was a pleasant day at first, but during the afternoon a storm of wind and snow sprang up from the direction of our line of march, and when we halted at night it was blowing a gale—a genuine poorga—which continued throughout the night and following day. When I lay down to sleep I sought shelter behind a shed, but soon had to leave it because I found myself nearly suffocated by the weight of snow on top of me. Then I noticed the natives, more wise than I, had lain down on the crest of the hill and were free from snow. Traveling the next day was simply torture, but it would have been equally bad to sit still out of doors, so we kept on. The night was a pleasant one and we slept well.

The next halt was on the rocky coast not a great distance from Chelagskoi, and a huge cavern in the face of the cliff afforded small protection from the wind, but made a most picturesque camping place. The following day we reached Erktreen, and right glad we were, for a frightful poorga was raging and the dogs could scarcely make any headway against it. There were plenty of houses here, and but little food. In fact, in the house where I slept, we fed the occupants instead of eating their provisions.

The next stretch was a long one, and we slept four nights in the snow. The natives were all very kind to me. They knew that Wanker was not helping me any more than he should, so they each had something for 'Keifey,' as is my Chukche name, and I believe I fared better than any one in the party.

About noon time of the third day out we reached Bassarika, a deserted village of five log houses, which at one time constituted a village of Russian trappers. Here we found a large quantity of bear meat and dried fish for dog food which they had cachéd on their way down the coast, and, taking a good supply upon our sleds, we gorged like genuine savages that night and slept soundly and warm.

As night approached on the day following we were near the native village of Diardlowran, the Barranno of the Russians. Three of the sleds halted on the beach at dark, while the sled to which I was attached and two others started to make a short cut across land to the village. One of the natives with us lived at that place, and was anxious to get home after an absence of two months and a half. But without landmarks on the bare waste of snow and no coast line to guide us even, he had to give up the search, though less than three miles from home, and we lay down in the snow to wait for daylight. But before dawn came the worst poorga I ever encountered, and when we started in the morning we could see less distance ahead than when we halted in the dark. It was a terrible struggle, that little march of about two miles and a half. The wind blew directly in our faces and drove the sharp particles of hard frozen snow against the eyeballs and cheeks, so that it was impossible to look to windward for more than a hasty glance. The dogs could not face the storm and lay down in the harness, so that we had to go ahead and drag them along, while we waded painfully through snow nearly waist deep. One sled was soon left behind, while Wile-dóte, the native of the neighboring village, and Wanker and I floundered on through the storm.

At last we reached a hillside swept by the wind, and found sled-tracks which Wile-dóte recognized as the right trail, and we trotted along merrily until the sleds were caught by the wind and swept over a precipice. I saw Wile-dóte and his team disappear over the edge of the cliff into a cloud of whirling snow, and knew that in a second we must go too. I could do nothing but close my eyes and set my teeth when I felt myself in the air and falling I knew not where. Fortunately it was a fall of but about twenty feet to a snow-bank, down which the dogs, the sled, and I rolled to the bottom, while I saw Wanker, who had been sitting on the other side of the sled, with his back to the cliff, shot over my head and reach the bottom first. I knew no one had been hurt, for the snow was very soft and we were almost buried by the drift before we could regain our feet; and I could not help laughing at the ridiculous figure poor Wanker cut as he passed over my head, rolled up in a little ball and desperately grasping his brake. He looked like a witch riding on her broomstick. Wile-dóte's sled was broken, and falling on his leg caused a slight but not very painful contusion.

We then began to look around to find some way out of this pit, but found it surrounded by a high wall of rock and snow, except one narrow drift that led again to the top of the hill. We plunged along as well as we could, but could only make a few yards' advance at a time, for the dogs had to be dragged along by main force. Time and time again we were compelled to throw ourselves down in the snow and rest for ten or fifteen minutes before making further exertion. Once again we were blown off the hill, but this time into a valley, which Wile-dóte recognized as the road to the village not more than half a mile away.

We now moved along more rapidly and soon found the coast, and a short turn to the right brought us directly into the houses before we could see them. Several times during the morning I had to remove from my face a perfect mould or mask of frozen snow, half an inch thick, and my nose, cheeks, chin, and forehead were badly frozen. My companions fared no better. Three of Wile-dóte's dogs perished during the storm, and I found, upon looking at my watch after entering the house, that we had been more than seven hours upon the road. The other sled got in toward night, but the three that halted on the beach did not overtake us until the second day after we left Diardlowran. At this village we found four Russians from Nishni Kolymsk, who were much interested in the recital of our adventures during the morning.

The next morning we again set out upon our journey, three of the Russians accompanying us. Wanker put me on the sled of one of these people, and right glad was I of the change, for now I felt sure that I would reach my destination. This man looked honest and intelligent, though he could not read, and said so. That night we halted at a deserted hut half filled with snow, but it was a sufficient shelter from a poorga that was raging at the time, and ever so much better than sleeping out of doors. Indeed, it was cheerful and cosey, with a fire blazing in the middle of the hut and a little of the smoke escaping through a hole in the roof, but most of it pervading the apartment. The tea-kettle hung over the flame and a large pot of reindeer meat was cooking on one side of the fire, while we ate frozen fish, which my new driver pulled from among the rafters. While we waited for the tea my new Russian friends sang a pretty little chorus, and I slept, dreaming of home, and feeling more at home than I had for weeks. I had at last reached the borders of civilization and had no longer to crawl at night into the huts of the savages; and yet I could not forget how often I had been so glad to crawl into those same dirty hovels to escape from storms and hunger.

The next day we reached quite a large deserted village, and Wanker here told me that the next day we would reach his house, and that there we would have to wait for Constantine, who was four days behind us, the sled he was with and one other having been separated from us during a poorga the first day out from Erktreen.

Before reaching Wanker's house we stopped at a log house to get some tea. This was the first inhabited house I had seen, and I regarded it with due interest. There was but one room, with the fireplace in the corner, on which was blazing a glorious fire that made my frozen nose glow with the heat. There stood the steaming tea-kettle, and as we entered, the lady of the house, attired in a loose robe, not gathered in at the waist, but flowing from the shoulders half-way down her leather boot-legs, cut some pieces of reindeer meat from one of two carcasses that leaned against the wall, with the skins still covering them, and fried them in a pan over the glowing coals. In the meantime a frozen fish was cut into slices and placed before us, with an additional plate of dried fish and some preserved cranberries, and afterward the hot tea that made the remainder of my journey quite comfortable. While we were partaking of the hospitality of the Russian native, three sledge loads of Chukches arrived and were similarly entertained. I thought it must be a considerable tax upon the time and hospitality of those who live upon the lines of travel to entertain so many guests, for no one passes their houses without entering, and no one pays anything for his entertainment. All the guests, excepting myself, even the Chukches, crossed themselves when they entered the house, as well as before, and after eating and when they left.

I told Wanker that I would rather go on to Nishni Kolymsk, but he would not listen to it, and insisted that I should remain at his house. I poured my complaint into the ear of my driver that day, and though he understood little of what I said he did seize the main point, which was that I staid at Wanker's against my will and preferred to go to Nishni Kolymsk. He said, 'Da, da,' and meant 'yes,' and here our conversation ended. He delivered me at Wanker's that night and departed early next morning.

There was one thing that struck me with considerable force when my course was turned from the northern coast of Siberia into the Kolyma River. The second day of my journey on that river, I noticed as we passed near the shore —first, higher grass than I had seen before, then a short growth of bushes, then stunted shrubbery, and afterward two solitary, lonely trees standing side by side. In the course of a few miles the trees became more numerous along the banks of the river until I reached Wanker's house, which is situated in a grove of trees thirty or more feet high.

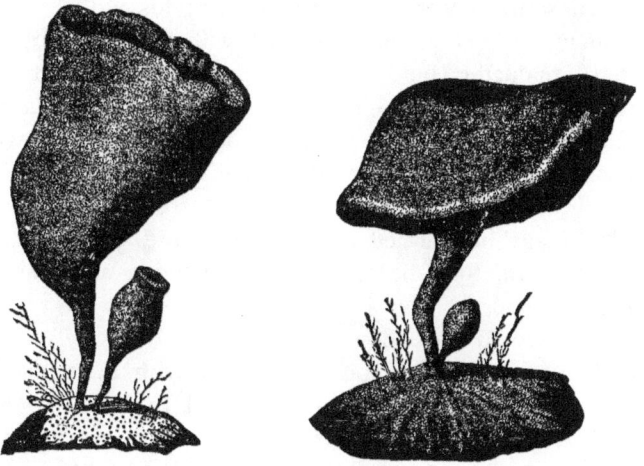

BEAKER SPONGES FROM THE SEA OFF THE MOUTH OF THE KOLYMA.

I had not expected to see all this climatic change in one day's travel.

At Wanker's house the entire family crossed themselves in front of the pictures of saints in one corner, and bowed as they muttered their prayers. Wanker, too, went through the same forms, but not, I thought, sufficiently to make up for the time he had lost in the Chukche's houses along the coast. He spoke the Chukche language perfectly, so that I felt certain that he was at least a half-breed. He wore their amulets to cure him when he was sick, and was with them a skillful shaman or medicine-man. No one could excel him in the performance upon the drum, and yet all these were laid aside at home, and he was apparently as pious as any of his family.

The day following my arrival at Wanker's my good friend the driver came early with a stranger, and I felt certain that my hour of deliverance was near at hand. And sure enough, the stranger read my letter from the consul and told me I should go along with him. Wanker got very red in the face, and submitted with bad grace to an arrangement that I was certain did not please him. But I saw that the quiet stranger had some power, and could enforce his will.

Glad enough was I to go away and with such a kind and considerate conductor, but I was overpowered when I found a covered sled in waiting to take me like a prince in triumph to my destination. It was a bitterly cold day, and I was pleased when we halted at a village half way to the town to get some hot tea and, as usual, with it frozen fish. Here the whole village had turned out to receive me, and the men stood in line with their heads bared and bowing as I passed them into the house.

A friendly crowd greeted me at Nishni Kolymsk, also, but though of my own race I could only talk with them in the language of the savages. My new friend took me to his house, and did everything in his power to entertain me and assist in carrying out my plans. I found that he was a Cossack, and acting commander during the absence of that official in Sredne Kolymsk. I managed to make myself understood, and he told me that at Sredne I would find some one who spoke French, and that he would send me to that place with a Cossack who would take me in three or four days. At Nishni Kolymsk I first heard of the loss of the Jeannette and that some of her people had survived.

After Constantine arrived and I had finished my business I started for Sredne Kolymsk with my Cossack guide, and bade good-bye to some of the kindest people I ever met. All seemed equally anxious to do something for me, and my landlord seemed really sad at parting. I had been at his

ARRIVAL AT SREDNE KOLYMSK.

house four days, and during that time he had devoted himself entirely to me, trying to make amends for the ill conduct of my traveling companion Wanker, who, by the by, had told the Russians we met at Diardlowran, that he had brought me to the Kolyma because I was big and strong, and he was going to keep me at his house until the winter was past, and then I would be a good hand to catch fish for him.

I reached Sredne Kolymsk on Sunday, the 5th of March, and was met in the street by a fine looking old gentlemen in a handsome uniform, who addressed me in French and informed me that he was the Prefet de Police for the district, and invited me to his house. It sounded most delightfully to hear once more a familiar Christian language, and not to be compelled to converse with intelligent people in the language of the savage. At this house I met also M. Kotcheroffski, formerly prefet of the district of Verkhoyansk, but who had just arrived to relieve my host, M. de Varowa, as the latter informed me, at the same time stating that he would start for Yakutsk in a few days, and extending me an invitation to accompany him. I gladly accepted his offer.

Sredne, or Middle Kolymsk, is a Russian settlement of about 500 inhabitants, including Russians, Yakuts, and a few Chukches. The houses are all built of hewn logs, are but one story high, and the windows are glazed with blocks of transparent ice. Some of the houses have windows of glass, but these are always much broken and mended, so that seen from the outside they look like stained glass windows of a church. The most conspicuous building there, as in all the little Russian towns, is the church edifice, which is of Oriental architecture, with a dome surmounted by a cross and exceedingly florid in its style of ornamentation. Adjoining the church and within the same enclosure is a small wooden tower, surrounded by a block house, which was built by the first settlers of Sredne as a means of defence against the savage Yakuts and Chukches. The town is irregularly built and extends over a considerable area of ground, the government buildings being situated about a mile from the center. By government buildings is meant merely the storehouses for grain and bread, and for the skins which are received for taxes. These buildings are of logs, with great heavy doors, and padlocks about the size of an ordinary valise, while the key is a load in itself.

I paid a visit to the storehouses while in Sredne, to witness the process of turning over the property to the new prefet or ispravnik, as he is termed, but it was a very uninteresting process and the weather so intensely cold that I did not stay long. A gang of laborers, heavily clad in skin clothing, were running around with bundles on their shoulders and dumping them upon one of the platforms of a pair of immense balance scales, such as I thought had long since become obsolete. The beam was suspended in the middle, and had a platform a yard square hung by the corners to either end of it. On one side were piled bundles of skins or grain in cow skin bags, and on the other were heaped up big iron weights about the size of a hundred pound shell, with handles. It looked as if the articles to be weighed were exactly counterbalanced by the proper amount of iron weights, and then they guessed how much iron there was.

I saw another curious balance here, a sort of combination of the beam with the steelyard, which is for weighing small articles. It has a scoop suspended from one end of the graduated steel rod, in which is placed the article to be weighed; on the other end of the rod is a fixed weight, and the balance is obtained by sliding the rod along the ring that holds it in suspension. I had been used to seeing the weight moved, and it was a novelty to see the whole beam sliding along instead. Pacing up and down near the scales with a gun upon his shonlder was a Cossack, who looked strangely bundled up in furs and under arms. Near the beam stood the new ispravnik, wrapped up so that nothing could be seen of him except his eyes. I do not remember ever having felt the cold more keenly, than during the first three days I was in Sredne. Unfortunately there is no thermometer in any of these towns north and east of Yakutsk, where observations of the weather would be so interesting.

The dwellings in Sredne, as well as throughout that part of Siberia, consist usually of three rooms, and are heated by an open fireplace, built of poles, which extend up through the roof and form a low chimney. The poles are covered with mud to protect them from the flames, and the wood is stood on end in the fireplace, resting against the back. There is plenty of wood, and it makes a brilliant flame and an abundance of glowing coals. On this same fireplace the cooking for the establishment is carried on apparently with equal skill by the men and women. The culinary arrangements are, however, of the simplest character, the staples of food being fish, rye-bread, and tea. All the lakes and rivers abound with most excellent fish, and the poorer classes eat nothing else. I can attest the excellent quality of the fish, especially raw and frozen.

Breakfast here consists of bread and tea, with, perhaps, frozen or dried fish, and later in the day meat, soup, and tea, and in the evening meat or fish and tea. It is impossible to imagine what these people would do without tea. It is the universal beverage and they drink from four to fifteen cups at one meal, sometimes with milk and sometimes with sugar. The sugar is not put into the cup with the tea, it is too precious for that, but a lump is served to each person, and as he sips his tea he nibbles at the lump which is his portion for the meal.

At Sredne Kolymsk, I saw several political exiles, socialists, nine in all, who are sentenced for various terms. There were also two at Nishne—one a socialist, and the other a Pole—who had been implicated in political intrigues inimical to the imperial government. His sentence had originally been for twenty-five years at Ahlokminsk, between Yakutsk and Irkutsk, but one day, in a fit of indignation at the government, he gave expression to his anger by spitting on a portrait of his late Imperial Majesty, and was sent to the most distant outpost of the government in Siberia. I found him a very pleasant old gentleman of polished manners and education, entirely distinct from the people with whom he is at present thrown; but he has grown gray and aged since he left his home in Warsaw, and says he feels almost equally at home in Siberia. It was rather difficult to talk with him, as he only remembered a few words of French, though he spoke German fluently, but I didn't.

I visited the socialists at their houses in Sredne, and found most of them pretty much the kind of keople I had imagined—a sort of intelligent lunatic. But there were exceptions. There were gentlemen whom I could not imagine guilty of an evil thought, and these I found were held in high esteem by the officers of the government who have them under their charge. They were all interested in the American stranger and seemed to imagine an affinity between my countrymen and the socialists. They were much surprised when I told them that their party was but poorly represented in the United States and that such as we had were foreigners, that I did not personally know of a single native American socialist.

I never saw religion so universal as the Greek religion in Siberia. Not only the Russian inhabitants, but the Yakuts, Tunguses, Amoots, and Chukches who reside near the settlements are all equally religious. It seemed to me to be a most convenient religion, for it consisted, as far as I could see, in crossing one's self and bowing before the pictures, and in fasting upon a fish diet when there was scarcely anything but fish to eat. The most pious old man I saw among them could scarcely restrain his anger at some infringement of his orders one day until he had finished his prayers. He then turned and opened upon the offending head such a volley of—well, if not oaths, they sounded as if they would have been when translated. It is a beautiful religion at any rate, and abounds in affectionate salutes. All these forms are particularly dear to the Yakut, and never omitted, at least in the presence of a white man. After prayers every one kisses every one else three times, once on each cheek and once on the mouth. This is universal—men, women and children, servants and masters, soldiers and their commanding officers. It is neither the ecstatic nor paroxysmal kiss nor yet the Platonic, but simply the kiss of devotion.

The entire household join in prayers, all standing before the chromos of saints with metallic rays attached to their heads in the most realistic fashion, and cross themselves and bow in unison unless some one particularly devout prostrates himself upon the floor and kisses the planks in the fervor of his religious zeal. It was a beautiful sight to me to see the gray haired prefet take the little Nanyah by the hand and lead her before the family altar, where they stood side by side at their devotions. When finished, she would cross her dear little hands and hold them suppliantly toward her companion, while he made the sign of the cross over her and dropped his hard hand upon hers. This concluded the devotion. It is a convenient religion for a lazy man, for in the 365 days that compose the year there are no less than 450 saints' days or holy days, and no good Christian would work upon a holy day. Were it not that the fish are so abundant I fear these people would starve to death.

I never could make out the exact position occupied by *la petite* Nanyah in the household at Sredne. She seemed to unite the duties of a plaything, a daughter, and a servant. I first saw her the day that I arrived at the house of the prefet. My attention had been attracted by a brilliant costume of the Amoots, and to show it to better advantage the ever-useful Nanyah was called upon as a lay figure. There was neither hesitation nor boldness in her manner. She was simply showing the dress, not herself. She had neither fear of the stranger nor hesitation to accommodate him by wearing this gaudy, savage costume. With her it was simply a pleasure to please others.

I was told that Nanyah was to be our traveling companion

to Yakutsk, that she was affianced to an officer of the regiment stationed there, and this would be the first time she had ever been away from Sredne Kolymsk.

During my sojourn in Sredne, as well as in Nishni Kolymsk, I was frequently invited to partake of the hospitality of some of the inhabitants. At all such entertainments it seemed to be a principle with the host to insist upon my drinking a glass of vodka—that is, diluted alcohol—about every five minutes. At first I thought I must submit myself to the custom of the country and sustain myself as best I could, and the consequence was that when dinner was over I had not the slightest idea whether I had eaten anything or not, but I was quite sure that I had drank something. Later I found out that all that was required was that you should sip the liquor and thus avoid the evil consequences of heavy drinking, and governed my drinking accordingly. I learned that the Russian rule is a glass of vodka before dinner, before each plate, during each plate, after each plate and after dinner—that is all."

From Sredne Kolymsk Mr. Gilder journeyed to Verkhoyausk, where he heard of the loss of the Jeannette and turned north to join Melville, as stated in Chapter XXXII. Meantime the news of the burning of the Rodgers was carried to Yakutsk by a special courier, and transmitted to the United States by telegraph from Irkutsk.

CHAPTER XXXVI.

STORY OF THE FORLORN HOPE.

THE following chapters giving additional particulars of Noros and Nindermann's journey to Bulun, and of Melville's November search for De Long, etc., are compiled from Mr. Jackson's letters. Mr. Nindermann's narrative, given below, commences on the 6th of October.

"On the 6th of October, Erickson's condition left no hope of recovery, and it was feared that he would be unable to move on further. I was alone in the hut and the captain asked me if I was strong enough to go to Kumak Surka, which he said was only twenty-five miles distant. He thought that I with a companion would be able to make the journey and return to them in four days. He told me that if we failed to find people at Kumak Surka, we should then go further to a place called Ajakit, which he said was about forty-five miles further to the south than Kumak Surka. 'If you find people,' he said, 'come back as quickly as possible and bring with you meat enough to feed us until we can get to the place.'

The captain asked me which of the men I would take with me on the journey, and I said Noros. He asked me if I would not rather take Iverson, but I said no, Iverson had been complaining of his feet for some days. He then agreed to my selection, and said further, 'Nindermann, you know that we have nothing to eat, and that I can give you nothing with you on your journey; but I will give you your portion of the dog meat.'

As we talked about these things the doctor walked up and looked at Erickson, and exclaimed, 'He is dead!' We were all awed. The captain then said, 'Nindermann, now we will all go southward.' This was about nine o'clock when Erickson died.

The captain then asked me where we could find a place to bury him; I answered that the earth was too hard frozen to dig a grave, and that we had no implements with us; we could do nothing else than make a hole in the ice of the river, and bury him there. The captain said yes, it must be so, and then told Noros and Kaack to sew the body up in a portion of the canvas belonging to the tent.

At midday we were ready to bury him; the flag was placed over him, and we had a little warm water with alcohol in it for our dinner. When we had drunk that the captain said: 'We will now bury our shipmate.' All were very still, and the captain spoke a few words to us, and when he was finished we took our comrade toward the river, and then made a hole in the ice with a hatchet. The captain then read the service for the dead, and Erickson's body was let into the river, and was carried away from our eyes by the stream. Three shots were fired over his grave, and then we went back to the hut. The weather was very bad, the wind was very strong, and the snow drifted fearfully. We had not much to say one to the other.

The captain told me to go out and see how the weather was. I went out, but the weather was so bad and the snow drifted so strongly that I could scarcely see anything; and I said it would be better to wait till the storm abated, for we could not see where we were going if we started out. I thought the day was just such a day as the one in which we buried Captain Hall. The captain then said, 'We will wait till to-morrow.' That evening we ate our last portion of dog meat. The captain said, 'This is our last meat, but I hope we will soon have some more.' Then we all laid down to rest.

On the 7th of October when we awoke the wind was pretty strong and the snow was still drifting. We made preparations to continue our journey. We left in the hut a repeating rifle, some ammunition, and a record. We took nothing with us but the records and papers, the captain's private journal, two rifles, and the clothes we wore. I suggested that all the papers should be left there in the hut, and that when we found people I would go back and fetch them; whereupon the captain answered:—

'Nindermann, the papers go with me as long as I live.'

When we left the hut we made a short cut across a sand-pit, about southeast, then struck a river, went along on the west bank of the river for some distance to the south, then, as the river took a turn, we had to go southeast again, then struck another small river where there was no water at all, going south for a short time, then going to the east for a short distance, when we struck the Lena, as the captain supposed it to be at the time. That is the river he was found on. The captain said, 'Nindermann, do you think the ice is strong enough to bear us?' I said, 'I will try it.' I went a short way on the river when I broke through, but was not very wet. When I looked around me I saw the captain quite near to me, and he had broken through up to his shoulders. I helped him out and we went back to the bank, made a fire, and dried our things. It was then midday, and we made some alcohol and warm water to drink."

On Sunday, October 9th, after divine service, Captain De Long sent Nindermann and Noros southward, repeating the instructions to Nindermann that he had given him the day before Erickson's death. He also gave him a copy of his small chart of the Lena River, and said:—

'That is all I can give you on your journey; information about the land or the river I cannot give you, for you know as much as I do myself. But go southward with Noros, who is under your command, until you reach Kumak Surka, and if you should not find any one there, then go on to Ajakit, which is forty-five miles southward from Kumak Surka, and should you fail to find people there, then go on to Bulun, which is twenty-five miles southward from Ajakit, and if there are no people there, go southward until you do find people. But I think you will find people at Kumak Surka. If you should shoot reindeer not farther away than one or two days' journey from us, come back and let us know.'

He gave me, says Nindermann, orders not to leave the western bank of the stream, because, he said, on the eastern bank I should find neither people nor drift-wood. He told me that he could not give me any written instructions, because if he did the people would not be able to read them, but I should do the best I could, and use my own judgment. He gave me strict orders that we should not wade through the water. He then said adieu to us, and that as soon as he was ready he would follow in our footsteps as rapidly as possible. Then all gave us three cheers, and my comrade and I left them. They were all in good hopes that we would be able soon to bring back assistance. My hopes, however, were not so bright, for I knew that it was very late in the fall and that in all probability the people had gone away to the south."

"We did not follow the river round, says Noros, but took a straight cut across the land. The mountains were ahead of us, and we knew that the river ran near them. It was an island we were on. There was a river on the other side of it. Nindermann and I reached the river and walked along it about five or six miles. We stopped before noon and had a little alcohol. After that we walked on till we came to a little canoe on the top of the bluff, and perched on the canoe we saw a ptarmigan. Nindermann shot at it with his rifle, and though he took out some tail feathers, the bird got away. We went down to the beach, where it was easier walking than on the bluff. We walked there about a mile, when we again took to the bluff, principally to look around us and to see if we could see any game.

Nindermann happened to get up on the bluff first, and exclaimed, 'They are deer—give me the gun.' We could see them; they were not more than half a mile away, but partly to the windward. So Nindermann took off his heavy clothes and lightened himself up, and then crawled along in the snow. I gave him the cartridges and said, 'Nindermann, make sure of your game; that may be the saving of the whole of us.' He said, 'I will do my best.' I was almost smoke-blind at the time and could not see very well, but I watched his movements very eagerly. I could make out his progress, and saw him crawling slowly up. There were several deer, perhaps a dozen; two or three were grazing and keeping the lookout and the others were resting on the ground. Nindermann got to within two or three hundred yards of them, when one of them caught sight or wind of him and gave the alarm to the rest. I saw Nindermann start up, and, seeing the deer making off, he fired three shots at them, hoping to bring down one with a chance shot. But he missed. They all escaped. Nindermann came back much disheartened. 'I could not help it,' he said; 'I could not do any better.' So we had to put up with it.

Then we started off again, and made another pretty good stretch till we felt exhausted and determined to seek shelter for the night. The best place we could find was beneath the high bluff, at a place where the earth had fallen away, and here we built a fire, had our alcohol, and there spent the night. We did not sleep much, it was so cold, and most of our time was occupied in keeping up the fire." (This camping-place was near the place where Captain De Long later built his last signal fire—perhaps a mile from the deserted raft.)

Next morning the two men started out again, believing they were on the south end of Tit Ary Island. The point which they were passing was, however, the bluff north of Stalboy. At their feet the wide Bykoff arm of the Lena flowed eastward, and was full of floating ice. A gale from the southeast soon came on.

"We had to go, says Noros, whichever way the wind blew us, and so we got away to the northwestward somewhere. Anyhow that day's travel took us out of our course so far that it took us nearly two days to get back again to a point opposite to the bluff on which we were when the gale commenced. We pushed on in spite of the wind and the drifting snow and sand. That night we could not find any shelter on the banks, and so we dug a hole in the drift for a shelter. This took us three or four hours to do, as we had nothing to work with except our hands and sheath knives; but at last we managed to dig a hole large enough for the two of us to creep into. After we had got in the hole the wind drifted the snow upon us and soon filled the entrance of our little place, and next morning we had to work a long time before we could get out of the drift again. We got up and started out; we did not use any of our alcohol to speak of—we were saving it up as much as we could."

On the 11th, toward night, after a hard day's tramp, they came to a small hut on the bank, and passed the night in it. It had a raised fire-place in the center, and they started a fire and kept it going by burning up the benches built around the room.

"We hated, says Noros, to leave the first shelter we had found since leaving the captain, but we went down to the river and started on. We had to face the wind from the southward, and we could hardly make any progress against it. We would have to stop once in a little while, unable to move a step further. We began to give it up in despair. At times we felt like going back to the hut, to wait there until death relieved us from our sufferings."

They walked slowly on, and after a while saw some mountains ahead, and they thought they saw a hut close by, but were not quite sure. There was water between them and the hut, and this they had to wade through up to their knees. They got across, and then found it was really a shelter-place, a little tent-like hut, built of sticks, and plastered outside with mud to keep out the wind. It was Mot Vai. Noros thought Nindermann had followed him, but instead of that he had gone a mile further off, and had found another hut. There they saw two crosses, which marked the graves of natives. They stayed here a day and a half, and ate some refuse eelskins and fish heads which they found there. It was poor food, but gave them some strength. They supposed they had arrived at Kumak Surka.

On the 14th they again started out, but the wind blew hard and they did not make much progress that day. At night they found shelter in a curious opening in the bank, two feet and a half broad, six feet high, and about fifteen yards in extent. It was, in fact, a kind of cave funnel, the other opening being on the top of the bank.

Next day, the 16th, they had breakfast of willow tea and portions of sealskin pantaloons, and then started out again. They crossed numerous sand banks and small streams frozen over, and toward evening struck the Lena proper, close to the high mountains on the western bank. That day, thinking they might find game on the other shore, they crossed over to the mountainous eastern bank of the Lena, where they spent a most wretched night in a ravine in a mountain side. They then crossed over to the western shore of the Lena again. They began to congratulate themselves that the streams were at last all frozen over and wading was now unnecessary. That night they had to camp under the shelter of a high bank, but, failing to find wood, they had neither supper nor shelter, and spent another wretched night.

Next morning, the 19th, they started out again after a meal of willow tea and sealskin, going south along the Lena. They made nearly no progress at all, and every five minutes had to lie down to rest on the ice. Toward night Noros was walking on the edge of the river about half a mile ahead of Nindermann, and on turning a point of land he saw a square hut perched in a gully between two high mountains on the west bank of the river; on going toward it he saw two other huts—tent-like structures of wood and plastered outside with mud. These were the huts of Bulcour.

After staying at Bulcour two or three days, living on some blue moulded fish which they found there, they decided to start again on the next day, 22d; but on that morning, although they had felt strong enough when sitting or lying down, they felt hopelessly weak when they stood up and attempted to walk, and therefore decided to rest there another day.

This delay proved fortunate for them. They were cooking their dinner when they heard a noise outside the door that 'sounded like a flock of geese sweeping by.' Nindermann, who could see through the chinks of the door, said, 'They are deer.' He picked up his gun and was creeping up near the door, when it was suddenly opened, and a native stood before them. He was a Tunguse; and seeing the gun in Nindermann's hands, he dropped on his knees, and pleaded, apparently, for his life. Nindermann threw down his gun and made signs to assure him that he would not be harmed; and finally he fastened a deer-team, with which he had driven up, and came inside.

"He began to talk, says Noros, but we could not understand what he was saying. We tried to explain to him that we wanted to go to Bulun. We were so glad when we saw him that we could have hugged him, for we knew then that we were pretty nearly all right. We tried to explain to him that there were others of our party away to the north, but he could not understand us. He examined Nindermann's clothes and then brought in a deer-skin, and then a pair of deer-skin boots, and made gestures as if to say that he would go away, but would soon return. He held up three fingers, and we thought he meant three days." Nindermann was for keeping him, but Noros advised that he should be permitted to do as he thought best. On following him out of the hut they saw four deer; they afterward learned that he had brought the two extra animals to put in a sled which he had left there some days previously, but which had been used by them for fire-wood.

After seeing the native drive away down the gully they went inside the hut to await events. As darkness came on they began to fear that he did not intend to come back. "We thought we had done wrong in letting him go, says

Nindermann. Night came on and we had got a little under way with our soup, when we heard sleds drive up, and saw our Tunguse coming with two other natives and five reindeer teams. The original Tunguse came rushing into the hut, bringing some frozen fish, deer-skin coats and boots. We went for the fish. He picked up all our things and put them on the sleds. We put on the coats and the boots and soon started off. This was about midnight. We were driven about fifteen miles, when we came to two large tents and many sleds, the deer not being in sight. The natives took us and washed our faces and hands and got us looking a little decent again. They had a big kettle of deer meat on the fire, and we were motioned to help ourselves at once. After that they made us some tea, and then spread deer-skins for us to sleep on. This was our first comfortable night since we left the captain."

The native had brought them to a camp of traveling Tunguses, who were on their way to Kumak Surka from a temporary settlement where they had been staying a little further to the north. In the caravan were seven men and three women, and seventy-five head of deer dragging thirty sleds. With this caravan Nindermann and Noros traveled two days, and arrived at Kumak Surka on the 24th of October. Here the two men were well taken care of, Noros at one hut and Nindermann at another.

They arrived at Kumak Surka during the evening, and amid the preparation of meals for a house full of people and the arrangement of bunks for the accommodation of the guests, there was no opportunity that night to engage attention to the subject of their errand. The next day, however, Nindermann had the field to himself after the morning meal had been discussed. Some one brought him the model of a Yakut boat, which they called a 'parahut,' and asked if his 'parahut' was like that. Then, with sticks to represent masts and spars, he showed them that it was bark rigged and moved by steam power also. All this they seemed to understand perfectly, and then asked how and where they lost the ship.

Pointing toward the north he made them understand it was very far in that direction, and, with two pieces of ice, showed them how the ship was crushed and sank down into the sea. Afterward he cut the models of three small boats, and put sticks in them to represent the men in each boat, and told them, as well as he could, how, with sleds and dogs and boats, they had crossed great seas of broken ice and open water, and finally reached the shore of their country. He then got a piece of paper and drew the coast line and sketched the boat, illustrating the manner in which the landing was effected. Drawing in the river from the coast line to the south, he showed that they walked down the east bank of the river, and marked the places where they found huts or encamped. He indicated the number of days they had been walking by putting his head down and closing his eyes as if to sleep and counting the number of sleeps with his fingers. He told them as plainly as he could that the captain, or 'kapitan,' as they called it, had sent him to get clothes and food and reindeer, to fetch them to the settlement, as they were very weak, and in a starving condition. He told them he had left the party sixteen days ago, and that two days before his departure they had had nothing to eat. He used every effort to convey his meaning to the savages who had befriended him, and induce them to go to the succor of the captain and his party, but was not successful. Sometimes it seemed as if they understood him perfectly, and at others he felt convinced that they had not understood a single thing he had told them. During the entire day he kept talking to them by signs and illustrations upon paper, but without avail.

The next day he renewed his efforts and resorted to every expedient to make them understand him. He did not ask them only to go alone, but wanted them to go with him. They would sigh and look distressed when he described the sufferings and condition of the party on the Delta, but when he urged that assistance should be sent to them the faces of his hearers were totally devoid of expression. He then thought of his companions as dead or dying, looking to his return as their only hope for deliverance. Weakened by fatigue, exposure, and famine, and feeling how utterly powerless he was when so much depended on him, this terrible strain was too much for him, and this strong, brave man, who had faced death and endured untold hardships without a quiver, sank into a corner and cried like a child. An old woman, the wife of the master of the hut, saw him and took compassion on him, and a long conference was held by the natives which resulted in their endeavoring to comfort him. Reaching a hand tenderly upon his shoulder they told him he should go to Bulun the next day. He had asked to be taken there, hoping to find some one by whom he could make himself understood, and it was to his anxiety to reach that town that they attributed his grief.

The next day he again asked them to take him to Bulun to see the commandant, and they told him they had already sent for the commandant, and were expecting him. During the evening the Russian exile, Kusmah, came to the hut, and Nindermann asked him if he was the commandant of Bulun. To this he answered 'Yes,' or at least Nindermann so understood him. Then Kusmah asked, "Parakod Jeannette?" and Nindermann replied, 'Yes.' He then told, as well as he could, the whole story of the loss of the Jeannette and the history of the retreat, illustrating by his little chart and by sketches.

Nindermann soon felt convinced that Kusmah did not understand either the chart or his description. Then he told him that on the journey on land one man had died and that there were eleven alive. While he was telling him this portion of the story Kusmah kept assenting, and seemed to understand perfectly. He would keep saying, 'kapitan, yes. Two kapitan, first kapitan, second kapitan, alluding to Melville and Danenhower. Nindermann then understood him to say he couldn't do anything until either one or the other of them had telegraphed to St. Petersburg for instructions. Therefore Nindermann wrote a telegram addressed to the American Minister in St. Petersburg, telling him the exact condition of affairs, and that the captain's party was starving and in need of food and clothing; and while talking, before the despatch was quite finished, Kusmah took it. Three days afterward Kusmah handed the despatch to Melville at Geemovialocke.

From Kumak Surka the two men were sent to Bulun, 100 versts further south, where they arrived October 29th. As soon as the commandant learned of their arrival he sent for them and gave them quarters for the day. The next day they were transferred to the house of the priest's assistant, but this gentleman did not appear to know the virtues of hospitality to shipwrecked men. After two days he sent them to the hut of a native, who also did not provide well for the guests.

Mr. Melville describes his meeting with Nindermann and Noros as follows:—

"Arriving at Bulun, on the 2d of November, I found Nindermann and Noros of the captain's party. They were in the stansea, the common reception place for traveling natives, and terribly broken down. They were suffering from diarrhsœa, and were feverish. They were totally unmanned, and burst out crying when they tried to tell me of their companions and of their own escape. Gradually I got from them as clear an account of their march as they could give, and a description of the place where they had left the captain's party. They complained to me that they did not get the proper kind of food, that after the commandant left they had been fed on stale fish that was not fit for any man to eat, and had no meat. A fire had been built in their place only twice a day, morning and night, and they had consequently suffered much from the cold.

I failed to find anybody in authority in the village; but Nindermann and Noros having made the acquaintance of the priest's assistant—the 'Malinki pope,' as he was styled—I visited him, and gave him to understand that the people must be better taken care of. He said he could do nothing, as he had no authority. I told him that there were two or three empty houses in the village, and that on the following day he must see that the two men had proper accommodation. That night I slept in the hole with the two men.

Next morning the man came, and, feeling that he had overstepped his authority, did not want me to have a house; but, finding where a good empty house was, I told him that as there was no authority in the village I would take the authority upon myself. So I inspected the vacant huts, selected the best, notwithstanding the protests of two or three people who had gathered around—the 'Malinki pope,' in particular—told the men to come, built a fire, and then took possession of the new quarters. I told the 'Malinki pope,' further, that I must have reindeer meat for the men, and that they must have as much bread as they could eat. I informed him, at the same time, that I was an officer of the United States—that the governor commanding the district, General Tchernieff, would not allow an American, cast on the Siberian shores, to be abused. This appeared to bring him and the rest of the Russians and natives to their senses. They immediately got me a bag of meal, a quarter of a reindeer, the pope himself sending a live reindeer, candles, sugar and tea for the use of the two men. Both of them believed that their companions had long since been dead when they themselves were found."

CHAPTER XXXVII.

ENGINEER MELVILLE'S NARRATIVE—CONTINUED.

(THE VOYAGE FROM SEMENOFFSKY AND SEARCH FOR DE LONG.)

MR. MELVILLE describes the voyage from Semenoffsky Island and separation of the boats as follows:—

"We remained at Semenoffsky Island over Sunday, and on Monday morning all three boats were launched. We had filled everything we could with snow to be melted for water. We made a good run along the island until noon, and had our dinner on the edge of the floe, with clear water to the southward.

Previous to this there had been some discussion as to the best point to land upon on the Siberian coast. Captain De Long asked the opinions of all the officers. Lieutenant Chipp was very decided that we should make for Cape Barkin, as once in its vicinity the boats could not mistake the coast, running as it does to the west or to the south in a direct coast line. When my opinion was asked, I urged that if an attempt was made to enter the Lena at all, it should be done by way of the eastern mouth; and I called to mind the fact that the captain of the 'Lena' had been unable to effect an entrance by any of the northern mouths, but had eventually entered the river by the eastern mouth. I also suggested that the mouths of the Yana or the Indigirka would be better places for landing, offering at least no perplexity of entrances. Captain De Long listened to both of us, and then decided the matter in his quiet manner by saying:—

'Mr. Melville, I think Mr. Chipp is right. We will make for Barkin, and then for the Light Tower and Sagaster, and the northern mouth of the Lena.'

Before leaving the floe, Mr. Chipp reported to the captain that his boat was very heavy, and that it was impossible for him to keep up with us. For this reason Captain De Long determined to relieve him of two men—he had then ten—and put one in the whale-boat and one in his own, the first cutter, leaving Mr. Chipp then with eight men all told—six men and two officers. These two men were Ah Sam, the Chinese cook, and Mansen, seaman, the latter of whom was given to the whale-boat. Up to this time Mr. Chipp had been relieved of carrying his pemmican. When we were at the edge of the floe, before starting out to sea, he was known to have but half a can of pemmican, but whether he received his *pro rata* of pemmican afterward none of us know. He did not get it when we were there.

The three boats left Seminoffsky in company and continued together until about seven o'clock in the afternoon, the wind increasing from a fresh breeze to a full gale, the first cutter and the whale-boat running with close reefed sails. The second cutter being a duller sailer than either of the other two, I do not know whether she had reefed sails or not.

At seven o'clock in the evening the gale was blowing very hard, and the boats were taking in so much water that it was absolutely necessary that each boat should take care of herself. The whale-boat was a hundred yards to the windward of the first cutter, and probably a hundred yards in advance, when I heard the captain or some of his people hailing, and then saw a signal. I looked round and saw Captain De Long waving his arm. Not knowing whether he wanted me to go on or to come down to him, I gybed the sail and ran the boat down to within hailing-distance, when he waved the whale-boat off, shaking his head and arm, making a signal for the second cutter, and I supposed he wanted to give Chipp his share of pemmican. Nindermann informs me that the captain only wanted to tell the boats to keep together; that there was no pemmican passed from the first to the second cutter; and that the sea was so heavy that the second cutter never came within hailing-distance of the captain's boat.

It is my opinion that Chipp never reached land, but that he was swamped during the gale. The second cutter was about the shape of a dry goods box. She was short and deep, and although flying the lightest of all three boats, she was bad to steer, and, as Mr. Chipp once said, 'eternally flying up in the wind.' Being short, if she was hove to, as she would undoubtedly have to be, as the others were, she would not lie as well."

The following is Mr. Melville's narrative of his search for Lieutenant De Long in November 1881:—

"At Burulak I secured two teams of dogs driven by Wassili Koolgiak and Tomat Constantine—the latter being one of the natives who had rescued Nindermann and Noros at Bulcour. I made Baishoff understand that all expenses would be paid; that I had no money, but my government and the Russian authorities would sanction everything I said or did. I told them I wanted ten days' food for myself, drivers and dogs. I had with me then a description I had taken down from the narratives of Noros and Nindermann of the whereabouts of Captain De Long and his party when they had left to come in advance for assistance. I got away that afternoon, and that night slept at Kumak Surka.

Next day I traveled fifty versts, and slept in one of the huts of Bulcour—the place where Nindermann and Noros had been found by the natives. This was the beginning of my search, following the river to the northward. During the night a snow storm arose and the natives would not move. I had not yet recovered from the frozen condition of my feet and limbs, so that I had to trust to the natives for my safety, and thought it best to wait until the gale was over. I was detained one day and the second night. Next morning it was calm enough, and I set out again. From Bulcour to the hut of Mot Vai is about 130 versts. The drivers told me it would be necessary to camp in the snow after going half the distance, and that if we were caught in bad weather it would be bad not only for them and their dogs, but for me, already so feeble.

We started out and visited a small hut twenty versts north of Bulcour, where Noros and Nindermann had stayed. I found evidence of their having been there where they had eaten their boots and burned the sleds. We camped on the snow that night. Next day we traveled as far as the place that Noros and Nindermann had designated as the two crosses. I searched the huts and saw evidences of their having been there, and by midnight arrived at the hut of Mot Vai, where we slept. In the morning, when getting ready to start out, I found a strange waist-belt, which upon examination I knew had been made on board the Jeannette. I thought I had struck the first evidences of some of De Long's party. Neither Noros nor Nindermann, in their description of their journey, made any mention of Mot Vai, and they had forgotten all about the place until they afterward visited the hut and recognized it as one of their halting places.

Very much to my surprise, I was then told by the dog drivers that they had no more provisions, either for dogs or men—and this was only the fifth day out. I then inquired of them how far it was to the nearest village. They told me North Bulun was about 120 versts distant, northwest. I gave orders to the drivers to take me there, in order to get a fresh supply of food. I stopped and slept at Khaskata, and visited a number of huts on the way north.

The next night, about midnight, I arrived at North Bulun. On my arrival there I found a considerable village of nearly 100 inhabitants. During the first half hour a man came in to give me a paper. He made me understand he had found it in a hut fifty versts to the eastward of North Bulun. I read it and saw it was one of De Long's records. Next morning natives brought me a gun and two other records, the most important of which was very nearly being lost, as a woman had carried it in her bosom until the lettering had become almost obliterated and had then thrown it away, and there had been some difficulty in finding it again. By these three records I learned where Lieutenant De Long had been, and of his course to the southward. I then went to look up the natives who had found the records, and told them they must take me to the most northerly hut, where one of the papers had been found.

Next morning I started for Ballock, the northermost hut, before starting making the people distinctly understand that I must have twenty days' provisions for myself, the dogs and their drivers. As there was nothing but frozen fish, I selected twenty good ones for myself, allowing myself one a day, telling the drivers they should get two apiece for themselves per day and sufficient for the dogs, all of which they perfectly understood. But in loading the sleds they put on the twenty fish I had selected, put on as few as they could for themselves, but none at all for the dogs. I found out afterward that the people had really no food at all to live on, and had given me all the fish they could spare. Of this I knew nothing at the time. We arrived at Ballock that night.

Next morning at daylight, following the direction of the record, I followed the main northern branch of the Lena, keeping the east bank aboard until I reached the sea. Then I hurried, and followed the coast for five or six miles, and, very much to the surprise of the natives, sighted the pole of the flagstaff which De Long had planted to mark the cache. They were very much astonished that I should tell them what would be found there. I found the things carefully placed on a groundwork of sticks to keep them clear of the earth, and then carefully covered with old sleeping bags and rags and bits of canvas. The wind had carried away the canvas and most of the covering, and the cache was covered with snow. I took the things out and loaded the sleds with everything that I found, with the exception of one oar. The ice had shoved up on the beach within a few yards of the cache. After searching the beach for a distance of five or six miles, and a mile or a mile and a half off shore looking for the first cutter, darkness came on. It commenced to blow hard, and so I determined to carry everything I had found to Ballock. On my arrival at Ballock again, very much to my astonishment, the drivers told me they had but one day's food for themselves and dogs, and I was, perforce, obliged to return to North Bulun for more provisions, carrying the relics with me.

At North Bulun I picked out everything of importance and value, throwing out the old sleeping bags, clothing, boots and worthless objects I had brought from the cache. The day following it blew very hard. After I had made arrangements to start, all the drivers but one said it was impossible to go out in such a wind, but I said I would go whether they all went or not. Finally, all the drivers agreed to start in the gale, and we went to the next shelter hut southward of Ballock. Thence I went to Usterda, the place where De Long had left the last record found, in which he stated that he was about to cross the river to the west bank and follow it until he reached a settlement.

After visiting Usterda I slept at a hut a mile further to the south, other huts being filled with snow. I crossed the river, as De Long had done, and followed the west bank southward, as his record had directed. Noros and Nindermann having informed me of the different huts the captain's party had stopped in, and of the hut in which Erickson died, I made the natives understand that I must visit every hut, old or new, on the Lena between Usterda and Mot Vai. Proceeding south about as far as I supposed the party would travel, I came across an old broken-down hut answering the description of Erickson's hut as given me by Nindermann. I searched it thoroughly, but found no evidence of the party having been there. I then proceeded south, and on the east bank of the river found another hut in good repair. I searched it thoroughly, inside and out, but found no evidences of the missing men.

It then came on to blow very badly, and the drivers told

me it was necessary to seek the shelter of a hut. The nearest to us was Sisteraneck, where I slept over night. Next day it was still blowing very hard, and the natives were loath to start out. As we had a very small amount of provisions on hand, and the drivers told me that the gales sometimes continued for ten days at a time, I urged them to move on, and they said they would go forty versts further, to Qu Vina. I searched the hut and all its surroundings, but found no evidences of the missing people.

By this time I felt that I was off the track. I had only three or four hours of light during the day to work in. I could place no dependence on the natives as regards food. Although I was unable to stand on my feet from the effects of previous freezing in the whale-boat, I was able, even in my semi-disabled condition, to stand the cold, and desired to continue the work; but I found the natives disinclined to venture out in the storm. They assured me that if we went out both myself and they would most certainly be frozen to death. So I made up my mind to return to Bulun.

The weather was so bad that the drivers would not leave Qu Vina that day, and so I had to wait there till the following day, when, the weather being fine, I started on the return journey, intending to stop at Mot Vai. As the weather continued fine I passed by Mot Vai without stopping, and camped in the snow further on the way, about eleven o'clock at night. Not having a tent we dug a hole in the snow, and there lay down for a sleep. During the night a terrific storm arose, with dense snow, and continued to rage for forty-eight hours, during which time I had no food except raw frozen fish. As soon as the gale abated we started for Bulcour, eighty versts distant, but we did not reach this place till after eighteen hours. A gale had arisen, the dogs could not work, but lay down and whined. But eventually we arrived at Bulcour and the shelter of the huts there.

On the journey down the loads proved so heavy carrying the things I had collected that the natives were obliged to walk all the way. I, being unable to walk, was carried on one of the sleds. When within twenty versts of Bulcour the sleds broke down, first one and then the other, in the dark night. The natives spent a long time in repairing their sleds, and it was not till some time near morning that we arrived at Bulcour. I then thought it best to leave the greatest part of my load at Bulcour, to make for Kumak Surka and then send back for them. The distance was fifty versts, which we covered in fourteen hours. On bad roads next day I arrived at Burulak, and the day following, about midnight, at Bulun, after being absent twenty-three days.

I found that the 'commandant' had made no effort in the search, but had been somewhere up north in the locality attending to his own private business. There was a report in the Russian newspapers that the Yakutsk government or somebody else Russian had sent the deputy ispravnik or some other person to aid and assist in the search. This was not so. There was neither a doctor nor anybody else sent to assist in the original search. Nobody accompanied me except the two Yakut dog drivers."

When Nindermann was searching for Lieutenant Chipp on the northern coast of the Delta, in April 1882, as he approached the place where Lieutenant De Long landed he drove out on the frozen bay, and found the first cutter imbedded in the ice and buried in a snow-drift. She had filled with water and frozen up as high as the rail both inside and outside. A few small articles were brought away by Nindermann as relics.

APPENDIX.

MELVILLE AT HOME.

The following account of the arrival and reception of Engineer Melville and his companions at New York city is copied and compiled from the New York *Herald:*—

"The party of relatives, comrades, and friends of the returning heroes, who had gone down to Quarantine to meet them on the Navy Yard boat, the Catalpa, spent Tuesday afternoon and night in waiting, most of them spending the night at the Staten Island hotels. Arrangements were made for calling the passengers of the tug together at any time of the night if the steamship was signalled. There was fortunately no necessity for doing so, and when the meeting did take place it was beneath the fairest of skies and amid the balmiest of breezes—a perfect autumn day.

About ten o'clock, Wednesday morning, word was received on the Catalpa that the Parthia had passed Fire Island. An hour later Mr. William P. Clyde's steam yacht, the Ocean Gem, having on board another party of welcome, glided past the Quarantine dock amid an exchange of cheers, and on toward Sandy Hook. On the yacht were Aldermen Roosevelt, McClane, and Brady, of the Aldermanic Committee; Colonel Church and Judge F. J. Fithian, of the Citizen's Committee; Chief Engineers Loring and Allen, and Past Assistant Engineers Kelly and Barry, of the United States Navy; Messrs. H. C. Ellis, J. Bryar, F. M. Canfield, John Collins, and others.

Health Officer Smith had kindly agreed to go out to the Parthia in the Catalpa, and when at half-past twelve she swung off from her dock upon the announcement that the Parthia was coming up the Narrows, she carried that official with her, as well as one of the gayest and most expectant parties ever seen. There were on board Mrs. John A. Demorest and Maggie Melville, sisters of the chief engineer; Mr. Alexander Melville, his brother; Miss Lydia V. Demorest, his niece; Miss Newman, the affianced of Nindermann, and her mother and brother; Captain J. A. W. Watton, the father of Mrs. De Long; Mr. Gustavus W. Lindquist, a mate of Nindermann on the Polaris expedition; Mr. John C. Morrison, who shipped the crew for the Jeannette; Surveyor Graham, Chief Engineer Maggee, United States Navy; Commander Kane, United States Navy; Paymasters Caswell and Skelding, United States Navy; Lieutenants Jacques and Drake, United States Navy; Past Assistant Surgeon Russell, of the Naval Hospital, Brooklyn; Mr. R. C. Stone, and others.

The Catalpa met the yacht Ocean Gem, which had turned back again, and then the two went down the Lower Bay in company. All were in a state of great expectation. When Dr. Smith was asked if it was not an unusual thing for him to go down so far to meet a steamship, he replied that this was an unusual occasion.

At a little after one o'clock the two parties approached the Parthia. A scene of the wildest enthusiasm, and which the participants will never forget, ensued. First the Ocean Gem ran up to the steamship and saluted her, the steamship blowing two whistles in response. Then the turn of the Catalpa came, and as she ran up toward the Parthia on the starboard side, they also exchanged salutes. Long before their voices could be made to reach across the distance which divided them, the passengers on both vessels were frantically waving their hats and handkerchiefs or whatever else was conveniently at hand to wave; and by the especially strong demonstration proceeding from the Parthia's after deck, it was evident to those on the tug that the party they had come to welcome was there. And so it proved, as the two came nearer, and shouts and cheers took the place of hats and handerchiefs.

'We've got him!' shouted a hundred voices from the Parthia. 'We've got him! He is here!' and they pointed in the direction where Melville was standing, and urged him to a more conspicuous place on the ship's side. He did not require much urging either, but scrambled upon the railing and shouted until he was hoarse, or would have been if he were not such an old sailor. His sisters cried their welcome to him, and he pulled his cap from his head like an overjoyed boy and flung it toward them. It fell into the water, though intended to reach the deck of the Catalpa; but no matter about the hat.

The wildest excitement prevailed when the Parthia took the lines of the tug, and preparations were making to open the freight port amidships for the health officer. Friends of Nindermann, Noros, and Berry saw their dear old faces above the railing of the steamship and laughed and cheered and cried; Melville and his family and fellow officers were hurriedly exchanging greetings, and all the other passengers on both vessels were crowding to the sides and hurrahing, except some in the steerage of the Parthia, who took up the familiar air—

> Home again! home again!
> From a foreign shore.

From a foreign shore, indeed! Wide open swung the iron doors of the freight port, and up went the doctor, helped by a dozen pairs of hands. At his heels was Lieutenant Jacques, who was supposed to be the only other person to board the Parthia; but Commander Kane, Paymaster Skelding and several others followed him. They brought down Melville, or rather they followed him, for Melville was too eager to be brought, and the first arms into which he fell, as he reached the deck of the tug, were those of Chief Engineer Maggee. They embraced like lovers, Melville dropping his head upon his old friend's shoulder and then kissing him on the cheek, both of them in tears the while. The shouting had to be done by the mere spectators now, for the voices of all the others were choked with emotion. Melville embraced his brother, and others of his companions in the navy, and then meeting Captain Watton, fell upon his neck, and they cried together. Those tears were for De Long, but not a word was necessary to make it understood.

Then Melville went back upon the steamship to look after his luggage, and two boxes that were to be transferred to the tug, —the two boxes which, as he afterwards said, he had not once lost sight of these many months, containing all that was found belonging to De Long and his companions, including the log and the private records. Melville's old comrades declared he looked almost the same as ever, except that he had lost a little flesh, and that his hair, which grew long upon his neck, was a little thinner. His rather tall and heavy figure looked pliant as ever, and his gray eyes, surmounted by a high forehead, which looked all the higher because of a little baldness, beamed with their old, affectionate lustre.

'Welcome, Noros!' cried a score of voices, as the athletic figure of a young man, with a bronzed face, blue eyes, and a light brown moustache, clambered with a sailor's agility through the port in the steamer's side down upon the rail of the tug, there to have his hands grasped and to be hugged about as enthusiastically as Melville had been greeted. Noros is the most youthful of any of the returned explorers. He does not look to be more than twenty-five years, and he is as shy as a girl. He looks like a New Yorker. He has rosy cheeks, a frank face, is fleshy, and appears none the worse for his terrible experiences, although, as he explained, he carries with him rheumatic pains which he fears will not easily be shaken off.

Nindermann was the next to make his appearance amid another burst of cheers and affectionate greetings. He is a short man, with a thick-set frame, and looks like what he is—a sturdy Swede. He has a long black moustache, reaching down to the corners of his chin, and his face and hands are tanned to the color of leather.

Then Melville came again on the tug and renewed his welcomes until he was conducted to the pilot-house, where Nindermann and Noros had gone before him, and where the ladies were awaiting them. They were left alone there for a time with those belonging to them, and the joy of such a meeting may easily be imagined.

The tall form of Commander Berry issued from the side of the Parthia, and that completed the party intended for the tug. Commander Berry's parting from those on the steamship was of the most affectionate kind, several of the lady passengers kissing him, and the men on the deck cheering him lustily when he descended to the tug. His welcome there was as sincere and demonstrative as his parting had been.

Meanwhile the steamship and tug were moving at a good rate of speed toward Quarantine. The navy officers had not been wasting their spare moments. Bottles of champagne were opened in the pilot-house, wherewith the family and friends of Melville were to drink his health; and Paymaster Skelding passed some of the beverage up to those on the Parthia, where it was hastily made way with, and the bottles were smashed upon the deck of the tug by way of a parting favor.

'Engineer Mellville,' said Lieutenant Jacques, as he stepped into the pilot-house, 'I have the honor to extend you a hearty welcome on behalf of the Secretary of the Navy, and the commander and officers of this station.'

The returned explorer bowed his thanks, and added that such a reception was more than he had looked for.

A scene of a different kind was soon to follow. Poor Captain Watton stood on the deck outside the pilot-house, and he and Melville met again. The captain asked him something about De Long.

'My God!' cried Melville, bursting into tears and grasping Captain Watton's hand, 'you have lost a son and I a friend. They may say what they like, but I assure you for Melville that he has lost a friend.'

The Catalpa had cut loose from the Parthia, whose passengers gave a parting yell for Melville that might have been heard in Coney Island, opposite to which these scenes transpired, and the Ocean Gem ran alongside the tug. Melville first and many others afterward, including some of the relatives of the honored guests, were transferred to the yacht. On her decks the scenes of glad greeting were repeated. As the yacht started for the city, Alderman McClane made a speech of welcome to Melville on behalf of the city authorities, tendering him the Governor's Room for the purpose of a public reception; and Colonel Church followed with a speech of welcome on behalf of the citizens of New York and of the country. A handsome lunch was spread in the cabin of the yacht, to which Melville and his companions were invited; but they were too much elated to remember their stomachs, and after a show of eating and some real drinking, a happy speech by Alderman Roosevelt, and a complimentary resolution to Mr. William P. Clyde for his courtesy and assistance, the party went on deck.

Here, on the after-deck, an extraordinary contrast was at one time presented; one of those rain-in-the-sunlight scenes which form so strange a phase of our human life. On two camp-stools, side by side and hand in hand, sat Melville and Captain Watton, talking together in low tones, and the tears coursing down the cheeks of both. Within arm's reach of them, and also side by side and hand in hand, sat Nindermann and his affianced bride; but they spoke only with their eyes, and their faces were so happy that they rained smiles on all around them."

A crowd of people awaited the arrival of the yacht at Twenty-third street. Mellville disembarked amid the greatest display of enthusiasm, was led off the dock between two files of marines, and, followed by the entire party, took carriages which were in waiting to convey them to the Hoffman House. Shortly afterward a delegation from Philadelphia waited on Melville and his companions, and tendered to them the hospitality of their city in the name of the committee of citizens they represented.

Mr. Melville had been invited to visit Public School No. 3, at the corner of Grove and Hudson streets, and was there at nine o'clock precisely. Many friends and relatives of the pupils were present. After being introduced, Mr. Melville, in a short speech said that he had himself received his first instruction at this very school; that he looked back to those days as the happiest of his life, and that he hoped all his juvenile hearers would 'make hay while the sun shines,' and grow up to be useful members of the community.

After Mr. Melville had returned to his hotel, two ladies dressed in deep black called upon him. They were the sisters of Lieutenant Chipp, and there were tears in the eyes of all three as they took their leave. Later in the day, Melville called on Mrs. De Long, at the residence of her father, Captain Watton, and conveyed to her the last messages of her dead husband. In the afternoon, at a public reception in the Governor's room at the City Hall, many citizens called on Melville and Noros.

In the evening about 150 gentlemen sat down to a banquet tendered to Melville at Delmonico's. Judge J. R. Brady presided, and in a short speech said that they had met to honor men who had shed glory upon the American name in the Arctic regions. As an explorer, Melville had distinguished himself by his fortitude, fidelity, courage, and heroism.

'But,' he continued, 'while the national heart throbs with great pleasure at his return, and while in every household in the

United States his name is as familiar as a household word, we must turn to the unfortunate comrades whose lives were lost in the same noble pursuit in which he was engaged. And, gentlemen, now I ask you to turn for a moment to the unfortunate De Long and his comrades, and to drink to their memory in silence and standing.' The toast was drank amid the most intense silence.

In response to cheers given in his honor, Mr. Melville spoke hurriedly as follows:—

'GENTLEMEN:—In behalf of myself and my two comrades—two sailor men who are here to-night—I will say two or three words—I won't count them, but I shall say only two or three, and, indeed, I should prefer to say nothing at all. I can only say that I feel that we did our whole duty, that we did all that we could do, and that if we had not tried to do that we would have been no men at all.'

Letters of regret from several distinguished gentlemen were then read. Among them was one from Rev. H. W. Beecher, who expressed admiration for the hero of the evening, and his companions in hardship, and concluded with the declaration that there was no invention of art of so much value as that which raises the standard of simple manhood. Mayor Grace then made a speech, from which the following are extracts:—

'There sit here beside us the survivors of a brave company, the history of whose fateful voyage we know so well. These men and their companions, whom we shall see no more, have displayed such courage and endurance as the world rarely sees. There is no one so thoughtless, none with so poor a memory, that their story is not graven on his heart. After twenty months of tortuous drifting, clamped in oceanic ice, their stanch ship—stanch as wealth and skill could devise—went down in the darkness of Arctic night. Then came months of wandering, and cold, hunger, and death; but their hearts were stancher than their ship. Their invincible courage never faltered. To you, sir, and to all the gallant crew, from the dead leader to the humblest surviving seaman, do all brave hearts owe their testimony, that, though our navy may be deficient in hulls of iron, she yet has her hearts of oak. At that parting scene—the most pathetic in the history of Arctic exploration—when on the banks of the Lena, standing knee deep in snow, the men gave three cheers to the two comrades who were going forth for rescue, the last words from the already closing grave were these:—'When you get to New York, remember me.' Yes, we do remember them. We remember their gallantry, their courage to dare, and still higher courage to endure.

'There is no man with capacity for growth who is not made better and stronger by contemplation of the characteristic bravery and will of these gentlemen and their dead comrades. It is these things which spring directly out of human nature which touch a sympathetic chord in every man's heart, where a Newton or a Kepler are cold abstractions. It is because these gentlemen have shown us in themselves the very types of courage and unselfish devotion, that this city and this country welcome them with a joy which is tempered only with grief for the loss of the brave men who will come home no more.'

Chief Engineer Isherwood said that Melville's brother engineers were not surprised when they read of his exploits. He did precisely what they should have expected from him. Engineers were trained to grapple with and overcome the forces of nature. The chief distinction between the ancient and the modern civilizations, lay in the fact that the ancients had no engineers.

Judge Brady remarked that in the navy it was impossible to get on without hatchways, and introduced Uncle Rufus Hatch, inviting him to say whether he was a 'bull' or a 'bear' on engineering. The Wall street sage made some amusing references to his recent trip through the Northwest, and *apropos des bottes* remarked that 'all of us' would have at the end of our lives a little obituary notice in the *Herald*—provided the survivors were able to pay for it. But when all ordinary obituaries had been forgotten, the names of Melville and his companions would still be fresh and brilliant in the pages of the history of heroism, and would be pointed to with pride by their posterity.

Senator Jones was then called upon to respond in behalf of the United States Senate. He delivered a glowing eulogy upon the heroism and self-sacrifice of the men of the Jeannette. As dangers thickened, and the chances of life decreased, he said, the humanity and fellowship of the sufferers increased. Those whom God permitted to survive did not save themselves at the expense of their fellow-sufferers. This was the highest manifestation of human virtue, and if we honor Melville for perilling his own life we ought to honor him still more for valuing the welfare and safety of his companions above his own. God grant that he might long continue to enjoy the honors that he deserves from his fellow-creatures. He was a man all Americans should be proud of. The good qualities he displayed in presence of danger were peculiarly American.

Judge Brady then said that he had not forgotten that there were two companions of Melville present—Messrs. Nindermann and Noros. He proposed their health, which was drunk with enthusiasm and three cheers.

'Bring them to the front!' was the cry after the toast had been honored; and the two seamen were led to the dais at the head of the table amid a round of applause, to which they blushingly bowed their acknowledgment.

Captain Parker responded to the toast to the health of Nindermann and Noros. He said that it was well to do honor to leaders like Melville; but they should remember that it was the faithfulness, courage, and obedience of the subordinates that rendered the glory of their leaders possible.

After speeches by several other gentlemen, the meeting dispersed with three hearty cheers for Melville, Nindermann, and Noros.

About noon the next day a deputation of citizens of Philadelphia and officers of the navy stationed there, proceeded to the Hoffman House to escort the Arctic voyagers to the City of Brotherly Love. This committee consisted of Commodore Rodgers, U. S. N., chairman; James A. Wright, Geo. W. Childs, Colonel John Price Wetherill, General Weitzel, U. S. A.; Chief Engineer Hilbert, U. S. N.; Pay Director A. W. Russell, U. S. N.; Joel Cook, O. E. McClellan, Edward W. Clark, and H. T. Kenny, of the Pennsylvania Railroad. The party traveled in the special car of President Roberts of the Pennsylvania Railroad; and on arriving at Philadelphia, and while stopping there, Melville and his companions received a welcome no less hearty than that accorded them in New York. Melville's interview with a deputation, fifty in number, from the Association of ex-engineers of the United States Navy was particularly interesting and affecting.

'God bless you, old fellows,' was Melville's first greeting, as he sprang among them.

From Philadelphia Mr. Melville proceeded to his home at Sharon Hill, Pennsylvania, and was cordially received by citizens of that town. While in New York he had received from them a congratulatory letter, which closed as follows:—

'But if you have not brought us tales of new lands and new seas which hide behind the glaciers of the Arctics, there has come to us over that polar messenger, the telegraph, other tidings of frightful sufferings, manfully borne—of partial rescue—and finally of a self-devotion and heroism in the search for your lost comrades, that throws a melancholy sweetness over the monotonous agony and the final deep tragedy of the voyage of the Jeannette.

'The whole civilized world is thrilled to the core with the story of your search for the dead. You, as the leader of that search, have earned a foremost place in the roll of Arctic heroes. And we, your neighbors, in welcoming you back to your home—in common with the rest of mankind—accord to you the respect and the homage due to one who holds life as of little worth when duty or humanity calls. May the past years of suffering be atoned for by an unclouded future—a future in which no long Arctic night will have a place, but where all will be warmth, and sunshine, and happiness. With heartfelt respect we greet you, neighbor.'

www.ingramcontent.com/pod-product-compliance
Lightning Source LLC
Chambersburg PA
CBHW022055150426
43195CB00008B/146